ENVIRONMENTAL SUSTAINABILITY AND AMERICAN PUBLIC ADMINISTRATION

ENVIRONMENTAL SUSTAINABILITY AND AMERICAN PUBLIC ADMINISTRATION

Past, Present, and Future

J. Michael Martinez

LEXINGTON BOOKS
Lanham • Boulder • New York • London

Published by Lexington Books
An imprint of The Rowman & Littlefield Publishing Group, Inc.
4501 Forbes Boulevard, Suite 200, Lanham, Maryland 20706
www.rowman.com

Unit A, Whitacre Mews, 26-34 Stannary Street, London SE11 4AB

British Library Cataloguing in Publication Information Available
The hardback edition of this book was previously catalogued by the Library of
Congress as follows:

Library of Congress Cataloging-in-Publication Data Available
ISBN 9781498509664 (cloth : alk. paper)
ISBN 9781498509688 (pbk. : alk. paper)
ISBN 9781498509671 (electronic)

♾™ The paper used in this publication meets the minimum requirements of
American National Standard for Information Sciences—Permanence of Paper for
Printed Library Materials, ANSI/NISO Z39.48-1992.

Printed in the United States of America

For Alex W. Thrower (1967–2013),

An extraordinary colleague and friend—

gone, but never forgotten

CONTENTS

LIST OF PHOTOGRAPHS

INTRODUCTION AND
ACKNOWLEDGMENTS

Alex W. Thrower, a long-time friend and onetime colleague, and I were musing over environmental issues during a lengthy telephone call one afternoon in June 2010. He and I had worked together during the early 1990s when we were both employed by an interstate compact agency near Atlanta, Georgia, specializing in energy and environmental matters. Although we had not worked as direct colleagues for more than a decade and a half at the time of our conversation, we had kept up our friendship across many miles and years. In 1999 and 2000, we even co authored academic articles on hazardous materials transportation as well as sustainability issues associated with the Waste Isolation Pilot Plant, a transuranic nuclear waste facility constructed in southeastern New Mexico.[1]

At the time of our 2010 discussions, I lived in Georgia and had just earned my doctorate in public administration from the University of Georgia (UGA). I was also working in the environmental affairs department for a privately held corporation addressing solid waste issues such as litter abatement and recycling. Alex lived in Richmond, Virginia, and had recently resigned from the United States Department of Energy to form a consulting firm. His specialty was advising governments and utilities on plans for disposing of high-level radioactive waste generated during civilian nuclear power plant operations. We no longer labored in the same field, but we had retained our mutual interest in the natural environment and the ways that government institutions and private sector entities can develop effective sustainability policies.

As Alex and I caught up on recent activities in our respective lives, I told him that I was writing a new book. I was especially interested in southern history during the period of the American Civil War and Reconstruction. He expressed the usual pleasantries and congratulations expected of a friend before posing a question that I have never forgotten.

"In all of your scholarly activities," he asked, "why have you never written a book about environmental issues? You have devoted most of your professional career to dealing with these matters, and yet you have never written about them apart from the two articles that we wrote together. I find that curious."

The question caught me off guard. Until that conversation, I had never contemplated writing a book about the environment even though, as he said, I had devoted much of my adult life to exploring such topics. I don't know why. Perhaps I was so immersed in environmental issues during my day-to-day life that subconsciously I wanted to explore other avenues of intellectual inquiry when I was away from my office. I might have believed that most of the books I had read on the environment were based on scientific data, and I was in no way, shape, or form an environmental scientist or engineer. I was, and remain, a policy person.

The most likely explanation is that I simply had not thought about it until Alex broached the subject.

Our telephone conversation ended and we went our respective ways. I had other writing commitments at the time, but I resolved to ruminate about developing a book on environmental sustainability at some time in the future.

That time is now.[2]

Thank you to my dear friend for making that suggestion during our long-ago conversation. Because Alex inspired me to undertake this project, I dedicate this book to him. When he died unexpectedly at the age of 45 in December 2013, I lost more than a colleague and a friend. I lost a blood brother. As corny as it may sound, his spirit is alive throughout these pages.

Speaking of these pages, it is important to understand what this book is about, and what it is not about, at the outset. It is not a comprehensive analysis of global environmental issues. In my view, such an undertaking would require enormous investments of time and resources, and it might be a fool's errand. Environmental issues, and the manner in which they are addressed, differ markedly among nations, continents, and regions. A book that seeks to analyze environmental issues in substantially all the world's nations requires a team of environmental scientists, policy-makers, ethicists, and other professionals to gather and assess the data. The tome would run to several thousand pages or, alternatively, it would require the authors to employ sweeping generalizations that may or may not be accurate. Rather than engage in such a massive undertaking, I chose to focus on what I know best—American environmentalism.

It is true that about 95 percent of the global population lives outside of the United States. A critic might argue that any book that ignores the overwhelming majority of the earth's population is provincial, at best, and simply inaccurate at worst. The point is well taken. Yet, the American brand of environmentalism is sufficiently distinct from the type of environmental protection practiced by many other countries such that it bears a closer examination apart from the global context.

Similarly, this book examines environmental issues through the prism of American public administration. In other words, it seeks to under-stand how American governmental institutions, especially at the federal level and within the executive branch, have approached, and perhaps ought to approach, questions involving the natural environment. Those who argue that focusing only on American public administration, or only on administration at the federal level, limits the breadth of the analy-sis are absolutely correct in this assertion. Yet, just as the book focuses only on American environmentalism, it is necessary to limit the topic to the federal executive branch activity in the United States. A state-level analysis would be valuable, but that is a topic for another time and place. As for focusing on the politics of sustainability within the overtly political branches of government, many existing works already tackle this ambi-tious topic.

As one might imagine from a book penned by someone holding a PhD in public administration, I am biased in favor of a robust bureaucracy. Such a position is hardly popular outside of the halls of academe these days—and even among scholars, opinions of executive branch agency participation in natural resource protection stretch across a broad con-tinuum. Rightly or wrongly, I believe that federal executive agencies can and should play a part in ensuring that American natural resources are protected. This view does not mean that I believe top-down "command-and-control" management is the best approach, nor am I the proverbial "tax-and-spend liberal" so feared and excoriated by politically conservative commentators. I simply believe that unelected public servants have an important role to play in environmental management. This belief is hardly radical. It does not necessarily risk branding me as a proponent of big, overarching government. In any case, the core question of the appropriate role of unelected officials in a democratic society is a broad topic best left for another time and place as well.

Instead, the issue at hand is whether a role exists for public administrators, especially those at the federal level, to pursue and promote environmental sustainability. I believe that a role does exist. The book, therefore, hopefully possesses a logical structure in service of this thesis. Part I addresses the fundamental concepts necessary to appreciate the topic of environmental sustainability. Thus, Chapter 1 grapples with the general concept, exploring the myriad definitions and points of contention among competing schools of thought. Chapter 2 discusses the integral role of economics in environmental issues. Sustainability, at its core, is about how economic and natural resources are acquired and used. Because economics, the so-called "dismal science," seeks to understand resource allocation and use, any discussion of the environment must include a discussion of economics. Yet, sustainability is not simply a question of economics; therefore, Chapter 3 focuses on environmental ethics. If the study of economics is largely, although not exclusively, a descriptive enterprise, ethics mostly becomes a normative endeavor. In other words, the study of environmental ethics is the study of how competing perspectives view, and ought to view, the appropriate human stance toward the natural environment.

Part II shifts gears, focusing on the processes and institutions of government and how they affect American environmentalism. Chapter 4 outlines the rise of the American administrative state. A major contention of the book is that American federal executive branch agencies are largely responsible for the development and implementation of environmental laws and policies. Assuming that this contention is factually accurate, understanding how those agencies originated and why their missions evolved is critical to understanding the role of American public administration in environmental sustainability. Chapter 5 builds on the insights developed in Chapter 4. After administrative agencies developed historically in the United States, they played a major role in the evolution of American environmental law. Accordingly, Chapter 5 explores the substantive results stemming from federal agencies engaging in rulemaking and litigation.

In addition to federal executive branch agencies, many private parties, especially nongovernmental organizations (NGOs), played, and continue to play, a key role in the development of modern American environmentalism. In Part III, the book discusses how and why an environmental movement originated during the latter half of the twentieth century. Chapter 6 explores the historical beginnings of the movement during the nineteenth century as well as its expansion in the decades that followed. It ends with the Three Mile Island (TMI) incident in 1979, a watershed event that I call (echoing Winston Churchill's famous phrase used in a different context) the "end of the beginning." Chapter 7 highlights the development of an environmental lobby, especially in the years after TMI. The term "lobby" is used broadly here, generally referring to a loose amalgamation of private interest groups that sometimes compete among each other for scarce resources. These groups wield a great deal of influence in the political world of Washington, D.C., as Chapter 7 discusses.

In Part IV, the final chapter synthesizes the discussions from previous chapters to reflect on the future of sustainable development in American public administration. Some federal agencies, most notably the United States Environmental Protection Agency (EPA), are specifically directed to undertake environmental initiatives; however, EPA is not the only agency that can influence environmental sustainability. Agencies across all levels of government and in many different subject matter areas can incorporate sustainability principles into decision-making. It is not always readily obvious how this task may be achieved, but it is important to understand the imperative to act.

Environmental Sustainability and American Public Administration: Past, Present, and Future is the result of more than three years of research and writing. As with any book, the errors and omissions are my responsibility alone. Having said that, I would be remiss if I did not thank the many colleagues, family members, and friends who have helped to make this work possible. Let me start by expressing my sincere appreciation to the wonderful folks at Lexington Books, especially Justin Race, my acquisitions editor who has since departed from the press, and Kate Tafelski, assistant editor for political science and African studies, who helped me cross the finish line. Without their time and talents, this book probably would not have seen the light of day.

I also benefited from the efforts of many fine librarians and archivists, notably the staff of the Horace W. Sturgis Library at Kennesaw State University (KSU), who provided guidance with the interlibrary loan process. KSU has been my academic home since 1998, and Sturgis library personnel have assisted me on most of my previous books. In an era where libraries are struggling to remain relevant with the digitization of research sources, the librarians at Sturgis saved me from untold hours of fruitless searching through Internet sources.

Maria Kopecky, outreach education coordinator at the Aldo Leopold Foundation, proved to be a source of great information on one of the greatest American environmentalists of the twentieth century. Jeff Nelson, a friend and colleague of many years at Dart Container Corporation, graciously allowed me to use a photograph of his father, the late great Gaylord Nelson, principal architect of Earth Day, without restrictions or remuneration. Since I was working on a tight (i.e., nonexistent) budget, his generosity was deeply appreciated.

I also appreciated the support and encouragement from my colleagues at Dart Container Corporation, my main employer since 1992. I extend my thanks (in alphabetical order) to Nick Anas, Christine Cassidy, Jonathan Choi, Pam Dolbee, Humberto Koike, Harry Kopp, Charlene Kuch, Jim Lammers, Frank Liesman, Ruben Nance, Matt O'Brien, Gerardo Pedra, Greg Perkowski, Paul Poe, Ashley Potts, Chuck Redmon, Cheryl Schmidt, AnnMarie Treglia, and Michael Westerfield. Former Dart colleagues Anne Mularoni and Ray Ehrlich greatly aided in my understanding of environmental issues over the years. I also appreciate the wise counsel and good judgment of current colleagues outside of Dart, including (in alphabetical order) Marcy Banton, Jay Bassett, Perry Bennett, Bill Carteaux, Lynn Cobb, George Cruzan, Peter de la Cruz, Chuck Elkins, Stacee Farrell, Marie Gargas, Brennan Georgianni, John Grant, Kanika Greenlee, Gloria Hardegree, Steve Harington,

Joel Heilman, Robert Helminiak, Matt Howe, Jon Kurrle, Mike Levy, Patty Long, Kendra Martin, Nancy Mayes, Jessine Monaghan, Suzanne Morgan, Samantha Padgett, Kevin Perry, Michael Power, Marla Prince, Allen Richardson, John Schweitzer, Dawn Smith, Rickey Smith, Jack Snyder, Michael Taylor, Rudy Underwood, Jeff Viola, Sarah Visser, Mark Walton, Eric Watts, Randy Weghorst, and Gil Ziffer.

Thanks also to friends, family, and academic colleagues who have been so supportive: Dr. Barry Bozeman, currently the Arizona Centennial Professor of Public Management and Technology Policy and Director of the Center of Organizational Research Design at Arizona State University, who served as my dissertation director while I studied at UGA; Dr. Jeffrey L. Brudney, the Betty and Dan Cameron Family Distinguished Professor of Innovation in the Nonprofit Sector at the University of North Carolina Wilmington, a long-time colleague and friend; Shirley Hardrick, housekeeper and babysitter extraordinaire; Laura Mead and her children; Phil and Carolyn Mead and their children; Martha and Dick Pickett; Dr. William D. Richardson, my mentor and dissertation director at Georgia State University, who now serves as the Odeen-Swanson Distinguished Professor of Political Science, chair of the Department of Political Science, and director of the W. O. Farber Center for Civic Leadership at the University of South Dakota; Keith W. Smith, a valued friend for 30+ years, since our law school days at Emory University; Barbara Wise and her children and grandchildren; and Bob and Peggy Youngblood. I now have nine grandchildren—Brianna Marie Carter, Aswad Elisha "Ellie" Woodson, Christopher Kainan Carter, Skylar Renee Carter, Emma Kay Lynne Woodson, Nero Blake Carter, Arya Rayne Carter, Rory Daulton, and Dawson Daulton—and they are always a delight and an inspiration.

I also must extend heartfelt appreciation to family members who are fellow writers: Chris Mead (cousin), Loren B. Mead (uncle), Walter Russell Mead (cousin), Robert Sidney Mellette (cousin), William W. Mellette (uncle), and Jim Wise (cousin). They have inspired me in myriad ways throughout the years.

Monroe, Georgia
July 2016

NOTES

1. Alex W. Thrower and J. Michael Martinez, "Hazardous Materials Transportation in an Age of Devolution," *The American Review of Public Administration* 29 (June 1999): 167–89; Alex W. Thrower and J. Michael Martinez, "Reconciling Anthropocentrism and Biocentrism Through Adaptive Management: The Case of the Waste Isolation Pilot Plant and Public Risk Perception," *The Journal of Environment & Development* 9 (March 2000): 68–97.

2. After my conversation with Alex, I wrote and published a book on environmental issues prior to this one: J. Michael Martinez, *American Environmentalism: Philosophy, History, and Public Policy* (Boca Raton, FL: CRC Press, 2014). Alex was the inspiration for that book and this one.

I
CONCEPTS

❶

DEFINING AND UNDERSTANDING
SUSTAINABILITY

"Sustainability" in the twenty-first century became an important concept in the debate concerning how the natural environment should be preserved and protected. Americans who would not have recognized the term a decade earlier suddenly spoke glowingly of the need for "sustainable development" and "sustainability in the marketplace." It was important, they said, to think of generations not yet born and protect their interests.

As the sustainability concept gained cachet, thoughtful environmentalists worried that a broad, over arching term would become a meaningless buzzword as it entered the national lexicon. Trendy concepts sometimes live and die in rapid succession, capturing headlines one year and lapsing into obscurity the next. If a desire for environmental protection is to lead to positive change, the vague "sustainability" concept must be translated into a concrete, measurable program complete with clearly delineated objectives and specific, quantifiable milestones. In the parlance of scholars, the variables must be operationalized so that a policy is formulated and a plan is implemented. Otherwise, sustainability is an amorphous notion, food for thought but little more than a grandiose, impracticable ideal.[1]

Environmentalists were wise to be concerned about the practicality of sustainability. As more citizens learned of the term and professed their

allegiance, the concept became less precise, encompassing any definition the speaker desired. In the environmental field, as in any field, the
absence of a fixed, more-or-less agreed-upon meaning makes it exceedingly difficult to determine whether a thing or a process—a consumer
product, a construction project, or a method of carrying out tasks in the
workplace—offers any level of environmental protection. A term that
means anything a speaker wants it to mean, ironically, holds no fixed
meaning at all.

With the increasingly common use of the term "sustainability" among
the citizenry, it did not help matters that associated colloquialisms were
equally vague and fuzzy. Dilettantes suddenly bandied about hollow
phrases that lacked virtually any content. "Green," "environmentally
friendly," "eco-friendly," "earth friendly," and similar labels became com-
monplace, but they did not communicate useful information because
they lacked context. In the marketplace, only one proper response exists
to the query, "Is your product or process 'green'?": "Is it 'green' compared with what other, presumably mutually exclusive options?" Absent
an understanding of what standards or features constitute "greenness,"
the question cannot be answered satisfactorily. Being "green" means
many things to many people. Without consensus on the definition, the
term is vacuous.

One commentator has observed that the concept is not vague or
imprecise, but putting sustainability into practice presents a challenge. "Environmental sustainability is a rather clear concept," Robert
Goodland observed. "However, there is much uncertainty about the
details of its application."[2]

Yet all hope has not been lost. Some organizations, notably the
International Organization for Standardization (ISO), have developed
standards for eco-labels in an effort to address the definitional problem. ISO standards 14020 and 14024, for example, recommend that
eco-labels in the marketplace adhere to several core principles such as
avoiding financial conflicts of interest, relying on sound scientific methods and testing protocols, and ensuring openness and transparency in
explaining how and why the product meets the standard. Ideally, ISO
standards relate to specific environmental products and processes in a
specific context. The goal is for a consumer to recognize the inclusion of
an ISO standard as tantamount to a Good Housekeeping seal of approval.

In choosing whether to purchase a product, the consumer ideally compares labels. "Ah, Product A is ISO certified, but Product B is not. All other things being equal, I will purchase Product A." Theoretically, the manufacturer of Product B realizes the market advantage of securing an ISO certification and therefore changes a manufacturing process to become "green" in accordance with the standard, moving away from a practice or process that generates a higher level of pollutants than do the alternatives. As a means of standardizing measures suitable for labeling, the ISO approach has been a step in the right direction, but it begs the broader question of defining sustainability writ large. The ISO effort is an example of a sustainable practice in action, but it is not a definition of the concept any more than pointing to a particular horse grazing in a field serves as a suitable definition of what it means to be a horse.[3]

OUR COMMON FUTURE

Perhaps the best known articulation of the sustainability concept originated in a report issued by the United Nations (UN) World Commission on the Environment and Development (WCED) in 1987. *Our Common Future* is often called the "Brundtland Report," named for WCED chairwoman Gro Harlem Brundtland, who served as the Norwegian minister for environmental affairs during the 1970s and later became prime minister of Norway and director-general of the World Health Organization. The report characterized development as sustainable if it "meets the needs of the present without compromising the ability of future generations to meet their own needs." To achieve this amorphous objective, public policies must balance "economic and social systems and ecological conditions."[4]

The report is unquestionably a political document, as it had to be. Whenever representatives of individual countries convene to debate matters of mutual interest, they must produce a written deliverable that accounts for a multitude of interests and interpretations, a compromise among competing parties and values. A report professing to reflect agreement among participants must be vague and imprecise on purpose so that the parties can present the results to their constituencies and offer an interpretation consistent with whatever various purposes are required to gain acceptance at home. So it was with *Our Common Future*.

The report was a starting point for discussing "sustainability," which was used virtually interchangeably with the term "sustainable development." Ideally, the terms should be differentiated. Sustainability refers to the overall goal of ensuring that consumption of natural resources does not exceed the regenerative capacity of the environment, while sustainable development is the process used to achieve the goal. Some commentators refer to sustainability as the output and sustainable development as the inputs that supposedly lead to the output.[5]

Such nuances may be teased out of the Brundtland Report, but they are not clear from the text. For this reason, the report's definition of sustainability has served as a starting point for discussions of sustainability, but it seldom has been the end of the debate. As with any work produced by a committee, *Our Common Future* has suffered from no shortage of critics. On the left, detractors have objected to the anthropocentric, or "human-centered," emphasis implicit in the definition. Meeting human needs is the focal point, as though the needs of other living things are less important or not important at all. Critics questioned whether any development can by definition be deemed "sustainable" if it impedes the ability of all animals to live on earth in a relatively unfettered state.[6]

For some audiences, the terms "sustainable" and "development" appear to be contradictory—or at least difficult to reconcile as a measure of environmental effects. The latter term presupposes that human beings will alter the natural environment to suit their needs and desires. Development necessarily entails manmade modifications to soil, vegetation, and trees, at a minimum. Even if these changes require few physical disturbances, they hold major consequences. An area that was previously uninhabited or sparsely inhabited can change when large numbers of people inundate new neighborhoods while demanding goods and services to suit their lifestyle choices. The developer can employ a multitude of processes and programs designed to minimize environmental effects, but even a well-constructed, "green" construction process invariably leaves behind a human footprint. Development always involves economic trade-offs.[7]

The concept of sustainability does not necessarily refer to economics, although eliminating economic considerations is difficult. The crucial component is a focus on natural resources and the conditions required for those resources to remain at least at the same level and quality as the present, and perhaps even in greater abundance in the future. To be sustainable is to preserve the status quo, at a minimum.

Environmentalists have noted that the Brundtland Report presupposes that "weak sustainability" is an appropriate philosophical construct. As discussed in Chapter 3 of this book, weak sustainability is the notion that trade-offs can be made between "natural" and "man-made" capital. In other words, weak sustainability adopts the economists' insight that substitutions among and between different types of capital can be, and should be, accommodated. Thus, a supporter of weak sustainability would countenance a construction project that intruded on wetlands as long as the construction company protected wetlands in another area or otherwise financially compensated persons harmed by the intrusion. No serious distinction is made between the *types* of capital. The challenge is to determine an equitable, more-or-less defensible valuation of natural wetlands compared with the economic benefits of a construction project. The goods can be substituted, provided an economic valuation can be calculated.[8]

Chapter 3 discusses the relative merits of weak sustainability. In this context, the criticism is that the Brundtland Report reflexively accepts a mainstream economic perspective. More expansive definitions based on the concept of biocentric (world-centered) environmentalism are not considered. By grounding the definition of sustainability in an anthropocentric framework, the report authors reduce the concept to a matter of assigning economic valuations to resources and establishing a system of trade-offs among apparently indistinguishable types of resources. For the committed environmentalist, this straightforward economic exercise underscores the crucial problem with sustainability as a unit of analysis. Natural capital is markedly distinct from manmade capital, but many economists do not recognize such distinctions.[9]

Mainstream economists, in the meantime, cite a separate criticism of the Brundtland Report's definition of sustainability. In their view, the difficulty lies not in the report's failure to recognize an expansive view of sustainability, but in the admonition that current consumers must preserve resources for future generations. This concern can be thought of as the "time extension" problem. Persons alive today can envision a world of the next generation—their children—and even the generation following that one—their grandchildren. Beyond that, it becomes conceptually challenging to think of three, four, or ten generations of people yet to be born. The world these future people will inhabit and the challenges they will face become increasingly difficult to imagine. In all likelihood, their needs and sensibilities will differ dramatically from the needs and sensibilities of the present generation. To assume that people living early in the twenty-first century can plan effectively for progeny living a century later is bordering on the ridiculous.

Moreover, generations yet to be born may be able to rely on inventions and technologies undreamt of in this less-than-enlightened age. A current generation that sacrifices today for people who have not yet graced the earth may be denying themselves necessities that will no longer be necessary for future peoples. To think that intentional deprivations will be for naught is dismaying to consumers who are not predisposed to accept sacrifices absent concrete assurances that future benefits will be worth current costs.[10]

Environmentalists bristle at what they see as selfish consumerism. To pawn off looming environmental problems on future generations in hopes that technological progress will mitigate destructive effects created today is beyond short-sightedness. It is half a step away from criminality. Broadly speaking, future generations will require the same things that current generations require—clean air, fresh water, and a non toxic environment. The means for achieving these goals may change as society and technology change, but the ends remain the same.[11]

Instead of focusing on the Brundtland Report's implied commitment to anthropocentricism, another perspective would be to concentrate on the concept of intergenerational equity. Setting aside the time extension problem and assuming for the sake of argument that future generations will need exactly the same types and quantities of resources required today, the guiding principle becomes clear, even if the means of adhering to those principles are murky. The anthropocentric argument is grounded in economics and efficiency, the typical mainstream analysis applied to any decision-making involving resource allocation. Emphasizing the notion of equity, by contrast, means that planners must establish a base line measure for determining the quality and quantity of natural resources currently available. Afterward, the policy is conceptually simple. Any use of resources must be measured against the baseline. An economic policy that diminishes the quality or quantity of those resources is prohibited while a policy that maintains the status quo or improves environmental quality is pursued.[12]

It takes little imagination or analysis to anticipate practical objections to this argument. Establishing a realistic baseline and expecting multiple nations to commit to the standard even if it harms their economy and perhaps their short-term national security is naïve. Policing international environmental standards raises a host of problems that have plagued international law for centuries. How do nations agree to enforce agreements when those same nations scoff at anything that smacks of a loss of sovereignty? What steps is the international community willing to take to punish a transgressor?[13]

Whether the Brundtland Report was a breakthrough because it propelled environmental issues onto the international agenda, as supporters argued, or it was a vacuous political compromise that paid lip service to ecology but was devoid of practical meaning, as detractors charged, it raised a difficult problem for anyone concerned about humankind's relationship to nature. Even the most committed environmentalist recognized that no matter how much one plans to preserve and protect natural resources, human beings will always use resources by virtue of their existence. To some extent, therefore, sustainability must allow for a measure of environmental degradation. The act of breathing, eating, engaging in locomotion, defecating, and dying affects the environment. The question is whether these acts can be offset by other human actions and therefore undertaken without exhausting finite resources.[14]

AGENDA 21

The UN had been involved in global environmental issues long before *Our Common Future* appeared in 1987. As early as 1972, the organization sponsored the first ever global environmental conference in Stockholm, Sweden. As a follow-up, the UN held the Conference on Environment and Development in Rio de Janeiro, Brazil, in June 1992. Popularly known as the Earth Summit, the Rio conference brought together government officials and activists to discuss the notion of sustainable development on a worldwide scale. During the summit, participants produced a 700-page, 40-chapter document known as Agenda 21, a reference to environmental needs for the twenty-first century.[15]

The authors, recognizing that environmental sustainability is a broad, all-encompassing subject, divided the document into four sections. The first, titled "Social and Economic Dimensions," aims to combat poverty, especially in developing nations where the resources are few and the government infrastructure is weak or non existent. The section discusses plans for changing patterns of consumption to preserve fragile, scarce resources, as well as promote the health of citizens who frequently have little or no access to quality health care and disease prevention. Section II, "Conservation and Management of Resources for Development," focuses most directly on the issues usually associated with the natural environment: protecting the atmosphere from air pollution, curbing deforestation, protecting fragile environments, conserving biodiversity, controlling pollution, along with managing biotechnology as well as radioactive waste. The third section, "Strengthening the Role of Major Groups," discusses the importance of organized entities, including non governmental organizations (NGOs), women and young people, local officials, and businesses along with indigenous peoples, including farmers. In "Means of Implementation," the final section, the authors outline the methods by which environmental protection can be achieved, such as science, technology transfer, education, international institutions, and financial mechanisms.[16]

As part of the document, the authors identified 27 core principles that lead to a sustainable natural environment. First and foremost, "Human beings are at the center of concerns for sustainable development. They are entitled to a healthy and productive life in harmony with nature." The language of this principle calls to mind Article 25 of the UN's well-known Universal Declaration of Human Rights. The article states, "Everyone has the right to a standard of living adequate for the health and well-being of himself and of his family, including food, clothing, housing and medical care and necessary social services, and the right to security in the event of unemployment, sickness, disability, widowhood, old age or other lack of livelihood in circumstances beyond his control."[17]

Many environmentalists the world over support the humanistic principles and sensible proposals for sustainable growth found in Agenda 21. It is difficult to fathom how anyone could object to innocuous calls for all nations to meet the basic needs of their citizens, improve living standards for the citizenry, and manage the world's natural resources in an efficient manner. The document encourages, but in no way requires, countries to develop comprehensible, reasonable, land-use plans to be implemented at all levels of government.

Yet, as with any comprehensive plan for changing the status quo, the devil is in the details. Agenda 21 supporters also recognize the difficulties inherent in urging poor, developing nations to provide a healthy, clean environment when those nations lack the economic resources and political stability to meet the basic needs of their people. Especially in nations riven by civil war, malnourishment, crippling diseases, and the lack of an adequate infrastructure or a history of effective self-governance, protecting the natural environment can be challenging, if not impossible.[18]

In other countries, notably the United States and the western democracies, conservative elements have taken umbrage at Agenda 21, launching a political campaign against the concept of United Nations-led environmental protection efforts. Right-wingers have objected to a UN program that encourages countries to set aside their own national interests in favor of "extreme environmentalism, social engineering, and global political control." Conservative commentator Glenn Beck is one of the most vehement critics of anything that smacks of environmentalism or international cooperation. Beck wrote several novels with co-author Harriet Parke about Agenda 21. (More precisely, Harriet Parke wrote the books and Glenn Beck applied his brand to the series of dystopian novels.) Well known for his belief in conspiracy theories, Beck envisioned Agenda 21 as a dangerous plan to abrogate American sovereignty and institute world government under the auspices of a diabolical United Nations. In *Agenda 21: Into the Shadows*, Parke/Beck wrote: "It was once named America, but now it is just 'the Republic.' Following the worldwide implementation of a United Nations-led program called Agenda 21, the once-proud people of America have become obedient residents who live in barren, brutal Compounds and serve the autocratic, merciless Authorities."[19]

DEMOCRACY AND THE NATURAL ENVIRONMENT

The debate over an appropriate definition of sustainability has never occurred in a vacuum. The context is almost as important as the definition, and the context has evolved. The nature of the environmental field—if it is an organized field of scholarly inquiry in the first place, which is another point of contention—changed at exactly the time that the term "sustainability" came into general usage. The nature of the change created one set of problems even as it solved another set.

The involvement of the nation's citizens in crafting public policy is a relatively recent phenomenon. Environmentalism as practiced in the United States in the 1960s and 1970s became a grassroots movement where citizens participated in decision-making concerning many highly salient problems, including the natural environment. Self-proclaimed environmentalists took up the mantle of protecting and preserving nature with an almost religious fervor. NGOs solicited donations from contributors in all walks of life. Parent-Teacher Association (PTA) members held recycling drives at their children's schools. Homeowners' associations sponsored community cleanups to retrieve litter deposited in neighborhoods. In later years, stay-at-home moms launched websites to empower their friends and like-minded individuals to publicize consumer product bans against household items that were treasured in years past, but which now became "pet peeves" of a vocal minority promoting alternate products thought to possess real or imagined "green" attributes. It became a brave new world of environmentalism.

Environmental protection, in a sense, has been democratized. The days when elites controlled access to information and formulated top-down policies (if any were formulated at all) about pollution control and abatement are over. The causes of the tectonic shift could be, and have been, debated endlessly. Perhaps the generation that recognized the first Earth Day on April 22, 1970, empowered future generations to demand accountability from governments and corporations that allow the environment to be polluted. Maybe the new laws and regulations enacted in the 1970s and 1980s finally bore fruit. A plausible explanation is that NGOs and individuals who campaign for clean air, water, and land have reached a large enough group of Americans that the environment is part of the ongoing national conversation about life and how it should be lived.[20]

However it happened, citizens speak out in favor of environmental issues as never before. As part of that ongoing conversation, citizens have taken up the mantle of sustainability. They urge all manner of businesses and government institutions to demonstrate a commitment to sustainable development. It is an attempt to incorporate environmental considerations into all manner of institutional decision-making, but it also creates an incentive for using creative methods of defining the term.

If sustainability means everything and nothing, the term or its synonyms can be used to create maximum distortion. In the commercial marketplace, environmental claims that a particular product possesses one or more "green" attributes leads to a proliferation of false or misleading statements. The problem has become so widespread that a term has developed: "greenwashing." A marketing claim must be qualified to such an extent that the claim of biodegradability, compostability, recyclability, or ability to be reused can be understood in context. A company must provide data to substantiate the claim or face charges of greenwashing. The U.S. Federal Trade Commission (FTC), the federal agency tasked with policing such claims, eventually created a series of green marketing guidelines to ensure at least a minimal level of context and consistency for companies that choose to promote an environmental message.[21]

Despite the presence of the FTC and other governmental entities in the field—a development that will be discussed throughout this book—much of the modern environmental movement has occurred outside of governments, among NGOs and concerned citizens. Beginning in the 1970s, the citizen environmentalist came to the forefront of a national, and sometimes international, debate. An environmentalist no longer needs to possess advanced university degrees in scientific disciplines or sport illustrious resumes showing clinical work at government laboratories, private sector businesses, or major research universities. An environmentalist holds that title because he or she self-identifies as one.[22]

In any democratic system, the process is as important as the outcome. Having one's voice heard and one's feelings validated are important components of democratized environmentalism. The participation of the middling sort in the affairs of the nation has been a blessing and a curse for governments that allow the people to engage in political and economic decision-making. When citizens make their opinions known and actively take part in governance, they buy into the results more often than if policies are promulgated on high and simply announced by elites. Yet, in the words of *The Federalist*, democracies everywhere have been "spectacles of turbulence and contention." People who perhaps possess neither the temperament nor the education to reach informed decisions sometimes act on incomplete data, misinformation, or outright prejudice. Finding a middle approach between removing the citizenry from decision-making altogether and following trends based on whim and mythology remains a challenge for twenty-first-century American environmentalism.[23]

THE PRECAUTIONARY PRINCIPLE AND THE PROBLEM OF UNCERTAINTY

As the environmental movement has become democratized, adherents have expressed support for the precautionary principle. Decisions involving environmental issues invariably require decision-makers to confront gaps in the data and missing information. Initiating a major construction project that may intrude on wetlands, marketing a new chemical, or limiting the amount of an industrial pollutant released into the atmosphere requires stakeholders to assume certain facts regarding future developments. Decision-makers cannot reach decisions with absolute certainty because data are always missing, incomplete, ambiguous, or conflicting. They must rely on presuppositions and guess-work, to some extent. Although analogous cases can provide valuable clues about the likelihood of specific outcomes, sometimes the unique nature of the resources in question transform the instant case into an unprecedented, or extremely rare, event. In such situations, decision-makers face a complex, multifaceted situation with numerous variables to consider. They cannot make a "perfect" decision, even assuming the definition of perfection could be established with consensus from all stakeholders.

Complex processes inherently involve uncertainty and risk. As one group of researchers exploring the risk of devastating floods has observed, "Because all information about the future is uncertain, [researchers] must make decisions under uncertainty every day, in a complex, evolving social, institutional, and political environment. Given these conditions, and the limited information and time they have to address numerous demands, practitioners often deal with uncertainty by finding the best information they can quickly and easily obtain and interpret, making the decision required for the moment, and then moving on."[24]

The literature on scientific decision-making under conditions of uncertainty recognizes that all decision-making processes involve uncertainties, although the nature and extent of those uncertainties varies. Some uncertainties are treated as "suboptimal" owing to missing variables. This strain of the literature suggests that the iterative nature of scientific research and decision-making eventually will fill in gaps in the data. Given enough time and research, the missing variables will be identified and supplied. Other sources suggest that the concept of "uncertainty" is far more profound; it is not merely a question of missing information. Rather, some types of knowledge are missing because epistemology is necessarily imprecise. Scientific answers depend on how scientific questions are framed, and framing questions into researchable hypotheses is a human enterprise. Because human enterprises are subject to the imperfections of human beings, questions can be developed that cannot be answered or at least answered in a manner that is precise and free from bias.[25]

Even as they wrestle with multiple constraints, decision-makers almost always seek to maximize utility; that is, according to expected utility theory, they choose a course of action that presumably yields the highest level of benefits with a lowest level of cost. The difficulty arises when uncertainty obfuscates some measures of costs and benefits. In virtually every case, decision-makers must grapple with unknown variables. Ideally, they will conceptualize uncertainty in terms of the following: (1) the frequency (probability) of an event; (2) assessments of credibility intervals around the estimates of probability; and (3) entropy, which refers to the uncertainty associated with one course of action versus a series of competing actions.[26]

The theory of information entropy dictates that when the probability of achieving a desired outcome among competing choices in the face of uncertainty is unknown or unknowable, a decision-making stalemate can occur because a clear decision rule is absent. This scenario sometimes is known as "analysis paralysis" because no matter how one assesses the data, he or she cannot resolve doubt when probabilities are equal or risks are unquantifiable. If all desirable outcomes are more or less equal or unknown, something more is needed if a decision is to be made. This lack of information about the probability of desired outcomes is captured in the term "equipoise," which refers to "equal beliefs, or equally distributed uncertainty about the relative effects of competing ... alternatives." "Equipoise" does not necessarily indicate that a precise quantitative assessment of variables can never be observed. Instead, the term has a looser meaning; it expresses the difficulty in decision-making that occurs when no one option appears superior to others and there exists a possibility that the doubt will never be resolved satisfactorily. In other words, when decision-makers confront a novel problem, their educated guesses and elegant research hypotheses cannot suggest a preferred course of action. No clear decision rule exists or is likely to exist in the foreseeable future. Some researchers call the choice between seemingly equivalent alternatives "Alternative Futures," or the choice between discrete alternatives where the outcome cannot be predicted with a reasonable degree of reliability beforehand.[27]

Another level of uncertainty exists involving a "Range of Futures," or the possibility that no discrete alternatives exist or, in any case, the alternatives have yet to be identified. This situation occurs when decision-makers must decide, for example, whether a new product containing a novel chemical can be manufactured and sold in the United States. Despite the exhaustive research conducted by chemical companies marketing the product, invariably the time needed to determine whether long-term, negative side effects will occur—decades, in some instances—has not elapsed. Because data are limited, it is possible that the range of potential side effects is greater than one might predict even when reviewing the side effects associated with similar products and chemicals from the same family of chemicals. Making comparisons and calculating risks when a Range of Futures is present is far more difficult than when Alternative Futures are involved because the former lacks precision in its data collection and analysis. Nonetheless, there is a high probability that given enough time and data, discrete categories can be developed and eventually decision-makers can discriminate among competing options. In other words, data are missing, but eventually they may become known.[28]

The worst-case scenario for decision-makers can be labeled "True Ambiguity." The situation is unprecedented, and knowledge about options is so incomplete that researchers cannot begin to calculate the quantity or quality of discrete choices. Unlike a situation with a Range of Futures, with True Ambiguity it is impossible to determine whether enough information will be collected and analyzed to improve the decision-making process. One might deem this scenario an "epistemological crisis" because the information necessary to make an informed choice may be unknowable. The difficulty with True Ambiguity is not simply that data are missing; a method of understanding data even if they were to be identified and collected is absent. Perhaps the method will never be found, or at least never found in a meaningful timeframe. A researcher faced with True Ambiguity should not despair that certainty is impossible and therefore become paralyzed with indecision, but he or she should recognize the travails associated with research when uncertainties outweigh certainties.[29]

In cases where uncertainties exist, "satisficing" is the order of the day. It is seldom possible (and perhaps not even desirable) to accumulate all the information necessary to make a fully informed decision. Sometimes the information could be gathered and assessed, but monetary or time constraints make it unlikely or impossible that the data will be available. In some instances, policy-makers deliberately obscure the reasons for their policy choices or they build in ambiguities so that the policy can attract political support that might not be available if the details of a policy were known beforehand. It is entirely possible, and often likely, that a legislative body will enact a statute or a regulatory body will promulgate a rule that lacks even rudimentary specificity. What the policy lacks during the formulation phase theoretically can be supplied during the implementation phase.[30]

Decision-makers develop heuristic tools to guide their thought processes. The precautionary principle is one such tool. According to the principle, when a decision must be made involving environmental protection and variables are missing or unknown, decision-makers should err on the side of caution. Instead of waiting until all information on possible consequences can be amassed, decision-makers should assume that environmental degradation will occur and act to eliminate or mitigate the damage as soon as they become aware of the risk. In some cases, they make take action to protect the natural environment even when the original threat never materialized or turned out to be far less severe than anticipated.

In essence, therefore, the precautionary principle is a tool for deciding who bears the burden of proof when risk and uncertainty exist.

In any decision-making process, one party must demonstrate whether it is preferable to act or refrain from acting in the face of a potential problem. On one hand, if a decision is made quickly, even when variables have not been identified and data gaps have not been plugged, the decision may be premature and exacerbate a problem owing to a dearth of high-quality, complete information. Private companies or society as a whole may incur unnecessary costs that impede their ability to undertake other projects. Private sector firms decry a government requirement that they spend millions of dollars to install pollution control devices to combat an environmental problem that was not as dire as originally feared. Under these circumstances, business leaders argue that the money they invested in superfluous environmental controls could have been better used to create new jobs through expansion, invest in new technology, or even finance environmental controls in other areas. The opportunity costs associated with using limited resources in an area where the costs were unnecessary outweigh the benefits received because the resources would have provided a higher return on investment if they had been used elsewhere.

On the other hand, if decision-makers wait until they had filled all gaps in the data, the underlying situation may reach a critical point and the problem might be larger and more daunting to address. Waiting for complete information means that decision-makers never act or they are so dilatory in acting that what originated as a minor problem has ballooned into a major crisis. If the burden of proof is placed on decision-makers advocating immediate action at the risk of suffering a host of adverse consequences, the best test of their credibility is to wait for those consequences to occur. By that time, it may be too late to stave off calamity.[31]

Climate change is the quintessential example of the precautionary principle in action. Political conservatives present a range of arguments against making policy changes to fight climate change. Some observers contend that climate change is a hoax and is based on faulty premises. The world is not growing warmer despite doomsayers' claims to the contrary. These critics cite popular theories about climate cooling that proliferated in some quarters during the 1970s. In their view, the hue and cry over climate change and the production of greenhouse gases are the inevitable result of politically liberal environmentalists who flitter from one crisis *du jour* to another in search of power, influence, and money through contributions from donors fearful of a host of deleterious effects that will never come to pass.

Still other conservatives accept the fundamental premise that the earth is trending toward warmer temperatures but they question whether human beings are responsible. Climate changes are cyclical, they argue. In some epochs, the world has endured an ice age while other eras have witnessed hotter periods. Even if human activity has triggered warmer global temperatures, the amount of variation is only a few degrees, which will not produce a significant impact across millennia. In short, a warming trend is not a cause for alarm.

Still other observers willingly admit that the earth is warming and that human beings are largely responsible for what is an alarming and significant change, but they question whether one nation, especially a mature nation such as the United States, can affect a positive outcome for the problem. As long as rapidly growing, industrializing countries such as China, India, and Brazil, among others, continue to emit greenhouse gases with little regard for global well-being, the incremental benefits of the United States reducing carbon emissions will be negligible. In the meantime, as all nations compete in the global economy, any country that labors under self-imposed constraints such as voluntarily reducing greenhouse gasses will hamper its competitiveness. No nation should hobble itself in the race for economic advantages unless other nations act in the same manner. Yet, political conservatives doubt that other nations will willingly sign onto an international agreement that places severe constraints on their ability to rely in fossil fuels unfettered by expensive pollution control devices. Even if these nations sign such agreements, they might cheat because they recognize that enforcement mechanisms under international law are pitifully weak.

Environmentalists combat these claims in several ways, all of which ultimately depend on the precautionary principle. The scientific community (to the extent that a community exists in the first place) is remarkably unified about the data on climate change. The overwhelming consensus is that the climate is growing warmer, humankind is a major reason for the change, and the results are significant. Although some naysayers continue to protest the state of the science, enough researchers have weighed in with credible evidence that the matter is mostly settled. The thorny question remains, however, about what, if anything, should be done to address the issue.[32]

The precautionary principle is especially useful to proponents of an activist public policy. If it is better to be safe rather than sorry, it is preferable to act now even if every question cannot be definitively answered. Scientists understand that the use of fossil fuels is a major contributor to global warming. It is in the best interests of everyone, regardless of the country involved, to enact policies that cut human sources of pollution. If the earth is treated as a common pool resource—that is, a resource that everyone can use, but no one assumes responsibility for caring for the resource after he or she consumes what he or she desires—the consequences can be catastrophic, especially for future generations. Once again, the idea of sustainability returns to the notion of persons who succeed the current population.[33]

Sustainability questions always turn on timing questions, usually in more ways than one. Reliance on the precautionary principle will always remain contentious because the concept does not provide specific guidance on an appropriate threshold level of evidence necessary for instituting action. Research proceeds in stages, and the appropriate stage of action depends on one's approach to data collection and evidence assessment. When an environmental problem initially is identified, researchers begin collecting evidence and sharing it with other researchers in the field. Early in the evidence-gathering mode, when the data are raw and undigested, their meaning generally is anything but conclusive. Gradually, trends in the evidence become clear, and researchers posit hypotheses upon which decision-makers base their decisions. Later, as multiple hypotheses emerge, different schools of thought may debate competing interpretations of the data. Occasionally, competing explanations are fused into a single theory that is more or less agreed upon by most researchers in the field.

Decision-makers must decide whether to formulate and implement public policies during the early or late stages of the investigation. The timing becomes the crux of the problem. If they act too early, before an issue is ripe, they may not understand the parameters of a problem, or even if a problem exists in the first place. If they act too late, when the issue is moot, the problem may be so large or severe that policy solutions may be ineffective. Decision-makers ideally will intervene when an issue has been identified, sufficiently persuasive data have been amassed, and policy solutions can resolve or substantially mitigate the problem.

Some environmentalists contend that a discussion of mitigation misses the point. If decision-makers wait to act until a problem has occurred, mitigation may not be possible. Instead, decisions must be reached and implemented *before* a problem becomes a full-fledged environmental crisis. The old adage that an ounce of prevention is worth a pound of cure applies here. Mitigation is tantamount to treating a heart attack after it occurs. It is far better to prevent the attack in the first place.[34]

THE POLITICIZATION OF SUSTAINABILITY

Concepts such as the precautionary principle are never precise because they are heuristic tools for addressing issues that defy easy quantitative analysis. Since they are imprecise and open to multiple interpretations, large, highly contested environmental ideas and concepts necessarily attract supporters and opponents who endlessly debated a proper course of action. These debates frequently occur in an atmosphere of ideological partisanship.

The debate over climate change highlights a crucial feature of twenty-first-century environmentalism: politics. The notion that politics will intrude into scientific or ecological decision-making is seen by many as anathema, for it implies that something nasty and underhanded has occurred. Rather than decide issues on a data-driven, scientific basis, decision-makers seemingly surrender to powerful forces that compel a conclusion based on inappropriate factors such as corporate interests, the number of jobs affected as well as other economic considerations, or the will of a misinformed majority. Although such questionable practices undoubtedly occur, politics need not be a corrupting practice in all circumstances.

If politics is thought of as the art of the possible, a political process is yet another form of arriving at a decision in the face of a democratized environmental movement and uncertainty in the data. The fear of political interference usually involves a scenario where a clear decision rule based on relatively well-established science overwhelmingly suggests that Option A should be selected when, in fact, well-financed lobbyists

descend into the political landscape spreading money around and fran-
tically peddling their influence so that Option B, the clearly inferior
choice, triumphs. If this situation occurs, the distaste for politics felt by
many Americans is understandable.

Yet, if the data are conflicting or incomplete, multiple parties espouse
multiple theories and competing points of view about the desired outcome, and the decision rule is not clear—and probably never will be—
politics can be helpful in resolving the matter. In a situation where the
costs and benefits are muddled or more or less equal, political considerations can provide clues to an acceptable outcome. Politics can and will
be a factor in resolving the issue, for better or worse.[35]

Virtually every institution of government exists in a political realm,
and so decision-makers must make a virtue of necessity. Because environmental policies frequently are promulgated on the federal level and
because many decision-makers are immersed in the political process,
a focus on politics is hardly surprising. Political concerns are always at
the forefront when public bureaucracies compete in the policy-making
arena to establish and maintain a policy domain. Researcher D.D. Riley
observed that public administrators must be politicians, at least in part,
because they can never perform their tasks merely as policy specialists
or technocrats. "If bureaucrats are going to enter the political arena they
will need to bring some coin of the realm—that is, they will need power,"
he wrote. "Knowledge provides some, but not enough, so bureaucrats
must find an expressly political base of power." Public organizations are
staffed by personnel who seek to establish a domain, distinguish the
agency from its competition, and develop effective political strategies for
maintaining—and perhaps strengthening—the agency's domain. Aside
from working with congressional committees and subcommittees in the
political realm, public administrators cater to clientele groups concomi-
tant with establishing a domain. These groups appeal to the agency to
respond to the groups' interests and, in turn, they provide knowledge
and information to public servants. Ideology and political consciousness
are never absent from an agency's agenda, to say nothing of other stakeholders—environmentalists, industry representatives, environmental
attorneys, and concerned citizens.[36]

The reality of environmental sustainability is that many interrelated
factors influence how the concept is perceived and how government

programs aimed at achieving sustainability are implemented. Anyone who hopes to understand sustainability as something more than a buzzword must delve into the nuances of the topic, especially two key, related subjects: economics and ethics. Chapter 2 explores the former and Chapter 3 discusses the latter.

NOTES

1. Sophia Imran *et al.*, "Reinterpreting the Definition of Sustainable Development for a More Ecocentric Reorientation," *Sustainable Development* 22 (March/April 2014): 134–35.

2. Robert Goodland, "The Concept of Environmental Sustainability," *Annual Review of Ecology and Systematics* 26 (1995): 19.

3. Magali A. Delmas and Maria J. Montes-Sancho, "An Institutional Perspective on the Diffusion of International Management System Standards: The Case of the Environmental Management Standard ISO 14001," *Business Ethics Quarterly* 21 (January 2011): 103–32; Ira R. Feldman, "ISO Standards, Environmental Management Systems, and Ecosystem Services," *Environmental Quality Management* 21 (Spring 2012): 69–79; Bo Weidema, "Has ISO 14040/44 Failed Its Role as a Standard for Life Cycle Assessment?" *Journal of Industrial Ecology* 18 (June 2014): 324–26.

4. World Commission on Environment and Development, *Our Common Future* (Oxford and New York: Oxford University Press, 1987), 40, 136.

5. Ivan Bolis, "Review: When Sustainable Development Risks Losing Its Meaning; Delimiting the Concept with a Comprehensive Literature Review," *Journal of Cleaner Production* 83 (November 2014): 7–20; Christine Byrch *et al.*, "Sustainable Development: What Does It Really Mean?" *University of Auckland Business Review* 11 (Autumn 2009): 1–7; Imran *et al.*, "Reinterpreting the Definition of Sustainable Development for a More Ecocentric Reorientation," 134–44; Michael Redclift, "Sustainable Development (1987–2005): An Oxymoron Comes of Age," *Sustainable Development* 13 (October 2005): 212–27.

6. See, for example, Benjamin Habib, "Sustainability is Not Enough: A Call for Regeneration," *Ethos* 23 (June 2015): 8; Erling Holden *et al.*, "Sustainable Development: *Our Common Future* Revisited," *Global Environmental Change* 26 (May 2014): 130–39.

7. Benjamin Habib, "Sustainability is Not Enough: A Call for Regeneration," 8; Vera Mignaqui, "Sustainable Development as a Goal: Social, Environmental and Economic Dimensions," *International Journal of Social Quality* 4 (Summer 2014): 71–72; Redclift, "Sustainable Development (1987–2005): An Oxymoron Comes of Age," 212–27.

8. Charles H. Eccleston and Frederic March, *Global Environmental Policy: Concepts, Principles, and Practices* (Boca Raton, FL.: CRC Press, 2011): 60–61; M.R. Masnavi, "Environmental Sustainability and Ecological Complexity: Developing an Integrated Approach to Analyse the Environment and Landscape Potentials to Promote Sustainable Development," *International Journal of Environmental Research* 7 (Autumn 2013): 995–1006.

9. Habib, "Sustainability is Not Enough: A Call for Regeneration," 8; Paul Sorensen, "Weak Sustainability and a Post-Industrial Society," *International Journal of Environmental Studies* 70 (December 2013): 872–76.

10. See, for example, Christine Carmody, "Considering Future Generations: Sustainability in Theory and Practice," *Economic Round-Up* 3 (November 2012): 65–92; J. Michael Martinez, *American Environmentalism: Philosophy, History, and Public Policy* (Boca Raton: CRC Press, 2014): 49–51; Thierry Ngosso, "The Right to Development of Developing Countries: An Argument Against Environmental Protection?" *Public Reason* 5 (December 2013): 41–60; Sorensen, "Weak Sustainability and a Post-Industrial Society," 872–76.

11. Habib, "Sustainability is Not Enough: A Call for Regeneration," 8; Mignaqui, "Sustainable Development as a Goal: Social, Environmental and Economic Dimensions," 71–72; Maurizo Sajeva *et al.*, "Giving Sustainability a Chance: A Participatory Framework for Choosing between Alternative Futures," *Journal of Organisational Transformation & Social Change* 12 (April 2015): 57–89.

12. Habib, "Sustainability is Not Enough: A Call for Regeneration," 8–10; M. Anaam Hashmi *et al.*, "Evaluation of Sustainability Practices in the United States and Large Corporations," *Journal of Business Ethics* 127 (March 2015): 673–81; Helen M. Haugh and Alka Talwar, "How Do Corporations Embed Sustainability Across the Organization?" *Academy of Management Learning and Education* 9 (September 2010): 384–96.

13. See, for example, Paul Anderson, "Which Direction for International Environmental Law?" *Journal of Human Rights & The Environment* 6 (March 2015): 98–126; Louis J. Kotzé, "Rethinking Global Environmental Law and Governance in the Anthropocene," *Journal of Energy & Natural Resources Law* 32 (May 2014): 121–56; Nicholas A. Robinson, "Fundamental Principles of Law for the Anthropocene?" *Environmental Policy and Law* 44 (2014): 13–27.

14. Alexandru-Ionuț Petrișor and Liliana Petrișor, "25 Years of Sustainability: A Critical Assessment," *Present Environment & Sustainable Development* 8 (2014): 175–90; Herman I. Stål, "Inertia and Change Related to Sustainability—An Institutional Approach," *Journal of Cleaner Production* 99 (July 2015): 354–65.

15. Roger Martella and Kim Smacziak, "Introduction to Rio + 20: A Reflection on Progress Since the First Earth Summit and the Opportunities That Lie Ahead," *Sustainable Development Law & Policy* 12 (Spring 2012): 4–7;

Miranda A. Schreurs, "20th Anniversary of the Rio Summit: Taking a Look Back and at the Road Ahead," *GAIA: Ecological Perspectives for Science & Society* 21, 1 (March 2012): 13–16.

16. United Nations, *Agenda 21: Earth Summit: The United Nations Programme of Action from Rio* (Heiskell, TN: CrabCube, Inc., 2013).

17. United Nations, *Universal Declaration of Human Rights* (Carlisle, MA.: Applewood Books, 2001), 7.

18. See, for example, Sarah E. Fredericks, "Ethics in Agenda 21," *Ethics, Policy & Environment* 17 (October 2014): 324–38; Viktor Kveton, Jiri Louda, and Martin Pelucha, "Contribution of Local Agenda 21 to Practical Implementation of Sustainable Development: The Case of the Czech Republic," *European Planning Studies* 22 (March 2014): 515–36.

19. Glenn Beck, *Agenda 21: Into the Shadows* (New York: Threshold Books, 2015), accessed May 25, 2016, http://www.glennbeck.com/agenda21/. See also Richard K. Norton, "Agenda 21 and Its Discontents: Is Sustainable Development a Global Imperative or Globalized Conspiracy?" *Urban Lawyer* 46 (Spring 2014): 325–60; Karen Trapenberg Frick, David Weinzimmer, and Paul Waddell, "The Politics of Sustainable Development Opposition: State Legislative Efforts to Stop the United Nations' Agenda 21 in the United States," *Urban Studies* 52 (February 2015): 209–32.

20. Christopher V. Hawkins and XiaoHu Wang, "Sustainable Development Governance: Citizen Participation and Support Networks in Local Sustainability Initiatives," *Public Works Management & Policy* 17 (January 2012): 7–29; "United Nations Activities: Advances in Sustainability and Democracy," *Environmental Policy and Law* 46 (March 2016): 2–9; James K. Wong, "A Dilemma for Green Democracy," *Political Studies* 64 (2016 Supplement): 136–55.

21. Lynn L. Bergeson, "The Federal Trade Commission Brings Actions Regarding Misleading and Unsubstantiated Environmental Marketing Claims," *Environmental Quality Management* 23 (Spring 2014): 75–79; Nick Feinstein, "Learning from Past Mistakes: Future Regulation to Prevent Greenwashing," *Boston College Environmental Affairs Law Review* 40 (2013): 229–57.

22. Lincoln Cushing, "Posters about Ecology and the Environment Before and During the 1970s," *Electronic Green Journal* 1 (December 2010): 1–5; Habibul Haque Khondker, "From 'The Silent Spring' to Globalization of the Environmental Movement," *Journal of International and Global Studies* 6 (April 2015): 25–37; Nikolay L. Mihaylov and Douglas D. Perkins, "Local Environmental Grassroots Activism: Contributions from Environmental Psychology, Sociology and Politics," *Behavioral Sciences* 5 (2015): 121–53.

23. Louise Conn Fleming, "Civic Participation: A Curriculum for Democracy," *American Secondary Education* 40 (Fall 2011): 39–50; Anthony Johnstone, "The Federalist Safeguards of Politics," *Harvard Journal of Law and Public Policy* 39 (2016): 415–85. The quote from *The Federalist* appears in James Madison, "Federalist 10," in Alexander Hamilton,

James Madison, and John Jay, *The Federalist Papers*, edited by Clinton Rossiter (New York: New American Library, 1961), 81.

24. Rebecca E. Morss, *et al.*, "Flood Risk, Uncertainty, and Scientific Information for Decision Making: Lessons from an Interdisciplinary Project," *American Meteorological Society* 86 (November 2005): 1596. See also Tarik Driouchi, Tarik, Michel Leseure, and David Bennett, "A Robustness Framework for Monitoring Real Options under Uncertainty," *Omega* 37 (June 2009): 698–710; Jean-Yves Jaffray and Peter Wakker, "Decision-making with Belief Functions: Compatibility and Incompatibility with the Sure-Thing Principle," *Journal of Risk & Uncertainty* 7 (December 1993): 255–71.

25. James D. Brown, "Prospects for the Open Treatment of Uncertainty in Environmental Research," *Progress in Physical Geography* 34 (February 2010): 75–100; Eileen Gay Jones, "Risky Assessments: Uncertainties in Science and the Human Dimensions of Environmental Decision-making," *William and Mary Environmental Law and Policy Review* 22 (Fall 1997): 1–70; Raanan Lipshitz and Orna Strauss, "Coping With Uncertainty: A Naturalistic Decision-making Analysis," *Organizational Behavior and Human Decision Processes* 69 (February 1997): 149–63; Daniel J.C. Skinner, Sophie A. Rocks, and Simon J.T. Pollard, "A Review of Uncertainty in Environmental Risk: Characterizing Potential Natures, Locations and Levels," *Journal of Risk Research* 17 (February 2014): 195–219; Amos Tversky and Daniel Kahneman, "Judgment under Uncertainty: Heuristics and Biases," *Science* 185 (September 27, 1974): 1124–31; Anastasios Xepapadeas and Catarina Roseta-Palma, "Instabilities and Robust Control in Natural Resource Management," *Portuguese Economic Journal* 12 (December 2013): 161–80.

26. Benjamin Djulbegovic, "Articulating and Responding to Uncertainties in Clinical Research," *Journal of Medicine and Philosophy* 32 (March/April 2007): 79–98; Sjak Smulders, "Environmental Policy and Sustainable Economic Growth," *De Economist* 143 (May 1995): 165–74.

27. Djulbegovic, "Articulating and Responding to Uncertainties in Clinical Research," 82. See also Ian G. Enting, "Assessing the Information Content in Environmental Modelling: A Carbon Cycle Perspective," *Entropy* 10 (December 2008): 556–75; Zooho Kim and Vijay P. Singh, "Assessment of Environmental Flow Requirements by Entropy-Based Multi-Criteria Decision," *Water Resources Management* 28 (January 2014): 459–74.

28. Djulbegovic, "Articulating and Responding to Uncertainties in Clinical Research," 83.

29. Sam Aflaki, "The Effect of Environmental Uncertainty on the Tragedy of the Commons," *Games and Economic Behavior* 82 (November 2013): 240–53; Takao Asano, "Precautionary Principle and the Optimal Timing of Environmental Policy under Ambiguity," *Environmental and Resource Economics* 47 (October 2010): 173–96; Ursula K. Heise, "Environmental Literature and the Ambiguities of Science," *Anglia* 133 (March 2015): 22–36; Antony Millner,

Simon Dietz, and Geoffrey Heal, "Scientific Ambiguity and Climate Policy," *Environmental and Resource Economics* 55 (May 2013): 21–46.

30. Michel Lara, Vincent Martinet, and Luc Doyen, "Satisficing versus Optimality: Criteria for Sustainability," *Bulletin of Mathematical Biology* 77 (February 2015): 281–97; John K. Stranlund and Yakov Ben-Haim, "Price-based versus Quantity-based Environmental Regulation under Knightian Uncertainty: An Info-gap Robust Satisficing Perspective," *Journal of Environmental Management* 87 (2008): 443–49.

31. Asano, "Precautionary Principle and the Optimal Timing of Environmental Policy under Ambiguity," 173–96; Michael Getzner, "Uncertainties and the Precautionary Principle in Cost-Benefit Environmental Policies," *Journal of Policy Modeling* 30 (2008): 1–17; J. Roger Jacobs, "The Precautionary Principle as a Provisional Instrument in Environmental Policy: The Montreal Protocol Case Study," *Environmental Science & Policy* 37 (March 2014): 161–71; Stephen John, "In Defense of Bad Science and Irrational Policies: An Alternative Account of the Precautionary Principle," *Ethical Theory & Moral Practice* 13 (February 2010): 3–18; Nancy Myers, "The Rise of the Precautionary Principle," *Multinational Monitor* 25 (September 2004): 9–15; Giannis Vardas and Anastasios Xepapadeas, "Model Uncertainty, Ambiguity and the Precautionary Principle: Implications for Biodiversity Management," *Environmental and Resource Economics* 45 (March 2010): 379–404;

32. Jonathan Aldred, "Climate Change Uncertainty, Irreversibility and the Precautionary Principle," *Cambridge Journal of Economics* 36 (September 2012): 1051–72; Daniel A. Farber, "Coping with Uncertainty: Cost-Benefit Analysis, the Precautionary Principle, and Climate Change," *Washington Law Review* 90 (December 2015): 1659–1726; Chris Shaw, "The Dangerous Limits of Dangerous Limits: Climate Change and the Precautionary Principle," *Sociological Review* 57 (October 2009): 103–23; Elizabeth Tedsen and Gesa Homann, "Implementing the Precautionary Principle for Climate Engineering," *Carbon & Climate Law Review* 2 (April 2013): 90–100.

33. Daan van Soest, Jan Stoop, and Jana Vyrastekova, "Toward a Delineation of the Circumstances in Which Cooperation Can Be Sustained in Environmental and Resource Problems," *Journal of Environmental Economics and Management* 77 (May 2016): 1–13;

Björn Vollan, Sebastian Prediger, and Markus Frölich, "Analysis: Co-managing Common-pool Resources: Do Formal Rules Have to be Adapted to Traditional Ecological Norms?" *Ecological Economics* 95 (November 2013): 51–62; Andrew B. Whitford, "Threats, Institutions and Regulation in Common Pool Resources," *Policy Sciences* 35 (June 2002): 122–39.

34. Christopher V. Hawkins and XiaoHu Wang, "Policy Integration for Sustainable Development and the Benefits of Local Adoption," *Cityscape: A Journal of Policy Development and Research* 15 (2013): 63–82; Robert Glenn Richey Jr., "The Effects of Environmental Focus and Program Timing on

Green Marketing Performance and the Moderating Role of Resource Commitment," *Industrial Marketing Management* 43 (October 2014): 1246–57.

35. Bernd Klauer *et al.*, "The Art of Long-Term Thinking: A Bridge between Sustainability Science and Politics," *Ecological Economics* 93 (September 2013): 79–84; James Meadowcroft, "What about Politics? Sustainable Development, Transition Management, and Long Term Energy Transitions," *Policy Sciences* 42 (November 2009): 323–40; Tim O'Riordan, "Environmental Science, Sustainability and Politics," *Transactions of the Institute of British Geographers* 29 (June 1, 2004): 234–47.

36. The quote appears in D.D. Riley, *Controlling the Federal Bureaucracy* (Philadelphia: Temple University Press, 1987), 60. See also Carolyn Bourdeaux, "Politics versus Professionalism: The Effect of Institutional Structure on Democratic Decision-making in a Contested Policy Area," *Journal of Public Administration Research and Theory* 18 (July 2008): 349–73; Laurie Kaye Nijaki, "Justifying and Juxtaposing Environmental Justice and Sustainability: Towards an Inter-Generational and Intra-Generational Analysis of Environmental Equity in Public Administration," *Public Administration Quarterly* 39 (Spring 2015): 85–116.

②

THE "DISMAL SCIENCE" OF ECONOMICS

The goal of advancing environmental sustainability ultimately involves allocating scarce resources from a menu of competing options. Protecting the natural environment is among the options, despite some activists' claims that environmental protection is, and should be, the paramount or even sole objective. According to the environmental activist perspective, natural resources are not amenable to traditional economic valuations. From the perspective of an ardent, biocentric (world-centered) environmentalist, a discussion of economic values degenerates into a simplistic calculation of profit and loss. Profit-loss considerations, in their view, are insufficient to capture the complexities of modern economics or, for that matter, the depth and breadth of environmental sustainability. Other observers acknowledge that environmental protection necessarily involves numerous values, including economics. First and foremost, economic theory emphasizes the most efficient use of resources possible. To that end, any discussion of environmental sustainability requires a discussion of economics and the means by which efficiency goals are realized.

As much as it pains some activists to admit it, for the overwhelming majority of human enterprises to be considered genuinely "sustainable," the activity must be economically feasible. In fact, some definitions suggest that sustainability requires the confluence of social, environmental, and economic forces. Whether it is a program to clean up litter in a blighted urban area, initiate a commodities recycling program, or forge a multinational agreement to curb carbon emissions that contribute to global warming, the costs must be met or the program cannot continue indefinitely. Human relationships typically are constructed on the foundation of self-interest. Economics, at its core, is the ultimate expression of self-interest, or at least one method for determining the factors that groups of individuals believe to be in their self-interest.

Self-interest, the sages assert, makes the world go 'round. Genuine altruism exists, but it is exceedingly rare. Religious mystics and ascetics probably are the only people who can consistently exhibit selflessness. Everyone else must recognize, at best, a mixture of "pure" and self-interested motives. Consequently, economic principles can be found at the core of almost every human activity. Citizens sometimes profess their desire to remedy environmental degradation, and they may support voluntary efforts for a time, but eventually the costs of the program must be borne by one party or the other. Anyone who is devoted to protecting the natural environment necessarily must possess a thorough grounding in, and understanding of, neoclassical economics. All the good intentions in the world will fail if they are not predicated on sound economic principles.[1]

Economic theory is a mixture of descriptive and normative values. As a descriptive enterprise, economists attempt to discern the interests and desires of a hypothetical rational maximizer who presumably seeks to maximize pleasure and minimize pain. This simple articulation of the Utilitarian credo is complicated by factors that sometimes skew the results. First, a consumer might not be a rational maximizer. He or she might be an ascetic or a masochist and therefore choose a course of action based on factors that are not amenable to a customary cost-benefit calculation. Even if a typical consumer is a rational maximizer, the person might be mistaken in the proper course of action because he or she does not recognize the values involved or fails to assign appropriate weights to the variables in the equation. In addition, external factors such as government intervention into the marketplace may interfere with normal expressions of preferences, thereby providing imperfect, flawed data on market equilibrium.[2]

The normative function of economics is a controversial subject because the skewed data probably color perceptions on what constitutes suitable public policy. If data are inconclusive, obtuse, or incomplete, relying on economics to reach a conclusion may be fraught with error. Moreover, even in cases where the data are more or less complete and uncontested, a government sometimes pursues policies for reasons that are economically inefficient. Due process of law and considerations of ethnic diversity and inclusiveness are notoriously inefficient, but such values may enjoy widespread popularity among citizens. Similarly, in some instances, protecting the natural environment may be economically inefficient and yet meet a social or political goal deemed superior to a straightforward cost-benefit analysis.[3]

Despite its limitations as a science of consumer behavior, economic theory provides a glimpse, imperfect though it may be, into individual desires in a manner that no other discipline can provide. Determining human behavior requires multiple sources of information to complement each other. Public opinion surveys can be skewed owing to interviewer biases or the reluctance of a subject to express a preference that is seen as callous or politically incorrect. For these reasons, pollsters must adjust their results and hedge their bets by citing a margin of error. Economics can provide useful tools for policy-making to augment other means for determining policy preferences. By observing how people act in the marketplace, as opposed to what they say about their behavior, economists hope to understand what motivates individuals far better than they might through other means.[4]

THE ORIGINS OF NEOCLASSICAL ECONOMICS

Although shrewd interpreters of human behavior have long recognized the desire of individuals to improve their financial circumstances in most instances, the idea of systematically studying human behavior and assigning values to consumer choices is a relatively new concept in the Western intellectual tradition. The discipline of economics was a product of the Enlightenment, the eighteenth-century philosophical movement that, on the heels of the Renaissance, supplanted the superstition of the Dark Ages of Western European culture. It was an epoch devoted to rooting out intolerance and magical thinking, replacing anthropomorphic idols with reasoned, deliberative, fact-based discourse grounded in hard data. As part of that sweeping movement, Enlightenment thinkers first set forth their theories of market forces and economic principles. They believed they had discovered the scientific principles of human behavior just as Sir Isaac Newton, the famed English scientist, had discovered the natural laws governing the universe.[5]

The acknowledged leader of this new science in the Western tradition was a Scottish moral philosopher, Adam Smith. A product of the Enlightenment, Smith argued that he was continuing the Newtonian tradition of uncovering immutable truths based on existential facts. Smith subscribed to the Enlightenment credo that if the appropriate scientific principles could be discerned, they would explain human behavior at any time, any place, and anywhere. Humankind's task was to discover those principles and act accordingly.

Smith did not perform his analyses in a vacuum. In his quest for scientific discoveries governing human behavior, he believed that economics and political science went hand-in-hand. The role of a democratic government was to ensure that free, unfettered markets were available for all who wished to compete. Because economics was ultimately a "science," it could be understood through the use of mathematical calculations that explained how human beings acted in particular ways. Based on those calculations, public and private sector actors could craft efficacious policies that improved the human condition.[6]

Smith is perhaps best remembered today for his "invisible hand" theory, but he was not a simpleton who mindlessly placed his faith in unrealistic abstractions. In fact, he sought a marriage of the abstract and the practical. In his first great work, *The Theory of Moral Sentiments*, first published in 1759, Smith posited a view of human beings as social creatures who develop what today is called "self-esteem" through their interactions with others. Moral judgments, he contended, develop when individuals perceive themselves in relation to others and eventually develop sympathy. In recognizing the interdependence of human beings, he laid the groundwork for his later work in economics and political science.[7]

Smith's best known work, *An Inquiry into the Nature and Causes of the Wealth of Nations*, published in the pivotal year of 1776, began with an understanding that all persons reason and act on the basis of self-interest. To understand what consumers desire, it is important to examine how people act through preferences expressed in the market-place. Asking the citizenry about its public policy needs frequently yields unsatisfactory results. Citizens do not always remain informed about crucial issues and, even when they do, their preferences do not necessarily reflect reasoned, deliberative, logically consistent choices. To appreciate individuals' choices, a policy-maker must examine what they do, not what they say. The "invisible hand" of consumers collectively acting on their preferences provides insight into what government decision-makers should do to satisfy their constituents, for people will "put their money where their mouth is," in the words of the old adage.

Some commentators have noted the apparent contradictions between *The Theory of Moral Sentiments* and *The Wealth of Nations*. A philosopher who delves into the nature of sympathy as a moral choice and yet presumes that consumers will choose self-interests as their prime decision-making rationale can be seen as inconsistent. Yet Smith's works can be reconciled by understanding the dynamic between the sympathies and the self-interest of human beings. Few individuals are entirely sympathetic, or empathetic, with others. People harbor a set of hopes and desires based on their own self-interested nature. Thus, human behavior is a mixture of selfless and self-interested characteristics. Smith did not view his works as contradictory. They were complements. He was simply exploring the range of human behavior, focusing on different aspects in his two great works.[8]

Smith lived at a time when learned men viewed rationality without the deep suspicion harbored by the Romantics of a later epoch. He believed that innovation arose from self-interest. Unlike the idealists who strove to perfect human nature, Smith accepted human beings as they were, not as he wished they might be. The more a self-interested entrepreneur believes he can pocket for himself, the greater his incentive will be to forge ahead against seemingly insurmountable odds to build an improved version of an existing good or create an altogether new good. As a result of this creativity based on an individual's understanding of his own interests, all of society benefits. Later economists suggested that a rising tide lifts all boats.[9]

The great French writer Alexis Tocqueville spoke of "Self-interest, properly understood" as the key to ordering a stable democratic regime, but what constitutes a proper understanding remains a fluid concept. In some instances, an individual may benefit from a course of action, but the action harms his neighbors. Thus, his self-interest has to be curbed in the interests of the greater good. An insight into the Utilitarian philosophy of ethics, as discussed more fully in Chapter 3, is that not everyone can realize his desires. Policy-makers must weigh interests and develop laws and regulations based on the greatest good for the greatest number. Government, therefore, always has and always will limit individual actions to promote a competing goal. Self-interest, therefore, is not necessarily a straightforward calculation of a specific individual's desires, at least insofar as public policy is concerned. Self-interest is a concept that is open to competing interpretations and evolving societal expectations.[10]

Adam Smith served as the starting point for neoclassical economics, and his progeny built on his foundation. The term "neoclassical economics" did not originate with Smith despite his now-famous association with the concept. Thorstein Veblen, a sociologist and economist of the late nineteenth and early twentieth centuries, coined the term in a 1900 article, "Preconceptions of Economic Science." Since that time, it has become a shorthand description of the operation of microeconomics in a western, highly industrialized nation.[11]

Neoclassical economists agree with Smith's conclusion that goods and services can be assigned a numerical value and values can be measured to indicate how individuals seek to maximize their interests. The desire to assign numbers to natural resources is deeply disturbing to many members of the environmental community who object to the idea that aesthetics can be treated as goods to be complemented and substituted as though they were any other marketable commodity. As discussed in Chapter 3, several schools of thought contend that such accounting impermissibly reduces environmental values to simply another good that can be traded. Owing to the interconnectedness of living matter and the long cycles of natural changes in temperature, climate, and ecological systems, treating forests and water sources as fungible economic commodities is narrow-minded and short-sighted.[12]

Despite the argument that natural resources differ not only in degree, but in kind, from other types of commodities, economists have long sought to develop a viable system of trading based on the preferences in consumer tastes. The core insight of economics, as Adam Smith and his

Enlightenment-era colleagues recognized, is that human beings must be accepted not as we would like them to be, but as they are in their most basic, elemental state. All the proselytizing in the world will not transform a self-interested being into an altruistic soul. Almost every man and woman will eventually slide back into his or her natural state. Rather than ground public policy as a noble, yet overly ambitious scheme of perfecting human nature, economists seek to understand why people act in certain ways. Applying this hard-got knowledge to policy questions can allow decision-makers to craft policies through tools such as the tax system to encourage or discourage certain behaviors. (The proper level of government meddling in free markets remains a fiercely contested point of debate among economists, with most mainstream proponents of capitalism opting for limited government intervention.)[13]

Exactly as individuals attempt to maximize their interests, firms seek to maximize profits. The entire premise of the capitalist system is that firms will respond to supply and demand cues from consumers and, to some extent, from governments that intervene in the marketplace. One difficulty in promoting environmental policies is that often the marketplace rewards short-term economic gain at the expense of long-term ecological health, which means that nature suffers unless and until government requires private sector entities to alter their practices. Such government regulation inevitably distorts markets, which causes free-market economists to cry foul. The divisions of opinion among industrialists and environmentalists across a spectrum of ideas reflect deep disagreements about the rights and responsibilities of human beings toward the natural environment and toward each other.[14]

What almost everyone can agree on is that government ideally exists to ensure that each party engaging in economic activity plays by the same rules. When disputes arise, as they invariably do, governments theoretically serve as neutral arbiters to ensure the free flow of goods, services, and ideas. The concepts are orderly and rational in theory, even if in practice they become convoluted and intricate.[15]

Controversies surround what constitutes "neutral" government action to guarantee a minimal level of "fairness" and what degenerates into unnecessary government intrusion and bureaucratically untidy over-regulation. Industrialists tend to argue that the Founders had it right when they embraced the concept of classical liberalism, namely that that government is best which governs least. Free-market economists intimate that unfettered market access is tantamount to maximizing human freedom. Therefore, any attempt by government to restrict markets is an attempt to limit human freedom. Environmentalists usually promote a different idea, the progressive credo that a government must either be part of the problem or part of the solution in improving citizens' lives. The best way to improve their lives is by advancing an agenda that places long-term environmental issues ahead of short-term economic profit.[16]

Neoclassical economists discuss economics and government as intertwined subjects, with each field influencing the other in an uneasy alliance. Fundamentally, their differing goals preclude a rapprochement, for economics is about maximizing the efficient use of resources. A democratic regime, by contrast, ideally promotes the benefits of pluralism, the rewards of diversity and conflicting opinions, the primacy of protecting liberty and property interests, and the necessity of safeguarding a minority from the tyranny of the majority. Governments seek to balance these competing values through a series of never-ending, controversial policies that change as constituencies and parties change their relative positions of power. A government based on the consent of the governed is a contentious, boisterous, bubbling cauldron of inefficiency. Add to the structural inefficiencies built into the American system of government through the U.S. Constitution, its amendments, statutory laws, and judicial opinions the growth of the administrative state beginning in the middle of the twentieth century and it is not surprising that the interests of free marketers and proponents of government controls would collide.[17]

Economists recognize that no market is ever free from some sort of government control; therefore, the task is to shape that control so that market forces are disrupted to the least extent possible. When markets are minimally affected by government forces, they are shaped by economic laws and principles that reflect consumer interests. A long-accepted maxim involves the concept of a general equilibrium where income distribution, the forces of production, and the prices and quantities of goods intersect. Moreover, supply and demand curves highlight the reciprocal relationship among these factors. When one variable moves from a point of equilibrium, other variables change, and the marketplace shifts until a new equilibrium point is reached. The relative proximity with which variables are tied to one another is expressed as elasticity. In other words, when one variable changes and triggers a change in another variable, the relationship is deemed to be elastic. If the change is not direct or does not trigger an immediate reaction, the relationship is held to be inelastic. From this general observation, economists use the concept of price elasticity of demand to refer to a percentage change in quantity demanded caused by a percent change in price. The price elasticity of supply measures how the quantity or amount of a good changes in response to price changes.[18]

A relatively unfettered, elastic market is essentially nothing more than a push-pull system of supply and demand curves. Free-market economists fear that government actors will create policies that affect these laws and principles without understanding the potentially calamitous results. In the environmental field, for example, policy-makers may impose a well-meaning policy on certain commodities to influence consumer behavior without considering the unintended consequences. Thus, a new law requiring plastics manufactures to use less material in their products next year may inadvertently cause them to increase the amount of material in their products this year so that they can comply with the new mandate that takes effect the following year. Instead of reducing the environmental impact of the product, as the legislators intended to do, they created inefficiency in the market. Manufacturers already possessed a market incentive to use the least amount of material possible—after all, if a producer can manufacture two plastic bottles instead of one with a given material, he will do it—but government policy-makers failed to consider this scenario. Instead, they drove up the cost of the product (since it costs more to increase the amount of plastic material in the product this year to compensate for the reduction next year) and their law did not support the original goal of source reducing the product. Free-market economists argue that this sort of market inefficiency occurs frequently.[19]

For all of the emphasis on general equilibrium, markets are never static for long. Increasing or stagnating wages, changes in production schedules, and substitutability among various types of products ensure that a market will fluctuate numerous times throughout the business cycle. In addition, consumer preferences change owing to multiple factors such as changing tastes in fashion, art, music, and books as well as consumers who seek out lower-priced commodities. Changes in consumer behavior necessitate changes in the marketplace, affecting virtually every party involved in the supply chain, from raw material suppliers to wholesalers and retailers.[20]

THE PROBLEM OF EXTERNALITIES

In theory, marketplace participants factor in all relevant variables that influence an exchange of goods or services. A material supplier, for example, must take into account the labor, insurance, transportation, and other factors necessary to produce a particular product. Such a supplier intuitively understands that he must keep his variable costs low, especially if he competes in a crowded, competitive marketplace, while he has little choice but to absorb the sunk costs associated with this enterprise. Not surprisingly, a rational supplier will not willingly absorb a cost that he cannot either pass on to the consumer or use as a market advantage.[21]

From these basic insights, the concept of negative externalities makes sense—and becomes a major factor in the debate over crafting effective environmental policies. An externality consists of the consequences of individual producer or consumer behaviors that are not formally factored into the cost-benefit equation. A positive externality occurs when society benefits from a transaction such as an individual acquiring an education. A well-educated citizen generally becomes more productive than a poorly educated citizen. The former probably will acquire gainful employment, pay taxes, and become a functioning, law-abiding member of society. A less well-educated person often faces fewer opportunities for lucrative employment, which means that he or she will pay fewer taxes and may actually acquire governmental assistance through transfer payments or liberal use of social welfare programs. Education, therefore, is a positive externality in the sense that society is not a direct participant in the transaction between the individual receiving the education and the school that provides it. Nonetheless, everyone more or less benefits from the transaction.[22]

In the environmental field, the externalities tend to be negative. The quintessential example of the negative externality involves industrial pollution. Using a hypothetical scenario, it is relatively easy to under-stand the concept. If the regulators in a specific jurisdiction determine that 10 parts per million (ppm) of an industrial pollutant can be safely emitted during an eight-hour period because the emission is so minis-cule that it is below regulatory concern, the effect of one manufacturer emitting 10 ppm is negligible. If 10 manufacturers in a small industrial park emit 10 ppm, however, the collective output (100 ppm) is no lon-ger below regulatory concern. In that instance, no one emitter possesses an incentive to internalize the cost of pollution abatement because a single firm's output is so low, and yet the cumulative effect may be dev-astating. The cost of the collective emissions of 100 ppm must be borne by society unless government insists that each firm internalize the cost or, alternatively, government develops a program to abate the collective level of pollution. Proponents of government intervention into the mar-ketplace fret over the imposition of negative externalities on society and insist that government must develop robust policies, backed up by firm enforcement, to combat these types of problems.[23]

GOVERNMENT INTERVENTION AND ECONOMIC POLICY

As discussed above, free-market economists decry government interven-tion in the economy. F.A. von Hayek, a well-known free-market econo-mist, observed that markets are more efficient when they are left alone to function according to private sector market signals. Governments interfere with supply and demand curves; that is, they confuse the mar-ket because governments introduce incentives that change consumer behavior, often resulting in inefficiencies.[24]

Despite the controversial nature of government intervention, such actions occur frequently nonetheless, even in economic systems that profess to encourage free markets. Representative governments justify their actions as necessary to mitigate the detrimental effects of capital-ism. If left in a state of absolute freedom, a market will reward some par-ties handsomely while leaving others destitute. Although the promise of economic advancement warms the hearts of many Americans, they generally chafe at the possibility that some percentage of the citizenry will be rendered financially impotent by the vagaries of the capitalist

system. Many citizens applaud capitalism in theory and recoil in practice, especially if they or their loved ones might be counted among the
less fortunate. For the small number of Haves, market developments
allow them to amass a wide array of material goods and enjoy a standard of living denied to the overwhelming majority of their peers. In
the meantime, Have-Nots suffer the ill effects of poverty and reduced
opportunity. By imposing rules on the behavior of elites (and others) in
the marketplace, governments seek to rein in behavior that takes advantage of the Have-Nots even if this means reducing some measure of
freedom enjoyed by the Haves.

A substantial number of Americans at least tacitly approve of intervention as long as it is not overly obtrusive. Even a self-proclaimed free-
market economist will not object to reasonable regulations that ensure
clear, consistent rules enforced against all so that persons and firms
guilty of egregious behavior will not profit from malfeasance. A more-or-
less honest market ensures that the valuations on which so many transactions depend generally are reliable. In a market where a significant
percentage of the actors are untrustworthy is a market bound to fail
and collapse. Thus, at a minimum, the role of government should be to
ensure that parties to a transaction play by the rules on pain of sanctions.
Determining which behaviors qualify as "egregious" and which actions
constitute "malfeasance" are not always simple matters, but government
must attempt to do so.[25]

Correcting market deficiencies and ensuring that parties can compete remain crucial governmental functions. Despite the best efforts of
regulators to ensure that a level-playing field exists, sometimes a monopoly develops in one sector of the economy, which means that only one
seller exists for a particular good. When only one seller exists, the seller
does not respond to market incentives because he faces no competition
for his product. To ensure that monopolies do not stifle competition and
upset markets, governments regulate market consolidation, ostensibly to
promote free trade. Again, virtually everyone save a genuine libertarian
probably would agree that government intervention to reduce or eliminate monopolies is beneficial to the marketplace.[26]

It is clear that a completely free market is seldom desired, much less
achieved. For economic conservatives, of course, the intervention should
be as minimal and brief as possible, providing for slight correctives that

encourage free enterprise to flourish, but nothing beyond that limited purpose. The idea of a redistribution of wealth in service of a preordained governmental goal is abhorrent. Yet after the concept of intervention is accepted as a legitimate use of governmental authority, the analysis shifts from whether to when, and how much. It becomes a matter of degree.[27]

When a market intervention occurs, government officials possess powers that allow them to police the conduct of private parties. In some situations, government can prohibit or encourage specific behaviors. In the scenario referenced above involving an environmental pollutant, regulators may determine that no amount of a pollutant can be emitted because the chemical is known through the best available scientific methods to be dangerous to the health or safety of human beings, animals, and/or the natural environment. Industries that rely on the pollutant in question may argue that the scientific data are not as robust or uncontested as the government suggests, in which case a debate ensues about the quality of the data. When all avenues of dissent have been exhausted—and assuming that the regulators are not persuaded to pursue a different course of action—government likely will require that the manufacturing concerns find alternate methods of producing their goods without using the offending chemical.[28]

In lieu of an out-and-out ban, government regulators may impose a tax on the negative externality. In this way, government policy seeks to influence the behavior of private parties acting in the marketplace by placing a tax burden on behaviors that are deemed injurious or providing a tax credit on behaviors that are encouraged. The influential Cambridge neoclassical economist A.C. Pigou famously championed the notion of a tax levied on businesses to force an externality to be internalized. A so-called "Pigouvian" tax is designed to reinstitute a balance by forcing firms to internalize their costs. Externalities that previously were hoisted onto third parties must now be factored into a particular firm's cost-benefit analysis.[29]

The difficulty with a Pigouvian tax is that it assumes that the parties possess more or less complete information regarding the transaction. If a participant does not realize that a tax has been imposed, he will not change his behavior, which was the purpose of imposing the tax in the first place. As an example, consider an environmental tax known

generally as an advance disposal fee (ADF), sometimes included as part
of an extended producer responsibility (EPR) program where manufacturers of a product with a short life must pay some or all of the disposal
costs. An ADF sometimes is offered by environmentalists as a mechanism for forcing manufacturers of disposable products to internalize
the cost of waste management by paying for the disposal ahead of time
in lieu of imposing the cost on governments, which then pass the cost
along by taxing members of the public. The ADF can be imposed on
the product at the wholesale or retail level, but it is designed to ensure
that consumers understand the presence of the tax and the reasons it has
been imposed. Presumably, consumers who realize that the tax has been
imposed may change behavior to avoid the tax. Thus, a consumer who
visits a grocery store and pays a tax of two cents for each plastic bag may
choose to ask for a paper bag or bring a reusable bag the next time he
visits the store to avoid paying the tax.

A free-market economist poses multiple objections to a Pigouvian
tax. In the case of an ADF, the consumer may not realize that he is paying a tax. If the tax is mentioned in a public service announcement or
if the consumer carefully examines the store receipt, he might realize
that he has paid a few extra pennies for a plastic bag and act to avoid
the tax. If the consumer does not notice that the tax has been levied or,
having noticed, finds it to be a trivial matter unworthy of further consideration, he will not change his behavior. Moreover, ADFs typically
create enormous administrative costs for both government agencies and
private companies. If the ADF funds are not used to improve the waste
management infrastructure—which is usually the stated goal of any such
funding mechanism—the tax does not achieve the goal for which it was
imposed. Creative, financially strapped legislators have been known to
transfer monies into the general fund even when the original funds were
earmarked for a special project. When or if this happens, the tax no longer serves the purpose for which it was created. It becomes yet another
feature of a financial bureaucracy.[30]

Assuming that a Pigouvian tax is imposed in a manner that changes
consumer behavior in the intended way, a measurement problem still
exists. Determining the true costs associated with disposing of plastic
bags, for example, is no easy task. Uncertainties abound. Assuming that
a more-or-less accurate valuation can be established at one point in time,

the evolving nature of the marketplace may change the future valuation. The costs associated with landfilling plastic bags in year zero will be substantially different in year 10 if, in the interim, a market for recycling plastic bags emerges. In short, free-market economists are quick to point out that governments do not wield their taxing authority in an efficient manner. For these reasons, many economists cite government officials as poor stewards for effective environmental management.[31]

Turning away from a Pigouvian tax, free-market economists sometimes point to the Coase Theorem developed by Ronald Coase, a 1991 Nobel Laureate in Economics. The theorem suggests that property resources, absent transaction costs, will end up in the hands of the party that places the highest value on the resource. If Coase is correct, his theorem explains why the private sector is so much more efficient than government. Individuals will take steps to acquire the resources they desire the most, assuming that they possess the necessary information to make informed decisions. If transaction costs are too high, consumers may change their behavior. Therefore, Coase indicates that the appropriate role for government is to develop public policies that minimize transaction costs.

Notice that Coase agrees with Pigou that government can play a significant role in changing consumer behavior; however, Coase relies on the private sector to take the lead in lieu of depending on government. A Pigouvian tax makes government the driver of the policy because government imposes impediments on consumers and businesses that do not comply with the desired policy. Coase suggests that government ought to clear the way for private parties to engage in transactions. Coase favors a carrot while Pigou favors a stick.[32]

Consider the implications of adopting the Coase Theorem. Although free-market economists seldom tout the virtues of the federal bureaucracy, they can point to an agency such as the Interstate Commerce Commission (ICC) potentially as a helpful government entity. Before it was abolished and some of its duties were transferred to the Surface Transportation Board in 1996, the ICC regulated, among other things, freight rates for railroads. By holding rates down, the ICC ensured that the costs associated with shipping goods were predictable and relatively modest. Because buyers and sellers could depend on stable freight rates, they could engage in commerce without worrying about rising transaction costs. In this instance, government promoted free enterprise by intervening to reduce transaction costs. (Of course, railroads could argue that government unconscionably interfered with the railroads' freedom to charge freight rates at whatever price the market would bear.)

In any case, Coase contended that Pigouvian taxes impede efficiency and undermine markets. The preferable course of action if a government must intervene into the private sector is for government to clear the way for market forces to work. Unlike Pigou, who tacitly accepted the legitimacy of government as a social engineer, Coase believed that the private sector would function more efficiently with minimal government intrusion. Nonetheless, even Coase recognized that no market is completely free from government oversight and participation. He was hardly a libertarian. The goal is to ensure that an intervention is minimally disruptive to market signals.[33]

Although many government interventions into the marketplace are far more intrusive than Coase might have preferred, they remain a standard feature of the American political system. In fact, government economic interventions, especially beginning late in the twentieth century, have become hallmarks of American governmental policy. Accordingly, understanding the types of economic policies is crucial.

Governments often create distributive policies that benefit a wide group of people who do not directly bear the cost of the policy. Agricultural price supports, federally insured educational loans for college students, tax deductions on interest for home mortgages, and loan guarantees backed by the federal government are among the best known examples of distributive policies. In each of these cases, government actors have identified a particular public good that should be advanced by government policies. Using the policy system to distribute these benefits ideally ensures that society is enriched by the large number of people who benefit. This conclusion assumes that the initial distribution more or less enjoys widespread public and political support.

When governments distribute goods, their objective is to determine the most efficient means of moving from one point to another. The policy of whether the good should be distributed already has been decided. The policy was formulated, presumably by a legislative body or a bureaucracy acting pursuant to a legislative mandate, at an earlier stage. At this juncture, effective implementation is the objective. The decision about whether a distribution should occur is more or less settled. (This conclusion assumes, of course, that policies, once formulated, do not change significantly during the implementation phase. A large volume of public administration literature argues that policies not only change during implementation, but in some cases—especially when the original policy was vague, ambiguous, or incomplete when it was formulated by the legislature—policies are partially formulated a second time by virtue of their implementation. Without delving into these issues, suffice it to say that distributive policies, at whatever stage they are created, involve moving goods and/or services from one point to another, regardless of how or why the policy originated.)[34]

Redistributive policies are far more controversial than distributive policies because virtually every stage of the policy is contested. Instead of serving as a conduit for distributing funds for popular programs, as distributive sometimes are, government takes resources away from one group in favor of another with redistributive policies. The quintessential example of redistribution—and one that meets with contentious debate—involves social welfare programs administered by the federal government. Citizens who are gainfully employed pay taxes to support a wide array of government programs. Social welfare programs rely on tax revenues to provide assistance to persons who are unwilling or unable to secure employment or, having secured employment, nonetheless cannot meet their basic material needs. These persons look to government to provide assistance in the form of transfer payments or a government voucher, such as food stamps. By redistributing funding from one group of people to another—setting aside the thorny question of whether recipients are, in fact, "deserving" of such largesse—government is requiring one group of citizens to fund the lifestyles of another group.

Redistribution of income from one set of people to another raises fundamental questions about the nature of government and its power over citizens' lives. Free-market economists and politically conservative officials worry that a government wielding the power to take from the rich and give to the poor, or something along those lines, is a government that can become oppressive. If property rights are to have any meaning, the market gives to some and takes from others without regard to the moral "worthiness" of a specific party.

Opponents of redistributive policies argue that government is figuratively placing a thumb on the scales when it chooses to transfer funds from one group to another. In a free market, parties theoretically choose for themselves how to use their funds. Natural inequalities have always existed, and always will. Redistribution interferes with individual choice, providing government with power to supplant a set of choices made by individuals with choices made by government. This sort of meddling, among other things, violates the concept of private property rights protected by a set of rules known and knowable beforehand. Robbing from Peter to pay Paul absent Peter's consent abridges Peter's property rights without due process of law. Due process of law, if it means anything, means that a government cannot decide ahead of time how the market will allocate resources. Instead, "due process" refers to a set of procedures, a series of promised steps that must be undertaken, not a specific outcome. According to this interpretation, government must not "cook the books" to ensure a result that government desires. Instead, government must enforce a series of pre established rules and allow the parties to reap the rewards, or pay the penalties, for their actions without regard to the prejudged desirability of the outcome.[35]

Redistributive policies affect a variety of government programs, including the natural environment, testing citizens' commitment to a rights-based economic system. Most directly, redistribution in the environmental realm sometimes relates to environmental justice, a concept that raises issues about race, class, and poverty in American society. Impoverished citizens typically live in areas that feature a large number of undesirable sites such as landfills, incinerators, water treatment plants, and electric utility transfer stations, to say nothing of abandoned, dilapidated buildings and a crumbling infrastructure. Because members of the community typically have little money to improve the neighborhood and even less political clout to insist on a clean, healthy environment, poor citizens suffer the negative effects of a degraded environment to a greater extent than do affluent Americans or the middle class. In a large number of cases, poor citizens tend to be people of color, especially black Americans and Latinos. Proponents of environmental justice contend that government must intervene to "equalize the playing field"; that is, government must ensure that one segment of society does not bear a disproportionate burden over another segment. If this means that landfills, incinerators, and other unseemly features must be located in more affluent areas, the price is necessary for a just, equitable society. Property owners who raise a hue and cry about declining prices and property values must understand that equity necessitates such redistribution in the interest of fairness.

The problem of locating undesirable facilities in close proximity to financially destitute persons has long presented a challenge in a free-market system. The efficiency principle dictates that a resource should be put to its best and highest use. Persons who own and control valuable assets such as expensive land and high-quality tangible assets will naturally seek to use them as efficiently as possible. If they can prevent the construction of a landfill or an incinerator in an affluent area because the presence of these facilities will decrease the value of their assets, they will do so. Yet, landfills and incinerators must be constructed somewhere; therefore, they will be placed in the less affluent section of town. If environmental justice supporters seek to change this evaluation, they are, in effect, redistributing the benefits and burdens of the marketplace. Such redistribution invariably creates tension and triggers a political backlash.[36]

Other types of government policies concerning the economy, although less contentious than redistributive policies, nonetheless generate considerable political controversy. Government sometimes allows members of a regulated community to self-regulate. Situations involving technical experts and members of professions present immense difficulties for government regulators. It is difficult for example to ask a non lawyer to oversee and regulate the work of a lawyer. Requiring someone who is not a medical doctor to judge the merits of work undertaken by a medical doctor can lead to poor results. A federal regulator who enters a manufacturing plant to ensure legal compliance may not be as well versed in the technical operation of the plant as someone is who works in the plant and has helped to develop the technology and machinery in use. A layperson simply does not possess the necessary expertise to determine the adequacy, or lack thereof, of a subject matter expert's actions. Even when government professionals are well positioned to oversee private sector professionals, the resources necessary to enforce the multitude of laws and regulations may be scanty or non existent. In these situations, government generally will allow the experts to police themselves through self-reporting.

Critics charge that self-policing invariably creates a conflict of inter-est. If one lawyer is called upon to oversee and punish another lawyer, he may be disinclined to mete out a harsh penalty. *There but for the grace of God go I*, he may say to himself. Moreover, the legal profession, espe-cially in small communities or in narrow fields, is a tight-knit enclave. Even on a larger stage, professionals tend to band together against out-siders. After all, no one outside of the community of experts can fully understand the experts' needs and desires. A layperson simply does not possess the necessary tools and judgment to oversee an expert, or so the argument goes.[37]

In the environmental realm, activists fret that powerful, wealthy, entrenched corporate interests may promulgate self-policing policies that are rubberstamped by government regulators anxious to avoid messy, expensive confrontations. In such situations, negative externali-ties that despoil the natural environment are firmly hoisted onto the shoulders of government taxpayers. Even worse, in some instances the externalities are not corrected and the environment suffers as a result. Free-market economists herald the virtues of neoclassical economics, but environmentalists counter that a hands-off approach amounts to nothing more than an abdication of government's responsibility to pro-tect the health and welfare of its citizens.[38]

Government policies, regardless of their type, sometimes become politically controversial because they involve a trade-off between two competing values, efficiency and equity. This is not to say that efficiency necessarily precludes equity; however, the values can diverge in many particulars. The efficiency principle dictates that a course of action should use the fewest resources in the shortest amount of time to achieve the stated objective. By contrast, equity is the notion that like cases should be treated alike. The American legal system, with its emphasis on the rule of law as well as due process of law, seeks to handle court cases in the most equitable manner possible. In many instances, relying on an equitable principle such as due process of law results in enormous inefficiencies. It is terribly inefficient to subscribe to the American Bill of Rights with its fundamental assumption that a criminal defendant is innocent until proven guilty in a court of law. Providing an indigent criminal defendant with a court-appointed defense counsel free of charge while also funding a prosecutor to seek a conviction against the same defendant is hardly a model of economic efficiency. Allowing a trial proceeding to drag on interminably while a parade of witnesses and a plethora of documents are presented is highly inefficient and consumes an enormous volume of resources. To introduce efficiencies into the process, prosecutors often encourage plea bargaining and other settlements to avoid trials. Such negotiations may lead to false convictions as defendants are pressured to avoid trial even when they are innocent. In these instances, efficiency and equity are divergent.[39]

Setting aside examples where efficiency and equity work at cross-purposes, the question for government policies affecting the environment is whether they can be both efficient and equitable. More to the point, the issue is whether economic and environmental issues can be reconciled. Even if a trade-off is necessary, can a principle or formula be found to govern the trade-off?[40]

Certain assumptions are necessarily built into economic and environmental calculations. First, individuals are self-interested rational maximizers. With few exceptions, they will make decisions based on what they believe to be necessary for commodious living in the short run. Appeals to a spirit of philanthropy can yield success, but self-interest is never far from the mix. Moreover, environmental activists who ask individuals to consider the long run—that is, dozens, hundreds, thousands, or millions of years—always encounter the distance problem. As discussed in Chapter 1, people may willingly forgo short-term pleasures for the sake of their children or grandchildren, but asking an individual to sacrifice a good or service today to assist persons who might live 100 or 200 years in the future can be a bridge too far.[41]

The policy process is never as simple or linear as textbooks might have us believe. The over arching difficulty in crafting policy proposals based on a generalized perception of public need is that a variety of potential impediments can skew the results. Aside from negative externalities, individuals may possess asymmetric information. They simply are not as well informed about public policy, and its ramifications, as their leaders are. Examining how the public votes, for example, is an imprecise indicator of the public desire. People vote for a variety of reasons—their friends and family vote a certain way, they find one candidate particularly attractive or especially distasteful, or they are responding to a memorable, clever political advertisement—some or all of which may not accurately reflect their interests or desires. In fact, members of the public may not understand differences among competing policies. Even if they could discern differences, they may be indifferent to the consequences of discrete policy choices. In the absence of a preferable means of determining the will of the populace, examining how people behave in the marketplace becomes the most realistic barometer of public sentiment.[42]

As with so much in economics, the notion that efficiency and equity can be traded as though each value is a commodity amenable to strict economic valuation remains a contentious proposition. Making trade-offs necessarily involves a relatively linear process, but comparing values through quantitative analysis may be nonsensical because some critics question whether these values can be reduced to comparable numbers. As discussed in Chapter 3 of this book, some environmental ethicists resist placing a price tag on environmental resources. Calculating the dollar value of clean air or the existence of a world without global warming is an exercise in futility. An environmental law that grants pollution permits and allow credits to be traded among polluters may be dangerous. Because environmental systems are exceedingly complex and exist across a vast expanse of time—hundreds of thousands, perhaps millions, of years—evaluating environmental resources or trading among environmental resources and economic resources simply does not involve an apples-to-apples comparison. It is genuinely a difference in kind, not degree.[43]

Environmental issues are so complicated that finding an achievable policy can be challenging. Indeed, the global warming issue presents a case in point. Mainstream scientists and policy-makers generally agree that the earth is growing warmer and that manmade processes are contributing to the temperature increase. The difficulty lies in finding a workable public policy to address the issue. Judging by the failures of previous treaties, asking dozens of sovereign nations to sign onto an enforceable international agreement is unrealistic. Even if a substantial majority of the countries somehow would agree to forgo the use of dirty fossil fuels and curtail industrial pollution, the consequences are unknown. Perhaps such a drastic step would reduce or eliminate global warming, but perhaps the earth might continue to grow warmer owing to natural processes. The actions of humankind may already have set into motion a chain of events that cannot be ameliorated. For persons who argue that we must do something, even if it proves to be too little, too late in the long run, an incremental policy is preferable to no policy at all. Yet the promise of potential benefits in the decades to come at the price of almost-certain severe economic deprivations in the short run, barring an incontrovertible worldwide catastrophe, is not enough to convince multiple policy-makers at all levels of government across the globe to surrender their near-term advantages. Whether this position represents a fatal myopia or prudent caution depends on one's view of environmental issues.[44]

Even if somehow valuations and comparisons can be made, the under-lying assumption in economics—namely, that the process is fundamentally rational and orderly—may be myopic. In her book *The Policy Paradox*, Deborah Stone argued that economic transactions, especially those involving high-profile public sector issues, invariably infuse politics with policy-making. To assume that a trade-off is a logically straightforward, inherently rational endeavor is to oversimplify political decision-making. Policy-makers, especially elected officials, must respond to the interests and desires of multiple constituencies. Accordingly, their policies reflect compromises and trade-offs that are not always economically rational, but reflect their perceptions of political realities. One set of preferences may be rejected for multiple reasons that are irrational, inefficient, and inju-rious to the public. Yet seemingly irrational decisions are made all the time in the political realm. An elected official refuses to throw his support behind a new technology to clean up the environment because he fears that the technology might displace low-skilled workers that make up a significant percentage of the voters in his district. Legislators stonewall and refuse to enact a measure that will set rigid standards for drinking water in a particular community because the billions of dollars required to comply with strict guidelines will balloon the deficit or require always unpopular tax increases that might imperil the reelection chances of some elected representatives. A governor refuses to support a much-needed environmental public works project because he fears that the credit for such a victory will go to a challenger from the opposite political party and thereby make the governor's party look bad by comparison. On and on it goes. If Stone is correct, trade-offs between efficiency and equity are skewed by multiple factors, especially political considerations that under-mine basic economic assumptions.[45]

In short, economics is necessary, but insufficient for understanding and evaluating the natural environment. No one who understands the acquisitive nature of man will deny that the dismal science is especially important, and yet contentious because the existence of free markets may harm the environment. To ameliorate the negative externalities, among other reasons, government actors frequently intervene in supposedly free markets. Their intervention usually does not satisfy everyone because the policies that governments champion during the intervention—distributive, redistributive, and self-regulating—are highly contested. In the meantime, while economists tout the importance of rationality and efficiency as they caution against too much government intrusion, political considerations can, and frequently do, alter outcomes. For many public sector officials, policymaking is a means to an end. Sometimes protecting the natural environment is the end, but that is not true in every case.

For many environmentally-conscious citizens, to ask whether economics should play a part in environmental decision-making is to frame the question poorly. Economics is but a single facet of a much larger issue. The decision is not merely a matter of valuations and tradeoffs, as discussed above, but involves a much deeper, philosophical inquiry. If environmental resources are fundamentally distinct from other types of more-or-less fungible resources, the question must be reframed. On what basis are environmental resources protected? If economic considerations are not determinative, how should environmental decisions be made? This question is addressed in Chapter 3.[46]

NOTES

1. Douglas A. Bosse and Robert A. Phillips, "Agency Theory and Bounded Self-Interest," *Academy of Management Review* 41 (April 2016): 276–97; D. Wade Hands, "Economics, Psychology and the History of Consumer Choice Theory," *Cambridge Journal of Economics* 34 (July 2010): 633–48; Nuno Ornelas Martins, "Classical Surplus Theory and Heterodox Economics," *American Journal of Economics and Sociology* 72 (November 2013): 1205–31.

2. Ali Besharat, Daniel M. Ladik, and François A. Carrillat, "Are Maximizers Blind to the Future? When Today's Best Does Not Make for a Better Tomorrow," *Marketing Letters* 25 (March 2014): 77–91; Christin Schulze,

Don van Ravenzwaaij, and Ben R. Newell, "Of Marchers and Maximizers: How Competition Shapes Choice under Risk and Uncertainty," *Cognitive Psychology* 78 (May 2015): 78–98; Milan Zafirovski, "A Rational Choice Approach to Human Studies: A Reexamination," *Human Studies* 26 (January 2003): 41–66.

3. Arthur Herman, "How America Got Rich: It Was Tax Relief, Not Keynesianism, That Propelled American Prosperity after World War II," *Commentary* 134 (September 2012): 20–25; W. Kip Viscusi and Ted Gayer, "Behavioral Public Choice: The Behavioral Paradox of Government Policy," *Harvard Journal of Law & Public Policy* 38 (Summer 2015): 973–1007.

4. Robert Andersen and Josh Curtis, "Social Class, Economic Inequality, and the Convergence of Policy Preferences: Evidence from 24 Modern Democracies," *Canadian Review of Sociology* 52 (August 2015): 266–88; Paul M. Kellstedt, Suzanna Linn, and A. Lee Hannah, "The Polls-Review: The Usefulness of Consumer Sentiment: Assessing Construct and Measurement," *Public Opinion Quarterly* 79 (Spring 2015): 181–203.

5. Alexander Dow, Sheila Dow, and Alan Hutton, "The Scottish Political Economy Tradition and Modern Economics," *Scottish Journal of Political Economy* 44 (September 1997): 368–83; Christopher J. Berry, *The Idea of Commercial Society in the Scottish Enlightenment* (Edinburgh: Edinburgh University Press, 2013); Jan Golinski, "Science *in* the Enlightenment, Revisited," *History of Science* 49 (June 2011): 217–31.

6. Christopher J. Berry, "Adam Smith's 'Science of Human Nature,'" *History of Political Economy* 44 (Fall 2012): 471–92; Mark Garrett Longaker, "Adam Smith on Rhetoric and Phronesis, Law and Economics," *Philosophy and Rhetoric* 47 (2014): 25–47;

7. John Dwyer, "Ethics and Economics: Bridging Adam Smith's *Theory of Moral Sentiments* and *Wealth of Nations*," *Journal of British Studies* 44 (October 2005): 662–87; Jerry Evensky, "Adam Smith's *Theory of Moral Sentiments*: On Morals and Why They Matter to a Liberal Society of Free People and Free Markets," *Journal of Economic Perspectives* 19 (Summer 2005): 109–30; Maria Pia Paganelli, "The Adam Smith Problem in Reverse: Self-Interest in *The Wealth of Nations* and *The Theory of Moral Sentiments*," *History of Political Economy* 40 (Summer 2008): 365–82; Maria Pia Paganelli, "The Moralizing Role of Distance in Adam Smith: *The Theory of Moral Sentiments* as Possible Praise of Commerce," *History of Political Economy* 42 (Fall 2010): 425–41; Craig Smith, "Adam Smith's 'Collateral' Inquiry: Fashion and Morality in *The Theory of Moral Sentiments* and *The Wealth of Nations*," *History of Political Economy* 45 (Fall 2013): 505–2; Jack Russell Weinstein, *Adam Smith's Pluralism: Rationality, Education, and the Moral Sentiments* (New Haven and London: Yale University Press, 2013).

8. E.K. Hunt and Mark Lautzenheiser, *History of Economic Thought: A Critical Perspective*. 3rd edition (Armonk, N.Y.: M.E. Sharpe, Inc., 2011),

382–85; L.D. Keita, *Science, Rationality, and Neoclassical Economics* (Cranbury, N.J.: Associated University Presses, 1992), 41–44.

9. See, for example, Sheldon Danziger, "Do Rising Tides Lift All Boats? The Impact of Secular and Cyclical Changes on Poverty," *The American Economic Review* 76 (May 1986): 405–10; L. Randall Wray and Marc-Andre Pigeon, "Can a Rising Tide Raise All Boats? Evidence from the Clinton-Era Expansion," *Journal of Economic Issues* 34 (December 2000): 811–45.

10. See, for example, John Patrick Diggins, *The Lost Soul of American Politics: Virtue, Self-Interest, and the Foundations of Liberalism* (Chicago and London: University of Chicago Press, 1986), 98.

11. Kenneth J. Arrow, "Thorstein Veblen as an Economic Theorist," *American Economist* 19 (Spring 1975): 5–9; Tony Lawson, "What is This 'School' Called Neoclassical Economics?" *Cambridge Journal of Economics* 37 (September 2013): 947–83; Rick Tilman, "Thorstein Veblen and the Disinterest of Neoclassical Economists in Wasteful Consumption," *International Journal of Politics, Culture and Society* 13 (1999): 207–23; Matthew Watson, "Desperately Seeking Social Approval: Adam Smith, Thorstein Veblen and the Moral Limits of Capitalist Culture," *The British Journal of Sociology* 63 (September 2012): 491–512.

12. Leonhard Dobusch and Jakob Kapeller, "Why is Economics not an Evolutionary Science? New Answers to Veblen's Old Question," *Journal of Economic Issues* 43 (December 2009): 867–989; Giuseppe Fontana and Malcolm Sawyer, "Towards Post-Keynesian Ecological Macroeconomics," *Ecological Economics* 121 (January 2016): 186–95; Robert L. Nadeau, "Methodological and Ideological Options: The Unfinished Journey of Ecological Economics," *Ecological Economics* 109 (January 2015): 101–108; Clive L. Spash and Anthony Ryan, "Economic Schools of Thought on the Environment: Investigating Unity and Division," *Cambridge Journal of Economics* 36 (September 2012): 1091–1121; Joseph Wayne Smith and Gary Sauer-Thompson, "Civilization's Wake: Ecology, Economics and the Roots of Environmental Destruction and Neglect," *Population and Environment: A Journal of Interdisciplinary Studies* 19 (July 1998): 541–75.

13. Olivier Guéant, Roger Guesnerie, and Jean-Michel Lasry, "Ecological Intuition versus Economic 'Reason,'" *Journal of Public Economic Theory* 14 (March 2012): 245–72; A.M. Tanvir Hussain and John Tschirhart, "Economic/Ecological Tradeoffs among Ecosystem Services and Biodiversity Conservation," *Ecological Economics* 93 (September 2013): 116–27; Kathleen Segerson, "The Role of Economics in Interdisciplinary Environmental Policy Debates: Opportunities and Challenges," *American Journal of Agricultural Economics* 9 (March 2015): 374–89.

14. John Patrick Diggins, *Thorstein Veblen: Theorist of the Leisure Class* (Princeton, N.J.: Princeton University Press, 1999), 14–15. See also Hunt and Lautzenheiser, *History of Economic Thought*, 38–90; Keita, *Science, Rationality, and Neoclassical Economics*, 77.

15. Adam Smith, *An Inquiry into the Nature and Causes of the Wealth of Nations* (London: J.M. Dent & Sons, Ltd., 1921), 104–09, 137–56. See also Elias L. Khalil, "Beyond Self-Interest and Altruism: A Reconstruction of Adam Smith's Theory of Human Conduct," *Economics and Philosophy* 6 (October 1990): 255–73.

16. Patrick M. Garry, *Liberalism and American Identity* (Kent, Ohio: Kent State University Press, 1992), 47–50.

17. See, for example, Marshall E. Dimock, *Free Enterprise and the Administrative State* (Westport, Conn.: Greenwood Press, 1972).

18. Yves, Nievergelt, "The Concept of Elasticity in Economics," *SIAM Review* 25 (April 1983): 261–65.

19. See, for example, Bernard Salanie, *The Economics of Taxation* (Cambridge, Mass.: MIT Press, 2003), 3, 23–30; John B. Shoven and John Whalley, "Applied General-Equilibrium Models of Taxation and International Trade: An Introduction and Survey," *Journal of Economic Literature* 22 (September 1984): 1007–51.

20. Francesco Bianchi and Leonardo Melosi, "Modeling the Evolution of Expectations and Uncertainty in General Equilibrium," *International Economic Review* 57 (May 2016): 717–56; Klaus Conrad, "Applied General Equilibrium Modeling for Environmental Policy Analysis," *Annals of Operations Research* 54 (1994): 129–42.

21. Douglas R. Johnson and David G. Hoopes, "Managerial Cognition, Sunk Costs, and the Evolution of Industry Structure," *Strategic Management Journal* 24 (October 2003): 1057–68.

22. Thalia González and Giovanni Saarman, "Regulating Pollutants, Negative Externalities, and Good Neighbor Agreements: Who Bears the Burden of Protecting Communities?" *Ecology Law Quarterly* 41 (2014): 37–79; Joshua C. Hall, "Positive Externalities and Government Involvement in Education," *Journal of Private Enterprise* 21 (Spring 2006): 165–75.

23. Nicholas Mercuro, "Interdisciplinary Paradigms for Environmental Policy: Interrelationships Among Ecology, Law, and Economics," in *Property Rights, Economics, and the Environment: The Economics of Legal Relationships*, Michael D. Kaplowitz, ed. (New York: Routledge, an Imprint of the Taylor & Francis Group, 2000), 247–79.

24. João Rodrigues, "Where to Draw the Line between the State and Markets? Institutionalist Elements in Hayek's Neoliberal Political Economy," *Journal of Economic Issue* 46 (December 2012): 1007–33; Edward J. Romar, "Noble Markets: The Noble/Slave Ethic in Hayek's Free Market Capitalism," *Journal of Business Ethics* 85 (March 2009): 57–66.

25. Philipp Doerrenberg and Andreas Peichl, "The Impact of Redistributive Policies on Inequality in OECD Countries," *Applied Economics* 46 (June 2014): 2066–86; Jacob S. Hacker and Paul Pierson, "Making America Great Again: The Case for the Mixed Economy," *Foreign Affairs* 95 (May/June 2016):

69–90; Jody W. Lipford and Bruce Yandle, "Determining Economic Freedom: Democracy, Political Competition, and the Wealth Preservation Struggle," *The Journal of Private Enterprise* 30 (Fall 2015): 1–18; Matthew Luttig, "The Structure of Inequality and Americans' Attitudes Toward Redistribution," *Public Opinion Quarterly* 77 (Fall 2013): 811–21.

26. Alden F. Abbott, "U.S. Government Antitrust Intervention in Standard-Setting Activities and the Competitive Process," *Vanderbilt Journal of Entertainment & Technology Law* 18 (Winter 2016): 225–46; Daniel A. Crane, "Is More Antitrust the Answer to Wealth Inequality?" *Regulation* 38 (Winter 2015–2016): 18–21.

27. Stephen K. Aikins, "Political Economy of Government Intervention in the Free Market System," *Administrative Theory & Praxis* 31 (September 2009): 403–408; Bradley W. Bateman, "Bringing in the State? The Life and Times of Laissez-Faire in the Nineteenth-Century United States," *History of Political Economy* 37 (Supplement 2005): 175–99; Nicholas Lemann, "Notorious Big: Why the Spectre of Size Has Always Haunted American Politics," *The New Yorker* 92 (March 28, 2016): 72–75.

28. Steven Cohen, "What is Stopping the Renewable Energy Transformation and What Can the U.S. Government Do about It?" *Social Research* 82 (Fall 2015): 689–710; Lily Hsueh, "Regulatory Effectiveness and the Long-Run Policy Horizon: The Case of U.S. Toxic Chemical Use," *Environmental Science and Policy* 52 (October 2015): 6–22.

29. James Andreoni, "Warm-Glow versus Cold-Pickle: The Effects of Positive and Negative Framing on Cooperation in Experiments," *Quarterly Journal of Economics* 110 (February 1995): 1–21; A.H. Barnett, "The Pigouvian Tax Rule under Monopoly," *The American Economic Review* 70 (December 1980): 1037–41.

30. "Analytical Framework for Evaluating the Costs and Benefits of Extended Producer Responsibility Programmes: Executive Summary," *OECD Papers* 5 (2005): 4–57; Donatella Baiardi and Mario Menegatti, "Pigouvian Tax, Abatement Policies and Uncertainty in the Environment," *Journal of Economics* 103 (July 2011): 221–51; Firouz Gahvari, "Second-Best Pigouvian Taxation: A Clarification," *Environmental and Resource Economics* 59 (December 2014): 525–35; Antonio Massarutto, "The Long and Winding Road to Resource Efficiency—An Interdisciplinary Perspective on Extended Producer Responsibility," *Resources, Conservation & Recycling* 85 (April 2014): 11–21; Jonathan S. Masur and Eric A. Posner, "Toward a Pigouvian State," *University of Pennsylvania Law Review* 164 (December 2015): 93–147; Takayoshi Shinkuma, "Reconsideration of an Advance Disposal Fee Policy for End-of-Life Durable Goods," *Journal of Environmental Economics and Management* 53 (2007): 110–21.

31. Hunt and Lautzenheiser, *History of Economic Thought*, 38–90; "Momentum for Plastic Bag Bans Spreading; Recycling Programs Earn Mixed Reviews,"

Solid Waste Report 45 (April 25, 2014): 5–6; David A. Weisbach, "Should Environmental Taxes Be Precautionary?" *National Tax Journal* 65 (June 2012): 453–74.

32. Ian A. MacKenzie and Markus Ohndorf, "Coasean Bargaining in the Presence of Pigouvian Taxation," *Journal of Environmental Economics Management* 75 (January 2016): 1–11; Steven G. Medema, "The Curious Treatment of the Coase Theorem in the Environmental Economics Literature, 1960–1979," *Review of Environmental Economics and Policy* 8 (January 2014): 39–57; Stephanie Rosenkranz and Patrick W. Schmitz, "Can Coasean Bargaining Justify Pigouvian Taxation?" *Economica* 74 (November 2007): 573–85; Pierre Schlag, "Coase Minus the Coase Theorem—Some Problems with Chicago Transaction Analysis," *Iowa Law Review* 99 (November 2013): 175–223.

33. Ronald H. Coase, "The Institutional Structure of Production," *The American Economic Review* 82 (September 1992): 713–19; Joseph Farrell, "Information and the Coase Theorem," *The Journal of Economic Perspectives* 1 (Autumn 1987): 113–29.

34. Christopher L. Foote *et al.*, "Just the Facts: An initial Analysis of Subprime's Role in the Housing Crisis," *Journal of Housing Economics* 17 (December 2008): 291–305; Anne Schneider and Helen Ingram, "Social Construction of Target Populations: Implications for Politics and Policy," *American Political Science Review* 87 (June 1993): 334–47.

35. Hans Peter Gruner, "Redistributive Policy, Inequality, and Growth," *Journal of Economics* 62 (February 1995): 1–23. See also Carol M. Rose, "Liberty, Property, Environmentalism," *Social Philosophy & Policy* 26 (July 2009): 7–8.

36. Richard Stillman II, *American Bureaucracy: The Core of Modern Government*, 3rd. edition. (Belmont, Calif.: Wadsworth/Thomson, 2004), 171, 173.

37. See, for example, M. Christine Cagle, J. Michael Martinez, and William D. Richardson, "Privatizing Professional Licensing Boards: Self-Governance or Self-Interest?" *Administration & Society*, 30 (January 1999): 734–70; Virginia Haufler, *A Public Role for the Private Sector: Industry Self-Regulation in a Global Economy* (Washington, D.C.: Carnegie Endowment for International Peace, 2001); Andrew A. King and Michael J. Lenox, "Industry Self-Regulation Without Sanctions: The Chemical Industry's Responsible Care Program," *The Academy of Management Journal* 43 (August 2000): 698–716.

38. See, for example, Daniel J. Fiorino, "Rethinking Environmental Regulation: Perspectives on Law and Governance," *Harvard Environmental Law Review* 23 (1999): 441–68; Andrew J. Hoffman, "Institutional Evolution and Change: Environmentalism and the U.S. Chemical Industry," *The Academy of Management Journal* 42 (August 1999): 351–71.

39. Darryl K. Brown, "The Perverse Effects of Efficiency in Criminal Process," *Virginia Law Review* 100 (March 2014): 183–223; Satya R. Chakravarty, "Equity and Efficiency as Components of a Social Welfare Function,"

International Journal of Economic Theory 5 (June 2009): 181–99; James C. Cox and Vjollca Sadiraj, "Direct Tests of Individual Preferences for Efficiency and Equity," *Economic Inquiry* 50 (October 2012): 920–31; Roger Koppl and Meghan Sacks, "The Criminal Justice System Creates Incentives for False Convictions," *Criminal Justice Ethics* 32 (August 2013): 126–62.

40. See, for example, Sudhir Anand and Kara Hanson, "DALYs: Efficiency versus Equity," *World Development* 26 (February 1998): 307–10; Michael L. Barnett, Nicole Darnall, and Bryan W. Husted, "Sustainability Strategy in Constrained Economic Times," *Long Range Planning* 48 (April 2015): 63–68; Robert A. Becker, "Intergenerational Equity: The Capital-Environment Tradeoff," *Journal of Environmental Economics and Management* 9 (June 1982): 165–85; Arthur M. Okun, *Equality and Efficiency: The Big Tradeoff* (Washington, D.C.: The Brookings Institution, 1975).

41. Anand and Hanson, "DALYs: Efficiency versus Equity," 307–10; Okun, *Equality and Efficiency*, 8, 50.

42. Susan M. Miller, "Administering Representation: The Role of Elected Administrators in Translating Citizens' Preferences into Public Policy," *Journal of Public Administration Research and Theory* 23 (October 2013): 865–97; Chris Tausanovitch and Christopher Warshaw, "Measuring Constituent Policy Preferences in Congress, State Legislatures, and Cities," *The Journal of Politics* 75 (April 2013): 330–42; Viscusi and Gayer, "Behavioral Public Choice," 973–1007; Susan Webb Yackee, "Participant Voice in the Bureaucratic Policymaking Process," *Journal of Public Administration Research and Theory* 25 (April 2015): 427–49.

43. Giuseppe Munda, *Multicriteria Evaluation in a Fuzzy Environment: Theory and Applications in Ecological Economics* (Berlin: Springer Science + Business Media, 2012); Bryan G. Norton, "Beyond Positivist Ecology: Toward an Integrated Ecological Ethics," *Science & Engineering Ethics* 14 (December 2008): 581–92; Bryan G. Norton, "Population and Consumption: Environmental Problems as Problems of Scale," *Ethics and the Environment* 5 (Spring 2000): 23–45.

44. Rachel Brewster, "Stepping Stone or Stumbling Block: Incrementalism and National Climate Change Legislation," *Yale Law & Policy Review* 28 (April 1, 2010): 245–312; Jason Delborne *et al.*, "Policy Pathways, Policy Networks, and Citizen Deliberation: Disseminating the Results of World Wide Views on Global Warming in the USA," *Science and Public Policy* 40 (2013): 378–92; Johannes Urpelainen, "A Model of Dynamic Climate Governance: Dream Big, Win Small," *International Environmental Agreements* 13 (May 2013): 107–25.

45. Deborah Stone, *Policy Paradox: The Art of Political Decision Making*, Revised Edition (New York: W. W. Norton, 2002): 376–83.

46. Xinyu Liu *et al.*, "Comparing National Environmental and Economic Performances through Emerging Sustainability Indicators: Moving Environmental Ethics beyond Anthropocentrism toward Ecocentrism," *Renewable*

and Sustainable Energy Reviews 58 (May 2016): 1532–42; Patricia A. Soranno *et al.*, "It's Good to Share: Why Environmental Scientists' Ethics Are Out of Date," *BioScience* 65 (January 2015): 69–73; Brian G. Wolff, "Environmental Studies and Utilitarian Ethics," *Bioscene: Journal of College Biology Teaching* 34 (December 2008): 6–11.

3

THE ETHICS OF SUSTAINABILITY

During the twenty-first century, the concept of sustainability became a crucial component of the American environmental movement. New government regulations encouraged private sector entities to develop sustainable policies and practices. Corporate boards of directors developed mission statements and tasked upper-level management with developing a list of best practices for incorporating sustainability into the business. Nongovernmental organizations (NGOs) lobbied world governments to be cognizant of systemic environmental challenges and respond with appropriate legislation to curb all manner of abuses. To anyone examining the evolution of American environmentalism since the 1960s, the focus on sustainability appeared to be a movement in the right direction toward incorporating environmental factors into decision-making.

Yet, all was not well on the environmental front. As discussed in Chapter 1, a major difficulty was that sustainability is a broad, imprecise notion, which means that it holds different meanings for different audiences. A term that is defined with overly broad parameters may be similar to having no definition at all. Moreover, a practice or product that is labeled as "sustainable" for one individual may be needlessly wasteful and harmful for another. If a company manufactures a product using fossil fuels, the company may believe that reducing its natural resource consumption should qualify as a sustainable practice while members of the environmental community regard such manufacturing enterprises as irredeemably profligate. Ongoing controversies about how to measure pollution and manage environmental quality ensure that multiple parties frequently fail to reach consensus. Even if parties more or less agree on a sustainable practice, the march of time and technological developments render a previously sustainable practice obsolete. Elected officials, conflicted about whether they should represent job-creating industries or environmentally conscious activists, find themselves between the proverbial rock and a hard place.

The starting point for most definitions of the term is the insight that human beings are obliged to leave future generations at least as well off as people are today. To be sustainable, a practice must be able to continue indefinitely without diminishing the quality or quantity of natural resources used to support the practice. Whether this means that trade-offs can occur to ensure no net loss of environmental quality remains a point of contention. Another definition suggests that sustainability refers to the confluence of economic, social, and environmental values. In other words, for an activity to be considered sustainable, it must balance all three values.

These definitions, while helpful, must be further developed if they are to hold genuine meaning for policy-makers. The absence of detail and context invariably results in conflicting opinions about which actions constitute sustainable practices. Even when the parties reach a consensus regarding definition of sustainability as a description of environmental quality, they may vehemently disagree on the normative component. The question of what ought to be considered "sustainable" requires a discussion of philosophical antecedents. If observers cannot agree on the foundations of sustainability, they will never be able to agree on a workable, implementable plan of action.[1]

GENERAL PHILOSOPHICAL IDEAS AND CONCEPTS

Environmental ethicists have debated at length the philosophical origins of American environmentalism. Some observers, notably Lynn White, Jr., have argued that the natural environment has received short shrift in the Western intellectual tradition. According to White and others, western philosophy is grounded on a Christian perspective of nature. The scriptures, according to this view, indicate that God created the earth for human beings to use as they see fit. Therefore, nature is useful only insofar as lower-order animals and plants are subservient to humankind. The environment does not hold intrinsic value. Instead, it is instrumentally valuable because it meets the needs of the creatures existing at the top of the food chain.[2]

The instrumental valuation of natural resources implicitly rests upon the theory of Utilitarianism, an idea that is as old as humankind but which reached full fruition as a philosophical school of thought during the nineteenth century. The theory's appeal is intuitively obvious. Adherents are not required to remake the nature of humankind. Human beings are naturally self-interested and acquisitive. They make decisions based on what they believe to be in their best interests even if they are sometimes mistaken in their calculations. The Utilitarians' philosophical insights are based on the principle of utility, which suggests that human beings seek to maximize pleasure and minimize pain. In the realm of public policy-making, decision-makers seek to craft policies that maximize the greatest good for the greatest number.

If Utilitarianism sounds suspiciously like neoclassical economic theory, it is little wonder. Both systems presuppose that human beings act on a principle of self-interest that they rarely, if ever, overcome. Enlightenment-era Utilitarianism and neoclassical economics trace their antecedents to the doctrine of moral sentiments, which posits that human beings instinctively understand which acts are useful in advancing their interests and which acts should be avoided. Unlike classical political philosophers, who believed that human nature was malleable and could be perfected through a proper education, the Utilitarians and neoclassical economists accepted human beings as they act in the real world, not as one might wish them to act.

It is no exaggeration to say that Utilitarianism has been one of the most influential philosophical doctrines of the modern era. Policy-makers working within a democratic political system understand that they cannot satisfy the needs of every constituent. The diverse interests and needs of the populace preclude unanimity of opinion; however, a middle ground frequently can be found. The successful elected official will navigate through numerous, frequently competing, constituencies to forge a compromise solution that allows effective public policy to be created and provides a path toward reelection. In fact, any political system based on a foundation of consensual self-government explicitly or implicitly accepts the premise that compromises are necessary to satisfy the largest number of constituents, even if the resultant policy falls short of the ideal.[3]

Jeremy Bentham, an English philosopher, is arguably the father of modern Utilitarianism, although much of his work was expanded by his godson, John Stuart Mill, who focused on Utilitarian features of public policy. Mill, in particular, understood that the concept of pleasure was not merely the instant gratification of selfish, hedonistic needs, but an expression of the needs of an enlightened populace. Persons might forsake a temporary satisfaction in exchange for a long-term goal or they might be willing to set aside individual preferences to adopt a policy in the interests of multiple individuals. The principal task of government, in Mill's view, is to encourage citizens to understand their role within a functioning polity. Without a conscientious, well-educated citizenry, the people likely will fall victim to demagoguery and possibly a loss of their cherished liberties.[4]

Even among observers who do not formally subscribe to the tenets of philosophical Utilitarianism, the utilitarian principle underlies their perspectives in subtle and not-so-subtle ways. They proceed from the assumption that the human animal will subscribe to the notion of the "good" as embracing pleasure and avoiding pain. Even a child knows to ask for more candy and cry out against swallowing bitter medicine. Ultimately, what makes Utilitarianism so compelling is its seemingly intuitive grasp of the human condition. Setting aside the complexities of any moral philosophy as well as competing interpretations of myriad schools of thought, at its core Utilitarianism does not require abstract theories, convoluted explanations, or myriad syllogisms to explicate its logic. The theory seems to conceptualize what virtually every human being has found to be true in his or her life. Trade-offs must occur, and a person attempts to maximize pleasure and minimize pain.[5]

Proponents of the instrumental view of environmentalism point to philosophical and literary sources in support of their perspective that maximizing the pleasure of human beings is the goal. In his dialogue the *Phaedrus*, Plato depicts his great teacher, Socrates, as a figure interested only in the affairs of man and uninterested in natural phenomena unless it directly touches a human life. Human beings matter and other things do not. Numerous passages in the Christian Bible refer to the dominion of human beings over lesser animals as well as the earth, although debates continue over "dominion" and whether this concept allows human beings to despoil the earth. Centuries later, William Shakespeare praises humankind—"What a piece of work is a man! How noble in reason, how infinite in faculty! In form and moving how express and admirable! In action how like an Angel! in apprehension how like a god!"—in Act II, scene two, of *Hamlet* while relegating nature to a subservient role.[6]

For all of its longevity and influence in Western philosophy, Utilitarianism has not been universally heralded as an incontrovertible philosophical system. Critics contend that measuring utility is never a simple calculation. Determining the greatest good for the greatest number depends on multiple assumptions. For example, what is "greatest" and what is "good"? Just as the term "sustainability" is imprecise and open to competing interpretations, so, too, is the term "utilitarian." The Utilitarian might argue that supporting an industry that creates jobs but harms the natural environment is beneficial because the need for good jobs outweighs the minimal environmental impact of a specific industry. If one company is precluded from building a manufacturing facility in one area, other companies can be regulated in a similar fashion. The final arbiter of who wins and who loses in the economic marketplace is an entity that possesses enormous power. Yet, as Lord Acton noted, power corrupts, and absolute power corrupts absolutely. To limit the freedom of contract and the right of business associations to engage in unfettered commerce is to allow an oppressive government to trample on the rights of its citizens.[7]

The rejoinder is that environmental impacts over time diminish the value of natural resources, which, in turn, affect far more people than does the creation of new jobs in a particular community. The direct economic impact of creating new jobs can be measured with a reasonable degree of precision, but determining the exact economic costs associated with the pollution from an industry that creates the jobs cannot be calculated with the same degree of precision. Any calculations must factor in a variety of variables that do not always meet with general consensus.

The distance problem also recurs here. An industry that constructs a new manufacturing plant can point to the economic benefits that will accrue in the immediate future, but the negative consequences associated with an incremental increase in pollution generally are much more nebulous and extend far into the future.[8]

Utilitarianism can complicate a comparison of policy choices because the philosophy assumes that measurements of pleasure and pain can be more or less reduced to discrete units of utility. In some instances, such comparisons can be made, especially when there is a quantifiable economic impact. In other instances, however, rational cost-benefit calculations are exceedingly difficult. In the area of natural resource consumption, systems are so interrelated and the time frames necessary to evaluate the detrimental impact created by human beings are so large that precision becomes almost impossible. It is tempting to say that a new construction project will only harm one species of animal, which is a minimal effect in the short run. Studies may indicate, however, that this species serves as an important food source for other species, which may be harmed by the loss of the first species. Over time, the loss or displacement of multiple species can alter the natural environment irreparably. In the final analysis, the construction project may trigger environmental consequences that few, if any, can predict beforehand. [9]

Related to measurement difficulties, Utilitarianism does not fully consider depths of preferences. A small number of constituents may adamantly desire a specific policy choice, but their policy preferences may be overwhelmed by a much larger constituency that is only minimally interested in the outcome. Large numbers of American citizens may approve of oil exploration in the Alaskan hinterlands without giving the matter much thought. Yet residents of the area, accustomed to enjoying a pristine natural environment, may object strenuously, arguing that the majority of citizens simply do not understand the full impact that oil exploration will have on the environment. If the decision is made based on majority rule, residents will be harmed with little recourse for effective redress of their grievances. Without some sort of weighted measurement, the larger number of people will always win the argument in a government based on democratic principles, even if this leads to a tyranny of the majority.

Apologists for the American political system contend that the design of government mitigates the ill effects of a tyrannical majority. They point to the U.S. Senate as a deliberative body where a majority can express views that, while not supported by the majority of Americans, the plurality believes to the critical. The point is well taken; yet some issues do not rise to the level of federal legislation. The Utilitarian perspective is fundamentally flawed because it seeks to measure the breadth, if not the depth of preferences. Attempts to shore up the theory's deficiencies, however noble and well-meaning, do not rehabilitate all of Utilitarianism's shortcomings.[10]

Perhaps the most devastating and incisive philosophical criticism of Utilitarianism came from the great German philosopher Immanuel Kant. Writing at the end of the eighteenth century, Kant was disturbed by what he called the "hypothetical imperative" he recognized in the work of the Utilitarian philosopher David Hume. Kant famously remarked that Hume's hypothetical imperative awoke him from his "dogmatic slumbers." Hume had argued that philosophical systems based on abstract metaphysical concepts are not helpful to a human life because they lack practical utility. According to Hume, moral judgments must be based on utility and feeling. Deep ruminations on moral questions are unnecessary and unwarranted. They simply clutter up human existence with pie-in-the-sky abstractions that do not touch the lives of ordinary men and women who must make moral choices in a flawed universe.[11]

Kant objected to this relativistic worldview. If a philosophy is only judged by its practical utility, the result is a situational ethic where any manner of activity can be justified as useful. Lying is acceptable because it benefits the liar and it does not cause pain for the listener. Thus, the adulterous spouse reasons, "I did not tell my wife about the affair because it would only get me into trouble and cause her undue grief. By lying, I am actually making both of us happier than if I told the truth." Theft is justified because I, who am so poor, needed the items I stole from the merchant, who is so rich. Authoritarian governments can rationalize pogroms because they benefit the greatest good for the greatest number and dispose of a small number of dissidents and malcontents efficiently.

Hume's hypothetical imperative allows a person to change his or her behavior as times and circumstances change. According to Kant, such a permissive ethic means that no absolute standard exists to judge whether an action is moral. An ethical system that allows a person to justify his or her actions in accordance with changing times and circumstances is tantamount to no system at all. To follow Hume is to embrace sophistry.[12]

Kant argued that if man is genuinely a rational, moral autonomous agent, he must obey immutable laws of conduct. In lieu of Hume's hypothetical imperative, Kant posited a "categorical imperative." In a rearticulation of the Golden Rule, Kant wrote, "Act only on the maxim whereby thou canst at the same time will that it should become a universal law." In other words, do unto others as you would have others do unto you. An ethical person asks himself or herself, "In undertaking this act, am I prepared to approve of others acting in exactly the same way? If I lie, cheat, or steal, am I prepared to live in a society where such behavior is condoned?" Kant believed that free, moral agents must determine their duty and follow that duty regardless of the outcome. Consequences be damned.[13]

In the realm of environmentalism, Kant's categorical imperative can be seen as the basis for treating natural resources as intrinsically valuable. Rather than asking whether clean air, clean water, or the scenic sunset is more or less valuable than the number of jobs an industry will bring to a community, the issue is whether the environment is an end in itself. In the Kantian philosophy, intrinsic value is not subject to bargaining and negotiation.[14]

ANTHROPOCENTRISM

Building on these general philosophical insights, environmental ethicists sometimes speak of two distinct views: anthropocentrism and biocentrism. Although some members of the environmental community prefer to move beyond the use of these terms, believing that such labels oversimplify the range of environmental perspectives, they remain a useful dividing line to understand the perennial debate between human-centered and earth-centered advocates. Accordingly, the terms will be used here to explore the ethics of sustainability.[15]

The former concept is based on neoclassical economic precepts as well as Utilitarian philosophical constructs. An anthropocentrist believes that all human transactions involve trade-offs. Consequently, the task is to define terms and data points as precisely as possible so that the trade-offs can occur as effectively and efficiently as possible.

An anthropocentrist is not necessarily a diehard supporter of industry. A policy-maker can support environmental causes while also recognizing the necessity of promoting smart industrial development. The goal is to ensure that industry carefully manages its resources to minimize environmental effects. This is a fine line to walk—and not every committed environmentalist believes that such a trade-off is possible—but anthropocentrists recognize that however committed they may be to natural resource protection, individuals must still eat, build houses, locate suitable employment, and enjoy a reasonable standard of life in an industrial economy.[16]

As discussed in Chapter 1, anthropocentrists support the definition of sustainable development found in the 1987 report of the World Commission on the Environment and Development (WCED), commonly known as the "Brundtland Report." Recall that the Brundtland Report characterized sustainable development as development that "meets the needs of the present without compromising the ability of future generations to meet their own needs." Similarly, five years later, in *Agenda 21*, the United Nations Conference on the Environment and Development defined sustainability as an effort "to ensure socially responsible economic development while protecting the resources base and the environment for future generations."[17]

Some anthropocentrists fall within what might be labeled the "weak sustainability" camp. For this group, economic mechanisms are the preferred method of changing consumers' behavior. Rather than calling for wholesale, systemic change, a proponent of weak sustainability seeks to use the existing political, legal, and economic infrastructures to affect incremental change. One of the best-known supporters of this position, Yale University economist William D. Nordhaus, argued in several works that international agreements hammered out among nations that rely on targeted reductions are preferable to setting arbitrary, unrealistic goals that are difficult, if not impossible, to enforce and fail to appreciate the myriad differences among the world's nations. Only by working within existing networks can policy-makers hope to improve environmental quality, especially in the international arena.[18]

A slightly more robust view of sustainability can be found among self-proclaimed intergenerational anthropocentrists. These persons contend that planning for future generations is a necessary component of any serious environmental strategy. Their jeremiads typically highlight the tragedy of the commons as an inevitable result of short-term, mainstream capitalist views. For a common pool resource owned by all, such as a natural park or a specific place known for its pristine beauty, individuals have an incentive to enjoy the resource, even to the point of exhaustion, without concern for its future use. After all, if I see the much ballyhooed scenery, with no plans to return, why should I care if anyone else enjoys the view? Americans fascinated by the Grand Canyon crowd into the last available lodging places to enjoy spectacular views of the canyon before the pollution that accompanied them spoils the resource for everyone who follows.

Intergenerationalists also argue that natural capital must be distinguished from standard monetary capital. Traditional neoclassical economists tend to regard all goods as fungible; that is, the item is more or less as a valuable as a similar item carrying the same price tag. All goods can be substituted. If one stock or piece of property or capital investment opportunity is diminished, a similar good can be found in short order. For anyone concerned about future generations, this sort of valuation is troubling. Natural capital is not fungible, and goods are not endlessly substitutable. If a natural habitat or a species is lost, the harm is irreparable. It is entirely possible that no substitutes can be found.[19]

The next step beyond traditional economic valuations sometimes is referred to as ecological economics. Instead of debating the value of natural resources using neoclassical tools, ecological economists and rely on a wider variety of measures to determine worth. Their methods are not without controversy, for ecologists cite the need for a dynamic, evolutionary approach to natural resource protection. The typical valuation requires a buyer or seller to examine the marketplace and fix a price based on what the market will bear. By contrast, an ecological economist seeks to integrate information from many sources into the valuation. According to one scholar, ecological economics relies on "nonlinear mathematics, general systems theory, non-equilibrium thermodynamics, and ecosystem ecology." If this description sounds abstract and difficult to envision, such concerns do not vex a committed ecological economist.

Individual tastes and preferences are not the appropriate focus for eco-logical economics. Rather, they seek to understand what the entire col-lectivity needs. They also suggest that a large scale is preferable to a small scale; in other words, rather than focus on what a group of indi-viduals desires for the next 10 or 20 years, economists should seek to understand what the planet earth requires over the next millennium.[20]

Some environmental ethicists go so far as to embrace adaptive man-agement, the notion that environmental protection is not simply one value among a competing set of values, but it is the paramount value. Human beings must understand that a large, complex, dynamic system is constantly in flux and probably cannot be understood in all its glory and complexity. Rather than try to conquer the environment and impose human rules on nonhuman systems, people should adapt, to the extent possible, their decision-making and activities to the needs of the environ-ment as opposed to assuming that nature should adapt to humankind. Because adaption is necessarily a fluid concept, proponents of adaptive management indicate that ecological systems must be monitored con-tinuously and, if natural resources are harmed, human plans must be altered to mitigate the harm, to the extent possible. Adaptive manage-ment theorists develop nuanced models that allow them to understand the effect of human activity on natural processes with the understand-ing that model building is an iterative, never-ending process. Unlike command-and-control management systems that develop deterministic prediction models, the adaptive management model must constantly be evaluated and changed as new data are collected.[21]

BIOCENTRISM

Despite some anthropocentrists' deep commitment to protecting the natural environment, they remain focused on the needs and desires of human beings. This emphasis on humankind as the appropriate unit of analysis disturbs radical environmentalists. Instead of considering the moral standing of humans, biocentrists believe that all living creatures possess moral standing and that no one animal should be valued above another. For this, and other reasons, biocentrism remains one of the most controversial philosophical positions in American environmentalism.[22]

Paul Taylor's book *Respect for Nature* is perhaps the best-known text in this area. "The biocentric outlook, we might say, provides a general 'map' of the natural world, enabling us to see where we are and how we fit into the total scheme of things," Taylor wrote. "It presents the realm of nature and life as a setting for human existence." Biocentrists refuse to justify human mischief on the basis of mainstream economic precepts. As Taylor explains, "Wte see ourselves as biological creatures." Whatever advantages that human beings enjoy over other creatures, humans cannot in good conscience rely on those advantages to determine their moral worth. For humans to consider themselves superior to other beings merely because they can overpower all would-be rivals is to adopt a might-makes-right ethic, which can lead to environmental despoliation without compunction.[23]

Much has been made of this schism between anthropocentrism and biocentrism, and not every environmental ethicist buys into such a neat, clean division. Indeed, for many observers, the idea of two competing concepts misses the point. Whether environmental protection is necessary because such action proves to be instrumentally valuable to human beings or because nature is intrinsically valuable may be an inconsequential distinction. If all parties agree that the objective is to preserve and protect nature for current and future generations, all other considerations are secondary. The point is well taken; however, because so much of the philosophical writing on the environment has relied on the anthropocentrism-biocentrism dichotomy, it is necessary to understand reputed differences in the schools of thought.[24]

In a famous 1973 article, Norwegian philosopher Arne Naess coined the term "deep ecology" as a way of explaining how a committed biocentric view differs from traditional anthropocentric concepts. What Naess dubbed "shallow ecology" is little more than simplified neoclassical economics with a stated concern for natural resource protection. Deep ecology, however, refers to the idea that the sum is greater than its parts. Nature must be considered as a holistic system. As a result, economic principles are not helpful in evaluating environmental issues because economics relies on the thoughts and actions of a self-actualized individual.

Deep ecologists believe that placing the human animal at the center of every ethical decision can lead to disastrous results because human beings are so short-sighted and their interests are so narrow and ego-centric. Descartes' famous maxim *cogito ergo sum*—I think, therefore I am—presupposed that the human individual and his or her needs and desires are the only verifiable concepts that man can know without question. Everything that exists beyond the individual's experience may be illusory and a figment of his imagination—or maybe not. The problem can never be resolved. This perspective holds enormous consequences. In an extreme case, it may lead to metaphysical solipsism, a kind of mental paralysis. Even when the response is not extreme, a human being's belief that his perspective is the only worthy perspective will lead him to harm other beings with insufficient regard for their needs or desires.[25]

Deep ecology rejects the Cartesian emphasis on the individual. The existence of the human ego is not the essential fact of life, nor can it be when human beings must share the planet with a diverse array of life forms. When individuals, especially those who live in western cultures, express dissatisfaction with their lives and the "rat race" of earning a living while juggling family responsibilities, they are in reality giving voice to the alienation that any creature feels when he does not live in harmony with his environment. He is speaking the wrong language.

The language of economics is a specific dialect of the human psyche and is deeply flawed—flawed as an expression of what lies in the human heart and flawed as a means of making decisions that affect the planet. Two well-known deep ecologists, Bill Devall and George Sessions, eloquently observed, "We must see beyond our narrow contemporary cultural assumptions and values, and the conventional wisdom of our time and place, and this is best achieved by the deep questioning process."[26]

Deep ecologists such as J. Baird Callicott and Laura Westra question why human beings assume that they can exercise dominion over the earth simply because they are stronger and more adaptable than other creatures. Moral worth is not a function of power and cunning. Otherwise, the principle of "might makes right" would be the pinnacle of ethics. Human beings must change their ways or catastrophic events will occur in the not-too-distant future as the biosphere is irredeemably harmed. According to Callicott and Westra, if might is to remain subservient to right, might must be employed in service of right.[27]

As with any philosophical construct, some deep ecologists embrace concepts and values that others do not accept. James Lovelock's Gaia principle is an excellent example. Lovelock and other Gaia enthusiasts from the Deep Ecology School argue for a position known as Gaia, the notion that organisms adapt and evolve continuously. Changes triggered by human activities can trigger environmental calamities in the short run, but they can be corrected by future adaptations. Co evolutionary Gaia is a theory that owes much to evolutionary biology. Changes among the species invariably result in stability and order in nature. All of these positions form the basis for Strong Gaia theory, which suggests that all living organisms are purposive and seek to create favorable conditions for the perpetuation of multiple species.[28]

Because Gaia relies heavily on evolutionary theory and, in some versions, indicates that nature possesses consciousness, it has been lampooned by detractors who see it as a New Age fad. Aristotle's belief that even inanimate objects seek to accomplish their goals has long been discredited, but Gaia, in its extreme form, appears to revive the old chestnut. Yet these metaphysical musings do not provide guidance on pressing environmental challenges, according to critics.[29]

The question of how (and why) human beings can consider environmental issues completely separate from human interests and desires has puzzled some scholars. Even ecologists who are otherwise sympathetic to deep ecology lament the ease with which some extremists can be parodied. Murray Bookchin, a prominent ecologist who has written widely on the subject, expressed skepticism about the "exotic tendencies" of those who "espouse deep ecology, biocentrism, Gaian consciousness, and eco-theology, to cite the main cults that celebrate a quasi-religious 'reverence' for 'Nature' with what is often a simultaneous denigration of human beings and their traits." Some extremists seem antagonistic to human needs and desires. Bookchin was appalled by a mystical account, *Gaia Meditations*, which spewed out a series of silly aphorisms such as, "Think of your next death. Will your flesh and bones back into the cycle. Surrender. Love the plump worms you will become. Launder your weary being through the foundation of life."[30]

Bookchin recognized that deep ecologists risk an overcorrection in arguing against mainstream economics and anthropocentrism. Although the point is well taken that human needs should be balanced with non human needs, spewing out bumper-sticker slogans and virtually impenetrable metaphysics does little to advance the biocentric cause. In fact, because the drivel can be dismissed as absurd, it may reinforce the existing paradigm that embraces neoclassical economics and human-centered theories of environmental protection. "The ecology movement is too important to allow itself to be taken over by mystics and reactionary misanthropes," Bookchin wrote.[31]

HENRY DAVID THOREAU AND THE AMERICAN ENVIRONMENTAL CREDO

No serious student of environmental ethics, whether he subscribes to the anthropocentric or biocentric point of view, can afford to ignore the writings of Henry David Thoreau, arguably the leading American environmental thinker of the pre-Civil War era. Thoreau is sometimes characterized as a misanthrope. Such a description is misleading. He did not hate the human race, nor did he negate the human condition so that he could "love the plump worms you will become." In fact, Thoreau loved life and sought to live it to the fullest capacity. His life-affirming philosophical musing on man's relationship with nature explains his continuing appeal more than a century and a half after his death. He has become an icon, and for good reason.[32]

Thoreau's work is often misunderstood because he was not a systematic, philosophically consistent writer spelling out syllogisms and clear, unequivocal prose. He was as much a poet as anything else, which meant that he employed eloquent language, but his meaning was not always clear or unambiguous. He was a fervent idealist, fearing the dehumanizing effects of technology and so-called progress, and yet Thoreau was not a reactionary Luddite longing for a return to yesteryear. He has been portrayed as a loner who traipsed into the wilderness in a deliberate attempt to turn his back on humanity. This popular conception, widely known and frequently discussed, is not supported by the historical record. Thoreau unquestionably enjoyed his celebrated excursions into wilderness lands, but he understood that man is a social animal. He always returned to society in search of human companionship.[33]

His origins were predictably humble, although his family was not quite destitute. He was born in Massachusetts in 1817. From his earliest years, young Henry David was a precocious child with a gift for grasping the nuances of human interactions. Despite his family's modest station, the young man eventually attended and graduated from Harvard University.

He might have enjoyed a lucrative career in law or business, but Thoreau was temperamentally ill-suited to follow a straight path into the commercial world. He taught school briefly before he fell under the spell of the Transcendentalists, especially Ralph Waldo Emerson, an idealistic New Englander who took a paternalistic interest in Thoreau. Similar to the English Romantics, Transcendentalists taught that human beings naturally possess a "pure" disposition, but society's institutions gradually and inexorably corrupt the individual.[34]

Transcendentalism developed during the 1830s and 1840s, an era when some observers began to despair over the growth of slavery in North America and the dehumanizing effects of industrialization throughout the western world. Rather than accept this new wave of pessimism, the Transcendentalists emphasized the power of the individual to build a better life through self-reliance and resistance to societal conventions, including organized religion and political parties. Human beings need not succumb to disillusionment and despair if they will only take control of their lives.

Transcendentalist concepts were tailor-made for an idiosyncratic soul such as Henry David Thoreau. Already exhibiting an individualistic bent, he believed that life consists of more than the world of physical existence. He also agreed with the Transcendentalists who rejected the dogmas of established churches that insisted on the primacy of sacred texts and adherence to a strict set of rituals. Instead of following the well-worn path, Transcendentalism championed personal intuition as the key to a successful life. A person must strive to understand his world through observation and self-reflection free from the clutter of modern technology. Unlike the Romantics, who tended to reject empiricism and the scientific method, Transcendentalists were not hostile to modernity. They simply believed that the individual must not become a slave to established doctrines and modes of thinking. In some ways, they reflected Socrates' centuries-old admonition that the unexamined life is not worth living.[35]

As he reached adulthood, Thoreau grew restless with his life as a teacher and occasional laborer in his family's pencil factory. It was not a hard life, but he worried that he had become too immersed in his routine and was not fully engaged with the world. After mulling over his options, he chose to turn away from the comfortable existence he had built and enter into the woods in search of a simple life free of encumbrances. It was a decision wholly in line with the Transcendentalist tradition.[36]

He was not abandoning the society of man or his friends and family. Thoreau was not a primitive survivalist who wished to test himself and discover whether he could stay alive when nature threatened him with blizzards and all manner of calamities. He entered the forest and lived in a cabin on the outskirts of Concord, Massachusetts, situated on land that his friend Emerson owned. If he became sick or needed medicine, he could trudge into town to seek assistance. The goal, as he explained in a stirring passage in his famous book *Walden*, was to simplify his life and provide himself with an opportunity for sustained self-reflection. He did not wish to complicate life by struggling for his daily bread. He wrote:

I went to the woods because I wished to live deliberately, to front only the essential facts of life, and see if I could not learn what it had to teach, and not, when I came to die, discover that I had not lived. I did not wish to live what was not life, living is so dear; nor did I wish to practice resignation, unless it was quite necessary. I wanted to live deep and suck out all the marrow of life, to live so sturdily and Spartan-like as to put to rout all that was not life, to cut a broad swath and shave close, to drive life into a corner, and reduce it to its lowest terms, and, if it proved to be mean, why then to get the whole and genuine meanness of it, and publish its meanness to the world; or if it were sublime, to know it by experience, and be able to give a true account of it in my next excursion.[37]

Thoreau recognized that human beings often are so focused on the day-to-day minutiae of life that they do not reflect on the meaning of their lives. They essentially set aside important questions and flitter from one self-imposed crisis to the next. The antidote, he believed could be summarized succinctly: "Simplicity, simplicity, simplicity!"[38]

As for nature, much of *Walden* is a paean to the virtues of a simple human life enjoyed close to a forest or mountain stream. Thoreau urged his readers not to intellectualize experience, for the natural environment is best experienced in all its immediacy and beauty without dissecting its component parts in a scientific manner. "The earth is not a mere fragment of dead history, stratum upon stratum like the leaves of a book, to be studied by geologists and antiquaries chiefly, but living poetry like the leaves of a tree, which precede flowers and fruit—not a fossil earth, but a living earth; compared with whose great central life all animal and vegetable life is merely parasitic. Its throes will heave our exuviae from their graves."[39]

He continues to speak to environmentalists of the twenty-first century because he understood that humankind cannot exist separated from the earth. Human beings are a part of nature and must learn to live in harmony with it. The traditional western concept of exercising dominion over other creatures is a recipe for environmental disaster. As Thoreau wrote, "We can never have enough of Nature. We must be refreshed by the sight of inexhaustible vigor, vast and titanic features, the sea-coast with its wrecks, the wilderness with its living and its decaying trees, the thunder-cloud, and the rain which lasts three weeks and produces freshets."[40]

Whether he was an anthropocentrist or biocentrist is difficult to say and completely beside the point. Thoreau's importance to environmental ethics is his insistence that human beings and nature are intertwined. They share a mutual fate, which means that one cannot exist without the other. For that reason, Thoreau is the logical starting point for anyone who seeks to understand sustainability in American environmentalism.

Critics concede that Henry David Thoreau could turn a phrase as well as anyone who wrote the English language during the nineteenth century. His philosophical observations are inspiring and enjoyable to read. Yet, the lack of specificity in his work and the sometimes self-indulgent moralizing do not provide guidance for a public servant who seeks to develop public policy. Thoreau's relentless individualism and his mistrust of manmade institutions, including government, as corrupting invariably mean that his reflections provide limited utility for a public administrator who desires to craft a workable plan for improving environmental quality.[41]

In the final analysis, Thoreau's work, as with virtually all the literature on environmental ethics, provides general insights—philosophical food for thought—about important values, but it is hardly practicable, nor was it designed to be. Human beings need nature to provide them with inspiration and sustenance. *Walden* can be read as a warning to persons who would divorce themselves from the natural environment. They who ignore nature do so at their peril. As an articulation of general philosophical concepts, a mission statement for environmentalists, his work is a valuable addition to the literature.[42]

Aside from nature's benefit to human beings, as all environmental ethicists realize, the question remains open as to the human responsibility to nature. Beginning in the second half of the twentieth century, mainstream American policy-makers began to grapple seriously with the means by which human beings could preserve and protect natural resources. Parts II and III of this book explore the processes and institutions existing inside of government devoted to addressing this question as well as the individuals and organizations outside of government committed to pursuing a goal of environmental protection. It is to these issues that we now turn.

NOTES

1. Robert Goodland, "The Concept of Environmental Sustainability," *Annual Review of Ecology and Systematics* 26 (1995): 1–24; Geoffrey Heal, "Defining and Measuring Sustainability," *Review of Environmental Economics and Policy* 6 (Winter 2012): 147–63; Adrian Parr, *Hijacking Sustainability* (Cambridge, MA: MIT Press, 2009); Robert M. Solow, "Sustainability: An Economist's Perspective," in *The Environmental Ethics & Policy Book*, 2nd edition, Donald VanDeVeer and Christine Pierce, eds. (Belmont, CA: Wadsworth, 1998), 450–55; Zoltan Somogyi, "A Framework for Quantifying Environmental Sustainability," *Ecological Indicators* 61, Part 2 (February 2016): 338–45.

2. Lynn White, Jr., "The Historical Roots of Our Ecological Crisis," *Science* 155 (March 10, 1967): 1203–1207. See also Jan Deckers, "Christianity and Ecological Ethics: The Significance of Process Thought and a Panexperientialist Critique of Strong Anthropocentrism," *Ecotheology: Journal of Religion, Nature & the Environment* 9 (December 2004): 359–87; Norman Wirzba, "Ecology and the Eyes of Faith: All Creatures," *Christian Century* 132 (July 22, 2015): 26–27, 29.

3. Shiri Cohen Kaminitz, "Economics and Ethics under the Same Umbrella: Edgeworth's 'Exact Utilitarianism,' 1877–1881," *Utilitas* 25 (December 2013): 487–503; Shiri Cohen Kaminitz, "J.S. Mill and the Value of Utility," *History of*

Political Economy 46 (Summer 2014): 231–46; Dudley Knowles, "Conservative Utilitarianism," *Utilitas* 12 (July 2000): 155–75; Sophie Rietti, "Utilitarianism and Psychological Realism," *Utilitas* 21 (September 2009): 347–67.

4. Robert Audi, "Can Utilitarianism be Distributive? Maximization and Distribution as Criteria in Managerial Decisions," *Business Ethics Quarterly* 17 (October 2007): 594; J. Mikael Olsson, "Higher Pleasures, Civic Virtue, and Democracy: A Reconstruction of Millian Themes," *Kritike* 8 (December 2014): 193–260; Dan Priel, "Toward Classical Legal Positivism," *Virginia Law Review* 101 (June 2015): 987–1022; Philip Schofield, "Jeremy Bentham on Utility and Truth," *History of European Ideas* (December 2015): 1125–42; Tom Warke, "Multi-Dimensional Utility and the Index Number Problem: Jeremy Bentham, J.S. Mill, and Qualitative Hedonism," *Utilitas* 12 (July 2000): 176–203.

5. Michael Hauskeller, "No Philosophy for Swine: John Stuart Mill on the Quality of Pleasures," *Utilitas* 23 (December 2011): 428–46; Much of the literature criticizing Utilitarianism questions whether a person violates his or her integrity by choosing to balance competing projects when the concept of integrity requires someone to "stick to his guns." See, for example, Edward Harcourt, "Integrity, Practical Deliberation and Utilitarianism," *The Philosophical Quarterly* 48 (April 1998): 189–98. The literature also distinguishes between act-Utilitarianism and rule-Utilitarianism, although such details are beyond the scope of the instant discussion. Tim Mulgan, "Utilitarianism for a Broken World," *Utilitas* 27 (March 2015): 92–114.

6. On Plato and the *Phaedrus*, see Cynthia Freeland, "Imagery in the *Phaedrus*: Seeing, Growing, Nourishing," *Symbolae Osloenses* 84 (2010): 62–72; Plato, *Phaedrus* (Millis, MA.: Agora Publications, 2009): 57, 92. On the biblical concept of dominion, see J. Baird Callicott, "Genesis and John Muir," *ReVision* 12 (Winter 1990): 31–47; Calvin DeWitt, *The Environment and the Christian: What Does the New Testament Say about the Environment?* (Grand Rapids, MI.: Baker Academic, 1991); J. Patrick Dobel, "Stewards of the Earth's Resources: A Christian Response to Ecology," *Christian Century* 94 (October 12, 1977): 906–09; Raymond E. Grizzle, Paul E. Rothrock, and Christopher B. Barrett, "Evangelicals and Environmentalism: Past, Present, and Future," *Trinity Journal* 19 (Spring 1998): 4–14; Peter J. Hill, "Environmental Theology: A Judeo-Christian Defense," *Journal of Markets and Morality* 3 (Fall 2000): 158–72; Jeanne Kay, "Human Dominion over Nature in the Hebrew Bible," *Annals of the Association of American Geographers* 79 (June 1989): 214–33; Joshua M. Moritz, "Animals and the Image of God in the Bible and Beyond," *Dialog: A Journal of Theology* 48 (Summer 2009): 134–46; Gwyn Rowley, "On 'Human Dominion over Nature in the Hebrew Bible' by Kay," *Annals of the Association of American Geographers* 80 (September 1990): 447–51; Francis A. Schaeffer and Udo W. Middelmann, *Pollution and the Death of Man* (Wheaton, IL: Crossway, 1970): 69; White, "The Historical Roots of Our Ecological Crisis," 1203–1207. On Shakespeare and the primacy of man, see

Sharon O'Dair, "'To Fright the Animals and To Kill Them Up': Shakespeare and Ecology," *Shakespeare Studies* 39 (October 2011): 74–83. William Shakespeare, *The Tragedy of Hamlet: King of Denmark* (New York: Airmont Books, 1965 [1603]).

7. Geir B. Asheim and Tapan Mitra, "Sustainability and Discounted Utilitarianism in Models of Economic Growth," *Mathematical Social Sciences* (Special Issue on Sustainability) 59 (March 2010): 148–69; Joseph DesJardins, "Is It Time to Jump Off the Sustainability Bandwagon?" *Business Ethics Quarterly* 26 (January 2016): 117–35; Gary Varner, "A Harean Perspective on Humane Sustainability," *Ethics & The Environment* 15 (Fall 2010): 31–50; Gary Varner, "Utilitarianism and the Evolution of Ecological Ethics," *Science and Engineering Ethics* 14 (December 2008): 551–73.

8. Daniel Arenas and Pablo Rodrigo, "On Firms and the Next Generations: Difficulties and Possibilities for Business Ethics Inquiry," *Journal of Business Ethics* 133 (January 2016): 165–78; M. Anaam Hashmi *et al.*, "Evaluation of Sustainability Practices in the United States and Large Corporations," *Journal of Business Ethics* 127 (March 2015): 673–81; Morela Hernandez, Laura J. Noval, and Kimberly A. Wade-Benzoni, "How Leaders Can Create Intergenerational Sustainability Systems to Promote Organizational Sustainability," *Organizational Dynamics* (Special Issue: Sustainability and Corporate Social Responsibility) 44 (April–June 2015): 104–11; Hermann Lion, Jerome D. Donovan, and Rowan E. Bedggood, "Environmental Impact Assessments from a Business Perspective: Extending Knowledge and Guiding Business Practice," *Journal of Business Ethics* 117 (November 2013): 789–805.

9. Gary Comstock, "Intuitive Level System Rules: Commentary on 'Utilitarianism and the Evolution of Ecological Ethics,'" *Science and Engineering Ethics* 14 (December 2008): 575–79; Nele Lienhoop, Bartosz Bartkowski, and Bernd Hansjürgens, "Informing Biodiversity Policy: The Role of Economic Valuation, Deliberative Institutions and Deliberative Monetary Valuation," *Environmental Science and Policy* 54 (December 2015): 522–32; Yves Meinard, Malgorzata Dereniowska, and Jean-Sebastien Gharbi, "Discussion: The Ethical Stakes in Monetary Valuation Methods for Conservation Purposes," *Biological Conservation* 199 (July 2016): 67–74; Norton, "Beyond Positivist Ecology: Toward an Integrated Ecological Ethics," 581–92; Gary Varner, "Utilitarianism and the Evolution of Ecological Ethics," 551–73.

10. Audi, "Can Utilitarianism be Distributive?" 593–611; Benjamin Eidelson, "The Majoritarian Filibuster," *Yale Law Journal* 122 (January 2013): 980–1023; Kaminitz, "J.S. Mill and the Value of Utility," 231–46.

11. Paul Guyer, "Kant's Answer to Hume?" *Philosophical Topics* 31 (Spring and Fall 2003): 127–64; James T. King, "The Moral Theories of Kant and Hume: Comparisons and Polemics," *Hume Studies* 18 (November 1992): 441–66; Manfred Kuehn, "Kant's Conception of 'Hume's Problem,'" *Journal of the History of Philosophy* 21 (January 1983): 175–93.

12. Oliver Sensen, "Kant's Conception of Inner Value," *European Journal of Philosophy* 19 (June 2011): 262–80; Michael Yudanin, "Can Positive Duties be Derived from Kant's Categorical Imperative?" *Ethical Theory and Moral Practice: An International Forum* 18 (June 2015): 595–614.

13. Patricia Kitcher, "Kant's Argument for the Categorical Imperative," *Noûs* 38 (December 2004): 555–84; Michael Ridge, "Consequentialist Kantianism," *Philosophical Perspectives* 23 (December 2009): 421–38; Norman Wilde, "Kant's Relation to Utilitarianism," *The Philosophical Review* 3 (May 1, 1894): 289–304.

14. Pierfrancesco Biasetti, "From Beauty to Love: A Kantian Way to Environmental Moral Theory?" *Environmental Philosophy* 12 (Fall 2015): 139–60; Clem Tisdell, "Local Communities, Conservation and Sustainability: Institutional Change, Altered Governance and Kant's Social Philosophy," *International Journal of Social Economics* 24 (December 1997): 1361–75.

15. Dario Martinelli, "Anthropocentrism as a Social Phenomenon: Semiotic and Ethical Implications," *Social Semiotics* 18 (March 2008): 79–99; Gregory M. Mikkelson and Colin A. Chapman, "Individualistic Environmental Ethics: A Reductio ad Exstinctum?" *Environmental Ethics* 36 (Fall 2014): 333–38; Markku Oksanen, "The Moral Value of Biodiversity," *Ambio* 26 (December 1997): 541–45; Joshua Rottman, "Breaking Down Biocentrism: Two Distinct Forms of Moral Concern for Nature," *Frontiers in Psychology* 5 (July 2014): 1–5; Kathleen R. Smythe, "Rethinking Humanity in the Anthropocene: The Long View of Humans and Nature," *Sustainability* 7 (June 2014): 146–53.

16. Frank J. Jankunis, "Milgram and the Prevalence of Anthropocentrism," *Theoretical and Applied Ethics* 2 (Winter 2013): 93–104; Michael Hemmingsen, "Anthropocentrism, Conservatism, and Green Political Thought," in *The Peace of Nature and the Nature of Peace: Essays on Ecology, Nature, Nonviolence, and Peace*, Andrew Fiala, ed. (Boston: Brill, 2015): 81–90.

17. World Commission on Environment and Development (WCED), *Our Common Future: From One Earth to One World* (Oxford and New York: Oxford University Press, 1987), 8; Wilfred Beckerman, "'Sustainable Development': Is It a Useful Concept?" in *The Environmental Ethics & Policy Book*, 2nd edition, Donald VanDeVeer and Christine Pierce, eds. (Belmont, CA.: Wadsworth, 1998): 463.

18. See, for example, William D. Nordaus, *Managing the Global Commons: The Economics of Climate Change* (Cambridge, Mass.: MIT Press, 1994).

19. Frederic Ang and Steven Van Passel, "Beyond the Environmentalist's Paradox and the Debate on Weak versus Strong Sustainability," *BioScience* 62 (March 2012): 251–59; Paul Sorensen, "Weak Sustainability and a Post-Industrial Society," *International Journal of Environmental Studies* 70 (December 2013): 872–76.

20. Quoted in Robert Costanza, Cutler Cleveland, and Charles Perrings, *The Development of Ecological Economics* (Cheltenham, UK: Edward Elgar

Publishing, 1997), 46–47. See also Giuseppe Fontana and Malcolm Sawyer, "Towards Post-Keynesian Ecological Macroeconomics," *Ecological Economics* 121 (January 2016): 186–95; Sacha Hollis, "Old Solutions to New Problems: Providing for Intergenerational Equity in National Institutions," *New Zealand Journal of Environmental Law* 14 (2010): 25–61.

21. Steve Barnard and Michael Elliott, "The 10 Tenets of Adaptive Management and Sustainability: An Holistic Framework for Understanding and Managing the Socioecological System," *Environmental Science & Policy* 51 (August 2015): 181–91; Charles L. Redman, "Should Sustainability and Resilience be Combined or Remain Distinct Pursuits?" *Ecology & Society* 19 (2014): 398–408.

22. Zdzislawa Piatek, "Ecophilosophy as a Philosophical Underpinning of Sustainable Development," *Sustainable Development* 16 (March/April 2008): 91–99; Van Rensselaer Potter, "Real Bioethics: Biocentric or Anthropocentric?" *Ethics and the Environment* 1 (Fall 1996): 177–83.

23. Paul Taylor, *Respect for Nature: A Theory of Environmental Ethics*, 25th Anniversary Edition (Princeton, N.J.: Princeton University Press, 2011), 156. See also Bebhinn Donnelly and Patrick Bishop, "Natural Law and Ecocentrism," *Journal of Environmental Law* 19 (2007): 89–101; James Sterba, "A Biocentrist Strikes Back," *Environmental Ethics* 20 (Winter 1998): 361–76.

24. See, for example, Nicholas Agar, "Biocentrism and the Concept of Life," *Ethics* 108 (October 1997): 147–68; Bob Pepperman Taylor, "Environmental Ethics and Public Policy," *Polity* 23 (Summer 1991): 567–83.

25. Alan Drengson, Bill Devall, and Mark A. Schroll, "The Deep Ecology Movement: Origins, Development, and Future Prospects (Toward a Transpersonal Ecosophy)," *International Journal of Transpersonal Studies* 30 (June 2011): 101–17; Nathan Kowlasky, "Whatever Happened to Deep Ecology?" *The Trumpeter: Journal of Ecosophy* 30 (2014): 95–100; Thomas Robert, "Darwinian Ethology and Naess' Principles of Deep Ecology," *The Trumpeter: Journal of Ecosophy* 31 (2015): 39–57.

26. Quoted in Bill Devall and George Sessions, "Deep Ecology," in *The Environmental Ethics & Policy Book*, 2nd edition, Donald VanDeVeer and Christine Pierce, eds. (Belmont, CA.: Wadsworth, 1998), 222. See also Peter B. Corcoran and Eric Sievers, "Reconceptualizing Environmental Education: Five Possibilities," *Journal of Environmental Education* 25 (Summer 1994): 4–8; Charles T. Rubin, *The Green Crusade: Rethinking the Roots of Environmentalism* (Lanham, MD.: Rowman & Littlefield, 1998): 179; George Sessions, "The Deep Ecology Movement: A Review," *Environmental Review: ER* 1 (Summer 1987): 105–25; Arne Naess, "The Shallow and the Deep, Long-range Ecology Movements," in *Deep Ecology for the 21st Century*, George Sessions, ed. (Boston: Shambala, 1995), 151–55.

27. See, for example, J. Baird Callicott, *In Defense of the Land Ethic: Essays in Environmental Philosophy* (Albany, NY: State University of New York Press,

1989), 129–48; J. Baird Callicott, "Non-Anthropocentric Value Theory and Environmental Ethics," *American Philosophical Quarterly* 21 (October 1984): 299–309; and Laura Westra, *Living in Integrity: A Global Ethic to Restore a Fragmented Earth* (Lanham, MD.: Rowman & Littlefield, 1998).

28. James Lovelock, *Gaia: A New Look at Life on Earth* (New York and Oxford: Oxford University Press, 2000). See also Andrew Free and Nicholas H. Barton, "Do Evolution and Ecology Need the Gaia Hypothesis?" *Trends in Ecology and Evolution* 22 (November 2007): 611–19; James W. Kirchner, "The Gaia Hypothesis: Can It Be Tested?" *Reviews of Geophysics* 27 (May 1989): 223–35; James W. Kirchner, "The Gaia Hypothesis: Fact, Theory, and Wishful Thinking," *Climatic Change* 52 (2002): 391–408; David M. Wilkinson, "Is Gaia Really Conventional Ecology?" *Oikos* 84 (March 1999): 533–36.

29. Charles H. Eccleston and Frederic March. *Global Environmental Policy: Concepts, Principles, and Practice* (Boca Raton, FL.: CRC Press, 2011): 30–33.

30. The quote is reprinted in John Seed *et al.*, *Thinking Like a Mountain: Towards a Council of All Beings* (Gabriola Island, B.C., Canada: New Society Publishers, 1988): 43.

31. Murray Bookchin, "Will Ecology Become 'The Dismal Science'?" in *The Environmental Ethics & Policy Book*, 2nd edition, Donald VanDeVeer and Christine Pierce, eds. (Belmont, CA.: Wadsworth, 1998), 230–35.

32. Andrew J. Corsa, "Henry David Thoreau: Greatness of Soul and Environmental Virtue," *Environmental Philosophy* 12 (Fall 2015): 161–84; Frank N. Egerton and Laura Dassow Walls, "Rethinking Thoreau and the History of American Ecology," *Concord Saunterer* 5 (Fall 1997): 5–20; Alan D. Hodder, "The Gospel According to this Moment: Thoreau, Wildness, and American Nature Religion," *Religion and the Arts* 15 (September 2011): 460–85. See also Richard J. Schneider, *Thoreau's Sense of Place: Essays in American Environmental Writing* (Iowa City: University of Iowa Press, 2000).

33. See, for example, Daniel Botkin, *No Man's Garden: Thoreau and a New Vision of Civilization and Nature* (Washington, D.C. and Covelo, CA: Island Press/Shearwater Books, 2001).

34. Robert D. Habich, "Emerson, Thoreau, Fuller, and Transcendentalism," in *American Literary Scholarship 2013: An Annual*, Gary Scharnhorst, ed. (Durham, NC: Duke University Press, 2015): 3–21; Sean Ross Meehan, "Ecology and Imagination: Emerson, Thoreau, and the Nature of Metonymy," *Criticism* 55 (Spring 2013): 299–329.

35. Charles Capper, "'A Little Beyond': The Problem of the Transcendentalist Movement in American History," *The Journal of American History* 85 (September 1998): 502–39; Dana RUS, "The Role of Transcendentalism in Shaping American Cultural Ideology," *Studia Universitatis Petru Maior—Philologia* 14 (January 2013): 247–54.

36. Botkin, *No Man's Garden*, 88–90; Curtis Kent, "The Virtue of Thoreau: Biography, Geography, and History in Walden Woods," *Environmental History* 15 (January 2010): 40–41.

37. Henry David Thoreau, *Walden, or Life in the Woods* (New York: Thomas Y. Crowell & Company, 1910 [1854]): 118.

38. Ibid., 119.

39. Ibid., 408.

40. Ibid., 419.

41. Botkin, *No Man's Garden*, xvi; Kent, "The Virtue of Thoreau," 31–33; Benjamin Kline, Ph.D, *First Along the River: A Brief History of the U.S. Environmental Movement*, 3rd. edition, (Lanham, MD.: Rowman & Littlefield, 2007): 32–34.

42. Danny Heitman, "Not Exactly a Hermit: Henry David Thoreau," *Humanities* 33 (September/October 2012): 14–17, 50.

II

PROCESSES AND INSTITUTIONS

4

THE RISE OF THE AMERICAN ADMINISTRATIVE STATE

Federal executive branch agencies have become integral players in formulating and implementing environmental laws and policies in the United States. As discussed in Chapter 5, it is difficult to fathom the development of modern American environmental law or policy without the active participation of federal administrative agencies. Agencies implement the will of Congress to the extent that legislative intent exists and can be discerned. In the absence of clear intent, administrators fill in the gaps of legislative statutes through rulemaking, adjudication, and policy interpretation. They also provide much-needed expertise across the spectrum of environmental issues. It is no accident of history that the development of federal environmental laws and regulations occurred well after the rise of the administrative state in the American regime.[1]

THE FOUNDERS AND PUBLIC ADMINISTRATION

Opponents of a large bureaucratic state contend that the American Founders would be horrified to discover how much the federal executive branch has grown since the early days of the republic. The Founders were men who loved liberty and sought to maximize human freedom by designing a classical liberal state with a minimalist government.

In modern parlance, they were antistatist. The mammoth institutional structure of the American federal government of the twenty-first century was undreamt of when the men who became known as the Founders assembled in Philadelphia in 1787 to correct the defects found in the Articles of Confederation. Their efforts focused on structure and process, leaving the details of policy formulation and implementation for another time. This emphasis on devising a constitution and its mechanisms in lieu of exploring the minutiae of administration is hardly surprising. They first needed to create an institutional structure before they could develop and improve its operating procedures.[2]

These men lived in a world far removed from the twenty-first century. The first census, undertaken in 1790, revealed a population of slightly fewer than four million souls, 18 percent of whom were enslaved peoples. They inhabited an area of approximately 430,000 square miles. It was a fraction of the 3.8 million square miles and 320 million people who populated the country at the dawn of the twenty-first century. The Founders knew nothing of automobiles, air travel, electronic communications, or modern views on race, gender, and sexuality. To fault them for failures to anticipate the growth of bureaucracy or define the concept of the administrative state with precision is to place too much responsibility at their doorstep.[3]

The point about the Founders' reaction to a large administrative state is well taken, but the insight must not be exaggerated. It is true that the men who framed the Constitution would be astonished at the state of the regime in the twenty-first century, but their reaction no doubt would be tempered by an understanding that times changed and government had to respond to the changes. (Whether the Founders would approve of the nature and scope of the changes remains an endlessly contentious point that will never be resolved.) With apologies to proponents of original intent, the Federalists believed that the framework for a government can be designed in a constitution, but the particular laws must be written to respond to subsequent, largely unforeseen exigencies. Writing under his pseudonym Publius, Madison observed in "Federalist 37" that "All new laws, though penned with the greatest technical skill, and passed on the fullest and most mature deliberation, are considered as more or less obscure and equivocal, until their meaning be liquidated and ascertained by a series of particular discussions and adjudications." If the laws must be written to respond to changed circumstances, government potentially will expand as the number and types of laws expand.[4]

More importantly, the seeds of a robust government were planted within the vague text of the Constitution itself. The language of the Necessary and Proper Clause (Article I, Section 8), the Commerce Clause (Article I, Section 8), and the Supremacy Clause (Article 6, Clause 2) were ripe for a broad interpretation even before Chief Justice John Marshall construed them in support of an empowered national government. The Constitution explicitly provided for federal engagement in constructing post offices and roads as well as in establishing an army and a navy. From these origins, the U.S. Postal Service grew, increasing from 4,837 employees in 1816 to 36,672 in 1861. In addition, the original cabinet-level agencies included only the Departments of State and the Treasury. Throughout the nineteenth century, the federal government created new administrative agencies as the complexity and size of government and the issues it deemed important expanded. Thus, the Interior Department came into existence in 1849, the Agriculture Department in 1862 (although it did not achieve cabinet-level status until 1889), and the Justice Department in 1870. Throughout the twentieth century, agencies sprang into existence and were shuffled about as times and needs changed. By the early twenty-first century, the federal executive department consisted of 15 agencies employing millions of civilian employees.[5]

That is not to say that the Founders were silent on the question of public administration. They did not speak of the administrative state in language that was employed in a later time, nor did they confine their discussion to one or a handful of official documents, but they spoke to the issue. Eighteenth-century statesmen frequently espoused their political views in correspondence, and there one can find hints of their sentiments on a variety of crucial questions of governance. For example, Thomas Jefferson, a prodigious letter writer, expressed his concerns over creating a centralized government repeatedly in letters to his colleagues and friends.

Jefferson believed that centralizing the functions of a government was a step along the road to tyranny. He expressed his fears in a letter to President George Washington on September 9, 1792. In his capacity as Washington's secretary of state, Jefferson believed that foreign affairs must be handled by the federal government, but that domestic affairs were properly left to the individual states. "When I embarked in the government, it was with a determination to intermeddle not at all with the legislature, & as little as possible with my co-departments," he explained. This observation fit perfectly with Jefferson's view of a minimalist government that would not interfere with the liberties of the people. Yet, Jefferson professed to have been duped by his rival within the administration, Secretary of the Treasury Alexander Hamilton. Jefferson argued that Hamilton's view of a robust Treasury Department was dangerous. "That I have utterly, in my private conversations, disapproved of the system of the Secretary of the treasury, I acknowledge & avow: and this was not merely a speculative difference," he wrote. Hamilton's "system flowed from principles adverse to liberty, & was calculated to undermine and demolish the republic, by creating an influence of his department over the members of the legislature." In short, Hamilton's executive branch department, staffed with unelected bureaucrats, threatened to overrule the wishes of elected representatives who were fulfilling the desires of the people. "These were no longer the votes then of the representatives of the people, but of deserters from the rights & interests of the people: & it was impossible to consider their decisions, which had nothing in view but to enrich themselves, as the measures of the fair majority, which ought always to be respected. If what was actually doing begat uneasiness in those who wished for virtuous government, what was further proposed was not less threatening to the friends of the Constitution."[6]

The concern that a robust public administration was a threat to the United States Constitution was not merely rhetoric. Jefferson and many of his contemporaries were suspicious of a powerful central government, believing that tyranny would result from placing too much power in too few hands. In a letter he penned to a Virginia supporter, Joseph C. Cabell, in 1816, Jefferson clearly set forth his understanding of the proper role of government in a country where consensual self-rule is a crucial feature. "The way to have good and safe government," he wrote, "is not to trust it all to one, but to divide it among the many, distributing to every one exactly the functions he is competent to. Let the national government be entrusted with the defence of the nation, and its foreign and federal relations; the State governments with the civil rights, laws, police, and administration of what concerns the State generally; the counties with the local concerns of the counties, and each ward direct the interests within itself." To embrace the Hamiltonian notion of a powerful, centralized government is to invite a royal government to oppress the citizenry. The only effective means of keeping a government tied to the needs of the people is to ensure that the people take part in operating the mechanisms of government. "Where every man is a sharer in the direction of his ward-republic, or of some of the higher ones, and feels that he is a participator in the government of affairs, not merely at an election one day in the year, but every day; when there shall not be a man in the State who will not be a member of some one of its councils, great or small, he will let the heart be torn out of his body sooner than his power be wrested from him by a Caesar or a Bonaparte."[7]

As for "virtuous government," Jefferson shared a view expressed by many eighteenth-century leaders that good character is a necessary ingredient in good government. Such concerns appeared quaint in subsequent epochs, and in truth these sentiments were never easily accepted, even by members of the Founding generation who agreed that the character of men dictates in no small measure the fate of political institutions. In establishing a republican form of government, the Founders appreciated that human beings must be taken not as we might wish them to be, but as they are—flawed, self-interested, passionate, and often driven by their acquisitive natures. This observation does not obviate the need for governors possessing desirable character traits, but it acknowledges that "good character" is a difficult quality to measure and cannot serve as a prerequisite for all elected officials. As "Federalist 51" famously observed, government would be unnecessary if angels governed human beings. Since divine beings cannot be counted on to intervene in government operations, human ambitions must be pitted against each other in a political stalemate that ensures the governors can craft efficacious public policy without necessarily becoming corrupted in the process.

Thus was the notion of institutional checks and balances born and implemented. Each branch of government would possess its own primary responsibility, but it also would share power with the others. No one branch would exercise too much independent authority lest it become omnipotent and oppressive. These "auxiliary precautions" would prevent a monarch from wresting power from the people or their elected representatives. Virtuous, noble elected officials would be highly desirable, but government would perform its essential functions even in the absence of high-minded individuals serving in public office.[8]

On the question of public administration, Jefferson's view of a small, relatively weak government was a popular perspective at the time, but he had met his match in the formidable Alexander Hamilton. Hamilton's view was that an energetic government—especially the executive branch—was required to ensure that citizens enjoyed the "commodious living" so desired by individuals who had escaped the yoke of an authoritarian regime and yet feared the chaos and disorder of an impotent sovereign. Displaying a remarkable prescience about the reasoning behind the expansion of the administrative state in the twentieth century, in "Federalist 70," Hamilton directly confronted oft-stated fears of a strong executive branch. "There is an idea, which is not without its advocates, that a vigorous Executive is inconsistent with the genius of republican government," he admitted. Yet such fears fail to appreciate the effect of a weak government. "Energy in the Executive is a leading character in the definition of good government. It is essential to the protection of the community against foreign attacks; it is not less essential to the steady administration of the laws; to the protection of property against those irregular and high-handed combinations which sometimes interrupt the ordinary course of justice; to the security of liberty against the enterprises and assaults of ambition, of faction, and of anarchy." Jefferson's opinion that that government is best which governs least is a poor excuse for improper administration. "A feeble Executive implies a feeble execution of the government," Hamilton contended. "A feeble execution is but another phrase for a bad execution; and a government ill executed, whatever it may be in theory, must be, in practice, a bad government."[9]

Hamilton tackled the question of administration in "Federalist 72." In a straightforward paragraph at the outset, he made his case:

> The administration of government, in its largest sense, comprehends all the operations of the body politic, whether legislative, executive, or judiciary; but in its most usual, and perhaps its most precise signification. It is limited to executive details, and falls peculiarly within the province of the executive department. The actual conduct of foreign negotiations, the preparatory plans of finance, the application and disbursement of

the public moneys in conformity to the general appropriations of the legislature, the arrangement of the army and navy, the directions of the operations of war—these, and other matters of a like nature, constitute what seems to be most properly understood by the administration of government. The persons, therefore, to whose immediate management these different matters are committed, ought to be considered as the assistants or deputies of the chief magistrate, and on this account, they ought to derive their offices from his appointment, at least from his nomination, and ought to be subject to his superintendence.[10]

The passage appears at odds with the concept of a politics-administration dichotomy that gained favor late in the nineteenth century but gradually lost its potency as scholars and practitioners reassessed the data, beginning especially in the 1930s. Hamilton recognized that the legitimacy of administering government functions is rooted, directly or indirectly, in the powers of the executive. He did not foresee a time when "deputies of the chief magistrate" would act separate from their principal's authority. By extension, to assume that public administrators are somehow neutral implementers of public policy, standing above or at least apart, from the political fray, is to mischaracterize the entire enterprise of government administration. The fundamental misconception of neutral public administrators became the conventional wisdom of a later age.[11]

A POLITICS-ADMINISTRATION DICHOTOMY AND THE EFFICIENCY PRINCIPLE

Since the origins of public administration (PA) as a subject of academic inquiry—generally thought to be in 1887 with the publication of Woodrow Wilson's essay "The Study of Administration," although the point is contested—theorists have sought to develop a "science" of public administration. One of the crucial points of debate among public administration practitioners and academics alike is whether a science of public administration is possible or, for that matter, even desirable. In large measure, the answer to the question depends on what it means to be a "science" or to be "scientific." In one sense, PA is more scientific

than it was in previous years; in another sense, it will never be completely scientific.[12]

In his 1887 essay, Wilson discussed a dichotomy between politics
and science. If public administration was to be morally neutral, subject
to operational rules and principles in the same manner that scientific
endeavors were predicated on presumably immutable laws, the dirty
business of electoral politics must be separated from pristine government administration. Elected officials must formulate policy and public
administrators must implement it.[13]

It is little wonder that early public administration theorists were
enamored of science. The German universities, with their emphasis
on the scientific method, were influential in the evolution of American
universities. The concept held great appeal: A researcher would muse
over a problem, sift through the available literature, set forth an educated guess—a research "hypothesis," in academic parlance—about how
something works, and develop a research design (with a research question, a standard of measurement, an instrument for collecting data, and
a mechanism for evaluating whether the data supported the research
hypothesis) that ultimately explained something significant about the
problem. To be a true experiment with great explanatory power, it
needed to be valid, reliable, and replicable by subsequent researchers.

The scientific method worked especially well in the hard sciences—
chemistry, physics, geology, biology, and the like. These disciplines
depended on explanations of external phenomena, perhaps not always
observable, but certainly subject to measurement, testing, and replica-
tion. Thus, the attributes and "behavior" of a particular gas in a chemist's
laboratory could be clearly measured and explained for all other chem-
ists to read about and replicate. As Thomas Kuhn later explained in *The
Structure of Scientific Revolutions*, eventually a more-or-less agreed-
upon explanation of why the gas behaved in a certain way under certain
conditions would be developed in the scientific community. This paradigm would be supported by subsequent experiments with the same
gas under the same conditions. If the results generally were the same,
the paradigm would stand up to repeated scrutiny. If anomalous results
occurred, researchers would attempt to offer alternate hypotheses
to account for the unexpected results. If enough unexpected results
occurred enough times, there would be a crisis that would undermine

the existing paradigm. Eventually, one or more researchers would offer up a different explanation, and a paradigm shift would occur. The old paradigm would be rejected and a new paradigm would take its place. The scientific method, therefore, became a process by which scientists communicated with each other and advanced the frontiers of scientific knowledge over time.[14]

The problem for researchers outside of the hard sciences was that the scientific method did not work very well when it was applied to subjects that could not be accurately measured, quantified, and replicated so that an agreed-upon paradigm could be developed. In the social sciences, for example, the research often was only as useful and accurate as the assumptions that the researchers built into their research design. Therein lay the rub. For every attempt to "scientifically" explain a social science problem unencumbered by bias, one or more hidden assumptions lurked somewhere within the research design. In many cases, well-meaning social scientists were unaware of the assumptions. An axiomatic proposition frequently was a presupposition that was open to interpretation and debate.

The early theorists thought they were applying the scientific method to solve the problem of government administration in the most efficient manner possible. Accordingly, Woodrow Wilson argued for divorcing politics from administration and developing a science of American public administration. The practice of nineteenth-century American politics, with the widespread influence of political machines and party bosses such as William Marcy Tweed in New York's Tammany Hall and the rampant corruption within the ranks of the federal executive branch, was distasteful to men such as Wilson who wanted to professionalize the ranks of American public administration and improve government performance. Neutral competence based on merit—what a person knows, not who he knows—was the key to reforming government. If politicians and corruption could not be rooted out completely, certainly public administrators could act in accordance with clearly defined, immutable, known and knowable principles. Science would provide the answer.[15]

Wilson subsequently backed away from his emphasis on the existence and desirability of a politics-administration dichotomy. In many of his later works—to say nothing of his career as an elected official—he came to see that politics plays an important and probably inseparable role in administration. Moreover, some scholars question whether Wilson's reputation as the founder of modern American public administration has been overstated. Other developments, notably enactment of the Pendleton Act in 1883, the first professional civil service regime in the American federal government, played a crucial role in the quest for a formal, neutral, scientific field of public administration. In the final analysis, settling the question of whether Wilson assumed a pivotal or supporting position in launching scholarly inquiry into public administration is less important than appreciating the influence of "science" on a system of professional government managers existing apart from elected officials and not necessarily dependent on electoral politics for their legitimacy.[16]

The idea that politics and administration could be bifurcated as a first step in developing a science of administration was accepted with little argument as the nineteenth century gave way to the twentieth. In *Politics and Administration*, Frank Goodnow supported Wilson's assertion that public administration could and should be separated from politics. He was among the first public administration scholars to focus on the role of administrative law in shaping the character of a regime. Goodnow argued that governments exercise two major functions. First, they engage in operations necessary to express the will of the body politic, and they engage in operations necessary to execute that will. Continuing the Wilsonian tradition, Goodnow believed that elected officials are responsible for formulating policy while public administrators must implement policy. Because elected officials ultimately are answerable to the people, they are driven by politics in virtually every action they undertake. Administrators, however, are not elected; therefore, they are, or should be, immune to direct political pressure. Political interference in administrative functions must be avoided.[17]

Wilson and Goodnow led the way toward orthodoxy in the study of administration, and others followed their lead. Frederick Taylor and Scientific Management—the idea that there is a "correct" way to perform tasks such as shoveling pig iron or administering a government program and we need but explicate the principles and instruct pupils accordingly—found its way into the orthodoxy, as did Max Weber's understanding of "ideal-types" when discussing bureaucratic organizations. In the case of the former, Taylor was especially interested in understanding the most efficient means of performing a task. Using time-and-motion studies, he hoped to isolate the best method for moving from Point A to Point B and thereby reproduce the method across all types of work. Taylor recognized that not every worker would be interested in achieving optimal output; therefore, he recommended tying pay to performance through "piece-rate" plans. Relying on a factory mentality, Taylor suggested that workers who produce more of a product should receive pay or bonuses that reflect increased production. If a worker realizes that he can improve his take-home pay by working harder and more efficiently, the worker will increase production and the firm will benefit as a result.

Later critics derided this overly simplistic understanding of labor relations and human psychology, but early in the twentieth century, Taylorism was popular among theorists seeking to improve organizational management. It was an appealing concept: For any given organization's tasks, a single "right," optimally efficient method exists. A manager must discover the appropriate method and ensure that employees follow the method as much as possible. Scientific management was a key ingredient in the growth of large organizations where individual workers are employed as cogs in a vast machine. Productivity and efficiency became proverbs in organizational management for both the public and private sectors. Decades after Taylor and his managerial system have been more or less repudiated, the emphasis on outputs as a measurement of a firm's success remain firmly ensconced in the mind of many a government or private sector manager.[18]

Taylor was not the only theorist to focus on the efficiency principle. Max Weber, another giant in the field of organizational management, was a German sociologist writing early in the twentieth century. Weber believed that "ideal types" existed for many practical endeavors. For a large organization, there needed to be a clear chain of command, a hierarchy—an "ideal type" of bureaucracy. He recognized that ideals are seldom realized, but a crucial theoretical construct was necessary to understand how organizations operate and how they can be improved.

The head of the organization sits at the top of the hierarchy. Beneath him, several assistant heads work, and they in turn have several assistants laboring below them. Subordinates report information up the chain of command where those higher up in the hierarchy make decisions based on that information and send orders down the chain of command. A division of labor and specialization of offices maximizes the organization's outputs. The hierarchy ensures that each person working inside the organization possesses a clear understanding of his duties and knows to whom he reports up the chain of command as well as subordinates who report to him. When each cog in the machine knows its role and acts in accordance with that role, efficiency (and, presumably, effectiveness) is enhanced.[19]

For Weber, a "bureaucracy" is not a pejorative description of a frustratingly opaque process, as the term is sometimes used today, but exists as an efficient means of operating a large, complex organization. Ironically, the dehumanization of bureaucracy, frequently cited as a severe drawback of the concept, is a benefit, in Weber's view. So many organizational decisions are based on emotions or the whims of eccentric individuals that developing and implementing standard operating procedures can be difficult when multiple personalities are involved. Weber contended that any organization that can root out such distractions becomes stronger because it eliminates or reduces irrationality. Decisions are reached based on reasonable, justifiable, defensible bases related to the mission of the organization. Dehumanization is a positive feature of a bureaucracy because it allows decision-makers to act on a rational basis in lieu of factoring in individual quirks and biases.[20]

Weber did not limit his analysis to an explication of organizational structure. He sought to understand how and why particular societies reach and justify specific conclusions. In exploring ideal types, Weber extended his analysis to "systems of domination," his term for the manner in which political regimes ensure citizen obedience and legitimize regime authority. Weber contended that power is predicated on three ideal types of authority: traditional, charismatic, and legal-rational. In the first case, power rests upon long-established ways of behaving. Because rulers have always acted a certain way, it is logical to continue acting in the same way. Often such societies are arranged in a hierarchy where a patriarchal figure governs based on heredity. Tribal authorities cite traditions and customs as the legitimizing principles of their primitive political systems, as do monarchies in more advanced forms of government.

The obvious problem in any system based on traditional authority is that it begs the question of whether tradition is a rational response to a changing world. Because something has always been done in a certain way does not necessarily imply that it should be done that way in the

THE RISE OF THE AMERICAN ADMINISTRATIVE STATE 101

future. Moreover, as the regime grows in size and complexity, the loss of kinship relationships means that the ties that bind citizens to the regime erode. If traditional societies grow too large, the regime may experience a legitimation crisis where persons governed by the central figure question his authority. Modern societies often reject the concept of traditional authority, although vestiges of hereditary rule survive in nation-states such as Great Britain, which recognizes a monarchy even though the institution has lost much of its formal power.[21]

According to Weber, the second type of authority is based on the personal qualities of a charismatic leader. This principle is not based on custom or tradition, but on the specific, sometimes intangible qualities of a specific individual. Benito Mussolini and Adolf Hitler are quintessential examples of a charismatic leader. These men positioned themselves as the one, true leader of the regime. All power flowed from the personal, messianic qualities of "the leader." In his personal manifesto *Mein Kampf*, Hitler asserted that a fascist regime with a single recognized leader was more accountable than a democratic regime featuring multiple leaders and overlapping systems of authority. Hitler believed that a political system with one charismatic leader at the helm reduced any ambiguity about the source of power or the origins of public policy. Therefore, a leader could not hide behind excuses such as, "it wasn't my fault because I had no responsibility" or "I had to share responsibility with others." In a regime built on a foundation of charismatic authority, clarity of purpose is a stellar characteristic.

A government based on charismatic authority need not be a totalitarian state, but it can degenerate into such a regime because the leader has no check on his use of power. In Hitler's self-serving diatribe, he suggested that a fascist state leads to increased responsibility, yet he failed to explain how abuses of power can be reduced or eliminated. Hitler would have responded that an "abuse" is not an abuse if the leader does not label it that way. In short, any action is justified by definition because the charismatic leader says it is. Aside from such patently problematic characteristics, a government built on a cult of personality ensures that a crisis will occur when the charismatic leader dies or is deposed. Although some democratically elected leaders manifest charismatic traits, they are not the ideal type of charismatic authority that Weber depicted in his work.[22]

Weber believed that the third ideal type of authority was preferable in a modern democratic state—legal-rational authority. As the name implies, legal-rational authority is based on a known and knowable set of rules that are clearly defined and attach to the formal institutions of authority as opposed to the individuals who hold office at a given point. The colloquial expression is that government exists based on the rule of law, not the rule of men.

Traditional authority and charismatic authority rely to some extent on personal relationships and the character of the man who would be king. By contrast, legal-rational authority de-emphasizes personal character-istics. According to Weber, such dehumanization is precisely the point. Critics deride bureaucracies owing to the "one size fits all" approach to management, but Weber believed that a system of rules scrupulously applied would result in the promulgation of efficacious policies. A gov-ernment that operates based on impersonal rules potentially will root out biases and cronyism that so often infect governments constructed on a leader's personal qualities. Legal rules can be structured to ensure that a leader cannot act on his whims, but must share authority with other duly selected officers of the government. An institutional structure deriving its authority from rules will provide for consistency, uniformity, and efficiency.[23]

Weber's typology influenced an array of American public adminis-tration scholars and practitioners early in the twentieth century. It was an era when administrators still grappled with the appropriate role of administrators in implementing public policy. Against this backdrop, Leonard D. White's classic 1926 textbook, *Introduction to the Study of Public Administration*, taught a generation of public administration students the fundamental, uncontested, and seemingly uncontestable tenets of orthodoxy. The Orthodox School took it for granted that a sci-ence of politics was possible and that administrators had removed the taint of politics from the public sector by developing a well-functioning bureaucracy. The high tide of orthodoxy came during the 1930s when Luther Gulick and Lyndall Urwick articulated the idea that the role of public agencies was to engage in POSDCORB (planning, organiz-ing, staffing, directing, coordinating, reporting, and budgeting). To that end, the same year that Gulick and Urwick postulated POSDCORB (1937), the President's Committee on Administrative Management (the

Brownlow Committee), established by President Franklin D. Roosevelt a year earlier, published its report outlining ways to make the federal bureaucracy more efficient and responsive to the chief executive.[24]

Unfortunately, by failing to question the assumption of whether a science of public administration was possible or even desirable, early theorists moved forward in developing a field or discipline or subspecialty—it wasn't quite clear what kind of inquiry it was—that would undergo a crisis shortly after the end of World War II. Their efforts to explicate the scientific principles of administration were reminiscent of Carl Sandburg's famously sardonic comment about idealism: "I'm an idealist. I don't know where I'm going, but I'm on my way." Theorists of orthodoxy were not quite sure what kind of academic inquiry they were engaged in, but no matter. They were well into their journey.

Enter an iconoclast named Herbert Simon, subsequently a Nobel Laureate. Simon was a logical positivist who contended that public administration had not been established on a scientific basis. In focusing on how institutions operate instead of examining how and why public administrators behave the way they do, theorists had studied the wrong issues. Simon argued in *Administrative Behavior* (1947) that it was important to examine administrators and how they make decisions. Simon developed a doctrine of "bounded rationality," which required researchers to look at the factors that go into public administrators' behavior under certain conditions. Administrators face institutional constraints, time pressure, budgetary shortfalls, and, yes, even political pressure, upon occasion. As a result, they make decisions that are not always optimal or ideal. They "satisfice," which means that they do not make the best decision that a rational maximizer would make under ideal conditions with complete information in hand, but they make a decision that will work satisfactorily in a particular situation. In a well-known academic article, "The Proverbs of Administration," Simon argued that many presuppositions in the PA literature—for example, "be efficient" or "don't be influenced by political pressure"—actually were truisms that did little to clarify the work of a public administrator. In addition, such homilies needed to be examined to uncover their hidden assumptions.[25]

A year later, another Young Turk challenged the tenets of orthodoxy. In *The Administrative State*, Dwight Waldo challenged the idea that public administration was somehow "neutral" and completely divorced from politics. Instead of attacking POSDCORB because it was not "scientific," as Simon suggested, Waldo was concerned about the problem of orthodoxy's normative assumptions. In Waldo's view, the field of American public administration contained a hidden political theory. Although proponents of orthodoxy believed that they had developed a neutral "science" of administration, that belief in and of itself was tantamount to a theory of politics. Hidden in orthodox public administration was the idea that "efficiency" is, and ought to be, the goal of government administration. Waldo noted that the American political system was founded, at least in part, on a deliberate theory of inefficiency. The Founders' concern that "too much power in too few hands" can lead to tyranny caused them to create what Vincent Ostrom and others have called a "compound republic." Separating powers into legislative (law-making), executive (law-enforcing), and judicial (law-interpreting) branches, creating a federal system of government that divides power between a central government and states, and requiring shared powers among and between branches and levels of government were incredibly inefficient acts. The inefficiency was the point. It prevented government from becoming too powerful and thereby oppressing citizens. Theorists who assume that efficiency is an uncontested proposition and the hallmark of a neutral science of public administration do not understand their history.[26]

In 1949, another assault on Orthodoxy appeared in the form of Paul Appleby's *Policy and Administration*. Appleby had already argued in favor of a "democratic" view of public administration—that is, the need for accountability within agencies to ensure that public administrators do not stray too far from the needs of a democratic society—an argument he originated in his book *Big Democracy*, published four years earlier. In *Policy and Administration*, he argued that there is no way to separate policy considerations from administrative operations. Specific policies may be articulated by political leaders, but those same policies are affected by administrators. A branch of public policy today—implementation studies—is devoted to examining exactly these effects.[27]

This trek through the literature suggests reasons why Yale University political scientist Robert Dahl expressed concern about the state of public administration in 1947. Dahl penned a famous essay identifying three major problems. In his day, the notion that the field contained hidden normative assumptions was just beginning to be discussed by his colleagues. A theory of human nature had been implicit prior to that time, but the structure and function of institutions had received the lion's share of attention before the 1940s. In addition, public administration was studied in those days as a decidedly American endeavor, with little attention afforded to administrative practices in other nations. Much has changed since Dahl's time, but much remains to be done.

According to Dahl, a first problem is the need to clarify normative values in the field. A number of theorists have focused on normative issues. Aside from Dwight Waldo, two famous theorists, Herman Finer and Carl J. Friedrich, engaged in a spirited debate about the need for, and nature of, bureaucratic controls. Finer argued that external controls are needed, while Friedrich contended that internal controls should be paramount. This debate centers on the question of how public administrators ought to be held accountable. Such a focus on administrative behavior would have been unlikely in the Age of Orthodoxy.[28]

A school of thought known as "New Public Administration" arose after the 1968 Minnowbrook Conference. This school of thought originates on the left of the political spectrum. Its proponents worry that questions of "social equity" have not been adequately addressed, especially in public agencies. The idea that a public administrator works isolated and apart from the larger society is worrisome. Instead, New Public Administrators contend that public administrators must work to incorporate equity into their jobs. H. George Frederickson probably is the best-known member of this school, but other theorists include Frank Marini, David K. Hart, and Susan Wakefield, among others. New Public Administration became so influential during the 1970s that one entire issue of the academic journal *Public Administration Review* was devoted to New Public Administration in 1974. The attractiveness of this approach has waned over time as the idealistic commitment to social equity has changed, but for a time this was indeed a serious effort to clarify normative values in public administration.[29]

A later effort was undertaken by a group of scholars at Virginia Tech. The scholars held a series of meetings followed by a book of essays dubbed the "Blacksburg Manifesto" aimed at "refounding public administration." The first groups of essays appeared in 1984, followed by subsequent editions in the 1990s and in the 2000s. Gary Wamsley served as the editor of the first group of essays. John A. Rohr arguably was the best known member of the group.

These administrative theorists were concerned that citizens had become so hostile toward the bureaucracy that the legitimacy of public administration was called into question. Rather than trace the lineage of the profession to the late nineteenth century, as many teachers and theorists had done, the Blacksburgers sought to travel back to the U.S. Constitution and the Founding period. In their view, PA was rooted in the U.S. Constitution; hence its legitimacy was not suspect. The effort to "refound" PA is an effort to see public administrators as constitutional officers. They must possess and practice civic virtue by seeing their role as one grounded in the Constitution.[30]

In *Ethics for Bureaucrats*, Rohr wrote that public administrators must identify "regime values" so that they can act ethically when they use administrative discretion in their jobs. They learn regime values by studying authoritative pronouncements on the rules of the regime, especially opinions announced by the U.S. Supreme Court. Education in ethics and character as well as the history and traditions of the regime are an integral part of the refounding school. Although he is not technically a Blacksburger, William D. Richardson, a political scientist at the University of South Dakota, has outlined the refounding position in some detail in his 1997 book, *Democracy, Bureaucracy and Character: Founding Thought*.[31]

As for Dahl's second point—that PA needs an improved understanding of human nature—a series of writers and researchers has done exactly that. The Human Relations School, which included researchers outside of the field of American public administration, also highlighted orthodoxy's shortcomings by focusing on behavior in lieu of institutions. For example, the Hawthorne Studies found that workers respond to attention more than they respond to physical conditions such as lighting. Building on this insight, Frederick Herzberg suggested that hygiene factors—the physical work environment, the conditions of the equipment, and the like—are necessary for workers to accomplish their tasks, but they are insufficient motivators. They needed external motivators such as advancement within an organization and acknowledgment of their accomplishments. Similarly, the American psychologist Abraham Maslow argued that psychological factors—his renowned hierarchy of needs—are important. After people have lower-order needs such as food, shelter and clothing satisfied, they seek to satisfy higher-order needs—a desire to be loved and to be self-actualized. In *The Functions of the Executive*, Chester Barnard indicated that people will work within what he called a "zone of indifference." Outside of that zone, they will refuse to work and even question the requirements imposed on them. In *The Human Side of Enterprise*, Douglas McGregor set forth Theory X, the idea that workers are indolent and must be ordered to do their jobs, and Theory Y, the idea that workers will labor independently when they are given the opportunity to set goals and participate in decision-making. Robert Golembiewski enjoyed a lengthy career writing numerous works on the need to transform organizations from rigid, impersonal hierarchies into places where workers can be more participative and, in a sense, "own" their jobs.[32]

The final problem that Dahl identified—namely that a comparative study of public administration is needed—also has been given attention since his time, although perhaps not as much as the first two problems. Studies have been undertaken by several scholars to compare the problems in American PA with the problems in PA in other countries. Laurence O'Toole, Jr. published studies comparing U.S. and foreign countries' administrative systems. During his lengthy academic career, John Rohr focused especially on France, a system where the state is much stronger and less fragmented than in the United States, which has a more-or-less "stateless" origin, according to theorist Richard Stillman II.[33]

One reason that comparative studies have been delayed in coming is that many public administration theorists have emerged from an academic discipline that often is tied to political science, especially that part of the field that focuses on American politics. Consequently, many political scientists with an interest in public administration have not been especially interested in foreign relations. Thus, they have not felt comfortable comparing foreign and American public administration because they do not know much about administrative functions in other countries. This decidedly provincial, American-centered focus is changing, particularly as more foreign students study public administration at American universities.

The advantage of comparative studies is that after the different historical and institutional circumstances between American and foreign public administration have been controlled for, the similarities in general administrative issues can be accentuated. Such a comparison can help to illuminate principles that arise from the commonality as well as highlight those aspects that are specific to one country or the other. Because the prospects for research in this area are so promising and because relatively little work has been done, comparative public administration is likely to see more research in coming years.[34]

With all the advances that have occurred in public administration since Dahl identified three problems in the field, the question remains: Has public administration achieved a "truly scientific stature"? Again, the answer depends on the definition of science. If a social science such as public administration is held to the same standard as the hard sciences, the answer must be "no." The idea that human behavior can be identified, quantified, and measured with the same degree of accuracy and precision as the behavior of inert matter or external phenomena has long been rejected by a large percentage of mainstream academic theorists.

With the demise of the Orthodox School of public administration, most mainstream thinkers and researchers—with, perhaps, the loud objection of extreme behavioralists and other diehard holdouts—have recognized that there is no way to root out presuppositions, biases, and vagaries inherent in the human condition. This realization is not to say that scientific processes and principles cannot be used to study social science problems, but it does recognize that the standards of research and interpretation applied to the hard sciences are inappropriate for the social sciences.

Public administration can be considered more scientific than it was in Dahl's era if "science" refers to the scientific method where a researcher identifies a problem, sifts through the literature, develops a research hypothesis, and develops a research design that explains something significant about the problem. In some cases, social science experiments may not be possible, although quasi-experiments such as surveys and field observations may prove to be useful. Such quasi-experiments can be valid, reliable, and replicable by subsequent researchers if their assumptions and biases are clearly identified beforehand.[35]

As subsequent chapters in this book illustrate, the recognition that public administrators are not morally neutral, technically proficient automations that carry out the will of elected officials holds enormous repercussions for American environmental law and policy. Administrators working within federal executive branch agencies play an integral role in promoting environmental sustainability in every phase. They assist in defining the term "sustainability," in formulating policies that influence sustainable practices, and in implementing and defending policies that protect and preserve the natural environment.

THE HISTORICAL EVOLUTION OF AMERICAN PUBLIC ADMINISTRATION

The scholarly understanding of the field of public administration evolved in tandem with larger social forces roiling the waters of American history. At the end of the Civil War, a generation of Americans, especially freedmen who threw off the shackles of servitude following ratification of the Thirteenth Amendment in December 1865, faced bleak economic prospects. The unwashed masses eked out a living mostly in agricultural pursuits, but they suffered through numerous vicissitudes such as harsh weather, the lack of available specie, dwindling capital, and a volatile marketplace. As a reaction to untenable conditions, a series of populist leaders championed "the people" over the affluent elite that seemingly exercised political power and developed economic policies to the detriment of the little man. Although the Populist Party disappeared as an organized entity early in the twentieth century, the concern for the needs of the lower and middle classes remained a staple of American politics for generations to come.[36]

On the heels of the populist revolt, America witnessed the birth of the Progressive movement. Progressives argued that the growth of private sector corporations, systematic corruption of the country's political parties, and weaknesses in federal governmental institutions threatened the survival of the middle class. Unlike classical liberals who believed that that government is best which governs least, Progressives offered a competing historical interpretation. Professing their love of liberty no less than any committed free market proponent, Progressives explained that government is either part of the problem or part of the solution. To be part of the solution, governmental institutions must intervene to ensure that citizens can partake in the American dream by earning a living and advancing along a socioeconomic continuum. Elected officials and private business leaders must be reined in lest they manipulate the lower classes for presumably nefarious purposes.[37]

Progressives called for "trust-busting" laws to curb the power of monopolies, promoted labor unions to allow workers to deal effectively with management, and lobbied against children working in factories instead of going to school.[38] One of the best-known and most success-ful Progressive causes, the settlement house movement, originated in England in the 1880s. Victorians increasingly worried about the effects of poverty; consequently, settlement houses arose to ensure that desti-tute souls received food, shelter, and clothing. Progressives established a series of settlement houses in the United States as the movement spread across the Atlantic. Settlement house activists eventually created a pro-fessional class of social worker to replace the amateurs who previously worked with the poor. A settlement house established in Chicago in 1889 by Jane Addams and Ellen Gates Starr and known as Hull House became a symbol of the new social activism of the Progressive era.[39]

Aside from recognizing a need to correct abuses outside of govern-ment, reformers sought to change the spoils system that had become entrenched in the political system. Usually traced to the administration of President Andrew Jackson (1829–1837), the notion was that a suc-cessful candidate for office should enjoy the patronage and perquisites that come with winning an election. "To the victor belong the spoils," the old adage suggested. As the nineteenth century progressed, however, observers of the American political system feared that cronyism and cor-ruption were rampant. The spoils system supposedly contributed to a variety of social and political ills, from the stolen presidential election of 1876 to the assassination of President James A. Garfield by Charles Guiteau, a "disgruntled office seeker," in 1881. Civil service reform, with its emphasis on merit and its hostility to nepotism and back-room deals, was a major Progressive goal. Creation of the first major professional civil service system on the federal level with the enactment of the Pendleton Act in 1883 appeared to be a crucial step in ensuring that a reformed government could meet the needs of its citizens free from undue bias and corruption.[40]

The Progressives instituted incremental reforms that were imple-mented by an expanding bureaucracy, but their efforts only came to full fruition beginning in the 1930s. As President Franklin Roosevelt initiated his programs known as the New Deal, government commissions and agencies were created to handle a wide array of problems. It became known as the "Golden Age of Tribunals." With the growth of bureaucracy came commissions to direct its growth. The Brownlow Committee recommended that the president exercise direct control over agencies. Executive assistants should work inside the White House to ensure that the president was kept informed of developments inside the agencies. The Attorney General's Committee on Administrative Procedure, which met from 1939 through 1941, found that a statutory foundation for administrative procedure was needed. The committee provided direction on judicial review of agency actions. As a result of these (and other) tribunals, Congress enacted the Administrative Procedure Act (APA) in 1946.[41]

The APA was designed to inform the public of bureaucratic procedures and rules, provide an outlet for public participation in rulemaking and adjudication, standardize formal rulemaking and adjudication procedures, and define the scope of judicial review. The administrative state had grown so large so quickly that each agency resembled its own little fiefdom with its own internal rules that appeared to be archaic and incomprehensible to all but the public servants working inside the agency. Thus, the APA was drafted to make sense out of the labyrinthine rules and procedures informally practiced within federal agencies.[42]

As the modern American administrative state continued to evolve through President Lyndon Johnson's Great Society programs of the 1960s, a "counter-bureaucracy" movement developed. A new narrative developed concerning the "out of control" bureaucracy that was unresponsive to the citizenry and dedicated to lavish, deficit spending. Proponents of New Federalism contended that American public administration was in need of serious reform so that states could exercise more authority and the private sector would be empowered to introduce much-needed efficiencies into the system. The Civil Service Reform Act of 1978 and subsequent efforts to curb federal authority through deregulation, budgetary impoundment, and judicial decisions limiting federal authority by reinvigorating the Tenth Amendment represented a desire to slow the growth and influence of American bureaucracy. To date, these reforms have met with limited success. Nonetheless, such changes affect public administration and sustainability.[43]

From the beginning, Progressives focused on environmental concerns. As the nation's population grew rapidly during the early years of the twentieth century and increasing industrialization spurred a robust modern economy, Americans increasingly purchased consumer goods. With factories arising to meet the demand, industrial pollution proliferated in tandem with the burgeoning economy. Citizens became consumers, and consumers purchased products and generated waste. In time, reformers realized that something or someone would have to intervene to curb unregulated environmental degradation. Only the federal government was large enough to serve as an effective check on citizen and corporate behavior.[44]

When the Progressives pushed for a robust federal government to tackle social ills and reformers established new federal agencies, the apparatus was in place to pursue evermore ambitious goals. The nation's public administration system, which had changed markedly since the founding period, responded. In light of a willingness to vest the federal government with power to correct private sector deficiencies, it was natural to task federal executive branch government agencies with environmental protection. Yet an additional step was needed: A legal and regulatory regime would have to be created. Until the mid-twentieth century, American environmental law mostly consisted of common law standards and causes of actions such as nuisance, trespass, and negligence. By the 1960s, it was clear that piecemeal approaches to environmental protection were insufficient. The story of how the American administrative state responded to environmental degradation by formulating and implementing modern environmental laws and regulations is the subject of Chapter 5.[45]

NOTES

1. Michael C. Blumm and Andrea Lang, "Shared Sovereignty: The Role of Expert Agencies in Environmental Law," *Ecology Law Quarterly* 42 (2015): 609–50; Luke Fowler, "Assessing the Framework of Policy Outcomes: The Case of the U.S. Clean Air Act and Clean Water Act," *Journal of Environmental Assessment Policy and Management* 16 (December 2014): 1–19; Jongkon Lee, "Environmental Legislative Standstill and Bureaucratic Politics in the USA," *Policy Studies* 35 (January 2014): 40–58.

2. See, for example, Martin Diamond, "Democracy and *The Federalist*: A Reconsideration of the Framers' Intent," *American Political Science Review* 53 (March 1959): 52–68; Frank Donovan, *Mr. Madison's Constitution: The Story Behind the Constitutional Convention* (New York: Dodd Mead & Company, 1965): 6; William D. Richardson and Lloyd G. Nigro, "Administrative Ethics and Founding Thought: Constitutional Correctives, Honor, and Education," *Public Administration Review* 47 (September/October 1987): 376–76; Martin H. Redish and Matthew Heins, "Premodern Constitutionalism," *William & Mary Law Review* 57 (April 2016): 1825–1912.

3. Henry Adams, *The United States in 1800* (Ithaca, NY.: Cornell University Press, 1974): 12; Rebecca Jean Emigh, Dylan Riley, and Patricia Ahmed, "The Racialization of Legal Categories in the First U.S. Census," *Social Science History* 39 (2015): 485–519; Kathryn E. Newcomer and James Edwin Kee, "*Federalist* No. 23: Can the Leviathan be Managed?" *Public Administration Review* 71 (November 2011): s37–s46.

4. James Madison, "*Federalist* No. 37," in Alexander Hamilton, James Madison, and John Jay, *The Federalist Papers*, Clinton Rossiter, ed. (New York: New American Library, 1961 [1788]): 229.

5. "Creation of the Executive Departments," *Congressional Digest* 40 (November 1961): 258–60; Dustin M. Dow, "The Unambiguous Supremacy Clause," *Boston College Law Review* 53 (May 1, 2012): 1009–44; Herbert A. Johnson, *Gibbons v. Ogden: John Marshall, Steamboats, and the Commerce Clause* (Lawrence: University Press of Kansas, 2010); John F. Manning, "The Necessary and Proper Clause and Its Legal Antecedents," *Boston University Law Review* 92 (July 1, 2012): 1349–80; Jed Handelsman Shugerman, "The Creation of the Department of Justice: Professionalization without Civil Rights or Civil Service," *Stanford Law Review* 66 (January 2014): 121–71; Harold W. Stanley and Richard G. Niemi, *Vital Statistics on American Politics 20011–2012* (Washington, D.C.: CQ Press, 2012); 255–56; Melvin I. Urofsky, "Thomas Jefferson and John Marshall: What Kind of Constitution Shall We Have?" *Journal of Supreme Court History* 31 (July 2006): 109–25.

6. Quoted in Thomas Jefferson, *The Portable Thomas Jefferson*, Merrill D. Peterson, ed. (New York: Penguin Classics, 1977), 455–56.

7. Quoted in Stephanie P. Newbold, *All But Forgotten: Thomas Jefferson and the Development of Public Administration* (Albany: State University of New York Press, 2010): 62.

8. James Madison, "*Federalist* No. 51," in Alexander Hamilton, James Madison, and John Jay, *The Federalist Papers*, 322.

9. Alexander Hamilton, "*Federalist* No. 70," in Alexander Hamilton, James Madison, and John Jay, *The Federalist Papers*, 423.

10. Alexander Hamilton, "*Federalist* No. 72," in Alexander Hamilton, James Madison, and John Jay, *The Federalist Papers*, 435–36.

11. Patrick Overeem, "The Value of the Dichotomy: Politics, Administration, and the Political Neutrality of Administrators," *Administrative Theory & Praxis* 27 (July 2005): 311–29; Reza Tahmasebi and Seyyed Mohammad Mahdi Musavi, "Politics-Administration Dichotomy: A Century Debate," *Administration & Public Management Review* 17 (December 2011): 130–43.

12. R. McGreggor Cawley, "Inserting Frontier into Dichotomies: Politics, Administration, and Agonistic Pluralism," *Administrative Theory & Praxis* 37 (December 2015): 227–41; Arthur S. Link, "Woodrow Wilson and the Study of Administration," *Proceedings of the American Philosophical Society* 112 (December 9, 1968): 431–33; Richard J. Stillman, II, "Woodrow Wilson and the Study of Administration: A New Look at an Old Essay," *The American Political Science Review* 67 (June 1973): 582–88; Mark R. Rutgers, "Beyond Woodrow Wilson: The Identity of the Study of Public Administration in Historical Perspective," *Administration & Society* 29 (July 1997): 276–300.

13. Woodrow Wilson, "The Study of Administration," *Political Science Quarterly* 2 (June 1887): 197–222. See also Marshall E. Dimock, "The Study of Administration," *The American Political Science Review* 31 (February 1937): 28–40.

14. Thomas S Kuhn, *The Structure of Scientific Revolutions*, 2nd edition, (Chicago: The University of Chicago Press, 1970). See also Barry Barnes, *T.S. Kuhn and Social Sciences* (New York: Columbia University Press, 1982); Alexander Bird, "Kuhn, Naturalism, and the Positivist Legacy," *Studies in History & Philosophy of Science Part A* 35 (June 2004): 337–56; Alisa Bokulich, "Heisenberg Meets Kuhn: Closed Theories and Paradigms," *Philosophy of Science* 73 (January 2006): 90–107; Jiahuan Lu, "Intellectual Paradigms in Public Administration: Why So Many and How to Bridge Them?" *Administrative Theory & Praxis* 35 (June 2013): 308–13.

15. Robert J. McGrath, "The Rise and Fall of Radical Civil Service Reform in the U.S. States," *Public Administration Review* 73 (July/August 2013): 638–49; Stephanie P. Newbold, "Toward a Constitutional School for American Public Administration," *Public Administration* 70 (July/August 2010): 538–46; David H. Rosenbloom, "The Politics-Administration Dichotomy in U.S. Historical Context," *Public Administration Review* 68 (January/February 2008): 57–60; Fritz Sager and Christian Rosser, "Weber, Wilson, and Hegel: Theories of Modern Bureaucracy," *Public Administration Review* 69 (November/December 2009): 1136–47.

16. Ari Hoogenboom, "The Pendleton Act and the Civil Service," *The American Historical Review* 64 (January 1959): 301–18; Patrick Overeem, "Beyond Heterodoxy: Dwight Waldo and the Politics-Administration Dichotomy," *Public Administration Review* 68 (January/February 2008): 36–45; Shugerman, "The Creation of the Department of Justice: Professionalization without Civil Rights or Civil Service," 121–71; B. Douglas Skelley, "The Persistence of the Politics-Administration Dichotomy: An Additional Explanation," *Public*

Administration Quarterly 32 (Winter 2008): 549–70; James H. Svara, "Beyond Dichotomy: Dwight Waldo and the Intertwined Politics-Administration Relationship," *Public Administration Review* 68 (January/February 2008): 46–52.

17. Frank J. Goodnow, *Politics and Administration: A Study in Government* (New York and London: The MacMillan Company, 1900). See also Laurence E. Lynn, Jr., "Restoring the Rule of Law to Public Administration: What Frank Goodnow Got Right and Leonard White Didn't," *Public Administration Review* 69 (September/October 2009): 803–12; Christian Rosser, "Examining Frank J. Goodnow's Hegelian Heritage: A Contribution to Understanding Progressive Administrative Theory," *Administration & Society* 45 (November 2013): 1063–94.

18. Frederick Winslow Taylor, *The Principles of Scientific Management* (Mineola, NY: Courier Dover Publications, 2009 [1911]). See also Maarten Derksen, "Turning Men into Machines? Scientific Management, Industrial Psychology, and the 'Human Factor,'" *Journal of the History of Behavioral Sciences* 50 (Spring 2014): 148–65; Cristina M. Giannantonio and Amy E. Hurley-Hanson, "Frederick Winslow Taylor: Reflections on the Relevance of *The Principles of Scientific Management* 100 Years Later," *Journal of Business & Management* 17 (April 2011): 7–10; Daniel A. Wren, "The Centennial of Frederick W. Taylor's *The Principles of Scientific Management*: A Retrospective Commentary," *Journal of Business & Management* 17 (April 2011): 11–22.

19. Werner J. Cahnman, "Ideal Type Theory: Max Weber's Concept and Some of Its Derivations," *The Sociological Quarterly* 6 (Summer 1965): 268–80; Michael W. Spicer, "Public Administration in a Disenchanted World: Reflections on Max Weber's Value Pluralism and His Views on Politics and Bureaucracy," *Administration & Society* 47 (January 2015): 24–43; Margaret Stout, "Revisiting the (Lost) Art of Ideal-Typing in Public Administration," *Administrative Theory & Praxis* 32 (December 2010): 491–519.

20. Abdullah M. Al-Wagdani, "Beyond Weberian Bureaucracy: Max Weber on Bureaucracy and His Critics," *Journal of the Social Sciences* 38 (2010): 11–28; Richard A. Hilbert, "Bureaucracy as Belief, Rationalization as Repair: Max Weber in a Post-Functionalist Age," *Sociological Theory* 5 (Spring 1987): 70–86; Nina Toren, "Bureaucracy and Professionalism: A Reconsideration of Weber's Thesis," *Academy of Management Review* 1 (July 1976): 36–46.

21. John Breuilly, "Max Weber, Charisma and Nationalist Leadership," *Nations and Nationalism* 17 (July 2011): 477–99; Michael M. Rosenberg, "The Conceptual Articulation of the Reality of Life: Max Weber's Theoretical Constitution of Sociological Ideal Types," *Journal of Classical Sociology* 16 (February 2016): 84–101; David E. Willer, "Max Weber's Missing Authority Type," *Sociological Inquiry* 37 (Spring 1967): 231–39.

22. Breuilly, "Max Weber, Charisma and Nationalist Leadership," 477–99; Joshua Derman, "Max Weber and Charisma: A Transatlantic Affair," *New German Critique* 113 (Summer 2011): 51–88. For Hitler's argument, see Adolf

Hitler, "Selections from *Mein Kampf*," in *The Quest for Justice: Readings in Political Ethics*, 3rd. edition, Leslie G. Rubin and Charles T. Rubin, eds (Needham Heights, MA.: Ginn Press, 1992), 245–49.

23. Jeffrey D. Houghton, "Does Max Weber's Notion of Authority Still Hold in the Twenty-first Century?" *Journal of Management History* 16 (September 2010): 449–53; Isher-Paul Sahni, "Max Weber's Sociology of Law," *Journal of Classical Sociology* 9 (May 2009): 209–33; Ann Swidler, "The Concept of Rationality in the Work of Max Weber," *Sociological Inquiry* 43 (January 1973): 35–42.

24. Leonard D. White, *Introduction to the Study of Public Administration* (New York and London: The MacMillan Company, 1946 [1926]); Luther Gulick and Lyndall Urwick, eds., *Papers on the Science of Administration* (New York: Institute of Public Administration, 1937); President's Committee on Administrative Management, *Report of the Committee* (Washington, D.C.: U.S. Government Printing Office, 1937). See also Peri E. Arnold, "The Brownlow Committee, Regulation, and the Presidency: Seventy Years Later," *Public Administration Review* 67 (November/December 2007): 1030–40; Kenneth J. Meier, "Governance, Structure, and Democracy: Luther Gulick and the Future of Public Administration," *Public Administration Review* 70 Supplement (December 2010): s284–s291; Alan Brunacini, "POSDCORB," *Fire Engineering* 168 (March 2015): 54–56; Herbert J. Storing, "Leonard D. White and the Study of Public Administration," *Public Administration Review* 25 (March 1965): 38–51.

25. Herbert A. Simon, *Administrative Behavior*, 4th edition (New York: The Free Press, 1997); Herbert A. Simon, "The Proverbs of Administration," *Public Administration Review* 6 (Winter 1946): 53–67. See also Lorraine Daston, "Simon and the Sirens: A Commentary," *ISIS: Journal of the History of Science in Society* 106 (September 2015): 669–76; Stefano Fiori, "Forms of Bounded Rationality: The Reception and Redefinition of Herbert A. Sion's Perspective," *Review of Political Economy* 23 (October 2011): 587–612; Bryan D. Jones, "Bounded Rationality and Public Policy: Herbert A. Simon and the Decisional Foundation of Collective Choice," *Policy Sciences* 35 (September 1, 2002): 269–84; Rouslan Koumakhov, "Conventions in Herbert Simon's Theory of Bounded Rationality," *Journal of Economic Psychology* 30 (June 2009): 293–306.

26. Dwight Waldo, *The Administrative State: A Study of the Political Theory of American Public Administration* (New York: Ronald Press, 1948). See also Robert L. Bish, "Vincent Ostrom's Contributions to Political Economy," *Publius: The Journal of Federalism* 44 (April 2014): 227–48; Vincent Ostrom, *The Political Theory of a Compound Republic: Designing the American Experiment*, 2nd. edition (Lincoln: University of Nebraska Press, 1987); Overeem, "Beyond Heterodoxy," 36–45; Richard J. Stillman II, "Review Article: Dwight Waldo's *The Administrative State*: A Neglected American Administrative State Theory

for Our Times," *Public Administration* 86 (June 2008): 581–90; Camilla Stivers, "The Significance of *The Administrative State*," *Public Administration Review* 68 (January/February 2008): 53–56; Svara, "Beyond Dichotomy," 46–52.

27. Paul H. Appleby, *Big Democracy* (New York: Knopf, 1945); Paul H. Appleby, *Policy and Administration* (University, AL.: University of Alabama Press, 1949); Roscoe Coleman Martin, editor, *Public Administration and Democracy: Essays in Honor of Paul H. Appleby* (Syracuse, NY.: Syracuse University Press, 1965).

28. Robert A. Dahl, "The Science of Public Administration: Three Problems," *Public Administration Review* 7 (Winter 1947): 1–11; Robert A. Dahl, *A Preface to Democratic Theory* (Chicago: The University of Chicago Press, 1956); Herman Finer, "Administrative Responsibility in Democratic Government," in *Combating Corruption/ Encouraging Ethics: A Sourcebook for Public Service Ethics*, William L. Richter, Francis Burke, and Jameson W. Doig , eds. (Washington, D.C.: The American Society for Public Administration, 1990), 44; Carl J. Friedrich, "Public Policy and the Nature of Administrative Responsibility," in *Combating Corruption/ Encouraging Ethics: A Sourcebook for Public Service Ethics*, eds. William L. Richter, Francis Burke, and Jameson W. Doig (Washington, D.C.: The American Society for Public Administration, 1990), 43; Michael Jackson, "Responsibility versus Accountability in the Friedrich-Finer Debate," *Journal of Management History* 15 (January 2009): 66–77; Debra W. Stewart, "Professional vs. Democracy: Friedrich vs. Finer Revisited," *Public Administration Quarterly* 9 (Spring 1985): 13–25; Jacinda Swanson, "The Economy and Its Relation to Politics: Robert Dahl, Neoclassical Economics, and Democracy," *Polity* 39 (April 2007): 208–33.

29. H. George Frederickson, *New Public Administration* (Tuscaloosa, AL.: University of Alabama Press, 1980); David K. Hart, "Social Equity, Justice, and the Equitable Administrator," *Public Administration Review* 34 (January 1974): 3–11; Frank Marini, "The Minnowbrook Perspective and the Future of Public Administration," in *Toward a New Public Administration: The Minnowbrook Perspective*, Frank Marini, ed. (New York: Chandler, 1971), 346–67; Susan Wakefield, "Ethics and the Public Service: A Case for Individual Responsibility," *Public Administration Review* 36 (November/December 1976): 661–66; Roger Wettenhall, "Minnowbrook: Just American or More?" *Administrative Theory & Praxis* 31 (June 2009): 255–60.

30. Meredith Hundley and Gary Wamsley, "John Rohr's Legacy: Constitutional Literacy and the Public Service," *Administrative Theory & Praxis* 34 (December 2012); 642–47; Gary S. Marshall and Orion F. White, Jr., "The Blacksburg Manifesto and the Postmodern Debate: Public Administration in a Time Without a Name," *American Review of Public Administration* 20 (June 1990): 61–76; Newbold, "Toward a Constitutional School for American Public Administration," 538–46; Gary L. Wamsley, *et al.*, *Refounding Public Administration* (Newbury Park, CA: Sage Publications, 1990).

31. John A. Rohr, *Ethics for Bureaucrats: An Essay on Law and Values*, 2nd. edition (New York and Bessel: Marcel Dekker, 1989); William D. Richardson, *Democracy, Bureaucracy, & Character: Founding Thought* (Lawrence: University Press of Kansas, 1997).

32. Jeevan D'Souza and Michael Gurin, "The Universal Significance of Maslow's Concept of Self-Actualization," *The Humanistic Psychologist* 44 (June 2016): 210–14; James A. Gazell, "Authority-Flow Theory and the Impact of Chester Barnard," *California Management Review* 13 (Fall 1970): 68–74; Robert T. Golembiewski, *Men, Management, and Morality: Toward a New Organizational Ethic* (New York: McGraw-Hill, 1965); Chan Su Jung and Soo-Young Lee, "The Hawthorne Studies Revisited: Evidence from the U.S. Federal Workforce," *Administration & Society* 47 (July 2015): 507–31; Ebrahim A. Maidani, "Comparative Study of Herzberg's Two-factor Theory of Job Satisfaction among Public and Private Sectors," *Public Personnel Management* 20 (Winter 1991): 441–48; Douglas McGregor, *The Human Side of Enterprise* (New York: McGraw-Hill, 1960); Dalitso Sulamoyo, "Building Beyond Already Established OD Success Rates: An Interview with Dr. Robert T. Golembiewski," *Organization Development Journal* 28 (Winter 2010): 11–19.

33. Laurence J. O'Toole, Jr., and Kenneth I. Hanf, "American Public Administration and Impacts of International Governance," *Public Administration Review* 62, Special Issue (September 2002): 158–69; John A. Rohr, "Ethics and Comparative Administration: A Constitutional Commentary," *Public Integrity* 10 (Winter 2007–8): 65–74; John Uhr, "John Rohr's Concept of Regime Values: Locating Theory in Public Administration," *Administration & Society* 46 (March 2014): 141–52; Richard J. Stillman II, "The Peculiar 'Stateless' Origins of American Public Administration and the Consequences for Government Today," *Public Administration Review* 90 (March/April 1990): 156–67.

34. Jody Fitzpatrick, *et al.*, "A New Look at Comparative Public Administration: Trends in Research and an Agenda for the Future," *Public Administration Review* 71 (November/December 2011): 821–30; Jamil E. Jreisat, "Commentary—Comparative Public Administration: A Global Perspective," *Public Administration Review* 71 (November/December 2011): 834–38; Christopher Pollitt, "Not Odious but Onerous: Comparative Public Administration," *Public Administration* 89 (March 2011): 114–27.

35. Raymond C. Hubbard and C. Kenneth Meyer, "The Rise of Statistical Significance Testing in Public Administration Research and Why This is a Mistake," *Journal of Business and Behavioral Sciences* 25 (Spring 2013): 4–20; Lu, "Intellectual Paradigms in Public Administration," 308–13; Jos C.N. Raadschelders, "The Future Study of Public Administration: Embedding Research Object and Methodology in Epistemology and Ontology," *Public Administration Review* 71 (November/December 2011): 916–24.

36. Peter H. Argersinger, *Populism and Politics: William Alfred Peffer and the People's Party* (Lexington: University Press of Kentucky, 2015). Peter H.

Alexander Tsesis, "Into the Light of Day: Relevance of the Thirteenth Amendment to Contemporary Law," *Columbia Law Review* 112 (November 2012): 1447–58.

37. The literature on Progressivism is voluminous. For a general introduction, see, for example, Daniel Gaido, "The Populist Interpretation of American History: A Materialist Revision," *Science & Society* 65 (Fall 2001): 350–53; Gabriel Gherasim, "Introductory Sketch to the Analytics and Pragmatism of American Progressivism," *Studia Universitatis Babes-Bolyai. Studia Europaea* 56 (September 2011): 119–30.

38. David Lee Amstutz, "Nebraska's Live Stock Sanitary Commission and the Rise of Progressivism," *Great Plains Quarterly* 28 (Fall 2008): 259–60; Eldon J. Eisenach, "Progressivism as a National Narrative in Biblical-Hegelian Times," *Social Philosophy & Policy* 24 (January 2007): 61–64.

39. Jean Bethke Elshtain, "A Return to Hull House: Reflections on Jane Addams," *Feminist Issues* 15 (1997): 105–113.

40. Hoogenboom, "The Pendleton Act and the Civil Service," 301–18; "Progress of the Civil Service System in the United States," *Congressional Digest* 16 (November 1937): 261–65.

41. Arnold, "The Brownlow Committee, Regulation, and the Presidency," 1030–40; Roni A. Elias, "The Legislative History of the Administrative Procedure Act," *Fordham Environmental Law Review* 27 (Winter 2016): 207–24; Walter Gellhorn, "The Administrative Procedure Act: The Beginnings," *Virginia Law Review* 72 (March 1986): 219–33; Joanna Grisinger, "Law in Action: The Attorney General's Committee on Administrative Procedure," *The Journal of Policy History* 20 (July 2008): 379–418; McNollgast, "The Political Origins of the Administrative Procedure Act," *Journal of Law, Economics, & Organization* 15 (April 1999): 180–217. See also Candice Millard, *Destiny of the Republic: A Tale of Madness, Medicine and the Murder of a President* (New York: Doubleday, 2011).

42. Arnold, "The Brownlow Committee, Regulation, and the Presidency," 1030–40; Daniel A. Farber and Anne Joseph O'Connell, "The Lost World of Administrative Law," *Texas Law Review* 92 (April 2014): 1137–89.

43. Steven Knudsen, Larry Jakus, and Maida Metz, "The Civil Service Reform Act of 1978," *Public Personnel Management* 8 (May/June 1979): 170–81; Richard P. Nathan, "There Will Always be a New Federalism," *Journal of Public Administration Research and Theory* 16 (October 2006): 499–510.

44. Gherasim, "Introductory Sketch to the Analytics and Pragmatism of American Progressivism," 136; Benjamin Kline, Ph.D., *First Along the River: A Brief History of the U.S. Environmental Movement*, 3rd. edition (Lanham, MD.: Rowman & Littlefield, 2007), 51–54.

45. Jonathan H. Adler and Andrew P. Morriss, "Common Law Environmental Protection," *Virginia Law Review* 101 (September 2015): 575–82; Michael S. Greve and Ashley C. Parrish, "Administrative Law without Congress,"

George Mason Law Review 22 (Spring 2015): 501–47; George P. Smith, II and David M. Steenburg, "Environmental Hedonism or, Securing the Environment Through the Common Law," *William & Mary Law & Policy Review* 40 (Fall 2015): 65–114.

5

THE DEVELOPMENT OF FEDERAL
ENVIRONMENTAL LAW

Before the modern era that originated in the late 1960s, proponents of environmental protection relied on traditional common law standards and causes of action. During the 1970s, lawyers and activists pushed legislatures and courts to expand legal provisions for protecting the environment. As Congress enacted new laws establishing a framework for handling hazardous materials, promoting clean air and water, and compensating landowners and the public for damages to the environment, the courts responded by expanding access to judicial review.

Against the backdrop of a growing bureaucracy described in Chapter 4 and with an expanding legal structure in place, administrative agencies promulgated a series of regulations designed to implement the new statutory requirements. The modern environmental regime thus was born. For environmental activists, the new era promised greater environmental protection and more citizen awareness. Some laws and regulations on both the state and federal levels contained what became known colloquially as "bounty hunter" provisions empowering private citizens to file lawsuits against suspected polluters and other violators of environmental laws and regulations. Bounty hunters could be anyone from concerned citizens or environmental groups to opportunistic nongovernmental organizations (NGOs) seeking to cash in on a quick payoff in attorney fees and civil penalties. Indeed, the laws typically provide that a portion of the civil penalties collected in bounty hunter actions will be paid to the group bringing the lawsuit rather than the public treasury.[1]

COMMON LAW STANDARDS AND THE ORIGINS OF AMERICAN ENVIRONMENTAL LAW

American environmental law is a patchwork of federal, state, and local laws and regulations enacted over the course of decades, beginning especially in the 1970s. Prior to that time, most laws involving environmental protection relied on traditional common law actions such as nuisance, trespass, negligence, and strict liability. Nuisance was a typical cause of action for environmental harm in an earlier era. According to this long-standing legal doctrine, no one may unreasonably interfere with the quiet enjoyment of another person's private property rights. The law distinguished between private nuisance, which referred to interference with private property rights absent a physical invasion, and public nuisance, which referred to an activity that affects the health, morals, safety, welfare, comfort, or convenience of the general public.[2]

Unlike nuisance law, which contemplated a noisy neighbor or a manufacturing plant that emitted an unpleasant odor, trespass was designed to regulate physical invasions of land. The most obvious example was a truck driven onto a plaintiff's property or persons physically traversing across a tract of land. In time, the concept of a physical invasion broadened so that nuisance and trespass became blurred, more a matter of degree than a sharp delineation in the law. A well-known 1959 case, *Martin v. Reynolds Metal Company*, provides insight into the evolution of trespass law. According to the Oregon Supreme Court in that case, "the defendant, in the operation of its aluminum reduction plant near Troutdale, Oregon caused certain fluoride compounds in the form of gases and particulates to become airborne and settle upon the plaintiffs' land rendering it unfit for raising livestock during that period." Reynolds Metal Company contended that the presence of gas was insufficient to establish that a physical trespass had occurred, but the court disagreed. "We have held that the deposit of the particulates upon the plaintiff's land was an intrusion within the definition of trespass. That intrusion was direct. The damages which flowed from it are consequential," the court concluded. Beginning with this case and many others, a physical invasion included encroachments from neighbors who did not actually traipse across the landscape.[3]

Negligence remained a staple of the common law complaint. If a property owner could demonstrate that an offender, typically a corporation, had breached a duty to produce a safe product and, in doing so, had caused damage to the plaintiff's legally protected interests, the aggrieved party could recover monetary damages and perhaps enjoin future actions. Causation was difficult to prove in environmental cases, however, because the nexus between the reputed action (such as the release of a chemical, air emission, or toxic effluent) and the onset of a debilitating illness was difficult to establish. A variety of intervening and extenuating factors sometimes mitigated damages and often resulted in a hopelessly confused situation. Moreover, statutes of limitation for filing a claim tended to be relatively short—typically, between two and five years—while the damage to property or human health might not appear until decades after the harm occurred. Thus, a tort claim theoretically could make the aggrieved party whole, but often it was an ineffectual remedy for a complex environmental problem.[4]

Strict liability avoided the difficulties associated with proving the elements of negligence, but the types of cases where the standard applied was limited. As the court expressed in a classic English case dating from 1865, an owner is liable for injuries that occur from a thing that "is likely to do mischief if it escapes." Reasonable care was not a recognized defense, but the "thing" in question had to be tied to an "abnormally dangerous activity." The question of what constitutes an "abnormally dangerous activity" has been, and likely will remain, controversial because different courts have applied different standards. Case-by-case adjudication has been the preferred approach. In some states, transporting or disposing of waste was deemed to meet this requirement, but not every court agreed. Moreover, environmental damage can result from activities that are not especially dangerous when carried out properly, but which can cause widespread damage when performed improperly or absent a particular industry's standard of care.[5]

The public trust doctrine was another common law standard used in environmental cases. Originally, the doctrine applied to navigable rivers and waterfronts held by the sovereign for use by citizens, although later it was expanded to include other natural resources. A famous court case dating from 1892, *Illinois Central Railroad Company v. Illinois*, set forth the standards associated with the public trust doctrine. According to the U.S. Supreme Court, two questions arise in such cases, namely whether the disposition of the property improves the public interest in navigation or use of the waterway and whether the disposition of the property substantially impairs the public interest in the remaining land and waters associated with the waterway. In the *Illinois Central Railroad Company* case, the state of Illinois granted submerged land to the railroad company but later repealed the grant. In a suit to quiet the title, the court held that the state had improperly granted the property to the railroad, thereby abdicating the public trust.[6]

Other cases have provided more detail on the doctrine. In *National Audubon Society v. Superior Court*, the Audubon Society cited the public trust doctrine to prevent the city of Los Angeles from drawing municipal water from Mono Lake. The California Supreme Court allowed some water diversions, but ultimately relied on the doctrine to prevent wholesale use of water from the lake. "The public trust doctrine serves the function in that integrated system of preserving the continuing sovereign power of the state to protect public trust uses, a power which precludes anyone from acquiring a vested right to harm the public trust, and imposes a continuing duty on the state to take such uses into account in allocating water resources," the court concluded. As of this writing, the doctrine remains a recognized means of protecting natural resources. Public entities are required to act in a fiduciary capacity to protect resources held in trust for the people. To abandon the doctrine is to treat public entities, in essence, as private parties. The courts generally refuse to blur the public-private distinction, for they understand that the public has a special duty to protect the citizenry from private entities that would exhaust a common pool resource.[7]

ADMINISTRATIVE ACTION AND STANDARDS FOR JUDICIAL REVIEW

Although common law causes of action and remedies exist to address environmental issues at the state and local level, most American environmental law is developed at the federal level through administrative action such as regulations, adjudications, and policy interpretations as well as decisions handed down in the federal courts. Owing to their singular role in implementing legislative standards, promulgating regulations through the rulemaking process, and filling in the gaps of ambiguous or incomplete statutes, federal public administrators play an important role in environmental law. Their decisions form the backbone of administrative regulations and serve as the starting point for many federal court cases.

Federal environmental law is rooted in the Administrative Procedure Act (APA) of 1946, the major statute that governs agency actions. The APA outlines the steps that must be taken for administrators to engage in the rulemaking process, the administrative version of lawmaking. According to § 553, administrators can initiate informal rulemaking by publishing a notice in the *Federal Register* setting forth a proposed rule, allowing for public comments during a prescribed period of time, responding to comments, and promulgating a final rule. In some instances, administrators may choose to undergo formal rulemaking, which necessitates a trial-type hearing with representation by counsel before an administrative law judge.[8]

Some administrative actions involve adjudication, a quasi-judicial form of dispute resolution. In these actions, a regulation is not at issue; rather, the application of the regulation to this particular party in this particular situation is the paramount consideration. The parties are provided with notice, the public can comment, and a theoretically neutral, independent decision-maker, typically an administrative law judge or agency hearing officer, will issue an opinion on the matter. The losing party has the option of appealing to the federal courts for judicial review.[9]

The APA allows for flexibility in authorizing hybrid procedures that combine features of both formal and informal rulemaking. A particular environmental statute—for example, the Clean Air Act—sometimes provides for a hybrid decision-making process, providing for notice and comment opportunities as well as a trial-type hearing under some circumstances. Sometimes federal regulatory authorities will forgo other types of administrative procedures and negotiate with members of the regulated community to arrive at a conclusion that presumably satisfies all parties.[10]

When parties have exhausted their administrative remedies and believe that their only reasonable recourse is to pursue additional legal action, they can file suit in federal court. As with many areas of the law, different courts apply different standards to determine whether to accept a case for review and, if so, the appropriate legal grounds upon which to base a decision. The courts have not always been consistent in determining when a matter should be subject to judicial review and when the agencies should resolve the matter. The court frequently defer to an agency unless administrators undertook an arbitrary and capricious action or violated a fundamental constitutional requirement.

Even in cases where the courts might be inclined to accept a case, judges and justices have developed rules to limit access to the courts. Standards of justiciability—that is, whether a court should be involved in the issue—apply not merely to administrative actions, but to any case that will come before a court. The first measure of justiciability is whether a party has standing to initiate a suit. The courts have established three tests to determine whether standing exists. The first is the injury-in-fact test. Clearly a person who owns property has standing to file a lawsuit because the person is directly affected if his property is damaged or seized. In environmental cases, the question is whether a person who joins an environmental organization or otherwise expresses an interest in protecting natural resources suffers enough of an injury to argue that he or she has standing to sue.[11]

Standing is not a fixed rule. Legal realists have long claimed that the law is what the judges say it is; consequently, judges and justices decide when to invoke strict standing rules and when to relax them. Environmental law cases demonstrate the wisdom of this observation. In *Sierra Club v. Morton*, a majority of the U.S. Supreme Court held that an environmental group, the Sierra Club, had not met the standing requirement to file a lawsuit against Disney for developing land in the Mineral King Valley because group members could not demonstrate actual damage. A year later, the court granted standing in another environmental law case, *United States v. Students Challenging Regulatory Agency Procedures (SCRAP)*. In that case, five students argued that an Interstate Commerce Commission (ICC) decision to allow across-the-board rate increases for railroads would hurt recycled materials because recyclables already shipped at a higher rate. By placing recyclables in a disadvantageous position, the ICC was inadvertently encouraging less recycling and more littering. The court granted standing to the students, although they later lost the case on the merits.[12]

In a 1978 case, *Duke Power Company v. Carolina Environmental Study Group, Inc.*, an environmental group challenged the Price-Anderson Act, a statute that limited liability for nuclear power utilities to $560 million for any one accident. Group members contended that the law had deprived them of their property (projected damages) without just compensation, which amounted to an unconstitutional "taking" under the Fifth Amendment, because a single nuclear accident probably would exceed $560 million in damages. The court granted standing.[13]

In two related cases from the early 1990s, the court tightened the liberal standing rule. In *Lujan v. National Wildlife Federation* and *Lujan v. Defenders of Wildlife*, the court held that a plaintiff must show an injury-in-fact damage to a legally protected interest. The cases suggest that a majority of the court believed that access to the court had been extended too far in environmental matters. Thereafter, a plaintiff was required to show "concrete" damage at a place certain and imminent harm at a time certain. A lawsuit that alleged a nebulous claim of damages at some unspecified future date would be denied standing. The greater the specificity of place and time, the more likely the court would be to grant standing to plaintiffs seeking redress.[14]

A second test for standing involves what the court has labeled a "zone of interest." In *Association of Data Processing Service Organizations v. Camp*, the court observed that the issue in any standing analysis is "whether the interest sought to be protected by the complainant is arguably within the zone of interests to be protected or regulated by the statute or constitutional guarantee in question." The problem with this test, however, is that it begs the question of whether Congress in enacting a statute intended to affect a particular party's interests. Determining what constitutes an interest for purposes of allowing standing can be within the eye of the beholder; consequently, such a broad test is not especially helpful in answering a standing question.[15]

Two other tests of standing occasionally appear in court cases. The first asks whether a party's actions caused the damage in question and the second asks whether a substantial likelihood exists that judicial relief will reduce or eliminate the injury. In the former case, it can be difficult to determine whether causation can be proved in cases of alleged environmental degradation without first accepting the case and investigating the causal chain. In short, a vicious tautology exists: Until a case is adjudicated and the facts are discovered, it is difficult to know whether the case should be accepted for adjudication. In the case of the applicability of judicial relief, the court is left to speculate as to whether the alleged environmental damage would occur with or without judicial intervention. Such inquiries, once again, may require a consideration of the merits of a case—an inquiry that normally occurs after the court has granted a plaintiff's standing claim and the litigants have filed their pleadings. Perhaps the best that can be said of standing after considering the multitude of tests is that the concept is fluid, and any party filing a lawsuit is well served by stating with as much particularity as possible the nature, extent, and timing of the alleged harm.[16]

Another tool to determine justiciability is whether a matter is ripe for judicial review. Ripeness refers to whether a matter has completed the administrative process and is subject to decision-making by a court of law. Section 704 of the APA mandates that only "final" agency actions are subject to judicial review. In *Port of Boston Marine Terminal v. Rederiaktiebolaget Transatlantic*, the U.S. Supreme Court set forth a standard for determining when an agency action has concluded. Writing for the court, Justice Thurgood Marshall noted that the "relevant considerations in determining finality are whether the process of administrative decisionmaking has reached a stage where judicial review will not disrupt the orderly process of adjudication and whether rights or obligations have been determined or legal consequences will flow from the agency action."[17]

In *Abbot Laboratories v. Gardner*, the court considered a case whether pharmaceutical companies could challenge a U.S. Food & Drug Administration (FDA) regulation before the regulation was enforced. The court determined that the drug companies would suffer substantial harm if they had to wait until the FDA initiated an enforcement action. Ripeness did not require some future threatened action. The courts would allow companies to initiate a lawsuit in advance of the harm as long as the regulation in question already had been promulgated as a final rule.[18]

The courts have carved out a list of reasons for determining why a party must exhaust its administrative remedies before seeking judicial review. Generally, the courts decline to interfere with the administrative process when the agency's use of its authority fulfills a legislative purpose for granting authority in the first place. Moreover, the courts want to protect agency autonomy by allowing the agency an opportunity to apply its expertise and correct its own errors. Allowing the administrative process to proceed unfettered by judicial intervention absent egregious circumstances encourages the participants to develop the facts of the case through agency proceedings. Such developments promote judicial economy by avoiding needless repetition of administrative and judicial fact-finding.[19]

Despite the courts' reluctance to intercede into administrative matters, in some instances it becomes necessary to allow judicial review. Courts accept cases where the agency exceeded the authority granted by its enabling statute or from the APA, misapplied the law, violated the agency's own administrative procedures, or construed the factual record in a manner that it could not justify.[20]

When choosing the standard for judicial review, agencies consider the nature of the case. In rare instances, the court will allow for a *de novo* review. Section 706 (2)(F) of the APA allows the court to serve as the trier of fact rather than relying on the facts as determined by the agency during the administrative process. In most instances, however, courts prefer to base their decisions on the record as established during agency proceedings.[21]

When deciding appeals from formal rulemaking undertaken by an agency, the courts look at the record. If the record includes "substantial evidence" supporting the agency's order or rule, a court will affirm the agency's findings even if the court would not have made the same findings. This standard provides for a great deal of agency discretion. When the courts accept a case following informal rulemaking, the standard provides for even more discretionary authority by the agency. The courts will not set aside the agency's decision as long as the result is not clearly erroneous and has some rational basis. The agency must have acted in an "arbitrary and capricious" manner for the court to overturn the decision.[22]

In granting judicial review, courts must determine the degree to which they will delve into the record. One school of thought champions the "hard look" review, which is to say that courts must exercise an aggressive oversight function to ensure that administrative agencies do not overstep their bounds. According to this analysis, administrative actions perform a useful function, but their actions must be scrutinized to ensure compliance with federal judicial standards. The leading case for this school of thought is *Citizens to Preserve Overton Park, Inc. v. Volpe*, a 1971 U.S. Supreme Court decision. The case originated when an environmental group, Citizens to Preserve Overton Park (CPOP), filed suit against the secretary of Transportation in the western district of Tennessee arguing that the secretary overstepped his bounds in approving the Tennessee Department of Transportation's plan to build an interstate highway that infringed on a city park in Memphis, Tennessee. The CPOP argued that "feasible and prudent" alternatives existed, which meant that the secretary could not use his discretion to build the park. The U.S. Supreme agreed that the secretary had failed to consider relevant factors when he rendered a decision based only on affidavits. It was a major victory for proponents of a federal bureaucracy restrained by an active, engaged judiciary. The court was willing to review the adequacy, or lack thereof, of an administrator's actions to determine whether he had followed reasonable procedures in a good-faith manner.[23]

Overton Park put agency personnel on notice that they must be able to provide a defensible justification for their actions when required to do so by a reviewing court. To ensure that they could withstand judicial review, administrators in the post-1971 era were well advised to build a thorough administrative record detailing the steps they undertook and the reasons for their actions. The lesson was clear: Judges and justices do not defer to agency expertise absent a showing that administrators acted in accordance with applicable procedures.

Undoubtedly, *Overton Park* was a groundbreaking case, but it was hardly the last word on judicial review of administrative action. Proponents of the "soft glance" approach have always contended that administrators are far better versed in the intricacies of an agency's subject matter than federal judges are. Therefore, agency personnel should be afforded suitable deference in using their discretion on both procedural and substantive matters in the absence of express congressional direction. *Vermont Yankee Nuclear Power Corporation v. Natural Resources Defense Council, Inc.* is the leading court case in this area. That 1978 case arose after the Atomic Energy Commission, a predecessor of the Nuclear Regulatory Commission, granted nuclear power plant licenses to two nuclear facilities over the objections of environmental groups. One group, the Natural Resources Defense Council, filed suit. The lower courts reversed the agency's decision because the judges were convinced that the agency had not weighed the relevant factors appropriately.[24]

In a stinging rebuke to the lower courts, the U.S. Supreme Court appeared to back away from a hard look review. Writing for the majority, Justice William Rehnquist argued that a court need not delve into the substance of an issue as long as the agency fulfilled the requirements of the APA as well as the environmental statute, if any, in question. In Rehnquist's view, "The Court of Appeals has unjustifiably intruded into the administrative process" by adding requirements to the APA. "Time may prove wrong the decision to develop nuclear energy," Rehnquist conceded, "but it is Congress or the States, within their appropriate agencies, which must eventually make that judgment. In the meantime, courts should perform their appointed function." Allowing a court to add procedural requirements to the APA, or any other federal statute, was impermissible.[25]

If *Vermont Yankee* represented a triumph of the soft glance judicial review for procedural requirements, *Chevron v. Natural Resources Defense Council* found the high court ruling in favor of the agency by emphasizing the need for courts to afford great deference to agencies in interpreting statutory requirements. The NRDC challenged the constitutionality of the U.S. Environmental Protection Agency's (EPA's) use of the "bubble" concept, which allowed manufacturing plants to avoid air emissions standards for new sources of pollution by assuming that a hypothetical "bubble" extended over contiguous property, thereby treating the emissions as part of an existing facility without having to apply for a separate air quality permit. The court proposed a linear decision-making process. First, it began with a question: Did Congress directly speak to the issue under consideration in delegating authority to the agency? If not—that is, if the statute was silent, vague, or ambiguous on the issue—then the agency would be deemed the appropriate authority for implementing a standard it developed in line with the legislative grant of authority. The agency's implementation plan need only be "reasonable," as judged by whether it had exceeded its delegated authority "arbitrarily and capriciously." If the agency had simply imposed its own interpretation where Congress failed to provide guidance, the agency had acted reasonably. Because Congress mentioned nothing about a "bubble" concept in the statute but also failed to provide guidance on the definition of a "modified" versus a "new" source of air pollution, EPA could develop the "bubble" concept in the absence of more definitive congressional direction. The case has been interpreted as the U.S. Supreme Court's general intention to defer to agencies in the rulemaking process.[26]

Following *Vermont Yankee* and *Chevron*, when federal judges intervene into substantive matters for which they have little or no expertise, they undermine the *raison d'être* for relying on administrative agencies in the first place. Public administrators, at least career civil servants who are not political appointees, are supposed to be subject matter experts. The reason they were hired was to bring their superior skills and deep understanding of substantive matters to bear on crucial issues within the agency's purview. Judges who take a hard look at an expert's decisions and impose requirements that may not be relevant—in fact, that may be harmful—will not improve the decision-making process, or so goes the argument. They will merely stymie the efforts of technical experts to implement regulations in the most efficacious manner possible.

It is difficult to reconcile the hard look and soft glance concepts in administrative law. Perhaps the best that can be said is that courts do not hesitate to delve into the reasons that administrators take action. If they are hauled into court and can demonstrate good faith and reasonable documentation for their actions, administrators' decisions will be afforded great weight. Only in cases where they failed to develop an adequate administrative record, acted in an arbitrary and capricious manner, or ignored a clear and specific legislative mandate will agencies find their decisions rejected or modified.[27]

As for remedies after judicial review is granted and a plaintiff is successful, much depends on the statute in question. Under the Federal Tort Claims Act, for example, recovery is prohibited if an administrator was exercising discretion allowed by law. Under the Equal Access to Justice Act, private parties can recover attorney fees if the government's position was not substantially justified. In environmental cases, the Freedom of Information Act (FOIA) is especially useful because it allows anyone to access information obtained, generated, and held by government unless it involves one of nine exceptions: (1) national security; (2) internal agency rules and procedures; (3) a statutory exemption; (4) trade secrets; (5) intra-agency and interagency memoranda; (6) privacy protection; (7) law enforcement purposes; (8) records of financial institutions; or (9) records of oil explorations.[28]

Two other statutes have proven to be valuable. The Federal Advisory Committee Act provides public access to technical advisory board information, including *Federal Register* notices with open access to the public. Similarly, the Government in the Sunshine Act requires that multi-member commission meetings must be publicly announced at least a week in advance. The act does not apply, however, to agencies headed by a single secretary or administrator, such as the U.S. Environmental Protection Agency.[29]

KEY ENVIRONMENTAL STATUTES

As environmental issues moved to the forefront of the American consciousness during the 1960s and 1970s, supporters recognized that common law standards and administrative processes under the APA were effective in protecting natural resources, but only in a piecemeal fashion. To ensure that environmental law provided a systematic approach, federal statutes were necessary. The turning point came during the early years of the Nixon administration.

One of the earliest of the new federal laws, the National Environmental Policy Act of 1970 (NEPA), was designed to emphasize environmental considerations when federal agencies engaged in physical operations. Section 102(2)(C), for example, required a federal agency to provide a "detailed statement" when the agency sought to undertake "a major federal action significantly affecting the quality of the human environment." The detailed statement, formally known as an "environmental impact statement" (EIS), must set forth the proposed federal action, identify the expected environmental impacts, and outline the costs and benefits of all reasonable alternatives. Unlike later environmental laws, which addressed substantive issues such as specific air emissions or water quality standards, NEPA was developed as an informational statute, not a regulatory scheme. NEPA ensures that an agency prepares an EIS, but the existence of an EIS does not forestall agency action, even in cases where the natural environment is harmed or another option would result in lesser damage.[30]

As part of the effort to highlight the importance of environmental concerns, NEPA created the Council on Environmental Quality (CEQ) to advise the president of the United States on environmental activities undertaken by federal executive branch agencies. Housed within the executive office of the president, the CEQ assumed responsibility for implementing NEPA as well as resolving disputes between EPA and federal agencies concerning the adequacy of an EIS submission. NEPA required the CEQ to prepare an annual report summarizing the state of environmental conditions in the United States.[31]

NEPA has been criticized in some quarters as a paper tiger, a statute that requires public administrators to jump through innumerable legal hoops without necessarily protecting natural resources. Preparing an EIS can be costly and time consuming, but agencies need not select an option that enhances environmental quality even after undergoing a rigorous analysis of the consequences of each course of action. Moreover, NEPA contains numerous exemptions. Under certain circumstances, an agency can prepare an environmental assessment (EA), a shortened version of an EIS, to determine whether an EIS should be completed. Using the EA as its basis, the EPA may reach a finding of no significant impact (FONSI), muting the statute's practical effect.[32]

Supporters admit that NEPA is not an ideal law, but they contend that it is preferable to having no law at all. By forcing federal agencies to incorporate environmental concerns into decision-making, public administrators must thoroughly consider a range of options they might otherwise have ignored. In addition, decision-makers must prepare a comprehensive administrative record, especially when developing an EIS. The record can serve as the basis for a lawsuit in situations where the agency acted in an arbitrary and capricious manner.[33]

NEPA was the first in a long line of federal environmental statutes enacted throughout the 1970s and 1980s. The Clean Air Act (CAA), the Clean Water Act (CWA), the Toxic Substances Control Act (TSCA), the Resource Conservation & Recovery Act (RCRA), and the Comprehensive Environmental Response, Compensation, and Liability Act (CERCLA, or Superfund) became part of a series of legal protections for the nation's natural resources. Activists hailed these far-reaching federal laws as important, although by no means comprehensive, steps in protecting and preserving the American landscape. Predictably, business leaders have argued that many environmental laws and regulations are overly complicated, needlessly costly, and do little, if anything, to protect the natural environment. The debate between proponents of increased environmental regulation and free-market capitalists has characterized much of federal environmental law since the 1970s.[34]

The CAA is one of the most recognizable and far-reaching environmental statutes of the era. It dates back to 1955, when Congress enacted the Air Pollution Control Act. Eight years later, legislators supplanted the earlier law with the first Clean Air Act. During the ensuing years, Congress passed a series of clean air measures, including the Motor Vehicle Pollution Control Act, the Air Quality Act of 1967, as well as CAA modifications in 1970, 1977, and 1990.[35]

The 1970 version of the CAA promulgated National Ambient Air Quality Standards (NAAQS) for six criteria pollutants: particulate matter, primarily from coal processes; sulfur dioxide from fossil-fuel combustion; ozone emissions from smog, automobile exhaust, and chemical facilities; nitrogen oxides from smog and fossil-fuel combustion; carbon monoxide; and hydrogens. Congress eventually added lead to the list. "Criteria pollutants" are chemicals that are not toxic when found in small concentrations in the atmosphere, but these precursors to pollution can damage air quality when they are combined with other chemicals. To ensure that efficient enforcement occurred, the 1970 CAA required states to prepare and submit state implementation plans (SIPs) to the EPA for review and approval. In the absence of an approved SIP, EPA could substitute a federal implementation plan (FIP) for a SIP.[36]

The 1970 CAA established New Source Performance Standards (NSPS) to control emissions for new or modified sources of air pollution. Any industry subject to NSPS requirements was required to use Best Available Control Technology (BACT), a stringent environmental standard. The statute developed National Emissions Standards for Hazardous Air Pollutants (NESHAPS), a requirement that went beyond NAAQS criteria pollutants to regulate less-widely emitted, but highly dangerous, toxic air pollutants. New federal motor vehicle emissions limitations required automobile manufacturers to reduce emissions of hydrocarbon and carbon monoxide as well as nitrogen oxide.[37]

Seven years later, Congress revised the CAA. One major change was to establish a standard known as Reasonably Available Control Technology (RACT) for major existing stationary sources of pollution. The amendments overlaid additional geographic-specific standards on top of the NSPS technology standards for new sources of pollution. In places deemed "non-attainment" areas, a "new source review" was required to determine whether new or modified major sources of pollution were using the Lowest Available Emission Rate (LAER). For "attainment" areas, Prevention of Significant Deterioration (PSD) plans were required to ensure that these places did not backslide.[38]

The last major CAA revision occurred in 1990, when Congress distinguished between primary NAAQS standards to protect public health and secondary standards to protect public welfare. Moreover, the law included more specificity concerning the geography of pollution. Five categories of non-attainment areas—marginal, moderate, serious, severe, and extreme—differentiated among states and regions where air pollution was a significant problem and where it was of lesser concern. The law established target dates for cleaning up each area. As for specific industries, a polluter designated as a "major source" of stationary emissions was required to obtain a permit under Title V of the amendments.[39]

The CAA remains one of the most comprehensive and controversial federal environmental statutes in American history. Activists generally applaud the effort to impose geographical requirements and stringent federal standards on regions where dirty air proliferates. Yet those same activists bitterly criticized the EPA's constantly shifting timetable. Each time the agency sets a deadline for air pollution cleanup, the date slips. Manufacturing industries, in the meantime, object to the cost of compliance and the plethora of rules and regulations imposed on private businesses. They argue that strict environmental laws and regulations impede American competitiveness in a global marketplace and do not necessarily improve overall environmental quality. Virtually everyone agrees that sound science should form the basis for federal environmental law, but few participants in the debate can agree on the appropriate sources and standards for the science.

The 1972 amendments to the Federal Water Pollution Control Act, commonly known as the Clean Water Act (CWA), became another controversial environmental statute. When Congress passed the law, the goal was to eliminate pollutants discharged into navigable waters by 1985. Thirteen years seemed to be an adequate timetable in 1972, but the ensuing years demonstrated the almost impossible task of tracking down and cleaning up water pollution. One section of the statute provided for federal financial assistance in constructing publicly owned waste treatment works (POTW). Before 1977, states relied on state and local systems that sometimes failed to protect public health. The CWA authors realized that this piecemeal approach resulted in variations in water quality throughout the country, and such a patchwork series of regulations could not be allowed to stand. The benefit of a federal statute was that a uniform, consistent national regulatory scheme would ensure an acceptable level of water quality across all 50 states.[40]

The authors wisely chose to differentiate among and between biological and chemical sources of pollution. Accordingly, the statute required different levels of treatments for POTWs, combined commercial and residential sewer systems, and industrial facilities. It also addressed a particularly troublesome problem, namely non-point-source pollution, defined as everything not characterized as point-source pollution, including farms, construction sites, mining operations, and urban runoff, as well as oil and hazardous waste spills. If authorities cannot locate the specific point where pollution enters waterways, cleaning up contaminants is especially tricky.[41]

The National Pollutant Discharge Elimination System (NPDES) was the defining feature of the CWA. Any sources that intended to discharge effluents into navigable waters were required to apply for an NPDES permit or face legal consequences. To obtain stormwater permits, POTWs were instructed to apply to EPA and provide detailed information such as topographic maps showing drainage areas, places where chemicals were used, and waste material storage and sampling data for effluent guidelines and permits.[42]

In addition to cleaning up air and water pollution, Congress enacted a series of sweeping environmental statutes during the 1970s that addressed hazardous materials before they were manufactured, while they were in common use, and as they were sent out for disposal. The

Toxic Substances Control Act (TSCA), for example, was drafted in 1976 to govern the manufacture, processing, distribution, use, and disposal of chemical substances in the United States. In balancing the needs of industry and consumers, TSCA adopted a middle approach. The act set forth a series of steps necessary to determine whether an industry could manufacture or market a specific chemical. According to the original statute, chemicals of concern would be identified. A dose response assessment would determine the magnitude of exposure and an exposure assessment would provide data on the nature and extent of human contact with the chemical. As part of the process, a risk characterization would describe the nature, magnitude, and uncertainty of the risks involved. A comprehensive risk assessment would combine all of these factors into a detailed overview of a chemical of concern. Section 8 of the act authorized EPA to obtain and disseminate information needed to set priorities and perform risk assessments, as appropriate.[43]

One of the most controversial features of the 1976 statute was the inclusion of economic factors in the analysis. Moreover, the law allowed for future technological innovations that might quantify risk and reduce "unreasonable" risk to the public. Section 5 contained a premanufacture review provision requiring a chemical manufacturer to provide a 90-day notice to EPA before the company could produce a new chemical or use an existing chemical in a "significantly new way." The agency was granted broad authority to determine whether the chemical could be manufactured or sold in the United States.[44] If, in the opinion of agency officials, a specific chemical was "imminently hazardous," the EPA administrator could prohibit the manufacture of the offending substance. A manufacturer who disagreed with the administrator's findings could seek administrative review. Under the APA, an aggrieved party that had exhausted its administrative remedies could seek judicial review.[45]

Decades after President Ford signed the original legislation, environmentalists and chemical manufacturers alike argued that TSCA should be updated. The former group contended that EPA required additional regulatory authority to establish a risk evaluation process, especially for the large number of new chemicals in use since 1976, while private sector chemical representatives desired a strong preemption measure to prevent states from enacting "little TSCAs" that created multiple, sometimes confusing or conflicting regulations. New Jersey Senator Frank R.

Lautenberg attempted to shepherd compromise legislation through the Senate, but he died before he could craft a bill with enough votes to pass both houses of Congress. Two years later, in 2015, Congressman John Shimkus (R-Ill.) and Senator Tom Udall (D-N.M.) championed a measure, HR 2576, officially known as the "Frank R. Lautenberg Chemical Safety for the 21st Century Act." With strong bipartisan support, the bill cleared both congressional chambers in 2016. President Barack Obama signed the updated TSCA measure into law on June 22, 2016. The bill appeared to be a genuinely popular compromise, with almost all stakeholders expressing their support for the new law.[46]

Aside from TSCA, environmental statutes from the 1970s focused on problems that had festered for years but had not yet received adequate federal legislative attention. One pressing need involved the lack of a well-functioning infrastructure for disposing of discarded materials, generally known as solid waste. State and local governments assumed responsibility for solid waste disposal before 1965. Congress enacted the Solid Waste Disposal Act of 1965 to address this need, providing grants to states and local governments to develop efficient waste disposal techniques. Five years later, the Resource Recovery Act continued this work. By 1976, Congress was prepared to overhaul the waste management system. The result was the Resource Conservation & Recovery Act (RCRA) creating a system to track hazardous waste "from the cradle to the grave." In 1984, Congress amended the statute to phase out land disposal of toxic chemicals and encourage industry to develop new technologies for detoxifying hazardous waste. RCRA included provisions handling underground storage tanks (USTs) and medical waste.[47]

RCRA adopted an expansive definition of "solid waste." Under § 1004(27), waste could be defined as "solid" regardless of whether it was a liquid or a gas. Some types of discarded material—for example, domestic sewage, industrial wastewater charges, irrigation return flows, mining wastes not removed from the ground, nuclear material, household waste, fertilizer used in agriculture, and certain high-volume wastes—were specifically excluded so that EPA could handle those materials separately.[48]

RCRA also defined the types of persons regulated by the statute. A "generator," for example, would be any person or entity that produced hazardous waste or caused a waste to be subject to regulation. Any entity that met this definition was required to obtain an identification number, appropriately store or package the waste, prepare a manifest, maintain records of manifests and reports, and dispose of waste at a permitted facility. Recognizing that some entities generated a miniscule amount of waste, the law held a "small-quantity generator" to a different standard than a large-quantity generator. Finally, the law established procedures for transporting waste to a licensed treatment, storage, and disposal (TSD) facility. Most notably, the 1984 RCRA amendments specified that landfills are designed to handle solid waste while hazardous waste must be treated before it can be disposed of on land.[49]

RCRA required TSD facility operators to submit a permit application describing its processes and the types of hazardous waste to be stored there. As part of the application, the TSD operators were directed to supply analytical information regarding relevant geological data, personnel training plans, emergency procedures and contingency plans, groundwater monitoring plans, closure plans, and a detailed accounting of financial responsibility. At EPA's discretion, the public could be invited to participate in a hearing process to determine whether the permit application should be approved. TSD facility operators were required to request a modification if they materially altered their operations, discovered new information about their processes, experienced problems complying with the permit terms, or found themselves subject to new regulatory requirements.[50]

A regulatory statute is only as effective as its enforcement mechanism. RCRA authorized EPA to conduct a facility assessment if the agency came to believe that a reasonable likelihood of a hazardous waste release existed. In such situations, EPA personnel could require the owner or operator of a TSD facility to engage in monitoring, testing, analysis, and reporting, as necessary, to ensure the safety and health of the public were not compromised.

Aside from EPA action, Section 7002 of the 1976 statute authorized any person to commence a civil action alleging a violation of any requirement or prohibition under RCRA. If the EPA administrator failed to perform a nondiscretionary function, a citizen could file a lawsuit compelling the administrator to enforce the statutory provisions. Citizen-plaintiffs were required to provide 60-days' notice of the intent to litigate or 90-days' notice for an "imminent hazard" action. If the citizen-plaintiff prevailed in the lawsuit, the citizen was entitled to recover litigation costs, reasonable attorney fees, expert witness fees, and civil penalties of up to $25,000 a day as well as an injunction and/or permit revocation. A citizen suit could not be pursued to enjoin the siting or licensure of a new TSD facility nor could it be used to sue EPA if the agency was diligently pursuing an enforcement action. In addition, citizen suits were prohibited if a state agency was diligently engaged in an enforcement action. Violations could not be wholly in the past.[51]

The final major statute enacted during the heyday of environmentalism during the 1970s and 1980s became one of the most controversial, and far-reaching, federal laws in this area. The Comprehensive Environmental Response, Compensation, and Liability Act (CERCLA), first enacted in 1980, was designed to fill in the gaps left by RCRA. RCRA's regulatory scheme applied to solid and hazardous waste prior to a release of material into the environment. CERCLA, by contrast, regulated hazardous substances after they were released.[52]

CERCLA resulted from an infamous set of circumstances involving the release of hazardous materials in a residential neighborhood. From 1942 through 1953, Hooker Chemicals, a chemical and plastics manufacturing facility, buried 21,900 tons of industrial wastes on a 16-acre site in Niagara Falls, New York. Following the customs of the day, Hooker covered the waste with a thin layer of clay. In 1953, the company sold the land to the Niagara Falls Board of Education for $1.00. Evidence indicates that Hooker never concealed the presence of waste material on the land. In fact, the deed explicitly revealed the existence of the waste and contained a liability limitation clause protecting Hooker from subsequent lawsuits. Years passed. By 1970, the land had been subdivided for residential use, and a housing development as well as neighborhood schools populated the area. Eventually, heavy rainstorms washed away the clay barrier, exposing toxic chemicals that seeped into household basements. Alarmed residents, many of whom did not know about the original uses of the land, complained about foul odors. The local newspaper, the *Niagara Falls Gazette*, investigated the complaints for two years. *Gazette* staff writer Michael Brown broke the story of potential health problems in the neighborhood known as Love Canal beginning in July 1978. As the story developed, it became clear that Love Canal homeowners had "suffered higher than normal rates of miscarriages, birth defects, epilepsy, and liver ailments." Responding to this new information, the New York Commissioner of Health declared a public emergency. In 1979, the commissioner ordered all families with children less than two years of age as well as pregnant women to relocate. The sordid tale attracted national headlines. "Love Canal" became a battle cry among environmentalists and highlighted the need for a comprehensive federal regulatory program to ensure that citizens would be kept safe from the risks of improperly discarded toxic chemicals.[53]

Congress eventually responded by enacting CERCLA to fill the gaps in RCRA and other federal environmental laws and regulations. One readily apparent problem was that many contaminated sites have been long abandoned, their original owners missing, dead, no longer in business, or otherwise unavailable. To provide relief for aggrieved parties, CERCLA established a fund for financing a cleanup and included a liberal mechanism for imposing liability on "potentially responsible parties" (PRPs). In an ingenious and yet controversial provision, CERCLA authorized the federal government to clean up a contaminated site using federal monies from the "Superfund" and sue PRPs for reimbursement to replenish the fund as well as provide for permanent remediation. If the agency chose not to handle the cleanup directly, it could issue administrative orders requiring the PRPs to clean up the sites with federal oversight.[54]

CERCLA was a revolutionary environmental statute. While the CAA, CWA, and RCRA regulated people, CERCLA regulated places. This shift in emphasis was necessary because the statute was aimed at specific parcels of land and, in many cases, it was unclear at the outset which people or entities had contaminated the site. CERCLA was a comprehensive, multi-media law governing land, water, and air. It contained no private rights of action. And in perhaps one of the most far-reaching of the law's provisions, CERCLA modified the common law doctrine of negligence by imposing liability without requiring proof of negligence. In essence, it imposed strict liability on PRPs.[55]

The statute contained four major programmatic elements. The first element identified EPA as the central authority for receiving reports concerning a release of hazardous substances. Any person in charge of a "facility" who knows of the "release" of a reportable quantity of a hazardous substance must notify EPA's National Response Center, a federally administered information clearinghouse. Failure to make the required notification can result in a fine of up to $10,000 or a sentence of up to a year in prison. The National Response Center, in turn, must notify the governor of an affected state as well as any appropriate government agencies. EPA compiles a list of problems sites throughout the country and can enter the property, conduct inspections, and take appropriate soil, air, and water samples. The agency possesses eminent domain authority.[56]

CERCLA authorizes federal officials to clean up sites where hazardous substances have been released through short-term removal or emergency response activities as well as long-term remedial activities. The 1980 version of the law allowed only $2 million of federal funds to be expended on short-term removal or emergency response activity prior to listing the site on the Superfund National Priorities List (NPL), a ranking of sites that require additional cleanup activities. All federal activities are governed by the National Contingency Plan (NCP), a set of regulations that specify the steps in cleaning up contaminated sites. EPA created the National Hazardous Substance Response Plan requiring cost-effective measures to be used, if feasible. All remedial actions must include a site investigation and analysis of remedial alternatives, compliance with NCP regulations on developing, screening, analyzing, and selecting cleanup methods, and a consideration of cost at every step in the process.[57]

A preliminary assessment must be performed to determine environmental and health risks and priorities among waste sites. EPA performs an analysis of the potential risks of each site to develop a numerical score on the Hazard Ranking System (HRS), a scale that evaluates toxicity, quantity, and waste concentrations. Based on the score, EPA assigns personnel and resources to coordinate cleanup activities. Following the NPL designation, EPA officials conduct a Remedial Investigation (RI) to determine the contamination level of a particular site. A Feasibility Study (FS) allows the agency to create a menu of remediation options. EPA issues a Record of Decision (ROD) to solicit public comments before initiating long-term cleanup activities. An EPA database, CERCLIS (Comprehensive Environmental Response, Compensation and Liability Information System), permits the agency to store information on the status of cleanup efforts, significant milestones, and the amount of liquid and solid media treated at NPL sites.[58]

The Agency for Toxic Substances and Disease Registry (ATSDR) partners with EPA throughout the CERCLA process. For its part, ATSDR establishes and maintains a national registry of serious diseases and illnesses of persons exposed to toxic substances and studies the health effects of exposure. The agency creates a list of areas closed to the public or restricted owing to toxic substance contamination.[59]

Arguably, the most recognizable of the statute's original provisions was the "Superfund," a financial arrangement developed to provide monies for cleaning up orphan sites if the original owner or operator could not be found or held accountable. The 1980 version of CERCLA specified that the trust fund would be established by sales taxes on chemical companies, although those provisions eventually were amended. Cost considerations, as always, became a major focus of the statute. It was almost immediately apparent that the cost of cleaning up contamination at most locations exceeded the amount of money available from the trust fund. CERCLA anticipated that Superfund would provide initial financing until PRPs could be identified and held accountable, but the fund was never intended to be a mechanism for the federal government to assume financial responsibility for cleaning up contaminated sites.[60]

The final program element outlined a mechanism for imposing liability on private parties. One of the difficulties with traditional common law standards for environmental contamination was that proving a causal connection between a hazardous waste spill and the responsible party presented a daunting challenge. In many instances of environmental contamination, the party directly responsible for the release was missing, insolvent, or unknown. To overcome this seemingly insurmountable evidentiary impediment, CERCLA established joint-and-several liability for the restitution of response costs incurred by the government or a private party. This provision, found in § 107, was among the most controversial sections of the original statute.[61]

By 1986, Congress resolved to amend the statute and improve upon its initial elements. The amendments revised statutory standards, strengthened the settlement and enforcement provisions, and specified a larger revenue base for financing and replenishing the trust fund. The Superfund Amendments and Reauthorization Act of 1986 (SARA) required that remediation must be "protective of human health and the environment" as well as cost-effective and afford "permanent solutions and alternative treatment technologies to the maximum extent practicable." These technology-forcing provisions placed the burden on private companies to seek out improved methods for site remediation or risk additional agency intervention.[62]

The amendments allowed for contribution rights among PRPs and established settlement rules for *de minimis* parties. Several provisions mixed EPA and private PRP funding to improve financial flexibility. Especially after 1986, a PRP had an incentive to join together with other PRPs to establish a working group dedicated to allocating costs and responsibilities lest a single recalcitrant party bear the full financial burden.[63]

With the passage of CERCLA, the federal environmental regulatory scheme was more or less complete. Congress eventually enacted a series of smaller environmental statutes to address "niche" problems, but they were limited in scope compared with NEPA, CAA, CWA, TSCA, RCRA, and CERCLA. Thus, the Federal Insecticide, Fungicide and Rodenticide Act (FIFRA) set forth legal requirements to register, classify, label, and distribute pesticides.[64] The Endangered Species Act (ESA) of 1973 protected organisms deemed too valuable to lose through extinction.[65]

Wetlands regulation was another area where the federal government stepped in to provide leadership. In 1899, Congress passed the Rivers and Harbors Act empowering the Army Corps of Engineers to regulate construction activities involving dredging, filling, or obstructing navigable waters. NEPA eventually expanded the Corps' authority to determine whether a federal agency could be permitted to undertake an action that might negatively affect wetlands. Section 404 of the CWA was interpreted as the key provision for protecting wetlands from "creeping" encroachment during the late twentieth and early twenty-first centuries. The section detailed the procedure for applicants to obtain permits for discharging dredged or fill material into navigable waters, an action that generally results in a loss of wetlands.[66]

By the end of the twentieth century, it was clear that environmental protection was no longer exclusively the province of state laws and common law standards. The federal government, acting through administrative agencies such as the EPA, was the lead actor in ensuring the protection and preservation of the nation's natural resources. The rise of the administrative state and the role of the federal government in establishing environmental laws have been, and continue to be, important chapters in the story of American environmentalism, but they are only part of the narrative. To understand twenty-first-century notions of sustainability, it is necessary to step outside of the institutional structure of American government and examine the role of nongovernmental actors. In the next section, this book will examine the history of the American environmental movement as well as the role of interest groups in advancing an environmental agenda.

NOTES

1. Alexis Applegate, "Common Law Preclusion and Environmental Citizen Suits: Are Citizen Groups Losing Their Standing?" *Boston College Environmental Affairs Law Review* 39 Supplement (2012): 1–14; Michael C. Blumm and Andrea Lang, "Shared Sovereignty: The Role of Expert Agencies in Environmental Law," *Ecology Law Quarterly* 42 (2015): 609–50.

2. Jonathan H. Adler and Andrew P. Morriss, "Common Law Environmental Protection," *Virginia Law Review* 101 (September 2015): 575–82; Henry N. Butler, "A Defense of Common Law Environmentalism: The Discovery of Better Environmental Policy," *Case Western Law Review* 58 (Spring 2008): 705–52; Bruce Yandle, "The Common Law and the Environment in the Courts: Discussion of Code Law and Common Law," *Case Western Reserve Law Review* 58 (Spring 2008): 647–61.

3. *Martin v. Reynolds Metal Company*, 221 Or. 86, 342 P.2d 790 (1959); *cert. denied* 362 U.S. 918 (1960).

4. Henry van Egteren and R. Todd Smith, "Environmental Regulations under Simple Negligence or Strict Liability," *Environmental & Resource Economics* 21 (April 2002): 369–96; Steven Ferrey, *Environmental Law: Examples and Explanations* (New York: Aspen Law & Business, 1997): 20.

5. Ferrey, *Environmental Law: Examples and Explanations*, 20–21. See also *Rylands v. Fletcher*, 3 H.C. 774, 159 Eng. Rep. 737 (1865).

6. *Illinois Central Railroad v. Illinois*, 146 U.S. 387 (1892). See also Alexandra B. Klass, "The Public Trust Doctrine in the Shadow of State Environmental Rights Laws: A Case Study," *Environmental Law* 45 (April 2015): 431–62.

7. *National Audubon Society v. Superior Court*, 33 Cal.3d 419, 452 (1983).

8. Daniel A. Farber and Anne Joseph O'Connell, "The Lost World of Administrative Law," *Texas Law Review* 92 (April 2014): 1137–89; Walter

Gellhorn, "The Administrative Procedure Act: The Beginnings," *Virginia Law Review* 72 (March 1986): 219–33.

9. Michael Asimow, "Five Models of Administrative Adjudication," *American Journal of Comparative Law* 63 (Winter 2015): 3–31.

10. Stephen F. Williams, "'Hybrid Rulemaking' under the Administrative Procedure Act: A Legal and Empirical Analysis," *The University of Chicago Law Review* 42 (Spring 1975): 401–56.

11. Elizabeth Fisher, Pasky Pascual, and Wendy Wagner, "Rethinking Judicial Review of Expert Agencies," *Texas Law Review* 93 (June 2015): 1681–1721; Alexander H. Türk, "Oversight of Administrative Rulemaking: Judicial Review," *European Law Journal* 19 (January 2013): 126–42.

12. *Sierra Club v. Morton*, 405 U.S. 727 (1972); *United States v. Students Challenging Regulatory Agency Procedures (SCRAP)*, 412 U.S. 669 (1973).

13. *Duke Power Company v. Carolina Environmental Study Group, Inc.*, 438 U.S. 59 (1978).

14. *Lujan v. National Wildlife Federation*, 497 U.S. 871 (1990); *Lujan v. Defenders of Wildlife*, 504 U.S. 555 (1992).

15. *Association of Data Processing Service Organizations v. Camp*, 397 U.S. 150 (1970).

16. Kevin A. Cole, "Standing of Third Parties to Challenge Administrative Agency Actions," *California Law Review* 76 (October 1988): 1061–1107; Ferrey, *Environmental Law: Examples and Explanations*, 39–44; Dru Stevenson and Sonny Eckhart, "Standing as Channeling in the Administrative Age," *Boston College Law Review* 53 (September 2012): 1357–1416; Christopher Warshaw and Gregory E. Wannier, "Business as Usual? Analyzing the Development of Environmental Standing Doctrine since 1976," *Harvard Law & Policy Review* 5 (July 2011): 289–322.

17. *Port of Boston Marine Terminal v. Rederiaktiebolaget Transatlantic*, 400 U.S. 62 (1970).

18. *Abbot Laboratories v. Gardner*, 387 U.S. 136 (1967).

19. Ferrey, *Environmental Law: Examples and Explanations*, 43–44; Gillian Metzger, "The Constitutional Duty to Supervise," *Yale Law Journal* 124 (April 2015): 1919–21.

20. Theodore J. St. Antoine, "The NLRB, the Courts, the Administrative Procedure Act, and *Chevron*: Now and Then," *Emory Law Journal* 64 Supplement (2015): 1529–52; Emerson H. Tiller, "Controlling Policy by Controlling Process: Judicial Influence on Regulatory Decision Making," *Journal of Law, Economics, and Organization* 14 (April 1998): 114–35.

21. Ferrey, *Environmental Law: Examples and Explanations*, 46; Christina Larsen, "Is the Glass Half Empty or Half Full? Challenging Incomplete Agency Action under Section 706(1) of the Administrative Procedure Act," *Public Land & Resources Law Review* 25 (April 2004): 113–30; St. Antoine,

"The NLRB, the Courts, the Administrative Procedure Act, and *Chevron*: Now and Then,"1529–52.

22. Ferrey, *Environmental Law: Examples and Explanations*, 46; Adrian Vermeule, "Deference and Due Process," *Harvard Law Review* 129 (May 2016): 1917–18.

23. *Citizens to Preserve Overton Park, Inc. v. Volpe*, 401 U.S. 402 (1971).

24. *Vermont Yankee Nuclear Power Corporation v. Natural Resources Defense Council, Inc.*, 435 U.S. 519 (1978).

25. *Vermont Yankee Nuclear Power Corporation v. Natural Resources Defense Council, Inc.*, 435 U.S. 519, 558.

26. *Chevron v. Natural Resources Defense Council*, 467 U.S. 837 (1984).

27. "Judicial Review of Agency Change," *Harvard Law Review* 127 (May 2014): 2070–91; "Notes: Rationalizing Hard Look Review After the Fact," *Harvard Law Review* 122 (May 2009): 1909–30.

28. Jonathan R. Bruno, "Note: Immunity for 'Discretionary' Functions: A Proposal to Amend the Federal Tort Claims Act," *Harvard Journal on Legislation* 49 (July 2012): 411–50; Margaret B. Kwoka, "FOIA, Inc.," *Duke Law Journal* 65 (2016): 1361–1437; William R. Sherman, "The Deliberation Paradox and Administrative Law," *Brigham Young University Law Review* 2015 (January 2016): 424–27.

29. Ferrey, *Environmental Law: Examples and Explanations*, 54–57; Sherman, "The Deliberation Paradox and Administrative Law," 414; Daniel E. Walters, "Note: The Justiciability of Fair Balance under the Federal Advisory Committee Act: Toward a Deliberative Process Approach," *Michigan Law Review* 110 (February 2012): 677–708.

30. The National Environmental Policy Act (NEPA) of 1969, 42 U.S.C. § 4321 *et seq.* (1969), especially § 102(2)(C), 42 U.S.C. § 4332(2)(C); § 202, 42 U.S.C. § 4341. See also Jamison E. Colburn, "Administering the National Environmental Policy Act," *Environmental Law Reporter: News & Analysis* 45 (April 2015): 10287–323.

31. Susan J. Buck, *Understanding Environmental Administration and Law*, 2nd edition, (Washington, D.C. and Covelo, Calif.: Island Press, 1996), 17–18; Colburn, "Administering the National Environmental Policy Act," 10287–323; Ferrey, *Environmental Law: Examples and Explanations*, 59–108; Olga L. Moya and Andrew L. Fono, *Federal Environmental Law: The User's Guide* (St. Paul, MN: West, 1997), 55–58.

32. 40 CFR § 1503.13. See also Charles H. Eccleston, "Does NEPA Suffer from the Pike Syndrome?" *Environmental Practice* 4 (March 2002): 8–9; Bradley C. Karkkainen, "Toward a Smarter NEPA: Monitoring and Managing Government's Environmental Performance," *Columbia Law Review* 102 (May 2002): 903–72; Sonja Klopf, Nada Wolff Culver, and Pete Morton, "A Road Map to a Better NEPA: Why Environmental Risk Assessments Should Be Used to Analyze the Environmental Consequences of Complex Federal Actions,"

Sustainable Development Law & Policy 8 (Fall 2007): 38–43, 84–85; Moya and Fono, *Federal Environmental Law*, 58. See also Lynton K. Caldwell, *Science and the National Environmental Policy Act: Redirecting Policy through Procedural Reform* (Tuscaloosa: University of Alabama Press, 1982).

33. Harvey Black, "Imperfect Protection: NEPA at 35 Years," *Environmental Health Perspectives* 112 (April 2004): A292–95; Roger C. Crampton and Richard K. Berg, "On Leading a Horse to Water: NEPA and the Federal Bureaucracy," *Michigan Law Review* 71 (January 1973): 511–36; United States House of Representatives, Committee on Resources, One Hundred Ninth Congress, First Session, Oversight Hearing, Thursday, November 17, 2005, *NEPA: Lessons Learned and Next Steps* (Washington, D.C.: U.S. Government Printing Office, 2006).

34. Bruce A. Ackerman and Richard B. Stewart, "Reforming Environmental Law: The Democratic Case for Market Incentives," *Columbia Journal of Environmental Law* 13 (1987): 171–99; Morris Altman, "When Green Isn't Mean: Economic Theory and the Heuristics of the Impact of Environmental Regulations on Competitiveness and Opportunity Cost," *Ecological Economics* 36 (January 2001): 31–44; Michael A. Berry and Dennis A. Rondinelli, "Proactive Corporate Environmental Management: A New Industrial Revolution," *Academy of Management Executive* 12 (May 1998): 38–50.

35. John Bachmann, "Will the Circle Be Broken? A History of the U.S. National Ambient Air Quality Standards," *Journal of the Air & Waste Management Association* 57 (June 2007): 662–63; Jonathan Davidson and Joseph M. Norbeck, *An Interpretive History of the Clean Air Act: Scientific and Policy Perspectives* (Waltham, Mass.: Elsevier, 2012), 7–10; "Evolution of Present Federal Law," *Congressional Digest* 49 (August/September 1970): 196–97.

36. The Clean Air Act (CAA) of 1970, 42 U.S.C. § 7401 *et seq.* (1970), especially § 109, 42 U.S.C. § 7409. See also Bachmann, "Will the Circle Be Broken?" 653–54; Davidson and Norbeck, *An Interpretive History of the Clean Air Act*, 5; Ferrey, *Environmental Law: Examples and Explanations*, 141–44.

37. §§ 111–12, 42 U.S.C. §§ 7411–12. See also Davidson and Norbeck, *An Interpretive History of the Clean Air Act*, 15; Ferrey, *Environmental Law: Examples and Explanations*, 149–50.

38. § 111, 42 U.S.C. § 7411; § 162, 42 U.S.C. § 7472; § 173, 42 U.S.C. § 7503. See also Bachmann, "Will the Circle Be Broken?" 654–60; Ferrey, *Environmental Law: Examples and Explanations*, 155–57; John-Mark Stensvaag, "Preventing Significant Deterioration Under the Clean Air Act: Area Classification, Initial Allocation, and Redesignation," *Environmental Law Reporter: News & Analysis* 41 (January 2011): 10008–23.

39. § 109, 42 U.S.C. § 7409; § 502, *et seq.*, 42 U.S.C. § 7661, *et seq.* See also Jed Anderson, "The Disappearing Distinction," *The Environmental Forum* 29 (December 2012): 30–33; Scott E. Atkinson and T.H. Tietenberg, "Approaches for Reaching Ambient Standards in Non-Attainment Areas:

Financial Burden and Efficiency Considerations," *Land Economics* 60 (May 1984): 148–59; Ferrey, *Environmental Law: Examples and Explanations*, 162–71.

40. The Clean Water Act (CWA) (Federal Water Pollution Control Amendments of 1972), 33 U.S.C. § 1251 *et seq.* (1972). See also Claudia Copeland, *Clean Water Act: A Summary of the Law* (Washington, D.C.: Congressional Research Service, April 23, 2010): 1–2; Jeffrey M. Gaba, "Generally Illegal: NPDES General Permits Under the Clean Water Act," *Harvard Environmental Law Review* 31 (March 2007): 419–20.

41. §§ 101–02, 33 U.S.C. §§ 1251–52. See also Copeland, *Clean Water Act*, 5–7; Gaba, "Generally Illegal," 424–32.

42. § 402, 33 U.S.C. § 1342. See also Gaba, "Generally Illegal," 424–55; Brian P. Gaffney, "A Divided Duty: The EPA's Dilemma under the Endangered Species Act and Clean Water Act Concerning the National Pollutant Discharge Elimination System," *The Review of Litigation* 26 (April 2007): 498–500.

43. The Toxic Substances Control Act (TSCA) of 1976, 15 U.S.C. § 2601 *et seq.* (1976). See also John S. Applegate, "The Perils of Unreasonable Risk: Information, Regulatory Policy, and Toxic Substances Control," *Columbia Law Review* 91 (March 1991): 261–333; Blake A. Biles and Lawrence E. Culleen, "TSCA, Redux," *The Environmental Forum* 27 (January/February 2010): 30; Courtney M. Price and Jennifer M. Smart, "Understanding the Toxic Substances Control Act: The Significance of Reporting and Recordkeeping Requirements," *William & Mary Environmental Law & Policy Review* 16 (1991): 1–29. Walter A. Rosenbaum, *Environmental Politics and Policy*, 4th edition, (Washington, D.C.: Congressional Quarterly Press, 1998): 138–42; "Toxic Substances Control Act Overview: Current Laws and Policies," *Congressional Digest* 89 (October 2010): 226–27.

44. Biles and Culleen, "TSCA, Redux," 30–31; Rosenbaum, *Environmental Politics and Policy*, 138–41; "Toxic Substances Control Act Overview," 226; "TSCA Reform: The Standard of Safety," *Environmental Law Reporter: News & Analysis* 41 (December 2011): 11082–83; William J. Walsh and Michelle M. Skjoldal, "Sustainability is Driving Toxic Chemicals from Products," *Natural Resources & Environment* 25 (Winter 2011): 16–17.

45. §§ 4–7, 15 U.S.C. §§ 2603–06. See also Biles and Culleen, "TSCA, Redux," 30–32; "Toxic Substances Control Act Overview," 227–28.

46. See, for example, Darryl Fears, "EPA Gains Power to Block Harmful Chemicals in Products," *The Washington Post*, June 23, 2016: A3; Donald B. Myers Jr. and Paul A. Locke, "Modernizing U.S. Chemical Laws: How the Application of Twenty-first Century Toxicology Can Help Drive Legal Reform," *New York Environmental Law Journal* 40 (2012): 35–78.

47. The Resource Conservation and Recovery Act (RCRA) of 1976, 42 U.S.C. § 6901 *et seq.* (1976). See also Ferrey, *Environmental Law: Examples and Explanations*, 251–52; Robin R. Jenkins, Elizabeth Kopits, and David

Simpson, "The Evolution of Solid and Hazardous Waste in the United States," *Review of Environmental Economics and Policy* 3 (Winter 2009): 104–20; Moya and Fono, *Federal Environmental Law*, 91–92; Travis Wagner, "Hazardous Waste: Evolution of a National Environmental Problem," *Journal of Policy History* 16 (October 2004): 308–18.

48. § 1004(27), 42 U.S.C. § 6903(27). See also Ferrey, *Environmental Law: Examples and Explanations*, 253–54; Moya and Fono, *Federal Environmental Law*, 95–98; United States Environmental Protection Agency, *RCRA, Superfund & EPCRA Call Center* (Washington, D.C.: U.S. Government Printing Office, Solid Waste and Emergency Response Publication No. EPA530-R-04-010, September 2003), 2.

49. § 3002, 42 U.S.C. § 6922; 40 C.F.R. Part 263. See also Ferrey, *Environmental Law: Examples and Explanations*, 264–66; Moya and Fono, *Federal Environmental Law*, 112–19; United States Environmental Protection Agency, *RCRA, Superfund & EPCRA Call Center*, 3–5.

50. §§ 3004-05, 42 U.S.C. §§ 6924–25. See also Ferrey, *Environmental Law: Examples and Explanations*, 268–72; Moya and Fono, *Federal Environmental Law*, 125–41; "RCRA Questions and Answers Provide Regulatory Insight," *Hazardous Waste Consultant* 30 (2012): 4.1–4.23.

51. § 7002(a), 42 U.S.C. § 6972(a). See also Ferrey, *Environmental Law: Examples and Explanations*, 281–82; Michael F. Hearn, "One Person's Waste is Another Person's Liability: Closing the Liability Loophole in RCRA's Citizen Enforcement Action," *McGeorge Law Review* 42 (April 2011): 471–73; Jason M. Levy, "Conflicting Enforcement Mechanisms under RCRA: The Abstention Battleground Between State Agencies and Citizen Suits," *Ecology Law Quarterly* 39 (2012): 380–82, 403–04; Moya and Fono, *Federal Environmental Law*, 137–41; Christopher Rizzo, "RCRA's 'Imminent and Substantial Endangerment' Citizen Suit Turns 25," *National Resources & Environment* 23 (Fall 2008): 50–51.

52. The Comprehensive Environmental Response, Compensation and Liability Act (CERCLA) of 1980, 42 U.S.C. § 9601 *et seq.* (1980). See also Martin A. McCrory, "Who's on First: CERCLA Cost Recovery, Contribution, and Protection," *American Business Law Journal* 37 (Fall 1999): 4–7; Emilee Mooney Scott, "Bona Fide Protection: Fulfilling CERCLA's Legislative Purpose by Applying Differing Definitions of 'Disposal,'" *Connecticut Law Review* 42 (February 2010): 957–90; Maryam Tabatabai, "Comparing U.S. and EU Hazardous Waste Liability Frameworks: How the EU Liability Directive Competes with CERCLA," *Houston Journal of International Law* 34 (Summer 2012): 656–57.

53. Phil Brown, Ph.D, and Richard Clapp, DSc, "Looking Back on Love Canal," *Public Health Reports* 117 (March/April 2002): 95–98; Buck, *Understanding Environmental Administration and Law*, 110–11; Lois Marie Gibbs, "Housewife's Data," *American Journal of Public Health* 101 (September 2011):

1556–59; Andrew J. Hoffman, "An Uneasy Rebirth at Love Canal," *Environment* 37 (March 1995): 4–9, 25–31; Moya and Fono, *Federal Environmental Law*, 156; Alicia Saunte Phillips, Yung-Tse Hung, and Paul A. Bosela, "Love Canal Tragedy," *Journal of Performance of Constructed Facilities* 21 (July/August 2007): 313–19; Scott, "Bona Fide Protection," 965–66.

54. § 107, 42 U.S.C. § 9607. See also Ronald G. Aronovsky, "Federalism and CERCLA: Rethinking the Role of Federal Law in Private Cleanup Cost Disputes," *Ecology Law Quarterly* 33 (2006): 24–34, 50–54, 104; Stefanie Gitler, "Settling the Tradeoffs Between Voluntary Cleanup of Contaminated Sites and Cooperation with the Government Under CERCLA," *Ecology Law Quarterly* 35 (2008): 344–50; Robert M. Guo, "Reasonable Bases for Apportioning Harm under CERCLA," *Ecology Law Quarterly* 37 (2010): 320–27; Amy Luria, "CERCLA Contribution: An Inquiry into What Constitutes An Administrative Settlement," *North Dakota Law Review* 84 (2008): 334–37; McCrory, "Who's on First," 5–7; Moya and Fono, *Federal Environmental Law*, 156–58.

55. Ferrey, *Environmental Law: Examples and Explanations*, 298–302; Moya and Fono, *Federal Environmental Law*, 158–60; Rosenbaum, *Environmental Politics and Policy*, 244–45.

56. §§ 103–04, 42 U.S.C. §§ 9603–04. See also Milos Jekic, "Lowering the Jurisdictional Bar: A Call for an Equitable-Factors Analysis Under CERCLA's Timing-of-Review Provision," *Kansas Law Review* 59 (2011): 157–90; Arnold W. Reitze, Jr., "Emergency Response and Planning Requirements Applicable to Unpermitted Air Pollution Releases," *Brigham Young University Law Review* 2005 (2005): 1078–81; Larry Schnapf, "How the CERCLA Notification Requirements Facilitate the Creation of Brownfields and What EPA Can Do to Address the Problem," *Sustainable Development Law & Policy* 11 (2010): 19–26, 63–65.

57. §§ 104–05, 42 U.S.C. §§ 9604–05. See also Ferrey, *Environmental Law: Examples and Explanations*, 306–10; Moya and Fono, *Federal Environmental Law*, 163–64; Reitze, Jr., "Emergency Response and Planning Requirements Applicable to Unpermitted Air Pollution Releases," 1075–1193.

58. §§ 104–05, 42 U.S.C. §§ 9604–05. See also Harold C. Barnett, "The Allocation of Superfund," *Land Economics* 61 (August 1985): 255; Ferrey, *Environmental Law: Examples and Explanations*, 307–09; Luria, "CERCLA Contribution," 333–64; Moya and Fono, *Federal Environmental Law*, 163–67; Maya Waldron, "A Proposal to Balance Polluter and Community Intervention in CERCLA Litigation," *Ecology Law Quarterly* 38 (2011): 402–13.

59. § 104(i), 42 U.S.C. § 9604(i). See also "Communicating Results to Community Residents: Lessons from Recent ATSDR Health Investigations," *Journal of Exposure Analysis and Environmental Epidemiology* 14 (November 2004): 484–91; Christopher J. Portier, Ph.D, "ATSDR in the 21st Century," *Journal of Environmental Health* 74 (March 2012): 30–31; Yee-Wan Stevens, Mildred M. Williams-Johnson, and William Cibulas, Jr., "Findings

and Accomplishments of ATSDR's Superfund-Mandated Substance-Specific Applied Research Program," *International Journal of Hygiene and Environmental Health* 205 (2002): 29–39; United States General Accountability Office, *Agency for Toxic Substances and Disease Registry: Policies and Procedures for Public Health Product Preparation Should be Strengthened* (Washington, D.C.: U.S. Government Printing Office, GAO Publication No. GAO-10–449, April 2010): 7–8.

60. §§ 111–12, 42 U.S.C. §§ 9611–12. See also Barnett, "The Allocation of Superfund," 255–62; Steven Ferrey, "Inverting the Law: Superfund Hazardous Substance Liability and Supreme Court Reversal of All Federal Circuits," *William & Mary Environmental Law & Policy Review* 33 (May 2009): 638–49; Brian L. Murphy, "Allocation by Contribution to Cost and Risk at Superfund Sites," *Journal of Environmental Forensics* 1 (September 2000): 117–20.

61. § 107, 42 U.S.C. § 9607. See also § 113, 42 U.S.C. § 9613; Ferrey, "Inverting the Law," 647–62; Guo, "Reasonable Bases for Apportioning Harm Under CERCLA," 322–27; McCrory, "Who's on First," 5–7.

62. § 121, 42 U.S.C. § 9621. See also Ferrey, *Environmental Law: Examples and Explanations*, 311–12; Ferrey, "Inverting the Law," 664–65; Moya and Fono, *Federal Environmental Law*, 158; Rosenbaum, *Environmental Politics and Policy*, 245; "The Unrealized Potential of SARA," *Environment* 29 (May 1987): 6–11, 40–44.

63. Ferrey, *Environmental Law: Examples and Explanations*, 311–12; Ferrey, "Inverting the Law," 638–49; Guo, "Reasonable Bases for Apportioning Harm Under CERCLA," 322–27; McCrory, "Who's on First," 5–7; Murphy, "Allocation by Contribution to Cost and Risk at Superfund Sites," 117–20.

64. The Federal Insecticide, Fungicide and Rodenticide Act (FIFRA), as amended by the Federal Environmental Pesticide Control Act of 1972, 7 U.S.C. § 136 *et seq.* (1972). See also Joseph Frueh, "Comment: Pesticides, Preemption, and the Return of Tort Protection," *Yale Journal on Regulation* 23 (2006): 299–309; John H. Minan and Tracy M. Frech, "Pesticides as 'Pollutants' Under the Clean Water Act," *San Diego Law Review* 47 (Winter 2010): 109–44; Douglas T. Nelson, *et al.*, "Real Environmental Protection: Not a Paper Exercise," *Environmental Law Reporter: News & Analysis* 42 (February 2012): 10166–71.

65. The Endangered Species Act (ESA) of 1973, 16 U.S.C. § 1531, *et seq.* (1973). See also Ferrey, *Environmental Law: Examples and Explanations*, 481–82; J.B. Ruhl, "The Endangered Species Act's Fall from Grace in the Supreme Court," *Harvard Environmental Law Review* 36 (2012): 488–97; Scott Schwartz, "The Hapless Ecosystem: A Federalist Argument in Favor of an Ecosystem Approach to the Endangered Species Act," *Virginia Law Review* 95 (September 2009): 1325–60.

66. § 404, 33 U.S.C. § 1344. See also Peg Bostwick, "Integrating State and Federal Needs Under the Clean Water Act," *National Wetlands Newsletter* 33

(July/August 2011): 5–6; David Evans, "Clean Water Act § 404 Assumption: What Is It, How Does It Work, and What are the Benefits?," *National Wetlands Newsletter* 31 (May–June 2009): 18–21; Ferrey, *Environmental Law: Examples and Explanations*, 423–27; Palmer Hough and Morgan Robertson, "Mitigation Under Section 404 of the Clean Water Act: Where It Comes From, What It Means," *Wetlands Ecology & Management* 17 (January 2009): 15–33; Margaret "Peggy" Strand and Lowell M. Rothschild, "What Wetlands Are Regulated? Jurisdiction of the § 404 Program," *Environmental Law Reporter: News & Analysis* 40 (April 2010): 10372–93.

For many Americans, the idea of environmental sustainability means that places of natural beauty, such as the Grand Canyon in Arizona, pictured here, are preserved and protected. Courtesy of the Library of Congress.

Environmentalists fear that current processes, such as strip mining, will leave the world diminished and limit the options for unborn generations. This scene shows a coal mine with strip mining dumps in the background. The photograph, taken in Cherokee County, Kansas, dates from May 1936. Courtesy of the Library of Congress.

Scenes such as this one are all too common because, in many cases, no one possesses an economic incentive to clean up pollution and thereby stem the tide of urban blight unless the costs of the program are borne by government or imposed on private parties. This photograph dates from 1940 and shows a polluted industrial area in **Dubuque, Iowa.** Courtesy of the Library of Congress.

The eighteenth-century Scottish philosopher Adam Smith, pictured here in a well-known drawing, is widely regarded as the father of modern economic theory. Courtesy of the Library of Congress.

Ronald Coase, a British economist who spent much of his career teaching at the University of Chicago, developed the Coase theory, the idea that parties will work efficiently as long as government intrusion is minimal and transaction costs are sufficiently low. Courtesy of the Coase-Sandor Institute for Law and Economics, University of Chicago Law School.

Henry David Thoreau, pictured here in 1856, became a famous American icon of the nineteenth century. Courtesy of the National Portrait Gallery, Smithsonian Institution, Benjamin D. Maxham Archive.

Woodrow Wilson, shown here in the 1880s, authored an important 1887 essay, "The Study of Administration," arguing that American public administration should be practiced according to scientific principles of government. Courtesy of the Library of Congress.

**The German sociologist Max Weber, pictured here, became an important propo-
nent of an "ideal-type" of bureaucracy.** Courtesy of the Library of Congress.

Love Canal became a potent symbol of environmental contamination in the United States. Courtesy of the U.S. Environmental Protection Agency.

John Wesley Powell, pictured here, was one of the most colorful naturalists of the nineteenth century. Courtesy of the Library of Congress.

Louis Agassiz, shown here circa 1865, was a towering scientific figure during the nineteenth century. Courtesy of the Library of Congress.

Harold Ickes, pictured here in 1939, became President Franklin D. Roosevelt's energetic interior secretary, and was the second longest-serving cabinet member in American history. Courtesy of the Library of Congress.

David Lilienthal, shown here in 1938, was a prominent utilities attorney who served as head of the Tennessee Valley Authority and later chairman of the U.S. Atomic Energy Commission. Courtesy of the Library of Congress.

Aldo Leopold, pictured here in 1944, wrote *A Sand County Almanac*, a collection of essays on nature that became popular during the twentieth century. Courtesy of the Aldo Leopold Foundation, www.aldoleopold.org.

Gaylord Nelson, a U.S. senator from Wisconsin, was the founding father of the original Earth Day in 1970. Courtesy of Jeff Nelson and the Nelson family.

William Ruckelshaus, shown here in May 1972, served as the first administrator of the United States Environmental Protection Agency. He later returned for a brief stint during the Reagan administration. Courtesy of the National Archives & Records Administration.

The partial meltdown at the Three Mile Island Nuclear Generating Station in Pennsylvania in March 1979 became a potent symbol of the potential catastrophe that may result from humankind's inattention to nature. Courtesy of the Centers for Disease Control & Prevention's Public Health Image Library.

President Theodore Roosevelt and his chief forester, Gifford Pinchot, converse during a trip on the steamship *Mississippi* in October 1907. Courtesy of the Library of Congress.

Rachel Carson became one of the most influential environmental writers of the twentieth century. Her landmark work, *Silent Spring*, virtually created the modern environmental movement and ushered in a new era of activism. Courtesy of the U.S. Department of Agriculture.

The renowned naturalists **John Muir** and **John Burroughs** pose together on Burroughs' 75th birthday in 1912. Courtesy of the Library of Congress.

III

MODERN AMERICAN ENVIRONMENTALISM

6

A BRIEF HISTORY OF THE MODERN
ENVIRONMENTAL MOVEMENT

To label the environmentalism of the past 100 years a "movement" and focus on the activities of a few prominent government officials is to risk mischaracterizing the phenomena. Mass movements typically do not begin with the "top down" orchestrated efforts of elites. They encompass a multitude of "bottom up" events undertaken by innumerable grassroots participants acting across many decades. Political leaders and public figures no doubt contribute to the timing and scale of movements, but the scope and direction result from the actions and reactions of many individuals whose names and faces are not well known. By the time a particular movement is recognized as such, it probably has been under way for many years. Accordingly, the movement to protect the natural environment in the United States is the result of numerous events and personalities.

The origins of the American environmental movement are virtually impossible to pinpoint for precisely these reasons. It is difficult to determine a specific time where an observer can conclude unequivocally, "many people were worried about a deteriorating environment and this was the beginning of modern environmentalism." Having said that, many historians trace the movement's roots to the nineteenth century, for this was the era when some astute Americans noticed the deleterious effects of population growth and industrialization. Presumably, an exhaustive history of efforts to protect the natural environment could be traced to antiquity, but the emphasis here is on American public administration, which also is a product of nineteenth-century theories and policies.[1]

THE EARLY EXPLORERS

Perhaps an environmental movement was inevitable, or at least necessary, the day that two men set out on a journey to explore the interior lands of the United States in 1804. Meriwether Lewis and William Clark answered their president's call to map out the acreage in the Louisiana Purchase and thereby assess its commercial and scientific possibilities. Their chief, Thomas Jefferson, possessed a restless mind; he had long been interested in determining whether a water route existed across the North American continent. To satisfy his curiosity and contribute to knowledge of the American landscape, he instructed his intrepid explorers to map out their route and collect specimens of plant and animal life along the way. The two-year Corps of Discovery Expedition succeeded beyond everyone's wildest imagination. Lewis and Clark passed into the annals of history as two of the greatest explorers of the nineteenth century. For his part, President Jefferson won accolades for his willingness to sponsor the celebrated venture that eventually opened up the American West to a fledgling nation and its people.[2]

The land was not completely pristine or unexplored. Aside from Native Americans, many of whom had journeyed through these lands for generations, even white Europeans had set foot on the continent in centuries past. During the sixteenth century, Spanish conquistadors traipsed through parts of the American South and into the Southwest. A hundred years later, French furriers tracked animals through many parts of what became the northern United States. Yet these explorations had been undertaken for many purposes, mostly commercial. Jefferson's Corps of Discovery Expedition was designed to gather systematic intelligence on the nation's land mass.[3]

Lewis and Clark succeeded in exploring the interior lands and bringing back useful information and breathtaking specimens to President Jefferson. Yet they accomplished far more than they realized at the time. In mapping out the miles of forest land, rivers, streams, and byways of the continent, they fired the imaginations of generations of Americans. In the decades that followed the expedition, American settlers flocked to the West. It became a mythical place of enchantment, a place where a man might start over from scratch and build a new life from the sweat of his own brow. Many a restless soul agreed with Henry David Thoreau that a meaningful life could only be had in western lands. "Eastward I go only by force; but westward I go free," Thoreau wrote in his inimitable prose. "Thither no business leads me. It is hard for me to believe that I shall find fair landscapes or sufficient wildness and freedom behind the eastern horizon. I am not excited by the prospect of a walk thither; but I believe that the forest which I see in the western horizon stretches uninterruptedly toward the setting sun, and there are no towns nor cities in it of enough consequence to disturb me. Let me live where I will, on this side is the city, on that the wilderness, and ever I am leaving the city more and more, and withdrawing into the wilderness."[4]

In opening the door to westward expansion and demonstrating that a man could enter the forest and emerge relatively unscathed, Lewis and Clark set into motion a mad scramble across the continent that lasted until the end of the nineteenth century. The consequences for the natural environment were profound. After fewer than 100 years, Frederick Jackson Turner famously declared that the frontier had closed. It was a wild ride during those nine decades between the Corp of Discovery's adventures and the taming of the West. The search for plentiful, inexpensive land, the displacement of Native Americans, the boom-and-bust cycle of various gold rushes, and the creation of cities and towns along the western frontier ensured that with each passing decade, life in the United States barely resembled life in the preceding decades.[5]

Westward expansion, with its attendant stories of a life free from mind-numbingly dull work and the ennui of day-to-day living, appealed to many Americans of the time. They suffered through many crises: the war of 1812; the passing of the founding generation; the financial panics of 1819, 1837, 1873, and 1893; escalating tensions over the expansion of slavery into the territories; and the fracturing of the union at mid-century. The national infrastructure was practically nonexistent. Political parties engaged in fractious debate, and they required decades to stabilize into a two-party system. Institutions of government were relatively weak and, in many cases, notoriously inefficient. Life in the United States during much of the nineteenth century was anything but ennobling.

Despite these severe impediments, Americans expressed optimism that their experience was somehow unique, far different from stultifying European traditions. The concept of American exceptionalism held that these people and this land were different than everything that had come before. If God could be said to be on anyone's side, he favored the American people and their bountiful lands. It was an idea that would characterize much of the nation's history. In time, prescient observers realized that Americans' unbridled faith in their ability to solve any problem and their unwillingness to recognize limitations on their expansive dreams would lead to devastating consequences when industrialization proceeded with few constraints or reservations.[6]

Beginning in the 1840s, this faith in America's unique promise came to be known as manifest destiny. Whatever problems had to be faced, whatever obstacles had to be surmounted, and whatever temporary inequities would need to be visited on select segments of the population, so be it. The American spirit would triumph—even if, upon occasion, certain peoples and lands were decimated along the way. As the prominent historian George Bancroft remarked in the first volume of his *History of the United States of America*, the country's motto reflected this journey to the Pacific Ocean: "Westward the star of empire takes its way."[7]

In the rush to exploit new lands in the western United States, a few wary Americans recognized that environmental destruction accompanied the human presence across the continent. George Catlin, a painter who traveled with William Clark during Clark's twilight years, was one such American. Catlin produced a two-volume work, *Letters and Notes on the Manners, Customs, and Condition of the North American Indians*. In one telling passage, he observed the destructive effects of human beings on the natural environment. "Many are the rudeness and wilds in Nature's work, which are destined to fall before the deadly axe and desolating hands of cultivating man."[8]

John James Audubon was another early naturalist who would be labeled an "environmentalist" during a later era. The illegitimate son of a French naval officer, Audubon was born in Haiti but spent most of his young life in France. He immigrated to the United States at age 18, in 1803, to escape the chaos of the Napoleonic wars. After working as a

farmer, the young man tried his hand in commerce, operatin
store. Unfortunately, the Panic of 1819 forced him into bank
debtor's prison.

After his release, the artistically gifted Audubon pursued an itinerant
life, which introduced him to scenes that sparked his imagination. He
became a well-known illustrator of nature, especially birds. His ambition knew few bounds. By the time he was 35 years old, Audubon had
resolved to paint every species of bird found in North America.[9]

To raise money for his vast undertaking, Audubon spent three years
traveling around England with his artwork. The book he later financed,
Birds in America, appeared in print serially between 1827 and 1838.
The groundbreaking work depicted 435 life-sized, hand-colored prints
of 497 species of birds that Audubon had identified. A subsequent
book that he coauthored with Scottish naturalist William MacGillivray,
*Ornithological Biography, or, An Account of the Habits of the Birds of
the United States of America*, showcased a variety of species and solidified Audubon's reputation as the foremost naturalist and illustrator of
his time.

He is remembered and revered in the twenty-first century as a tireless advocate on behalf of nature. Audubon was not a lobbyist in the
modern sense of the word. He did not reach out to elected officials in
an effort to influence the legislative process. Instead, he worked with his
brushes. His art shows the delicacy and beauty of birds existing in their
natural habitat. Anyone who gazes on his illustrations cannot help being
swept away by the immediacy of his scenes and the fragility of natural
creatures.[10]

Thirty-five years after Audubon's death, George Bird Grinnell, a Yale-
educated naturalist and associate of Theodore Roosevelt and Gifford
Pinchot, cofounded the first Audubon Society, an early forerunner of
the National Audubon Society, founded in 1905. Grinnell never knew
John James Audubon personally, although he did meet with the great
man's widow, Lucy. Based on his understanding of John James' sensibilities, Grinnell chose the name "Audubon" to highlight his group's fidelity
to nature and its creatures.[11]

Another early naturalist, George Perkins Marsh, carved out a remarkable career as a diplomat and scholar, truly a renaissance man of nineteenth-century America. He spent most of his professional career as a

diplomat, and his facility for learning languages was legendary. Marsh traveled extensively in Europe as well as in the American West. His opportunities to compare lands on both continents led to important insights, especially in the context of the times.

Marsh lived in an epoch when many thinkers were first learning of Charles Darwin's theories of natural selection. A conservative reaction held that the British naturalist was profane and misguided. Darwin's theories suggested that human beings were animals—certainly poised at the top of the food chain, but not demonstrably a different breed of being than a lower-order beast. Darwin struck fear in the hearts of observers who believed that human beings were unique creatures, existing apart from nature. Natural selection theories posited that humans were different in degree, not kind, from other animals. For conservatives fearful that Darwinian theories undermined the Christian view of God, this sort of radical thinking would not do.[12]

Among the many implications of the Darwinian enterprise was the realization that if human beings were not outside of, and superior to, nature, their duty to other beings was reasonably clear. They must not despoil the environment because they were obliged to leave the premises in the best possible condition for their fellow creatures as well as for future generations of Homo sapiens. If humankind was somehow special and separate from nature, the environment could be shaped to suit his will. Darwin suggested a different way of thinking. Human beings were constantly destroying natural lands with no regard for the consequences. This practice would have to change.[13]

The insight that human beings must care for the earth informed the work of naturalists writing in the years after Darwin's theories circulated. In his acclaimed 1864 book *Man and Nature; or Physical Geography as Modified by Human Action*, Marsh cautioned that "man is everywhere a disturbing agent. Wherever he plants his foot, the harmonies of nature are turned to discords." This insight may appear intuitively obvious to a twenty-first century denizen, but it was a rare acknowledgment at the time. Marsh saw human beings as both creatures of the earth and yet also beings that exist on a higher plane. "The fact that, of all organic beings, man alone is to be regarded as essentially a destructive power, and that he wields energies to resist which, nature—that nature whom all material life and all inorganic substance obey—is wholly impotent, tends to prove that, though living in physical nature, he is not of her, that he is of more exalted parentage, and belongs to a higher order of existences than those born of her wombs and submissive to her dictates."[14]

As he considered the differences between the United States and European nations, Marsh recognized that most of the natural forestland in the Old World had been destroyed through centuries of misuse and unwise land management practices. Although the New World was largely untapped, Marsh feared that American forests would be decimated in much the same manner as the European forests if policy-makers did not institute prudent forestry practices. It was a revelatory assessment during the Gilded Age where a large percentage of the population believed that industrialization equaled progress, and progress was beneficial to virtually everyone save persons too indolent or impoverished to compete within the marketplace.

Even if nature cannot defend herself against the ravages of humankind owing to her impotence in the face of assaults, she occasionally displays her wrath in dramatic fashion. According to Marsh, when hurricanes, tornadoes, earthquakes, and other natural calamities occur, nature "avenges herself upon the intruder, by letting loose upon her defaced provinces destructive energies hitherto kept in check by organic forces destined to be his best auxiliaries, but which he has unwisely dispersed and driven from the field of action." Human beings must recognize their own destructive tendencies and curb their worst impulses; otherwise, "the whole earth, unless rescued by human art from the physical degradation to which it tends, becomes an assemblage of bald mountains, of barren, turfless hills, and of swampy and malarious plains."[15]

Marsh's dire predictions were echoed by other commentators. John Wesley Powell, a grizzled Civil War veteran, was among the most colorful of these early naturalists. He had lost an arm fighting in the Battle of Shiloh in 1862, but the destruction of an appendage did not destroy his zest for life. He was a restless soul who demonstrated a scholarly aptitude but not a disposition to live a sedentary life. After the war, Powell served as a professor of geology at Illinois Wesleyan University and co-founded the Illinois Museum of Natural History, but he was not satisfied with these endeavors. The peripatetic adventurer set out to explore the Rocky Mountains.

Powell's 1875 book *The Exploration of the Colorado River and Its Canyons* recounted his trek along the Colorado River in the 1860s through the scenic vistas of the Grand Canyon. Powell lovingly detailed his recollections of a landscape "so destitute of animal and vegetal life" that it "would not support large numbers." Only the hardiest human beings could live in such inhospitable environs, and yet the value of nature was not in its direct effect on human needs and desires. Natural vegetation and rock formations held value even if human beings did not harvest them for profit. It was not quite a direct endorsement of bio-centrism, but Powell's stirring words certainly could be interpreted as a forceful acknowledgment of nature's transcendence.[16]

THE POLICY-MAKERS AND THINKERS

No discussion of the American environmental movement would be complete without including John Muir, an explorer, author, and natu-ralist extraordinaire. He became an environmental activist long before such a breed was common. Muir cofounded the Sierra Club, one of the most influential environmental lobbying organizations in American his-tory. Building on the work of Thoreau, Marsh, Powell, and others, Muir recognized that environmental consciousness, while important, was only the beginning of a long journey toward natural resource preservation.[17]

Muir hailed from Scotland. In 1849, when he was 11 years old, his family moved to Wisconsin, where young John grew up on a farm. It was an ideal setting for a solitary youth who enjoyed exploring the forests and grasslands around his home. As a child, he also discovered a natu-ral talent for problem solving, for he was constantly tinkering with and improving his family's farm machinery.[18]

It was not uncommon during the nineteenth century for young man, even one as obviously gifted as John Muir, to forgo a college educa-tion and set out to make his mark on the world at a tender age. Yet this self-taught tinkerer and rapid reader chose to study at the University of Wisconsin-Madison, where he learned of Transcendentalism as well as the works of Ralph Waldo Emerson and Henry David Thoreau. These iconoclastic New Englanders appealed to Muir's sense of adventure, self-reliance, and love of the outdoors. His university years left Muir with a desire to study nature, especially botany. He would devote much of his life to exploring untamed swaths of land and championing public policies to preserve and protect the natural environment.[19]

Of all the places he traveled, Muir particularly appreciated California, notably the area that became Yosemite National Park. As early as 1868, he realized that these lands were special and deserving of protection. In his many written works, Muir described the wonders of nature and the potentially destructive power of man. He was not a hopelessly idealistic misanthrope, one of the shrill environmentalists so easily parodied owing to their denunciation of all things human. At the same time, Muir argued against the myopic presuppositions of neoclassical economists who would not recognize the worth of resources that cannot be easily assigned a numerical value.[20]

Muir cultivated friendships with high-ranking government officials in hopes of educating them on the need for protecting the natural environment. One influential friend, Gifford Pinchot, a Yale-educated forestry expert, proved to be a valuable connection, although the two men eventually had a falling out. Pinchot had become interested in protecting forest lands at an early age. As with so many naturalists of his era, he supplemented his academic education with practical, hands-on experience working in the wilderness.[21]

Pinchot believed that human beings could cultivate forests for human benefit without necessarily decimating the land. He eventually became a proponent of the conservationist ethic, as opposed to Muir's preservationist approach. Pinchot agreed with Muir than Americans must take care not to destroy the land, but their views differed on how the objective would be achieved. For Muir, human beings are inherently destructive beings. Wherever they encroach on pristine lands, the result invariably damages the earth. Therefore, land must be segregated from human use and preserved indefinitely. Pinchot contended that extreme measures are not required to protect the environment. With the exception of creating national parks and monuments, Pinchot cautioned against removing public lands from private consumption. He would allow logging companies to harvest timber from public lands under some circumstances, provided they did not clear-cut old growth forests and as long as they mitigated the damage with remediation efforts. It was a decidedly anthropocentric perspective.[22]

It was little wonder that Gifford Pinchot, unlike Muir, was such a pragmatic public figure and willing to compromise. Pinchot was a politician, serving as a member of the National Forest Commission created by the National Academy of Sciences. Later in his career, he became chief of the Division of Forestry at the U.S. Department of Agriculture. When the U.S. Forest Service was established, he served as head from 1905 until 1910. He capped his public service career as governor of Pennsylvania. A long association with Theodore Roosevelt furthered his professional aspirations.[23]

Muir enjoyed a convivial relationship with Roosevelt, but the two did not see eye to eye on every issue. They learned to live with each other, agreeing whenever possible and respectfully disagreeing on occasion. The same was not true for Muir and Pinchot. Matters deteriorated beyond repair over the issue of sheep grazing in national parks. Muir and Pinchot originally agreed that the practice must be curtailed, but Pinchot later changed his position. Incensed, Muir believed that Pinchot had kowtowed to the Wool Growers Association and sabotaged Muir's efforts to battle against the practice. During a heated exchange with his former friend, Muir hissed, "I don't want anything more to do with you."

A contentious debate over water rights further divided the two men. Early in the twentieth century, as San Francisco's population grew, the city desperately needed new sources of water. City planners concocted a scheme to dam the Tuolumne River that flows through Yosemite National Park and thereby create a freshwater reservoir. John Muir worried that such bold action would lead to unintended consequences. Echoing an argument that would be propounded by multitudes of environmentalists throughout the years, he deplored the arrogance of human beings who would callously manipulate natural resources for their own purposes without regard to the consequences visited on the ecosystem. Muir complained to President Roosevelt, a political leader who claimed to be a friend of the natural environment, asking for assistance in defeating this proposal. Although he was sympathetic to Muir's concerns, the president refused to interfere, believing that San Francisco's need for water outweighed the possible harm to the environment. Despite many delays, the project eventually moved forward and the dam was built. It was a bitter defeat. The destruction of the Hetch Hetchy Valley in Yosemite radicalized John Muir. Convinced that Gifford Pinchot had poisoned

Theodore Roosevelt against Muir's position, the great naturalist broke all ties with his former friend and associate.[24]

The split between John Muir and Gifford Pinchot to some extent reflected a split between preservationists and conservationists. The former school of thought, associated with Muir, seeks to preserve the natural environment by limiting human encroachment on pristine lands while the latter, commonly linked with Pinchot, argues for a proper balance between nature and human needs. This fault line directly or indirectly runs through almost every environmental issue in the United States. At its core, the debate centers on the appropriate role of human beings and nature, and whether the natural environment exists for its instrumental value in meeting human needs or whether it possesses intrinsic value apart from Homo sapiens.

Both Muir and Pinchot counted Theodore Roosevelt as a close associate. Roosevelt certainly agreed with their desire to propel environmental questions to the forefront of the national agenda. A tireless Progressive who always appeared to be in constant motion, Roosevelt believed that government should be involved in all manner of activity designed to cure, or at least mitigate, social ills. He also was a life-long enthusiast for the strenuous, outdoor life. The Bull Moose, as he came to be known, enjoyed studying wildlife and hunting. If his penchant for gunning down innumerable specimens with little or no compunction strikes modern environmentalists as incongruous, Roosevelt would have responded with a thoroughly anthropocentric explanation. He believed that nature provided a bountiful harvest for humankind, but political leaders must protect natural resources to ensure that the harvest would continue in perpetuity.[25]

As president of the United States, Theodore Roosevelt did more for environmental protection than any of his predecessors and more than most of his successors. He unabashedly set aside lands for national parks and monuments, extolling the virtues of the forests, deserts, and streams of the American landscape, especially in the far West. Throughout a long career at all levels of government, he set a highly visible example of the man who rejuvenates himself by exploring the wilderness and learning to love the natural life.[26]

For all of his energy and zest for life as well as his written works on nature, however, Theodore Roosevelt was a man of action, a practical policy-maker and elected politician. He was not a deep thinker, not the way Jean Louis Rodolphe Agassiz, a Swiss-born Harvard biologist and geologist, was. Agassiz resembled Roosevelt in the sense that he was an energetic and charismatic figure that effortlessly drew people into his orbit. Handsome, witty, charming, and erudite, the great professor contributed immensely to the scientific literature of the nineteenth century, although he sullied his reputation with repulsive racial theories that were discredited by numerous scientists of a later time.[27]

Born in 1807, Agassiz studied in universities all over Europe, eventually becoming a protégé of the Prussian scientist Alexander von Humboldt as well as the French paleontologist Georges Cuvier. He made his name as one of the first scientists to discover the existence of the ice age. By the time Agassiz visited the United States during the 1840s, his career seemed to have reached a plateau. He was determined to change the course of his life and career, and so he did.

Invited to deliver a series of public lectures in Boston, Agassiz dazzled his audiences with his natural self-confidence, wit, and ability to explain complex scientific concepts in easily understood language. Even his occasional difficulties speaking grammatically correct English was endearing to some appreciative listeners. The effect was not lost on the city's elite. Harvard University administrators had been searching for a means of revamping the science curriculum. Recognizing that Agassiz could assist in this effort, they offered the renowned scholar a faculty appointment. He was exactly the big name researcher who could breathe life into the program and continue the university's ascent into the academic stratosphere. He accepted. Beginning in 1848, the European scientist became a permanent resident of the United States.

Harvard was fortunate to find this man when it did. His contributions to the American science curriculum were vast and deep. Agassiz believed that academic pursuits should be undertaken without the contamination of theology, politics, or economics, an axiomatic proposition in the twenty-first century, but novel in the nineteenth. Science had often been taught as a series of facts to be memorized. In their lessons for students as well as their research, scientists knew that they must not contradict the teachings of the Christian church. Agassiz objected to such dogma. Prejudging the outcome according to religious or philosophical biases undermines the scientific process. He also believed in a hands-on approach; that is, science is advanced by examining specimens and conducting experiments. Only through inductive reasoning—developing generalizations and theories after carefully observing natural phenomena—could a researcher hope to understand the world. This kind of pedagogical insight was not unique, but it was sufficiently rare to make Agassiz a legendary teacher and scientist. A generation of scientists would come of age under Agassiz's tutelage, and decades after their classroom work had ended, they would vividly recall his scientific experiments. He further ensured his place in the pantheon of great American scientists when he helped to found the Museum of Comparative Zoology at Harvard in 1859.[28]

He was an inspiring figure as he collected hundreds, if not thousands, of specimens, dead and alive. One well-known story, recounted innumerable times, told of Agassiz living with a tame bear who followed him around town. Supposedly, the bear became intoxicated during a student-faculty party. On many occasions, students gleefully recalled the professor bounding into class with live specimens, including snakes, jutting from his coat pockets. At a time when most professors insisted that their students regurgitate large quantities of memorized facts, Agassiz delivered lively, memorable lectures about the specimens that he had distributed throughout the class. He expected his pupils to handle the specimens, disassemble them, and explore nature in all its glory and wonder. The professor made his biology and zoology classes fun for the students.[29]

He charmed his peers as well. During his years at Harvard, Agassiz came to know the great thinkers and writers of New England, including Ralph Waldo Emerson, Henry David Thoreau, Nathaniel Hawthorne, Henry Wadsworth Longfellow, John Greenleaf Whittier, Charles Sumner, and Oliver Wendell Holmes, Sr. The professor frequently scheduled dinners and meetings of this loose association, which became known as Agassiz's Club. Even among these men of stellar intellect and sterling reputation, Agassiz stood out from the crowd.

In fact, Holmes was so impressed with his colleague that he penned several poems in honor of the great man. In "A Farewell to Agassiz," written in 1865 as the professor embarked on a well-publicized expedition to Brazil, Holmes adopted a jocular tone:

Heaven keep the great Professor!
May he find, with his apostles,
That the land is full of fossils,
That the waters swarm with fishes
Shaped according to his wishes,
That every pool is fertile
In fancy kinds of turtle,
New birds around him singing,
New insects, never stinging,
With a million novel data
About the articulata,
And facts that strip off all husks
From the history of mollusks.[30]

In 1884, more than a decade after Agassiz's death, Holmes recalled the legendary group meetings in his poem "At The Saturday Club." This is how he described Agassiz:

The great PROFESSOR, strong, broad-shouldered, square,
In life's rich noontide, joyous, debonair.
His social hour no leaden care alloys,
His laugh rings loud and mirthful as a boy's,—
That lusty laugh the Puritan forgot,—
What ear has heard it and remembers not?[31]

Agassiz enjoyed a long, productive career expounding on his view of natural history. Yet he was not infallible. When he first encountered Darwin's famous book *On the Origin of the Species*, Agassiz expressed deep skepticism that organisms evolved from their original, primitive state into something far more complex and advanced. He would spend the rest of his life unpersuaded. Although he taught that religion had no place in the inductive scientific process, Agassiz believed, as did so many prominent men of his day, that a study of nature was in essence a study of God. He could not acknowledge that evolution, which suggests that a single species can, given enough time, more into another, distinct species, was a godly process. God does not make mistakes or change species over time. In Agassiz's view, Darwin's theories were "ingenious but fanci-ful," and his work was "the sum of wrong-headedness."[32]

As other men of academic renown embraced Darwin's theories, Agassiz found himself swimming against the current. The man who had done so much to advance the cause of science suddenly was no longer at the cutting edge of academe. He had spent most of his life as the learned professor who showed others the errors of their ways. He simply could not fathom the possibility, nay the probability, that he had become the very thing against which he had so long railed: the stodgy, old-fashioned proponent of antiquated notions that had lost their scientific currency. Even as the evidence of his erroneous theories mounted—and per-haps because of the voluminous new data—Agassiz became evermore entrenched in his views, a dogmatic old man who seethed with resent-ment that lesser men would dare to question his scientific literacy.

He was not satisfied to hold his views placidly or go gentle into that good night. The great professor engaged in verbal duels with a num-ber of academic men, including the American botanist Asa Gray. Their dispute took an especially nasty turn as each man vilified the other in a variety of public forums, especially through their written work. In one telling passage, Gray lamented, "This man, who might have been so use-ful to science and promised so much here has been for years a delusion, a snare, and a humbug, and is doing us far more harm than he can ever do us good." It was a devastating critique and, try as he might, Agassiz simply could not overcome the weight of the opposition's arguments.[33]

He continued to collect his specimens and write his articles, but, as one historian observed, a "shadow fell over the brilliant career." The man who had prided himself on his scientific acumen became another polemicist who refused to credit contrary opinions. The intellectual jousting eventually took its toll on his health. An 1869 nervous break-down left him unable to work for a year. When he finally died in 1873, the scientific world noted his passing with genuine regret, but his utility to American environmentalism had already passed. Louis Agassiz was a brilliant man who contributed much to his adopted nation's understand-ing of nature and science, but he was very much a creature of his age.[34]

The man's legacy is difficult to assess. Undoubtedly he contrib-uted much to nineteenth-century scientific progress, but his quirky

acceptance of certain fashionable notions of the era caused later generations to wince at their crude foundations. Modern scientists are appalled
at Agassiz's belief in polygenism, the notion that the races of man were
created separately and could best be understood by examining the climatic zones where they lived. Although he was not a supporter of slavery, Agassiz's theories can be used to justify the institution of human
bondage. God created each race separate and distinct from the other
race. Thus, if black people appeared to be inferior, it was because God
planned for them to be the subordinate race. Agassiz's insistence that
evolution was hogwash led the great man to this intellectual cul-de-sac.
He simply could not admit that social and cultural factors would influence so dramatically the differing conditions among the races.

And so one of the great naturalists of the nineteenth century ended
his career ignominiously. He was one of the great thinkers of his era—a
man who rejected conventional wisdom and insisted on the power of
inductive scientific processes—but he fell victim to his own hubris. In
replacing the status quo, Agassiz became the status quo and, in turn, was
replaced.[35]

TWENTIETH-CENTURY ENVIRONMENTAL POLICY

In 1873, the year of Agassiz's death, Mark Twain and Charles Dudley
Warner published *The Gilded Age: A Tale of Today*, a book satirizing
an era that masked its social problems beneath a thin façade of gold
gilding. The term soon gained popular acceptance as a description of
the years between the 1870s and the turn of the twentieth century. The
Gilded Age was marked by rapid industrialization and urbanization as
well as an influx of immigrants onto American shores. As increasingly
large numbers of people crowded into cities, wages rose, but so, too, did
prices. With explosive economic activity came the dark side of industrialization: the plight of the poor and ever-increasing levels of pollution.
Americans recognized that their activities were detrimental to nature,
but understanding a problem and fixing it often are two vastly different
enterprises.[36]

By the turn of the century, Progressives gained enough political power
to enact measures aimed at ameliorating poverty, reducing child labor,

curbing predatory lending practices, and ensuring consumer safety in the marketplace. They were an eclectic lot, these social and political reformers, but they pursued common goals. Progressives believed that the old ways of doing things were broken and outdated. Business and politics had been stymied by unprecedented corruption that allowed rich, powerful elites to prosper at the expense of the poor and middle class. They argued for the elimination of the smoke-filled back rooms where deals had been hammered out with little concern for the societal consequences.

The Progressives expressed far more faith in government than their predecessors dreamed possible. Ever since the Founding period, political thinkers had believed that governments were inherently oppressive; therefore, they subscribed to the motto that that government is best which governs least. The promises of societal improvements are best fulfilled by limiting government controls and allowing the private sector to thrive. Yet a century later, the evidence of private sector abuses was widespread. Children labored in dangerous factories under unsafe and unsanitary conditions. Giant monopolies restricted the ability of the small businessman to get ahead in his chosen profession. Political bosses controlled politicians and rammed through policies that disenfranchised the needy and downtrodden. The era of the classical liberal who believed that government was inherently oppressive had given way to a new understanding about the appropriate role of the state.

The solution to social ills was to recast the role of government as either part of the problem or part of the solution. No longer could government officials, especially at the federal level, stand by blithely and allow citizens to fend for themselves. Government policies, based on the latest and best scientific management principles, would rectify social problems.[37]

Some progressive programs worked better than others. Laws to limit child labor and reduce business monopolies were effective and long-lasting, genuine Progressive achievements. Their desire to create fields in social science such as political science, sociology, and economics also reverberated throughout academe to the present day. Frederick Taylor and his Scientific Management school became popular in the quest to professionalize public and private institutional operations. Theodore Roosevelt, one of a trio of American presidents deemed to be Progressive, was a conservationist who helped to protect the natural environment during an age when such policies clearly were in their infancy. Yet the push to amend the U.S. Constitution prohibiting the sale and use of alcohol was an abysmal failure that contributed to organized crime during the 1920s. It was one thing to rely on governmental institutions to improve the quality of life for those Americans lacking the means to triumph in the brutal world of economic gamesmanship; it was another thing to enforce laws on social engineering.[38]

Moreover, the Progressives triggered a backlash among guardians of the status quo. By the standards of subsequent years, it was a modest network of reforms, but for Americans accustomed to laissez-faire economic policy, the Progressive agenda smacked of a powerful, potentially oppressive government. Reactionary forces saw something far more sinister than pockets of government overreach: Socialism, with its authoritarian dictates, stalked the land. The debate between those who would employ the power of government to achieve social goals and those who would leave progress to private entities remains a point of contention to the present day.[39]

As Americans during the Progressive era gradually accepted a larger role for government in the daily lives of citizens, their willingness to support federal environmental policies increased. This realization is not to suggest that most citizens heartily endorsed radical land management policies; however, they appreciated the need to protect natural parks as well as curb the activities of overly enthusiastic timber and mining companies that might decimate large swaths of land.

For all of Theodore Roosevelt's celebrated efforts to protect nature, American environmental policy came of age during the administration of Franklin Delano Roosevelt (FDR), Theodore's distant cousin. FDR had a long history of enjoying nature and outdoor activities even after he was stricken with poliomyelitis in 1921. Coupled with his belief that government could solve many social ills, Roosevelt's willingness to use the mechanisms of the federal executive branch to address environmental issues proved to be one of the lasting legacies of the New Deal.[40]

His use of government institutions for natural resource protection and restoration can be seen especially by examining the record of the Civilian Conservation Corps (CCC), an agency modeled on a military hierarchy and designed to employ people to construct parks, revamp hiking trails, plant new trees, and repair decrepit roads and bridges in poor areas hit hard by the economic downturn. Initially, the Corps was open to unmarried men between the ages of 18 and 23, although later the age limit was raised to 28. Eventually, the CCC reached out to 25,000 World War I veterans, 25,000 "Local Experienced Men" to serve as mentors and guides to younger workers, and 10,000 Native Americans. It was an ambitious effort that required coordination from various federal agencies, including the War, Interior, and Agriculture departments. The CCC became one of the best-known New Deal institutions.[41]

The president tapped Robert Fechner, an American Federation of Labor leader, to serve as the first CCC director. It was a brilliant choice. Fechner was a self-made man who had earned only an elementary school education, but he had managed to pull himself up to the top of the American labor hierarchy owing to his tenacity, sense of fairness, and flexibility in finding solutions to seemingly intractable problems. FDR understood that the CCC concept was controversial among labor proponents who feared that the agency would exploit workers and thereby destroy the gains made by organized labor in recent years. With Fechner, a prominent labor leader at the helm, the administration could argue that the intent was not to harm the labor movement; rather, it was to put people back to work who otherwise would not have been able to secure meaningful employment elsewhere.

Within a few months of its inception in 1933, the CCC was up and running. Tents sprang up in many areas across the country to house the influx of young men streaming into the program. The crude housing eventually was replaced by wooden, military-style barracks. Although it was not an army unit and workers did not drill or train with weapons, their lives in other respects resembled the military. CCC men awoke to reveille at 6:00 a.m. and retired to taps at 10:00 p.m. They were expected to be orderly, disciplined, and unquestioning in obedience to authority.

The program operated from 1933 until 1942. FDR did not plan for the agency to become permanent, but as a means of saving young men from hopelessness (and homelessness) at a time when they normally would enter the workforce. With the advent of World War II, many young men who would have labored on CCC projects entered the military to fight on the nation's behalf. Some CCC duties were transferred to other agencies while other duties simply were no longer performed by government.[42]

Outside of the CCC, Roosevelt looked to another extraordinary public servant to serve as the administration's environmental champion. Harold L. Ickes was a progressive Midwestern Republican and a University of Chicago graduate who supported Theodore Roosevelt's Bull Moose Party in 1912. When Franklin Roosevelt tapped him to serve as secretary of the Interior Department in 1933, he was not well known nationally. The selection of a Republican to serve in a Democratic administration might have seemed odd. Yet those who knew Ickes recognized him as something of an iconoclast, willing to step beyond his party in the service of ideals he deemed important. FDR believed that the man's gruff exterior and willingness to buck authority was exactly the sort of champion the Interior Department desperately needed.[43]

The department was tasked with overseeing the use of public lands as well as managing and conserving natural resources. For decades before Franklin Roosevelt became president, the department had been rocked by scandals and a well-deserved reputation for profligacy. The most infamous episode occurred during the 1920s when Albert Fall, secretary of the Interior under President Warren G. Harding, leased navy petroleum reserves at Teapot Dome, Wyoming, to private oil companies in exchange for bribes. Since that time, the Interior Department had improved its image only marginally. Ickes was determined to change the image as well as the reality of a department in crisis. Despite his Republican Party bona fides, Ickes was a progressive who successfully fought entrenched interests on behalf of common citizens, including Native Americans, during a rough-and-tumble career on the margins of politics. As a cabinet member, he would now be in the thick of the battle.

The new Interior secretary liked nothing so much as being in the middle of things. He positively reveled in controversy, calling himself "America's No. 1 Curmudgeon, or Sour Puss." Observers agreed that the man could be prickly and difficult to fathom. One member of Congress expressed disgust with this "prodigious bureaucrat with the soul of a meat ax and the mind of a commissar." Walter Lippmann, the famous mid-twentieth-century newspaper reporter and syndicated columnist, characterized Ickes as the "greatest living master of the art of quarreling." Horace M. Albright, National Park Service director during Ickes' opening months at the Interior Department, bluntly called his former boss "the meanest man who ever sat in the Cabinet office in Washington." One contemporary, reviewing Ickes' career, charitably concluded that the secretary was "a remarkably complex and profoundly suspicious man who thrived on rancorous debate and unending controversy."[44]

Although he supported civil liberties and was a champion of progressive causes, Ickes realized that desperate times call for desperate measures. If he wanted to turn the agency around, he believed he must institute draconian policies and instill fear into the hearts of slackers everywhere. He was known to prowl the halls of the agency in search of sloths and shirkers. Famous for his explosive tirades and insistence on perfection, Ickes cleaned house. In time, his efforts improved the agency's reputation and ensured that the Interior Department and the National Park Service, an agency within DOI, focused on the core mission by improving efficiency and environmental quality.[45]

Ickes not only assumed the mantle of leadership at the Interior Department, but he headed up the Public Works Administration (PWA), an alphabet-soup agency that, among other things, initiated large public works projects in areas devastated by the economic downturn. Ickes' masterful management of both organizations assured him a place in the pantheon of effective public administrators. Long after his time in office, he is remembered as the curmudgeonly department secretary who championed some of the country's most cherished national parks, including Kings Canyon in California, Shenandoah in Virginia, and Olympic in Washington state. Never satisfied to rest on his laurels, Ickes pushed the government to acquire land that became the Grand Tetons National Park. On Ickes' watch, in 1940 the federal government established the U.S. Fish and Wildlife Service to aid in "conserving the nature of America" by establishing wildlife refuges and sanctuaries.[46]

Although not as well known as Ickes, David Eli Lilienthal also made a name for himself during the New Deal as an accomplished public servant committed to environmental protection. He began his career as a Midwestern lawyer practicing in Chicago and working on high-profile cases. In one instance, he assisted in writing a legal brief in *Michaelson v. United States* (1924), a prominent case where the United States Supreme Court held that striking railroad workers were entitled to jury trials when they were charged with criminal contempt. He also worked with the legendary attorneys Clarence Darrow and Arthur Garfield Hays, co-founder of the American Civil Liberties Union, to defend a black physician from Detroit, Michigan, Dr. Ossian Sweet. Sweet's case became a cause célèbre. The good doctor was tried for murder when he and his friends defended his home from a white mob incensed that a black man had purchased a house in a previously all-white neighborhood. Gunshots fired from the Sweet home during the melee struck two white men, killing one. Surprisingly, Dr. Sweet and his codefendants won an acquittal from an all-white jury.[47]

It was heady stuff for a young lawyer, but Lilienthal found his true calling later in his career as a public utilities attorney. As a member of the Wisconsin Public Service Commission, the dynamic young man attracted widespread attention for his legal acumen as well as his indefatigable investigations of the gas, electric, and telephone utilities. He became adept at playing bureaucratic politics. After Lilienthal's patron, Wisconsin Governor Philip La Follette, son of the famed Progressive Robert M. La Follette, Sr., suffered a defeat in the 1932 gubernatorial election, Lilienthal realized that his position was diminished. He sought an appointment inside the incoming Roosevelt administration. It was his best hope to influence public policy development and implementation on a grand stage. In 1933, President Roosevelt appointed Lilienthal to a three-person board overseeing the new Tennessee Valley Authority (TVA). Thus began a rocky tenure characterized by dramatic accomplishments and enormous controversy.[48]

TVA was Franklin Roosevelt's answer to revitalizing the depressed area in parts of Alabama, Kentucky, Mississippi, and Tennessee. Residents were rural and poor. They had been hit especially hard by the Great Depression, which meant that much of their farmland was uncultivated and of little use to people who could not afford to purchase feed, seed, and accoutrements necessary to till the land for profit. TVA established a gigantic hydroelectric plant that generated inexpensive electricity for residents while also creating construction jobs and educating citizens on productive uses of land.

At first blush, TVA appeared to be exactly the sort of colossal public works project that was sorely needed in a country starved of financial resources and desperate for a plan to combat the depressive economic cycle that had gripped the nation's businesses. Who could object to an infusion of capital that got the nation working again? As an added benefit, the success of this high-profile effort could demonstrate to critics of democracy and capitalism around the world that government programs could ensure the success of private enterprise. With the creation of the public corporation, however, FDR's critics believed they had seen incontrovertible evidence of the president's sinister goals to socialize the country.[49]

Corporations were supposed to be private entities that competed in free markets, not creatures of the federal government. By providing low-cost electric service while acting as a market participant, TVA distorted private sector supply and demand curves, which interfered with pricing. Such actions, the administration's detractors contended, introduced inefficiencies into markets that interrupted the natural flow of commerce. Far from ameliorating the Great Depression, New Deal programs such as TVA merely moved the United States from a free market to a controlled economy. Yes, the economic downturn of the 1930s was unprecedented in scale, but it did not represent a fundamental departure from the nature of the business cycle. It was different in degree, but not in kind. By overspending in an effort to jumpstart the economy through artificial means, the administration was creating government deficits through make-work programs that ultimately delayed the day of reckoning.[50]

The TVA flooded 153,000 acres of land in the Tennessee Valley region, creating a large outdoor recreation area and two major new dams, Norris and Wheeler, to generate hydroelectric power. No one was a more enthusiastic booster for the agency than David Lilienthal, who proudly wore the sobriquet "Mr. TVA." He was joined on the Authority board by Harcourt Morgan, an agricultural expert who previously served as president of the University of Tennessee, and Arthur E. Morgan, an engineer and educator who served as the first TVA chairman.[51]

Arthur Morgan and Lilienthal did not get along, and as time went on the two men clashed repeatedly. Their disputes involved two markedly different personalities—Morgan was an old-fashioned moralist who was set on his ways while Lilienthal was the proverbial brash young man on the move, impatient with the staid, conformist TVA chairman—but it was more than that. Lilienthal's vision for TVA was that the agency would be a grassroots expression of participatory democracy; that is, the Authority spoke in "a tongue that is universal, a language of things close to the lives of the people." Communities where the TVA operated would employ local people, educate them, invite them to participate in decision-making, and better the lives of everyone involved. If the agency never quite lived up to this ideal, Lilienthal's philosophy was the quintessential expression of New Deal idealism.[52]

Lilienthal spelled out his view of an activist government in a commencement address that he delivered at the University of Virginia on June 14, 1948. Titled "The Citizen as Public Servant," the speech argued that all citizens should give back to their communities by working inside of government, at least for a small portion of their adult lives. Referring to the challenges facing Americans at mid-century, he remarked that "This period will not only call for steadfastness and faith, but for great skills in self-government, great judgment and open-mindedness in the development of public policies, and creativeness in all the arts of government. In these circumstances we must summon all of our talents for citizenship, for self-government, for public service as we chart our course through these dark waters." Lilienthal was careful to note that he was not rejecting the primacy of private enterprise. He simply wanted a more robust form of citizen participation in government service. "What I urge is a fluid kind of citizen-service, in which men and women move from private life into public service for a period of years, and then back to private life."[53]

This sort of activism did not sit well with Arthur Morgan. The chairman lobbied President Roosevelt not to reappoint Lilienthal when the young man's three-year term expired in May 1936. In fact, Morgan threatened to resign as chairman if the president reappointed Lilienthal. FDR used his considerable powers of persuasion to mollify Morgan even as Lilienthal won his reappointment. Later, after Morgan had left the board, Lilienthal served as chairman.[54]

Today the TVA experiment is remembered as the best of times and the worst of times. It has become a symbol of the New Deal's tremendous promise as well as its failure to live up to that promise. The Authority did indeed provide for the needs of the poor people of the Tennessee Valley, and it did bring jobs and a small measure of prosperity to the region. Yet it was hardly a model of participatory democracy. Moreover, for every environmental problem it solved, such as providing hydroelectric power and revitalizing land use, it also created other problems. Whenever human beings engineer large construction projects such as dams and river rerouting, they interfere with nature's processes, displacing some species and habitats even as they improve the lives of animals and plants in other areas. The ultimate success or failure of TVA depends on who is asked and the standards by which its successes are measured.[55]

In addition to the activities of government institutions such as the CCC, the Interior Department, and the TVA during the Roosevelt era, environmental activists began to emerge at mid-century. Few Americans epitomized the new breed of American environmentalist better than Aldo Leopold. Although he spent much of his life in government service as an employee of the U.S. Forest Service, Leopold had accepted a position as a professor of game management in the Agricultural Economics Department at the University of Wisconsin-Madison by the time that Franklin Roosevelt became president. Nonetheless, in 1934, at Roosevelt's request, Leopold accepted a position on a three-member blue ribbon panel on wildlife restoration.[56]

Combining the poetic sensibilities of Thoreau with the scientific rigor of later environmental scientists, Leopold influenced virtually all the American ecologists who followed him. Born toward the end of the nineteenth century, just as the American frontier closed, young Aldo knew even as a child that he wanted to work as a naturalist. Educated in forestry at Yale University, he eventually joined the ranks of the Forest Service and set out on a storied career.[57]

Stationed in the Southwest during his first assignment, Leopold enjoyed numerous opportunities to observe nature as well as human-kind's destructive effects on the environment. In an essay titled "Thinking Like a Mountain" which, would become famous when it was published many years later, he recalled that his early orders were to kill mountain lions, wolves, and bears, many of which preyed on livestock. Leopold initially believed that his task was an environmentally sound practice. Ridding the area of beasts that interfered with human interests appeared to be a noble undertaking, in his view, because he was protecting animals that the predators killed. He soon changed his mind.

Eating lunch with his colleagues one day, he spied a family of wolves next to a river. "In those days we had never heard of passing up a chance to kill a wolf," he mused many years later. "In a second we were pumping lead into the pack, but with more excitement than accuracy: how to aim a steep downhill shot is always confusing. When our rifles were empty, the old wolf was down, and a pup was dragging a leg into impassable slide-rocks. We reached the old wolf in time to watch a fierce green fire dying in her eyes." It was a revelatory moment, an episode Leopold never forgot. "I realized then, and have known ever since, that there was something new to me in those eyes—something known only to her and to the mountain. I was young then, and full of trigger-itch; I thought that because fewer wolves meant more deer, that no wolves would mean a hunters' paradise. But after seeing the green fire die, I sensed that neither the wolf nor the mountain agreed with such a view."[58]

Leopold never became a full-fledged deep ecologist, but he nonetheless understood that human beings see nature from a self-centered perspective that does not always factor in the natural balance that exists in the wild. He discussed this balance in another famous essay, "The Land Ethic." Leopold wrote of the "interconnectedness of all things," arguing that ecological systems cannot be understood and appreciated unless people realize that "the individual is a member of a community of interdependent parts." According to Leopold, the "land ethic simply enlarges the boundaries of the community to include soils, waters, plants, and animals, or collectively: the land." He did not base his conclusions on mythical or mystical tales of nature's wonders. He was at heart a pragmatist. Instead, Leopold set forth what later scholars would discuss as a holistic, systems approach to environmental management. "A land ethic of course cannot prevent the alteration, management, and use of these 'resources,' but it does affirm their right to continued existence, and, at least in spots, their continued existence in a natural state." In other words, "Conservation is a state of harmony between men and land."[59]

Aldo Leopold wrote about ecology through much of his professional life, but *A Sand County Almanac* was by far his most influential work. He penned most of the essays and vignettes during his twilight years, and they represented the culmination of his insight into a new environmental ethic. First published in 1949, a year after his death, *A Sand County Almanac* contains Leopold's most poetic ruminations on nature. The essays are beautifully written and designed for lay persons with no special knowledge of, or training in, ecology to read and enjoy. To date, the book has sold more than two million copies and has been translated into many languages.[60]

Other environmentalists followed in Leopold's footsteps and sought to profit from his example. Some cut their teeth as government workers while others earned their reputations in the private sector. In some cases, they shuttled back and forth through a revolving door of government service and nonprofit organizations. They brought with them keen insight into the ways that government entities and private organizations could forge partnerships in the name of environmental protection.

Few of the new breed were as influential as Robert "Bob" Marshall, 14 years younger than Leopold. Raised in a liberal Jewish family, Marshall learned about power and its uses at the feet of his father, Louis, who was a partner in the prestigious Washington, D.C. law firm of Guggenheimer, Untermeyer, and Marshall. Bob also learned about environmental protection from his father, who actively fought to protect the Adirondack Forest Preserve in New York. The father's combativeness would be a useful lesson for the son in the latter's career, which frequently was steeped in controversy and contentiousness.[61]

In 1935, Aldo Leopold joined forces with Bob Marshall to form an environmental group, the Wilderness Society, designed to "protect wilderness and inspire Americans to care for our wild places." Later, Marshall became head of the Division of Recreation and Lands for the U.S. Forest Service and worked in the Forestry Division of the Bureau of Indian Affairs. During his tenure in public service, Marshall came to see that "people cannot live generation after generation in the city without serious retrogression—physical, moral, and mental." His reverence for nature and his distaste for urban life reflected the views of Jean Jacques Rousseau and Henry David Thoreau, two thinkers who understood the corrosive power of organized society to degrade the human psyche.[62]

Marshall was a polarizing figure during his era. An unabashed liberal at a time when many conservatives were challenging Franklin Roosevelt's conception of an activist federal government, a preservationist when many proponents of environmentalism were staunch conservationists, and a gay man living in a country that stigmatized homosexuality, Marshall grew exhausted from the battles he fought during his short life. He somehow seemed doomed from the start.[63]

Marshall's idealism was in full view in his two best known works. Arguing for the establishment of a "green utopia," he published a pamphlet, *The Social Management of American Forests* (1930), and a book, *The People's Forests* (1933), calling for public ownership of all U.S. timber lands. He worried that without a strong central government to direct environmental policy, private interests would slowly, inexorably encroach on the nation's forests. Marshall wanted all Americans to enjoy forest lands, which meant that wooded acreage had to be judiciously preserved. To instill a sense of the wonder and responsibilities associated with a love of nature, he suggested that programs be created to allow the less affluent to visit wilderness areas, even at public expense.[64]

His radical proposals, dripping with not-so-implicit socialist ideas, attracted the attention of a U.S. House of Representatives investigative committee examining "un-American activities." Committee chairman Martin Dies, a prominent Democratic congressman from Texas and an infamous reactionary who seethed with anger and resentment over FDR's New Deal, launched an investigation into the activities of eight federal officials with reputed ties to Communist causes. Bob Marshall was one of the committee's targets. It was a dangerous time to be targeted by the committee. Careers and reputations could be, and often were, destroyed with little more than a well-placed rumor or innuendo. Marshall's colleagues recognized the danger and took evasive action, even if he did not. Although some forestry officials distanced themselves from Marshall to protect their programs from unwanted scrutiny, he remained steadfast in articulating his beliefs. The Dies investigations imperiled U.S. wilderness programs with the taint of Communist conspiracies, but Marshall believed that he would weather the storm.[65]

He was never hailed before the committee. During an overnight train journey from Washington, D.C. to New York City, the 38-year-old environmentalist unexpectedly died in his sleep. Marshall's untimely death saved him from a protracted battle. With no family to care for, he left his $1.5 million estate (equivalent to $25 million in 2012 dollars) to a variety of causes, including a trust established for "preservation of wilderness conditions in outdoor America, including, but not limited to, the preservation of areas embracing primitive conditions of transportation, vegetation, and fauna."[66]

After his death, Marshall's reputation grew and his influence spread. When President Lyndon B. Johnson signed the Wilderness Act into law in 1964, Marshall's and Aldo Leopold's Wilderness Society had been instrumental in pushing the legislation, which protected nine million acres of wilderness lands. Later that year, the federal government created the Bob Marshall Wilderness Area in Montana. Time and distance had revealed that Bob Marshall was not a threat to the American republic, but a conscientious defender of environmental causes.[67]

It was fitting that Marshall's legacy extended into 1964. The 1960s saw a rise in environmental activism, especially after Rachel Carson published her groundbreaking book *Silent Spring* in 1962. As discussed in Chapter 7, Carson initiated the modern environmental movement that eventually led to the ascendancy of numerous nongovernmental organizations (NGOs) dedicated to environmental protection. Moreover, Carson's call for average citizens to become involved in environmentalism in lieu of leaving the issue to elites paved the way for grassroots movements such as Earth Day celebrations.

Earth Day eventually became one of the most high-profile events in all of American environmentalism. The first celebration dates from April 22, 1970, but the concept was born earlier. The idea originated with Democratic U.S. Senator Gaylord Nelson, a long-time environmentalist. Nelson hailed from Wisconsin, a Midwestern state with a long history of progressivism. During his governorship from 1959 until 1963, Nelson earned high marks as the "conservation governor" after he championed the creation of an agency, the Department of Resource Development, to administer state parks. He also created the Youth Conservation Corps, which put 1,000 young people to work in "green jobs." Nelson's Outdoor Recreation Action Program (ORAP) was an innovative program for acquiring land to convert into public parks and wilderness areas.[68]

Implementing environmental protection programs on the state level was no small achievement, but Nelson wanted more. When he stepped into the United States Senate, he was determined to expand his conservation programs from Wisconsin onto a national stage. He was aided by the publication of *Silent Spring* not long before he arrived in Washington, D.C. After reading the book, Senator Nelson realized that the indiscriminate use of dichlorodiphenyltrichloroethane (DDT), the chemical Carson targeted in the book, constituted a genuine health hazard and must become the focus of his legislative agenda. He sponsored legislation to ban DDT use in the United States, but he failed to garner sufficient congressional support to enact the measure. Nelson was ahead of his time. The U.S. Senate remained an essentially conservative institution, and any attempt to initiate widespread change met with fierce resistance from entrenched powers.[69]

Recognizing that he would face seemingly insurmountable barriers if he continued to push for a legislative solution, the senator stumbled upon a different approach. He was sitting on an airplane flying back from witnessing the environmental degradation caused by a massive oil spill in California in 1969 when he experienced an epiphany. His tactics needed to change. Rather than pursue a top-down approach such as sponsoring legislation, perhaps he could empower a grassroots network to push for change from the bottom up. At the time, college "teach-ins" were popular vehicles for raising consciousness and encouraging citizens, especially young people, to participate in political activities. Opposition to the Vietnam War had politicized a generation of young people. Senator Nelson realized that this same group of activists could energize the environmental movement and effect change in ways that he could not.[70]

Throughout that fall, Nelson delivered speeches about his evolving notions of an environmental teach-in. He eventually attracted attention from influential national publications such as *Time* magazine and the *New York Times*. As momentum built, the senator selected April 22, 1970, as the date for a "National Teach-In on the Crisis of the Environment." It was a shrewd move. He chose a date between university spring breaks and examination periods so that students on college campuses across the country could take part in the festivities. Although Nelson did not use the term "Earth Day," soon his teach-in gained widespread recognition.[71]

He knew that the event should not become the Gaylord Nelson Show. It must be larger than one individual. Thus, in November 1969, he organized a steering committee of scientists, environmentalists, and students to handle the deluge of questions from the press and persons interested in participating in the April 22 teach-in. In a savvy bipartisan maneuver, the Democratic senator convinced liberal Republican Congressman Paul McCloskey of California to co-chair the event. Nelson and McCloskey directed their respective staffers to develop a platform, recruit student volunteers, schedule fundraisers, and coordinate media materials such as posters, buttons, an official documentary, and even a popular song.[72]

Senator Nelson also understood that the event must not be a single day of celebration that was promptly forgotten as soon as the banners were torn down and the calendar moved toward May. To that end, he formed Environmental Teach-In, Inc., an independent nonprofit organization headquartered in Washington, D.C. A former Stanford University student body president and Harvard Law School student, Denis Hayes, stepped in to head the new group. Under Hayes' leadership, Environmental Teach-In staff developed a public relations campaign that featured a newsletter, resource packets, posters, and a campaign to encourage citizens to write their elected officials about the need to protect the natural environment. The group sponsored a full-page advertisement in the *New York Times* on January 18, 1970. The phrase "Earth Day" appeared there for the first time.[73]

The text for the advertisement was deliberately provocative, a call to action that could only be ignored at humankind's peril. "A disease has infected our country. It has brought smog to Yosemite, dumped garbage in the Hudson, sprayed DDT in our food, and left our cities in decay. Its carrier is man." With this sobering assertion, the organizers outlined their goals for the event. "Earth Day is a commitment to make life better, not just bigger and faster; to provide real rather than rhetorical solutions. It is a day to re-examine the ethic of individual progress at mankind's expense. It is a day to challenge the corporate and governmental leaders who promise change, but who short-change the necessary programs."[74]

The 1970 event succeeded beyond Senator Nelson's wildest expectations. What had started as an idea for improving environmental awareness blossomed into a national, and eventually international, campaign for human beings to focus on their destructive activities and their impact on the health of the planet. More than 20 million people came together that April 22, convening in public parks, on college campuses, and in a variety of public spaces. They listened to speeches by political figures and entertainers, enjoyed songs by professional singers as well as inspired amateurs, and focused their attention on oil spills, pesticides, air pollution, toxic substances, and the loss of wilderness acreage and wetlands. New York City featured perhaps a million people as Mayor John Lindsay directed city officials to block off Fifth Avenue and allow a mass rally to take place in Central Park. Movie stars Paul Newman and Ali McGraw showed up to lend support. In Washington, D.C., folk singer Pete Seeger played his guitar and sang protest songs. The events generated enormous media coverage. CBS News featured a one-hour prime-time television special, "Earth Day: A Question of Survival," hosted by the venerable news anchorman Walter Cronkite.[75]

Senator Nelson appeared at an Earth Day celebration in Denver, Colorado, and accepted an invitation to speak to the crowd. "Earth Day is dramatic evidence of a broad new national concern that cuts across generations and ideologies. It may be symbolic of a new communication between young and old about our values and priorities," he said. Yet a single event, no matter how important, is not enough to accomplish meaningful, systemic change. Sustained action is crucial. "Earth Day can—and it must—lend a new urgency and a new support to solving the problems that still threaten to tear the fabric of this society ... the problems of race, of war, of poverty, of modern-day institutions." These problems will not be solved overnight. They require Americans to remake themselves, as citizens have done many times throughout history. "Our goal is not just an environment of clear air and water and scenic beauty. The objective is an environment of decency, quality and mutual respect for all other human beings and all other living creatures."[76]

Earth Day met the senator's initial objectives. The event raised environmental awareness and pushed untold numbers of citizens to engage in the political process when they otherwise might have stayed on the sidelines. As discussed in Chapter 5, the numerous environmental laws enacted at the federal level during the 1970s (to say nothing of state environmental laws) might not have been introduced, much less signed into law, were it not for the Earth Day awakening. By encouraging a ground-swell of public participation, Gaylord Nelson allowed average Americans in all walks of life to participate, which empowered communities. In explaining his tactics, the senator observed, "No one could organize 20 million people, 10,000 grade schools and high schools, 2,500 colleges and 1,000 communities in three and a half months, even if he had $20 million. The key to the whole thing was the grass-roots response."[77]

A grassroots response can raise awareness for a short time, but sustaining the awareness is challenging. In the wake of the 1970 celebration, the question was how the environmental community could build Earth

Day into something that produced measurable results. Fortunately for Senator Nelson and his supporters, environmentalism was alive and well. Denis Hayes and other organizers scrambled to solidify their organizations. Hayes moved to create the Earth Day Network, a series of organizations devoted to promoting environmental awareness year-round and campaigning for policy changes inside governments. Environmentalists of the 1970s understood that NGOs, quasi-governmental agencies, state and local governments, private citizens-turned-activists, and others interested in promoting environmental education and improving public policy could work together. By turn of the century, some 19,000 organizations in 192 countries were working with the Earth Day Network.[78]

THE END OF THE BEGINNING

If the 1970s were to become the environmental decade—a decade that would reverse at least some of the negative effects of pollution, proliferating toxic chemicals, and loss of wetlands—they needed a champion inside the ranks of government to ensure that progress continued. The decade also needed a large-scale environmental catastrophe that would highlight once and for all the damage that human beings can do to the environment.[79]

The decade found its first major governmental champion in William Ruckelshaus. He was a Harvard-educated lawyer who began his career in the private practice of law before moving in and out of government service. In 1970, President Richard Nixon tapped the 37-year-old lawyer to serve at the first head of the U.S. Environmental Protection Agency (EPA), a newly established independent agency that would coordinate policies across all federal executive branch departments to provide for clear, consistent, and coherent environmental policy. EPA was not part of a larger executive branch agency, which meant that it would be relatively autonomous, a step removed from political pressure in regulating air pollution, water pollution, drinking water contamination, hazardous waste disposal, pesticides, and toxic substances.[80]

EPA soon became a troubled agency mired in controversy largely because its mission was to stop organized entities, especially private-sector corporations, from releasing emissions into the atmosphere or discharging effluents into waterways without providing documentation that such pollutants did not harm environmental quality or endanger public health. As with anyone who repeatedly says "no" to the plans of others, the agency developed a reputation as recalcitrant and obstructionist, a job-killing bureaucracy staffed with unelected zealots. Agency officials sometimes were vilified as true believers in the environmentalist credo pursuing a liberal agenda under the guise of natural resource protection. For their part, many EPA scientists and researchers believed that their enemies, often political appointees in Republican presidential administrations, were interested in protecting large corporate campaign contributors at the expense of the environment, essentially adopting the neoclassical perspective that economic issues outweigh other, presumably lesser considerations.[81]

Ruckelshaus' appointment was designed to placate parties on both sides of the divide, to the extent possible. He was widely regarded as a principled man of integrity who would administer the agency without playing favorites or bowing to political pressure—refusing to demonize corporations or ignore the concerns of environmentalists. To some extent, Ruckelshaus succeeded. In a press release he issued not long after he assumed his duties in December 1970, he vowed to work with all stakeholders to craft an equitable solution. "The job that must be done now to restore and preserve the quality of our air, water, and soil can only be accomplished if this new Federal agency works closely with industry and with other levels of government," Ruckelshaus promised. "The technology which has bulldozed its way across the environment must now be employed to remove impurities from the air, to restore vitality to our rivers and streams, to recycle the waste that is the ugly by-product of our prosperity."[82]

Ruckelshaus spent much of his tenure establishing the agency's organizational structure and lending his good name and credibility to the institution. One of the first orders of business was to create 10 regional offices around the country "to work with state and local officials and private organizations to insure maximum participation in environmental programs." The new administrator also recognized the importance of filing lawsuits against cities that were not enforcing federal environmental laws to compel compliance within the private sector. The suits not only required municipal officials to enforce federal law, but they pushed other noncompliant entities who were not yet litigants to act with dispatch lest they be hauled into court. In later years, the EPA brought actions against private parties as well. The federal courts became a critical enforcement mechanism for the environmental gains that followed.[83]

Ruckelshaus remained at the EPA helm from December 1970 until April 1973, but this "extraordinary public servant" was in high demand, and he never stayed at one position for long. He was dispatched to serve as acting director of the Federal Bureau of Investigation (FBI) and, eventually, deputy attorney general of the U.S. Department of Justice. During the infamous "Saturday Night Massacre," Ruckelshaus and his boss, Elliot Richardson, resigned rather than obey President Nixon's order that they fire Archibald Cox, the special prosecutor investigating malfeasance in the Watergate scandal. He returned to the EPA from 1983 until 1985 to restore public confidence in the agency following several highly publicized debacles during the Reagan years.[84]

Ruckelshaus did much to repair EPA's tarnished reputation during the 1980s, but it may have been too little, too late. Public perception was that the natural environment in the United States was badly contaminated, and the problem was growing worse. Although the 1970s witnessed the enactment of major federal environmental statutes, those laws frequently were reactions to disastrous events such as the Love Canal episode recounted in Chapter 5. In any case, the Three Mile Island (TMI) nuclear incident in 1979 was perhaps the most notorious environmental mishap during an era filled with mishaps. TMI was the catastrophe (or very nearly one) that galvanized environmentalists everywhere.

The Three Mile Island Generating Station, owned in the 1970s by the Metropolitan Edison Company, a subsidiary of GPU, Inc. (formerly General Public Utilities Nuclear) energy division, was a nuclear reactor located in Dauphin County, Pennsylvania, near Harrisburg, the state capital. Around 4:00 a.m. on Wednesday, March 28, 1979, a mechanical or electrical failure prevented pumps from sending water to the steam generators located in reactor number two. Water is a crucial component of a nuclear reactor because it removes heat from the core. This initial failure triggered a series of events. The reactor's turbine generator shut down, as did the reactor itself. In the wake of this development, pressure built to unsustainable levels. A pilot-operated relief valve opened to relieve the pressure, but the valve never closed when the pressure dropped to normal levels. In the meantime, control panel instruments did not alert the reactor staff that the valve was open. Consequently, cooling water from the reactor poured through the valve. The staff was confused. No one recognized that the plant had lost coolant. Workers reduced emergency cooling water levels and overheated the reactor. Nuclear fuel caused approximately half of the core to melt down, although the most dangerous radioactive material did not escape from the plant.

Notified of the incident, the U.S. Nuclear Regulatory Commission (NRC) sent a team of investigators from the NRC operations center in Bethesda, Maryland, to investigate. The EPA and the U.S. Department of Energy followed suit. Before long, the event attracted national and international news coverage. Each day the matter appeared to be resolved, only to recur with frightening intensity. Plant neighbors worried that unseen radiation was seeping from the plant walls and no one was taking their fears seriously. Finally, after concerns about a radiation release reached a fever pitch on March 30, Pennsylvania Governor Richard L. Thornburgh directed that pregnant women and children should be evacuated from the area as a safety precaution.

One last crisis loomed. The day after the governor ordered the precautionary evacuation, chemical reactions inside the pressure vessel dome created a hydrogen bubble that posed a risk of a containment breach. Experts feared that the bubble might expand and eventually lead to a catastrophic explosion along with an accompanying release of dangerous levels of radiation. Fortunately, the bubble dissipated and utility personnel brought the crisis under control. Nonetheless, those days at the end of March 1979 were tense for area residents, NRC officials, and utility executives. The incident also eroded public support for nuclear energy for decades afterward.[85]

The aftermath of the TMI debacle was in some sense the end of the beginning of American environmentalism. Owing to the efforts of Progressives such as Theodore Roosevelt, John Muir, and Gifford Pinchot, environmental concerns became crucial public policy issues in the United States during the early years of the twentieth century. Later, public servants such as Harold Ickes and David Lilienthal ensured that plans to protect natural resources and improve the lives of citizens as a result would be implemented with vim and vigor. They set the stage for Aldo Leopold and Bob Marshall, among others, to champion environmental issues as they skirted between the public and private sectors. Finally, dedicated public servants typified by William Ruckelshaus at EPA ensured that the environmental laws and policies developed during the 1970s would be enforced rigorously.

Yet the 1970s, that much-discussed decade of enormous environmental progress, ended on a sour note. TMI demonstrated the limits of manmade technology. Even if the technology were not flawed, the human beings who reacted to glitches and confusing data were unable to problem solve effectively. The incident not only curtailed nuclear power development in the United States for decades, but it also highlighted humankind's inability to protect the environment from destruction caused by Homo sapiens.

As environmentalism evolved during the 1970s and beyond, dedicated public servants laboring inside government agencies remained integral to the success of national environmental policy. Yet the private sector also grew evermore influential. NGOs assumed an important role in shaping environmental policy beginning in the 1970s and continuing to the present day. Chapter 7 explores the rise of environmental NGOs in making and implementing public policy in the modern, post-1970s era.[86]

NOTES

1. See, for example, J. Michael Martinez, *American Environmentalism: Philosophy, History, and Public Policy* (Boca Raton, FL.: CRC Press, 2014); Carolyn Merchant, *American Environmental History: An Introduction* (New York: Columbia University Press, 2007); Paul S. Sutter, "The World with Us: The State of American Environmental History," *The Journal of American History* 100 (June 2013): 94–119.

2. See especially Stephen E. Ambrose, *Undaunted Courage: Meriwether Lewis, Thomas Jefferson, and the Opening of the American West* (New York: Touchstone Books, a Division of Simon & Schuster, 1996). See also William A. Koelsch, "Thomas Jefferson, Geographers, and the Uses of Geography," *Geographical Review* 98 (April 2008): 260, 264–69; Ingo Schwarz, "Alexander von Humboldt's Visit to Washington and Philadelphia, His Friendship with Jefferson, and His Fascination with the United States," *Northeastern Naturalist* 8 (2001): 43–56.

3. Ida Altman, "The Revolt of Enriquillo and the Historiography of Early Spanish America," *The Americas* 63 (April 2007): 587–614; Richard Flint, *No Settlement, No Conquest: A History of the Coronado Entrada* (Albuquerque: University of New Mexico Press, 2008); Andrés Reséndez, *A Land So Strange: The Epic Journey of Cabeza de Vaca: The Extraordinary Tale of a Shipwrecked Spaniard Who Walked Across America in the Sixteenth Century* (New York: Basic Books, 2007); Richard White, "Discovering Nature in North America," *The Journal of American History* 79 (December 1992): 877–85.

4. Henry David Thoreau, "Walking," in *The Writings of Henry David Thoreau*, Vol. V: *Excursions and Poems*, Bradford Torrey, ed. (Boston and New York: Houghton Mifflin and Company, the Riverside Press, Cambridge, 1906 [1865]): 217–18.

5. Frederick Jackson Turner, "The Significance of the Frontier in American History," *Annual Report of the American Historical Association for 1893* (Washington, D.C.: U.S. Government Printing Office, 1894): 199–227. See also Robert H. Block, "Frederick Jackson Turner and American Geography," *Annals of the Association of American Geographers* 70 (March 1980): 31–42; Ronald H. Carpenter, "Frederick Jackson Turner and the Rhetorical Impact of the Frontier Thesis," *Quarterly Journal of Speech* 63 (April 1977): 117–129; T.R.C. Hutton, "Beating a Dead Horse: The Continuing Presence of Frederick Jackson Turner in Environmental and Western History," *International Social Science Review* 77 (January 2002): 47–57; Alex Wagner Lough, "Henry George, Frederick Jackson Turner, and the 'Closing' of the American Frontier," *California History* 89 (March 2012): 4–23; Wilbur Zelinsky, *The Cultural Geography of the United States* (Englewood Cliffs, N.J.: Prentice Hall, 1973), 34–35.

6. Mike Dunning, "Manifest Destiny and the Trans-Mississippi South: Natural Laws and the Extension of Slavery into Mexico," *Journal of Popular Culture* 35 (Fall 2001): 111–27; Sally Frahm, "The Cross and the Compass: Manifest Destiny, Religious Aspects of the Mexican-American War," *Journal of Popular Culture* 35 (Fall 2001): 83–99; Daniel Walker Howe, *What Hath God Wrought: The Transformation of America* (Oxford and New York: Oxford University Press, 2007), 762–64; Michael A. Morrison, *Slavery and the American West: The Eclipse of Manifest Destiny and the Coming of the Civil War* (Chapel Hill: University of North Carolina Press, 1997).

7. Quoted in Howe, *What Hath God Wrought*, 704.

8. Quoted in George Catlin, *Letters and Notes on the Manners, Customs, and Condition of the North American Indians*, vol. I (London: Tosswell and Myers, 1841): 260. Italics appear in the original. See also John Hausdoerffer, *Catlin's Lament: Indians, Manifest Destiny, and the Ethics of Nature* (Lawrence: University Press of Kansas, 2009); Benjamin Kline, Ph.D, *First Along the River: A Brief History of the U.S. Environmental Movement*, 3rd. edition (Lanham, MD: Rowman & Littlefield, 2007): 34–35.

9. Michael K. Steinberg, "Audubon Landscapes in the South," *The Mississippi Quarterly* 63 (Winter 2010): 314–15.

10. Albert Boime, "John James Audubon: A Birdwatcher's Fanciful Flights," *Art History* 22 (December 1999): 728–55; Steinberg, "Audubon Landscapes in the South," 313–14.

11. Douglas Brinkley, *The Wilderness Warrior: Theodore Roosevelt and the Crusade for America* (New York: HarperCollins, 2009): 10–11, 184–89.

12. Edward J. Larson, "The Reception of Darwinism in the Nineteenth Century: A Three Part Story," *Science & Christian Belief* 21 (April 2009): 3–24; John G. West, "The Church Darwin," *First Things: A Monthly Journal of Religion & Public Life* 254 (June/July 2015): 21–23.

13. John Angus Campbell, "Charles Darwin and the Crisis of Ecology: A Rhetorical Perspective," *Quarterly Journal of Speech* 60 (December 1974): 442–49; Christian Diehm, "Darwin and Deep Ecology," *Ethics & The Environment* 19 (Spring 2014): 73–93; Trevor Pearce, "'A Great Complication of Circumstances'—Darwin and the Economy of Nature," *Journal of the History of Biology* (August 2010): 493–528.

14. George Perkins Marsh, *Man and Nature; or Physical Geography as Modified by Human Action* (New York: Charles Scribner, 1864): 36.

15. Ibid., 42. See also Kline, *First Along the River*, 46–47; Philip Shabecoff, *Earth Rising: American Environmentalism in the 21st Century* (Washington, D.C. and Covelo, CA: Island Press, 2001): 2.

16. John Wesley Powell, *The Exploration of the Colorado River and Its Canyons* (New York: Penguin Books, 2003 [1875]), 83. See also Kline, *First Along the River*, 47.

17. Steven J. Holmes, *The Young John Muir: An Environmental Biography* (Madison: The University of Wisconsin Press, 1999): 3–4.

18. Holmes, *The Young John Muir*, 17–18; James W. Shores, "A Win-Lose Situation: Historical Context, Ethos, and Rhetorical Choices in John Muir's 1908 'Hetch Hetchy Valley' Article," *The Journal of American Culture* 29 (June 2006): 191; Donald Worster, "John Muir and the Modern Passion for Nature," *Environmental History* 10 (January 2005): 9.

19. Brinkley, *The Wilderness Warrior*, 540–41; Holmes, *The Young John Muir*, 138–39; Shores, "A Win-Lose Situation," 191.

20. John Muir, *The Mountains of California* (New York: Penguin Books, 1985 [1894]): 88.

21. Brian Balogh, "Scientific Forestry and the Roots of the Modern American State: Gifford Pinchot's Path to Progressive Reform," *Environmental History* 7 (April 2002): 198–207; Brinkley, *The Wilderness Warrior*, 340; Char Miller and V. Alaric Sample, "Gifford Pinchot: A Life in Progress," *Journal of Forestry* 97, 1 (January 1999): 28.

22. Paul V. Ellefson, "The Safety of Our Forests and the Prosperity of Out People," *Journal of Forestry* 98 (May 2000): 15; Kline, *First Along the River*,

55–56; Char Miller, "Thinking Like a Conservationist," *Journal of Forestry* 100 (December 2002): 44–45; Gifford Pinchot, "The Economic Significance of Forestry," *The North American Review* 213 (February 1921): 157–67.

23. Brinkley, *The Wilderness Warrior*, 340–47; Kline, *First Along the River*, 55–58; Stewart L. Udall, *The Quiet Crisis* (New York: Holt, Rinehart, and Winston, 1963): 126–45.

24. Brinkley, *The Wilderness Warrior*, 789–90; Kline, *First Along the River* 58–60; Shores, "A Win-Lose Situation," 192–94.

25. Ben A. Minteer and Stephen J. Pyne, "Restoring the Narrative of American Environmentalism," *Restoration Ecology* 21 (January 2013): 6–11; Glen Sussman and Byron W. Daynes, "Spanning the Century: Theodore Roosevelt, Franklin Roosevelt, Richard Nixon, Bill Clinton, and the Environment," *White House Studies* 4 (April 2004): 339–41.

26. Brinkley, *The Wilderness Warrior*, 340–47, 541–45; Miller and Sample, "Gifford Pinchot," 29–30; Shabecoff, *Earth Rising*, 3.

27. See for example, Christoph Irmscher, *Louis Agassiz: Creator of American Science* (Boston: Houghton Mifflin Harcourt, 2013); David McCullough, *Brave Companions: Portraits in History* (New York: Simon & Schuster, 1992): 20–21.

28. Christoph Irmscher, "The Ambiguous Agassiz," *Humanities* 34 (November/December 2013): 16–17; Irmscher, *Louis Agassiz*, 42–47, 111–16, 118–20; McCullough, *Brave Companions*, 22–31; Louis Menand, *The Metaphysical Club: A Story of Ideas in America* (New York: Farrar, Straus and Giroux, 2001): 97–99.

29. Irmscher, "The Ambiguous Agassiz," 18; Irmscher, *Louis Agassiz*, 9–13, 111–12; McCullough, *Brave Companions*, 28–29.

30. Oliver Wendell Holmes, "A Farewell to Agassiz," in *The Complete Poetical Works of Oliver Wendell Holmes* (Boston and New York: Houghton Mifflin and Company, the Riverside Press, Cambridge, 1895): 204.

31. Oliver Wendell Holmes, "At the Saturday Club," in *The Poetical Works of Oliver Wendell Holmes in Three Volumes, Vol. III* (Boston and New York: Houghton Mifflin and Company, the Riverside Press, Cambridge, 1891): 122.

32. Irmscher, "The Ambiguous Agassiz," 18–19; Irmscher, *Louis Agassiz*, 4–5, 23–24, 126–29, 147–52; James R. Jackson and William C. Kimler, "Taxonomy and the Personal Equation: The Historical Fates of Charles Girard and Louis Agassiz," *Journal of the History of Biology* 32 (Winter 1999): 515, 524, 549; McCullough, *Brave Companions*, 31–33; Menand, *The Metaphysical Club*, 120–28.

33. Quoted in McCullough, *Brave Companions*, 33. See also Irmscher, "The Ambiguous Agassiz," 18–19, 51; Irmscher, *Louis Agassiz*, 133–34, 135–45, 147–48; Menand, *The Metaphysical Club*, 125–28.

34. McCullough, *Brave Companions*, 34. See also Irmscher, "The Ambiguous Agassiz," 18; Jackson and Kimler, "Taxonomy and the Personal Equation," 549–50.

35. Irmscher, "The Ambiguous Agassiz," 18–19, 51; Irmscher, *Louis Agassiz*, 346–48; Jackson and Kimler, "Taxonomy and the Personal Equation," 549–50; McCullough, *Brave Companions*, 34–36.

36. Mark Twain and Charles Dudley Warner, *The Gilded Age: A Tale of Today* (New York: The New American Library, 1985 [1873]). See also Shen Hou, "*Garden and Forest*: A Forgotten Magazine and the Urban Roots of American Environmentalism," *Environmental History* 17 (October 2012): 813–42; Domenic Vitiello, "Monopolizing the Metropolis: Gilded Age Growth Machines and Power in American Urbanization," *Planning Perspectives* 28 (January 2013): 71–90.

37. Nicholas Lemann, "Notorious Big: Why the Spectre of Size Has Always Haunted American Politics," *The New Yorker* 92 (March 28, 2016): 72–75; Jerry L. Mashaw, "Federal Administration and Administrative Law in the Gilded Age," *Yale Law Journal* 119 (May 2010): 1362–1472.

38. Brinkley, *The Wilderness Warrior*, 5–6; Michael A. Lerner, "Going Dry," *Humanities* 32 (September/October 2011): 10–13, 48; Susan J. Pearson, *The Rights of the Defenseless: Protecting Animals and Children in Gilded Age America* (Chicago and London: The University of Chicago Press, 2011); Frederick Winslow Taylor, *The Principles of Scientific Management* (Mineola, NY: Courier Dover Publications, 2009 [1911]); Daniel A. Wren, "The Centennial of Frederick W. Taylor's *The Principles of Scientific Management*: A Retrospective Commentary," *Journal of Business & Management* 17 (April 2011): 11–22.

39. Peter Dreier, "The Fifty Most Influential Progressives of the Twentieth Century," *Nation* 291 (October 4, 2010): 11–21; Simina Raţiu, "The Anti-Utopian Pessimism of the Late Nineteenth and Early Twentieth Century," *Caietele Echinox* 25 (December 2013): 65–75.

40. See especially Douglas Brinkley, *Rightful Heritage: Franklin D. Roosevelt and the Land of America* (New York: Harper, 2016).

41. Neil M. Maher, *Nature's New Deal: The Civilian Conservation Corps and the Roots of the American Environmental Movement* (Oxford and New York: Oxford University Press, 2008); Neil M. Maher, "A New Deal Body Politic: Landscape, Labor, and the Civilian Conservation Corps," *Environmental History* 7 (July 2002): 435–61; Edward J. Martin, "Economic Rights, Sustainable Development, and Environmental Management," *Public Administration & Management* 16 (April 2011): 126–27, 137–38.

42. Melissa Bass, "The Success and Contradictions of New Deal Democratic Populism: The Case of the Civilian Conservation Corps," *The Good Society* 21 (2012): 250–60; Brinkley, *Rightful Heritage*, 170–86, 582–84; Robert Fechner, "The Civilian Conservation Corps Program," *The Annals of the American Academy of Political and Social Science* 194 (November 1937): 129–40.

43. Jack Alexander, "Reformer in the Promised Land," *Saturday Evening Post* 212 (July 22, 1939): 5–7, 66–71; Brinkley, *Rightful Heritage*, 163–66;

Harold L. Ickes, "A Department of Conservation," *Vital Speeches of the Day* 3 (September 1, 1937): 693–95.

44. The comment on "America's No. 1 Curmudgeon, or Sour Puss" appears in Donald C. Swain, "Harold Ickes, Horace Albright, and the Hundred Days: A Study in Conservation Administration," *Pacific Historical Review* 34 (November 1965): 456. The comment on Ickes as a "prodigious bureaucrat" appears in Swain, "Harold Ickes, Horace Albright, and the Hundred Days," 456. The Walter Lippmann quite appears in Barry Mackintosh, "Harold L. Ickes and the National Park Service," *Journal of Forest History* 29 (April 1985): 78. The Horace M. Albright quote appears in Mackintosh, "Harold L. Ickes and the National Park Service," 79. The contemporary who characterized Ickes as "a remarkably complex and profoundly suspicious man" is quoted in Mackintosh, "Harold L. Ickes and the National Park Service," 78. See also M. Judd Harmon, "Some Contributions of Harold L. Ickes," *The Western Political Quarterly* 7 (June 1954): 238–52; W. Scott Nobles, "Harold L. Ickes: New Deal Hatchet Man," *Western Speech* 22 (Summer 1958): 158–63.

45. Harmon, "Some Contributions of Harold L. Ickes," 239; Mackintosh, "Harold L. Ickes and the National Park Service," 79–84; Swain, "Harold Ickes, Horace Albright, and the Hundred Days," 456–58.

46. Brinkley, *Rightful Heritage*, 544–48; Kline, *First Along the River*, 64–67; Robert D. Leighninger, Jr., *Building Louisiana: The Legacy of the Public Works Administration* (Jackson: University Press of Mississippi, 2007).

47. *Michaelson v. United States*, 266 U.S. 42 (1924). On the Sweet case, see, for example, Kevin Boyle, *The Arc of Justice: A Saga of Race, Civil Rights, and Murder in the Jazz Age* (New York: Henry Holt, 2004); Thomas J. Fleming, "The Murder Trial of Dr. Ossian Sweet," *Ebony* 25 (October 1970): 106–8, 110–12, 114.

48. A leading source of information on Lilienthal's background is Steven M. Neuse, *David E. Lilienthal: The Journey of an American Liberal* (Knoxville: University of Tennessee Press, 1996). See also "David E. Lilienthal is Dead at 81; Led U.S. Effort in Atomic Power," *New York Times*, January 16, 1981: A1.

49. Lilienthal's expression of faith in the TVA premise appears in his well-known tract, *TVA: Democracy on the March* (New York: Penguin Books, 1944), especially at 196–200. See also Brinkley, *Rightful Heritage*, 203, 204; David Ekbladh, "'Mr. TVA': Grass-Roots Development, David Lilienthal, and the Rise and Fall of the Tennessee Valley Authority as a Symbol for U.S. Overseas Development, 1933–1973," *Diplomatic History* 26 (Summer 2002): 335–74; Howard Segal, "Down in the Valley: David Lilienthal's TVA: Democracy on the March," American Scholar 64 (Summer 1995): 423–28.

50. See, for example, H.W. Brands, *Traitor to His Class: The Privileged Life and Radical Presidency of Franklin Delano Roosevelt* (New York: Doubleday, 2008): 252–53.

51. Robert Barde, "Arthur E. Morgan, First Chairman of TVA," *Tennessee Historical Quarterly* 30 (Fall 1971): 308; Brinkley, *Rightful Heritage*, 203–206; Aaron D. Purcell, "Undermining the TVA: George Berry, David Lilienthal, and Arthur Morgan," *Tennessee Historical Quarterly* 57 (Fall 1998): 171–72.

52. Ekbladh, "'Mr. TVA,'" 344–46; Purcell, "Undermining the TVA," 174–81.

53. David E. Lilienthal, "The Citizen as Public Servant," *Vital Speeches of the Day* 14 (July 15, 1948): 580–81.

54. Barde, "Arthur E. Morgan," 314; Purcell, "Undermining the TVA," 174–82.

55. Barde, "Arthur E. Morgan," 299–300; Brinkley, *Rightful Heritage*, 205; Ekbladh, "'Mr. TVA,'" 344–46; Purcell, "Undermining the TVA," 174–81.

56. Brinkley, *Rightful Heritage*, 272–74; Danny Heitman, "Earthy Wisdom: Aldo Leopold's Land Ethic," *Humanities* 34 (November/December 2013): 30.

57. Stephen J. Frese, "Aldo Leopold: An American Prophet," *History Teacher* 37 (November 2003): 100–103; Heitman, "Earthy Wisdom," 32.

58. Aldo Leopold, *A Sand County Almanac; with Essays on Conservation from Round River* (New York: Ballatine Books, 1990 [1949]): 138–39. See also Heitman, "Earthy Wisdom," 32–34; Philip Shabecoff, *A Fierce Green Fire: The American Environmental Movement* (Washington, D.C. and Covelo, CA: Island Press, 2003): 82–83.

59. Leopold, *A Sand County Almanac*, 239, 240, 243. See also Bill Devall, "The End of American Environmentalism?" *Nature and Culture* 1 (Autumn 2006): 159; Heitman, "Earthy Wisdom," 34–35.

60. Frese, "Aldo Leopold," 99–100; Heitman, "Earthy Wisdom," 29–30; Kline, *First Along the River*, 62–63; Max Oelschlaeger, "Ecological Restoration, Aldo Leopold, and Beauty: An Evolutionary Tale," *Environmental Philosophy* 4 (Fall/Spring 2007): 149–61; Gavin Van Horn, "The (Religious) Naturalist's Eye: An Introduction to 'Aldo Leopold: Ethical and Spiritual Dimensions,'" *Journal for the Study of Religion, Nature, and Culture* 5 (2011): 397–409; Barbara E. Willard, "Rhetorical Landscapes as Epistemic: Revisiting Aldo Leopold's *A Sand County Almanac*," *Environmental Communication* 1 (November 2007): 218–35.

61. Bibi Booth, "Robert Marshall (1901–1939)," in *Environmental Activists*, eds. John Mongillo and Bibi Booth (Westport, CT: Greenwood Press, 2001): 174; Phil Brown, "Wilderness Advocate," *New York Conservationist*, 62 (August 2007): 3–5; James A. Glover, *A Wilderness Original: The Life of Bob Marshall* (Seattle, WA: The Mountaineers Book, 1986): 89–90; Donald Dale Jackson, "Just Plain Bob was the Best Friend Wilderness Ever Had," *Smithsonian* 25 (August 1994): 92–94.

62. Quoted in Robert Gottlieb, "Reconstructing Environmentalism: Complex Movements, Diverse Roots," in *American Environmental History*, Louis S. Warren, ed. (Oxford, U.K.: B.H. Blackwell, 2004), 246–47. See also Booth,

"Robert Marshall (1901–1939)," 176; Brown, "Wilderness Advocate," 6; Glover, *A Wilderness Original*, 238.

63. Brown, "Wilderness Advocate," 5–6; Gottlieb, "Reconstructing Environmentalism," 247–48; Jackson, "Just Plain Bob was the Best Friend Wilderness Ever Had," 96–100.

64. Robert Marshall, *The Social Management of American Forests* (New York: League for Industrial Democracy, 1930); Robert Marshall, *The People's Forests* (Iowa City: University of Iowa Press, 2002 [1933]). See also Brown, "Wilderness Advocate," 5–6; Glover, *A Wilderness Original*, 163; Gottlieb, "Reconstructing Environmentalism," 247–48.

65. Glover, *A Wilderness Original*, 244–45; Dennis K. McDaniel, "The First Congressman Martin Dies of Texas," *Southwestern Historical Quarterly* 102 (October 1998): 130–61.

66. Quoted in Gottlieb, "Reconstructing Environmentalism," 248. See also Booth, "Robert Marshall (1901–1939)," 176; Brown, "Wilderness Advocate," 6.

67. Peter A. Appel, "Wilderness, the Courts, and the Effect of Politics on Judicial Decision-making," *Harvard Environmental Law Review* 35 (2011): 290; Booth, "Robert Marshall (1901–1939)," 177; Brown, "Wilderness Advocate," 6; Gottlieb, "Reconstructing Environmentalism," 248; Jackson, "Just Plain Bob was the Best Friend Wilderness Ever Had," 99–100.

68. Bill Christofferson, *The Man From Clear Lake: Earth Day Founder Senator Gaylord Nelson* (Madison: The University of Wisconsin Press, 2004): 273, 284; Devall, "The End of American Environmentalism?" 161; David J. Webber, "Earth Day and Its Precursors: Continuity and Change in the Evolution of Midtwentieth-Century U.S. Environmental Policy," *Review of Policy Research* 25 (July 2008): 314.

69. Christofferson, *The Man From Clear Lake*, 464–79; Sheila Terman Cohen, *Gaylord Nelson: Champion for Our Earth* (Madison: Wisconsin Historical Society Press, 2010): 66.

70. Cohen, *Gaylord Nelson*, 68–69; Adam Rome, *The Genius of Earth Day: How a 1970 Teach-In Unexpectedly Made the First Green Generation* (New York: Hill and Wang, 2013): x; Webber, "Earth Day and Its Precursors," 318.

71. Christofferson, *The Man From Clear Lake*, 531; Cohen, *Gaylord Nelson*, 68–69; Mark Hertsgaard, "Save Earth Day," *The Nation* 294 (May 7, 2012): 3; Webber, "Earth Day and Its Precursors," 318–19.

72. Christofferson, *The Man From Clear Lake*, 517; Cohen, *Gaylord Nelson*, 71; Rome, *The Genius of Earth Day*, 85.

73. Christofferson, *The Man From Clear Lake*, 8, 520–21; Cohen, *Gaylord Nelson*, 83; Hertsgaard, "Save Earth Day," 3; Shabecoff, *Earth Rising*, 186.

74. Quoted in Rome, *The Genius of Earth Day*, 164. See also Christofferson, *The Man From Clear Lake*, 524.

75. Douglas Brinkley, *Cronkite* (New York: Harper, 2012): 431–34; Christofferson, *The Man From Clear Lake*, 2–8; Cohen, *Gaylord Nelson*, 3–4, 71;

Hertsgaard, "Save Earth Day," 3; Kline, *First Along the River*, 81; Webber, "Earth Day and Its Precursors," 318.

76. Gaylord Nelson, "Earth Day Speech, Denver, Colorado," in *The Environmental Movement, 1968–1972*, David Stradling, ed. (Seattle: University of Washington Press, 2012): 85–86.

77. Quoted in Kline, *First Along the River*, 81. See also Hertsgaard, "Save Earth Day," 3–4; Shabecoff, *A Fierce Green Fire*, 105–12; Webber, "Earth Day and Its Precursors," 319.

78. Cohen, *Gaylord Nelson*, 71–75, 82, 83; Riley E. Dunlap and Angela G. Mertig, "The Evolution of the U.S. Environmental Movement from 1970 to 1990: An Overview," *Society & Natural Resources: An International Journal* 4 (1991): 209–18; Denis Hayes, "Earth Day! A Call to Unite in Defense of Our Planet," *Mother Earth News* 309 (April/May 2005): 24–31; David Rejeski, "Any Big Ideas Left?" *The Environmental Forum* 28 (September/October 2011): 36–41; Shabecoff, *A Fierce Green Fire*, 107–12.

79. See, for example, Habibul Haque Khondker, "From 'The Silent Spring' to Globalization of the Environmental Movement," *Journal of International and Global Studies* 6 (April 2015): 25–37; Nikolay L. Mihaylov and Douglas D. Perkins, "Local Environmental Grassroots Activism: Contributions from Environmental Psychology, Sociology and Politics," *Behavioral Sciences* 5 (2015): 121–53.

80. Richard N.L. Andrews, "The EPA at 40: An Historical Perspective," *Duke Environmental Law and Policy Forum* 21 (Spring 2011): 226–31; Susan J. Buck, *Understanding Environmental Administration and Law*, 2nd edition, (Washington, D.C. and Covelo, CA: Island Press, 1996), 21–22; Devall, "The End of American Environmentalism?" 161; Kline, *First Along the River*, 92; Robert V. Percival, "Checks without Balance: Executive Office Oversight of the Environmental Protection Agency," *Law and Contemporary Problems* 54 (Fall 1991): 129–35; Walter A. Rosenbaum, *Environmental Politics and Policy*, 4th edition, (Washington, D.C.: Congressional Quarterly Press, 1998), 82.

81. Andrews, "The EPA at 40," 235–53; Buck, *Understanding Environmental Administration and Law*, 23–24; Kline, *First Along the River*, 102–104; Rosenbaum, *Environmental Politics and Policy*, 107–12; Shabecoff, *Earth Rising*, 122–23.

82. Quoted in Marcos Luna, *The Environment since 1945* (New York: Facts on File, an Imprint of Infobase Learning, 2012): 105–106. See also Raanan Lipshitz and Leon Mann, "Leadership and Decision Making: William R. Ruckelshaus and the Environmental Protection Agency," *Journal of Leadership and Organizational Studies* 11 (June 23, 2005): 41–53; Reiner H. Lock and J.B. Ruhl, "Interview: William Ruckelshaus," *Natural Resources & Environment* 5 (Summer 1990): 36–39, 62–66.

83. Daniel J. Fiorino, "Streams of Environmental Innovation: Four Decades of EPA Policy Reform," *Environmental Law* 44 (Summer 2014): 737–38;

Lipshitz and Mann, "Leadership and Decision Making," 42–45; Lock and Ruhl, "Interview," 37.

84. Andrews, "The EPA at 40," 235–53; Fiorino, "Streams of Environmental Innovation," 740–41; Lipshitz and Mann, "Leadership and Decision Making," 42–48; Lock and Ruhl, "Interview," 36.

85. Raymond L. Goldsteen, Karen Goldsteen, and John K. Schorr, "Trust and Its Relationship to Psychological Distress: The Case of Three Mile Island," *Political Psychology* 13 (December 1992): 693–707; Nathan Hultman and Jonathan Koomey, "Three Mile Island: The Driver of U.S. Nuclear Power's Decline?" *Bulletin of the Atomic Scientists* 69 (May 1, 2013): 63–70; United States Senate, Committee on Environment and Public Works, Subcommittee on Clean Air and Nuclear Safety, *Three Mile Island: Looking Back on 30 Years of Lessons Learned: Hearing Before the Subcommittee on Clean Air and Nuclear Safety of the Committee on Environment and Public Works, United States Senate, One Hundred Eleventh Congress, First Session, March 24, 2009* (Washington, D.C.: U.S. Government Printing Office, 2015); Samuel J. Walker, *Three Mile Island: A Nuclear Crisis in Historical Perspective* (Berkeley: University of California Press, 2004): 71–172, 209–44.

86. See, for example, Wesley Longhofer, *et al.*, "NGOs, INGOs, and Environmental Policy Reform, 1970–2010," *Social Forces* 94 (June 2016): 1743–68; Christopher Rootes and Liam Leonard, "Environmental Movements and Campaigns against Waste Infrastructure in the United States," *Environmental Politics* 18 (November 2009): 835–50.

7

INTEREST GROUPS AND THE ENVIRONMENTAL LOBBY

Ask the average citizen walking down the street whether interest groups—usually referred to, with a sneer, as "special interest groups"—are a positive or a negative feature of the American political system, and the response invariably will be that these groups are harmful. Newspaper stories about the disproportionate power of the National Rifle Association (NRA) (on the right) and People for the Ethical Treatment of Animals (PETA) (on the left), among many, many other groups, have convinced the citizenry, which probably did not need much convincing, that interest groups are a large part of what is wrong with the country. According to popular myth, professional lobbyists representing these organizations—derisively identified as "high-paid lobbyists"—scurry about in state capitals and on Capitol Hill in Washington, D.C., pedaling ideas that are extremely unpopular with citizens at large but which attract political support either directly owing to large contributions to political action committees (PACs) or, more likely, because outside groups use soft money donations to manipulate state and federal elections. The level of cynicism normally is high even if the level of information frequently is low.

Certainly some interest groups, occasionally labeled "non-governmental organizations" (NGOs), use superior access and seemingly inexhaustible financial resources to squelch information they oppose and promote ideas they support, but the existence of interest groups is not necessarily detrimental to the policy process. As with so many aspects of American politics and administration, interest groups run the gamut from wretched, self-serving bastions of like-minded individuals to noble, well-meaning, self-appointed guardians of the republic. The challenge is to separate the wheat from the chaff.

THE ROLE OF INTEREST GROUPS
IN THE AMERICAN POLITY

The American Founders realized that interest groups probably would be involved in the policymaking process. The pluralist model dictates that persons will associate with other persons of a similar outlook and disposition to advance their mutual causes in the halls of power. Despite their long-standing fear of factions, the Founders understood that groups will always form unless they are stifled by coercion or chicanery, for the "causes of faction are thus sown in the nature of man."[1]

This view of humankind as inherently self-interested and acquisitive was radically different from the view entertained by the ancients. In the classical world of western man, philosophers assumed that governments existed to uplift human beings, removing them from a depraved condition and educating them on the proper course of human conduct. Plato famously believed that an enlightened monarch—his philosopher-king—was desirable because his wisdom and sound judgment would ensure that a well-adjusted, harmonious regime would exist. In this conception of good government as springing from the mind and bosom of a wise father, competing groups battling each other for political power do not symbolize the stability of a vast marketplace of ideas. Citizens jockeying for position are distasteful, unbecoming, and potentially dangerous. Democratic brouhahas are a few steps removed from anarchy, a chaotic cauldron of cacophony that endangers everyone within the regime. Officers of the Athenian democracy, after all, executed the great Socrates, Plato's model of what a philosopher-king should be. If democrats can perpetrate such crimes against philosophy, they are capable of all manner of mischief.

The ancient antipathy for democracy carried forward into the eighteenth century, but the Federalists believed they had found a suitable

mechanism for rehabilitating democratic government. The trouble with
the Greeks' conception of government was that it assumed a benevolent
dictator would be on hand to govern judiciously, but history was replete
with examples of wise kings who died and left behind idiot sons or merciless tyrants in their wake. Moreover, the ancients presupposed that
human nature was perfectible. If they could only be shown the light,
both the governors and the governed would seek out the good.

The Greeks also believed that a regime molded citizens' character
by promoting timeless virtues. Anyone who was properly educated in
regime values would recognize their importance and govern accordingly.
The "good" would never be known with certainty, but men of good character could point the way. It was a noble, uplifting, harmonious philosophy that satisfied anyone who believed in permanent, immutable truths
that characterized a fulfilled human life.[2]

In the centuries that followed the demise of classical political thought,
a series of modern theorists championed a different view. Their names
echo across the broad canvass of western intellectual thought, including
Niccolo Machiavelli, Francis Bacon, René Descartes, Thomas Hobbes,
and John Locke. They and their progeny contended that human beings
have a dark side that often resists enlightenment. While some souls will
reach for the light, the masses will not make the effort. Rather than
assume that human nature can change—and who says that government
is the appropriate source of change even if it were possible?—modern
thinkers argued that human beings should be accepted not as we would
wish them to be, but as they exist. It was this pragmatic understanding of
individual psychology that influenced the American Founders to design
a government based on human beings as base and self-interested.

Aside from the perspective that human beings cannot always be
uplifted to a higher plane, modernists assailed the concept of a "good"
that can be known and the timelessness of virtues. The Greek philosophy
was perhaps well-suited to a small, homogenous city-state where citizens
could reach agreement on the appropriate ends of government and the
goals of human life. In the modern era, where people of distinct racial
and ethnic identities residing in multiple nation-states possess different
values and pursue conflicting ends, a tidy view of political philosophy
and faith in an orderly universe were no longer accepted. Socrates, Plato,
and Aristotle witnessed their share of human strife, but they had never

seen the endless wars of later centuries, the fall of Rome, the advent of the Dark Ages, and the scourge of the Black Plague. The harmony of the ancients' views did not fit with the chaos of seventeenth- and eighteenth-century European and American lives.[3]

The clearest expression of the American Founders' understanding of factions—or at least the Federalists' understanding—can be found in the writings of James Madison, Alexander Hamilton, and John Jay. In *The Federalist Papers*, the trio sought to address the pathology of democracy and defend the new order of consensual government reflected in the U.S. Constitution, unratified at the time of their writing. In the famous "Federalist 10," Madison, writing as the fictitious Publius, described democracies as "spectacles of turbulence and contention," types of government which "have ever been found incompatible with personal security or the rights of property; and have in general been as short in their lives as they have been violent in their deaths." Yet he was not as willing as the ancients to reject popular representation by elected deputies. In a clear rejoinder to the Greeks, Publius cautioned against over correcting for the deficiencies in democratic rule. "Theoretic politicians, who have patronized this species of government, have erroneously supposed that by reducing mankind to a perfect equality in their political rights, they would, at the same time, be perfectly equalized and assimilated in their possessions, their opinions, and their passions." Publius recoiled in horror at this notion. Harmony cannot be imposed by governments, for inevitably it becomes the coercive "harmony" of a tyrant.[4]

The Gordian knot can be cut by crafting a regime where people can compete with each other and participate in government, but not descend into a seething cauldron of violent, clashing opinion. A popularly elected government must be established with correctives built into its structure to reduce or eliminate the abuses of a tyranny of the majority. According to Publius, establishing a republic is the most efficacious means of providing for good government. A republic, he explained, is "a government in which the scheme of representation takes place, opens a different prospect, and promises the cure for which we are seeking." The distinction between a democracy and a republic, he contended, was not merely a semantics game. "The two great points of difference between a democracy and a republic are: first, the delegation of the government, in the latter, to a small number of citizens elected by the rest; secondly, the greater number of citizens, and greater sphere of country, over which the latter may be extended."[5]

Here was a recipe for controlling the negative effects of faction. When citizens elected deputies to represent their views in the legislative body of a large republic, a multiplicity of interests could be represented and the ideas of all could be discussed and debated. This plan is essentially an expression of the adage "if you can't beat 'em, join 'em." Rather than discourage the masses from participating in government by placing faith in a benevolent father figure who may or may not pursue a judicious course, a good government allows the governed to provide consent—within reason. Their passions and opinions are channeled into institutions that respond to legislative enactments following due reflection and mature deliberation. "In the extent and proper structure of the Union, therefore, we behold a republican remedy for the diseases most incident to republican government," Publius explained.[6]

Appropriately structuring the institutions of government is crucial to the long-term success of the plan. Separating power into three distinct branches that make laws, enforce laws, and interpret laws, respectively, and providing for shared power where no one branch can act without the consent of a coordinate branch ensures that too much power is not vested in too few hands. As Hamilton, writing as Publius, noted in "Federalist 9," "The science of politics, however, like most other sciences, has received great improvement. The efficacy of various principles is now well understood, which were either not known at all, or imperfectly known to the ancients." Plato did not understand the beneficial features of a republic, for he observed a direct democracy in ancient Athens. Publius understood: "The regular distribution of power into distinct departments; the introduction of legislative balances and checks; the institution of courts composed of judges holding their offices during good behavior; the representation of the people in the legislature by deputies of their own election: these are wholly new discoveries, or have made their principal progress towards perfection in modern times. They are means, and powerful means, by which the excellences of republican government may be retained and its imperfections lessened or avoided."[7]

Publius recognized that factions always have existed and always will exist, but a well-constructed government can ameliorate their effects. Groups cannot be eliminated without inadvertently creating a tyranny, but an effective mitigation scheme means that factions (both inside and outside of government) can and must be pitted against each other. As Publius (Madison) observed in "Federalist 51," "Ambition must be made to counteract ambition." In this way, the interests of one party will check the interests of another. "It may be a reflection on human nature, that such devices should be necessary to control the abuses of government. But what is government itself, but the greatest of all reflections on human nature?" In one of the most famous passages in *The Federalist Papers*, Publius laid bare the rationale for establishing a republican form of government containing checks and balances on power. "If men were angels, no government would be necessary. If angels were to govern men, neither external nor internal controls on government would be necessary. In framing a government which is to be administered by men over men, the great difficulty lies in this: you must first enable the government to control the governed; and in the next place oblige it to control itself. A dependence on the people is, no doubt, the primary control on the government; but experience has taught mankind the necessity of auxiliary precautions." Auxiliary precautions—a republican form of government, a system of federalism, separation of powers, and checks and balances—allow groups inside and outside of government to compete for power without destroying consensual self-government.[8]

Publius viewed groups as a necessary evil, but this negative perception did not bestow blessings on an interest group theory of democracy. That task fell to Alexis de Tocqueville, a Frenchman who traveled to the United States during the 1830s and became an astute observer of the democratic experience. Tocqueville marveled at Americans' desire to participate in "voluntary associations." He was referring to interest groups, or associations of like-minded individuals united by a common passion or interest. "Americans of all ages, all conditions, all minds constantly unite," he remarked in his tome *Democracy in America*. In his view, these associations were part of the rich tapestry of American life. "Not only do they have commercial and industrial associations in which all take part, but they also have a thousand other kinds: religious, moral, grave, futile, very general and very particular, immense and very small; Americans use associations to give fêtes, to found seminaries, to build inns, to raise churches, to distribute books, to send missionaries to the antipodes; in this manner they create hospitals, prisons, schools."[9]

The Frenchman recognized that Europeans of his day did share Americans' affinity for joining up with kindred spirits in these types of associations. Group membership in the United States filled a need that was not met by family or community organizations, to say nothing of political parties, which were still evolving. "As soon as several of the inhabitants of the United States have conceived a sentiment or an idea that they want to produce in the world, they seek each other out; and when they have found each other, they unite," he wrote. His favorable impressions practically leap from the page. "From then on, they are no longer isolated men, but a power one sees from afar, whose actions serve as an example; a power that speaks, and to which one listens."[10]

Examining the American phenomenon at precisely the time when groups were becoming important in the American system, Tocqueville understood that voluntary associations can serve a necessary function in a democratic society; namely, they answer the age-old question, "who watches the watchers?" "Federalist 51" posited that one "must first enable the government to control the governed; and in the next place oblige it to control itself." If a government fails in the latter function, voluntary associations can provide public information on the failure of government officials to control themselves. Groups that watch the watchers became part of the scheme of pitting rival ambition against rival ambition that Publius found to be the *sine qua non* of a healthy republic. In such instances, group members act as whistleblowers when elected officials engage in malfeasance. The majority of groups are not organized to keep watch on government, but at least some groups will exercise this function. Lest anyone mistake the crucial role played by voluntary associations, Tocqueville dramatically stated, "In democratic countries the science of association is the mother science; the progress of all the others depends on the progress of that one."[11]

Tocqueville's views on the primacy and desirability of group association provided the foundation for a robust literature on the role of interest groups in twentieth-century American politics. David Truman's famous 1951 book *The Governmental Process* argued that interest groups play a significant role in the public policy process. Truman accepted Tocqueville's insight that Americans willingly join associations of like-minded individuals who share their values and goals. These associations, at least some of them, influence the policy process. Although the three branches of government are the institutions that formally develop laws and policies, external groups affect the process through lobbying activities and by engaging in public debate on salient issues. The competition among groups enriches the debate, although government actors must establish the conditions for groups to act in an appropriate manner.

The interest group theory of democracy espoused by Truman provides benefits for the American political system that were not readily apparent to the Founders. One of the criticisms of a republic is that elected representatives are supposed to discover "the will of the people," at least in theory, and act accordingly, but impediments exist. Some elected officials see themselves as trustees for the people, freely substituting their judgment for the judgment of their constituents, as opposed to delegates who seek to discern the mind of the men and women whom they represent. Even a conscientious delegate faces obstacles in determining constituents' desires. The people may be so divided or inattentive to an issue that preferences cannot be identified. Sometimes constituents entertain conflicting opinions on related issues, communicating no clear policy preferences. Sometimes public opinion changes so rapidly that policy choices cannot be pursued with confidence. These obstacles frustrate an elected official's ability to act on the will of the people.

Interest group membership provides a partial answer to the problem of determining popular will. Individuals who care about public policy and seek to have a voice in policy development join organizations that lobby in the halls of power. A gun-rights enthusiast sometimes will contribute money, and perhaps his time, to the NRA efforts to prevent gun control legislation from being enacted. A retiree will join the American Association of Retired Persons. When the AARP perceives a threat to Social Security or other policies that senior citizens hold dear, the organization asks its members to contact their elected officials to communicate their policy preferences. On and on it goes.

Interest groups also employ subject matter experts who can provide credible technical information to elected officials to assist in informed decision-making. As an example, an elected official may be undecided about his vote on an agricultural issue involving soybeans. Assuming that the official has not traded his vote for another elected representative's vote on a different issue and assuming that the elected official is not voting as the party elders dictate, the decision will be made based on available data about soybeans. It will be helpful to know what a trade association of soybean farmers thinks about the issue because in all likelihood the association employs professionals knowledgeable on the topic. They have studied the issue assiduously and should be well acquainted with the latest data and analyses on soybeans.

In consulting lobbyists for interest groups potentially affected by pending government action, lawmakers and regulators recognize that no source of information is neutrally competent. Lobbyists undoubtedly are biased toward their own interests, but they also have a useful perspective on the subject matter. Collecting data and information from a variety of groups can provide balance as well as a window into the range of competing opinions on an issue. Under these conditions, interest groups perform a valuable educative function in the American political system.[12]

The Governmental Process ignited an ongoing debate over the proper role that interest groups should play in a compound republic, with some commentators buttressing Truman's arguments and others attacking his premises. Critics challenged the book's assertion that interest group membership accurately reflects the policy wishes of a substantial plurality of citizens. As Mancur Olson cogently explained in his classic work, *The Logic of Collective Action*, all groups do not possess the same level of power or resources. Pluralist theory assumes that every group starts on more-or-less equal footing, but this presumption does not reflect reality. A small number of groups are elites with large budgets and outsized influence in government circles. Moreover, when groups grow larger and increase their membership, they suffer from a multitude of problems, including the free rider problem where a subset of the group refuses to bear the burdens of membership, such as paying dues and performing tasks on behalf of the group, but enjoys the benefits of group membership. In addition, gauging policy preferences by sifting through membership rolls is not a fruitful endeavor. Individuals may join the NRA, PETA, or other groups for reasons other than because they approve of a group's policy goals. They may simply enjoy receiving the group's newsletter or they seek group discounts on car rentals. They may join a group because a friend, family member, or neighbor joined and the new member seeks outlets for camaraderie.[13]

Political scientist E.E. Schattschneider viewed pluralist theory as a convenient myth. In *The Semisovereign People: A Realist's View of*

Democracy in America, he observed that the "range of organized, iden-
tifiable, known groups is amazingly narrow; there is nothing remotely
universal about it." To think that a semblance of public expectations
or policy preferences can be gleaned from examining the number and
types of groups clamoring in favor of one public policy of another is to
subscribe to magical thinking. Schattschneider contended that interest
groups do not resolve the conundrum of democracy because the differences between group participants and persons who do not associate
with groups are akin to the differences between voters and non voters.
It is not possible to discern the will of the people, because "the people"
are not members of groups that wield genuine influence on matters of
public policy. The groups that effect large changes in public policy are
elite groups associated with business interests, and these groups are not
representative of Americans.[14]

Theodore Lowi echoed Schattschneider's devastating critique. In
his well-known tract *The End of Liberalism*, Lowi wrote that an ever-
increasing number of political decisions are made by unelected officials
(i.e., public administrators) and interest groups—in fact, so many that
the notion of consensual self-government is placed in serious jeopardy.
He traced the rise of the administrative state to Franklin Roosevelt's
New Deal during the 1930s, a period when evermore authority was
transferred to the federal government. With this transfer of authority,
Congress faced a vast array of complex issues that required specialized
knowledge. Yet members of Congress tend to be jacks of all trades, mas-
ters of none. They have so many demands placed on their time and
so few resources for delving into the complexities of policies that they
delegate authority to administrative agencies. The agencies employ
career public administrators who possess the necessary in-depth knowledge and expertise to review the relevant data and develop specific,
detailed regulations necessary for decision-making. Congress retains
oversight authority for directing the actions of agency personnel, but
legislators generally fail to exercise this authority. As is often the case
when generalists oversee the work of specialists, members of Congress
are flummoxed when they intervene into agency actions. Rather than
becoming immersed in arcane policy details, therefore, congressmen
and senators turn a blind eye, focusing their time and energy on raising
funds of their reelection bids, meeting with constituents, and engaging

in activities at the behest of their political party. Lowi feared that the modern Congress has committed "legiscide," the figurative act of killing itself by delegating too much authority to nonelected public administrators to make crucial public policy decisions absent the appropriate congressional oversight.

On top of repeated acts of legiscide, members of Congress allow interest groups to lobby on behalf of their interests with few, if any, safeguards in place to control their actions. Federal laws prohibit out-and-out bribes paid to members of Congress or unelected public administrators, but lobbyists can influence the legislative and regulatory processes in myriad ways. Lobbyists inundate government officials with information on their respective issues, frequently crowding out the ideas of individuals unaccustomed to the rough-and-tumble world of political influence-peddling. Because interest groups are not required to engage in transparent decision-making, they can present ideas that are not always in the best interests of the polity. As Lowi sees the political landscape, interest groups are far from beneficial to the policy process. They are self-serving bastions of elite interests that work with unelected public administrators to bypass Congress—thereby bypassing the theoretical will of the people—and pursue their own agendas, which more often than not contravene citizens' interests. For Lowi, it is worrisome that the two areas where many important political decisions are made in the American political system—in the federal executive branch agencies and among external interest groups—are areas where no one is directly accountable to the electorate.[15]

Another attack on the interest group theory of democracy focuses on a key presupposition that Tocqueville stated in *Democracy in America*. The belief that Americans join voluntary associations has been accepted as axiomatic for much of American history. Data from the nineteenth and twentieth centuries apparently supported this conclusion as figures indicated that citizens enthusiastically joined social and civic clubs, fraternal organizations, church groups, and bowling leagues, among many other types of organizations. During the 1990s, however, Harvard University political scientist Robert Putnam challenged this assumption in his influential book *Bowling Alone: America's Declining Social Capital*. Putnam argued that Americans were turning away from group membership and becoming increasingly isolated. He cited data on the declining membership rolls among a variety of groups to suggest that even if interest groups somehow contribute to the health of the political process, the waning interest in group participation suggests that interest groups may be less important than they once were.[16]

Putnam generated a wide variety of responses among commentators. Supporters believed that he had stated a credible thesis while detractors argued that he had misinterpreted the data. *Washington Post* columnist Robert J. Samuelson was among the legion of Putnam's critics. Samuelson could barely contain his skepticism over Putnam's "intellectual ambition and journalistic superficiality." As Samuelson explained in a blistering critique of *Bowling Alone*, "Putnam argues that civic life is collapsing—that Americans aren't joining, as they once did, the groups and clubs that promote trust and cooperation. This undermines democracy, he says." Samuelson dismissed Putnam's work as "mostly bunk" because "although Americans may be sour, the reason is not that civic life is vanishing." On the contrary, "Americans mingle across racial, sexual and ethnic lines more now than ever."[17]

An analysis of the value of interest groups may say more about the opinions of the person performing the analysis than the intrinsic value of interest groups in the American policy process. Whether they are desirable, interest groups are numerous. Since the 1970s, the number of interest groups involved in environmental issues alone has grown tremendously. In 2006, the academic journal *Environmental Politics* found 92 environmental organizations that maintained an office in Washington, D.C. Many groups do not maintain a Washington presence, however, preferring to lobby for issues on a local or state level. Some groups are loosely organized by only a handful of organizers devoted to a single issue. When they are added to the ranks, the number of environmental interest groups swells into the hundreds.[18]

RACHEL CARSON AND THE BIRTH OF THE MODERN ENVIRONMENTAL LOBBY

The proliferation of interest groups interested in environmental issues is hardly surprising. At least since the Progressive era at the turn of the twentieth century, private organizations have sought to influence American environmental policies, especially at the federal level. Environmental groups achieved their first major successes under the Theodore Roosevelt administration. As discussed in Chapter 6, Roosevelt was keenly aware of the need to protect nature from indiscriminate manmade damage, and he acted with dispatch to champion strong conservationist policies. Although he enjoyed a reasonably good relationship with preservationists such as John Muir, the president was primarily an anthropocentric conservationist. He famously lent his prestige to Gifford Pinchot, the pioneering environmentalist who served as the first head of the U.S. Forest Service. In 1907, Roosevelt appointed Pinchot to the Inland Waterways Commission, an entity established to investigate the wise use of water resources.[19]

Although informal groups enjoyed moderate success in pushing an environmental agenda early in the twentieth century, it wasn't until much later that organized interest groups coalesced around environmental issues. Their ascendancy originated in the 1960s. If anyone can be said to have created the conditions for a strong environmental movement featuring influential interest groups, it was Rachel Carson. She was the rare scientist who could delve into the minutiae of an issue and translate the results into easily understood, engaging prose. Her landmark book *Silent Spring* all but created the twentieth-century environmental movement. After Houghton Mifflin published the book in September 1962, every major work on environmental degradation was compared to it. Publishers loved touting a just-published study as "the new *Silent Spring*," a groundbreaking exposé that would change the world. Rachel Carson's death from cancer not long after the book appeared solidified her image as a breakthrough muckraker, bravely penning her magnum opus as her ailing body shut down. One appreciative writer observed that, "It is said that ladies often have the last word. Rachel Carson will have hers from beyond the grave."[20]

She was well-suited for his career as a scientific gadfly from the very beginning. Born on a 65-acre family farm in Springdale, Pennsylvania, in 1907, Carson spent her formative years exploring the outdoors as well as vociferously reading everything she could find about nature and wildlife. Even as a child, she was interested in forging a career as a naturalist. She began writing stories about animals at the age of eight. By the time she was 11 years old, she had published her first story. She studied biology in college and pursued graduate studies in zoology and genetics. Eventually, Carson would combine her love of a good story with her desire to highlight nature in a series of well-received, influential books.[21]

Her original plan was to earn a doctorate, but family obligations forced her to surrender that dream. Later, she joined U.S. Bureau of Fisheries in a temporary position writing copy for radio programs on various educational topics. Carson excelled at her assignments, impressing her supervisor with her uncanny ability to express complex topics in clear, concise prose. Her intelligence and abilities earned her a permanent position as an aquatic biologist with the Bureau of Fisheries.[22]

Carson commenced her writing career in earnest during the 1930s. One piece in *The Atlantic Monthly* attracted the attention of editors at Simon & Schuster. They approached the young naturalist to gauge her interest in writing a book on marine life for popular readers. Carson agreed to undertake the challenge. The result, *Under the Sea Wind*, appeared in 1941. It garnered strong critical reviews, but sales were modest. Undaunted, Carson produced another full-length work on marine life, *The Sea Around Us*. The second time around, the response to her writing was phenomenal. *The Sea Around Us* eventually sold two million copies and earned the National Book Award.[23]

In the wake of her extraordinary success, Carson devoted herself full time to writing. Although she tackled many subjects in her career, she became internationally famous for her study of an organochlorine insecticide known as dichlorodiphenyltrichloroethane (DDT). During the 1940s and 1950s, DDT appeared to be a miraculous agricultural product. Sprayed on crops to control all manner of pests, the chemical was especially effective at eliminating mosquitoes and thereby reducing malaria and typhus. The armed services had relied on DDT heavily during World War II, especially as American troops stormed the beaches of numerous tropical islands in the Pacific Theater. Tasteless and odorless, the substance appeared to hold few, if any, side effects and worked wonders on the target population. Many municipalities sprayed DDT on playgrounds and grassy fields as a means of combating pesky insects that plagued communities during the spring and summer months.[24]

As she examined the scientific evidence on DDT, Carson questioned the conventional wisdom regarding its safety. She was especially worried about the allegations contained in a 1957 lawsuit about DDT indiscriminately sprayed on Long Island, New York. As a result of her investigations, Carson became convinced that the use of this chemical was one of the most pressing environmental concerns in the nation. The book she wrote on this subject would become one of the landmark environmental studies in American history. In the process, it generated enormous controversy.[25]

Carson's literary agent, Marie Rodell, suggested the title. Anxious to capture the popular readership that had propelled *The Sea Around Us* onto the bestseller lists, Carson agreed. This work was not designed to be a dry, academic tome. It was meant for a wide, popular readership, which required the kind of language that grabbed the reader and held his attention. She opened the book with a provocative, poetic passage: "There was a strange stillness. The birds, for example—where had they gone? Many people spoke of them, puzzled and disturbed. The feeding stations in the backyards were deserted. The few birds seen anywhere were moribund; they trembled violently and could not fly. It was a spring without voices."[26]

Her thesis was that human beings frequently spray toxic pesticides onto lawns in communities teeming with people who may be negatively affected, but the companies that produce the chemicals, the scientists who study them, and the government regulators who grant permission to use them possess an incomplete understanding of how the chemicals work. Her argument was that even a small amount of DDT used on one occasion is dangerous. DDT supporters fail to account for bioaccumulation, the notion that the cumulative effect of chemicals that build up in the bloodstream can harm animals, including human beings, exposed to those chemicals. She feared that human arrogance led people to discount the dangers of chemical overuse until it was too late to prevent a variety of health and environmental problems from occurring. "One of the most sinister features of DDT and related chemicals is the way they are passed from one organism to another through all the links of the food chains," she observed.[27]

Carson was deeply disturbed by the reaction she witnessed whenever someone called attention to concern over a chemical use. Chemical manufacturers, she charged, circle the wagons, vigorously arguing that the risks are overblown or nonexistent. In egregious cases, they alter their research findings, fabricating data to demonstrate that the chemical is safe for human health and environmental quality.

Aside from side effects, she noted that over time the chemicals become less effective as pests develop a resistance to the original chemical. To eradicate the more resilient target population, pesticide manufacturers are forced to increase the potency of the chemical, thus initiating an arms race of sorts. Instead of supporting this vicious cycle of ever-increasing pesticide use, Carson recommended the use of organic materials.[28]

Her strident voice and dramatic storyline ensured that *Silent Spring* would generate criticism and praise in almost equal measure, depending on who was debating its merits. Favorable reviews from the *New York Times* and *The Washington Post* as well as word-of-mouth reviews ensured a wide audience. Everyone seemed to be talking about the book. It rocketed up the bestseller charts, selling more than 600,000 copies during the fall of 1962. The Book-of-the-Month Club tapped the work as its featured selection.[29]

Even the president of the United States took notice. When asked to comment, John F. Kennedy promised that his administration was aware of the allegations and would vigorously pursue the matter. Federal agencies that had been reluctant to act in the years before *Silent Spring* was published suddenly became actively engaged in chemical monitoring and research. The impact was felt well into the 1970s, as Congress enacted a slew of environmental laws aimed at regulating chemical manufacture and use.[30]

Predictably, industry representatives denounced the book as inflammatory and one-sided. Rachel Carson was a popular writer using poetic language, hyperbole, and dramatic examples to increase book sales. Instead of relying on data and writing in the standard scientific jargon used by reputable researchers, she was hyping an issue that was not as dire as she would have the reader believe. Because she was not a toxicologist or a chemist, she was writing about matters far beyond her area of expertise, or so the argument went. The more misogynistic detractors dismissed her work as the delusions of a misinformed, hysterical woman. Vanderbilt Medical School's William Darby was among the most vehement critics. Writing an especially vitriolic review in *Chemical and Engineering News* titled "Silence, Miss Carson!" Darby snidely suggested that the book would appeal to "the organic gardeners, the anti-fluoride leaguers, the worshippers of 'natural foods,' and those who cling to the philosophy of a vital principle, and pseudo-scientists and faddists." Real scientists would reject such claptrap, he intimated. On and on went the litany of criticism.[31]

Silent Spring's merits as a credible work of science would be debated for decades after its publication. Whatever else it did, though, Carson's seminal work transformed the environmental movement, becoming a cultural landmark that heightened public awareness in a way few other events did, with the possible exception of Earth Day. It is difficult to imagine the environmental lobby existing in its current state without *Silent Spring*, or some book like it, serving as a foundation. It became a bible for environmentalists who believed that public policy must be shaped and changed by dedicated outside parties who would not allow government officials to abdicate their responsibility for preserving and protecting nature.[32]

A TRIO OF AMERICAN ENVIRONMENTAL INTEREST GROUPS

Although it is not possible to examine the origins and goals of hundreds of environmental interest groups in this chapter, it is instructive to review the origins, history, and purposes of three influential organizations: The Sierra Club, the National Audubon Society, and the Natural Resources Defense Council. Each of the three groups employs different strategies and tactics, and pursues slightly different objectives, but they all share a concern for the destructive effects of modernity on the natural environment. The three groups are among the most prominent and effective nongovernmental environmental organizations working in the United States.

The Sierra Club is one of the oldest continuously operating environmental groups, dating from 1892. The club began as the result of a conversation between the legendary naturalist John Muir and Robert Underwood Johnson, editor *The Century Magazine*. According to oft-repeated lore, the two men were sitting around a campfire in the Tuolumne Meadows of central California one night in 1889 discussing their shared passion, protecting the pristine beauty of the Yosemite Valley. The year after this conversation occurred, Congress created Yosemite National Park.[33]

As recounted in Chapter 6, Muir had spent much of his life promoting environmental preservation. His love of nature was rooted in a spiritual connection with the land, and his devotion to the cause was unwavering and fierce. He became friends with many of the most influential policymakers of his day, and he was especially drawn to figures that could help in the quest to preserve nature. As a prime example, Muir's celebrated friendship with the naturalist and essayist John Burroughs yielded dividends for American environmentalism. Although both men would be prickly and confrontational, they shared the same passions. Like Muir, Burroughs was not a scientist. He was a nature lover who wrote in clear, eloquent prose of his love of the outdoors. He and the Scottish ecologist were kindred spirits. After Muir died in 1914, Burroughs fondly recalled his friend. "A unique character—greater as a talker than as a writer," Burroughs reflected. "He loved personal combat and shone in it. He hated writing and composed with difficulty, though his books have charm of style; but his talk came easily and showed him at his best. I shall greatly miss him."[34]

Muir was sophisticated enough to understand that his love of nature and his personal campaigns to protect wilderness lands, while important, were insufficient to succeed in the long run. He was an old man. He would not live forever. The federal government had done much to preserve western lands, but he feared that more efforts were needed to prevent industry from encroaching on natural areas. Recalling his long conversation with Robert Underwood Johnson, he resolved to form an organization that would continue his good work long after he had left the scene.

Muir soon found that he was not alone. Reaching out to J. Henry Senger, an environmentalist from the University of California, Muir discovered other committed environmentalists who shared his concerns. Senger introduced the naturalist to a small band of willing compatriots in the San Francisco Bay area, among them Stanford University President David Starr Jordan, attorney Warren Olney, artist William Keith, and professors from several California universities. The band of brothers met in Olney's office on May 28, 1892, and formally incorporated the Sierra Club "to explore, enjoy, and render accessible the mountain regions of the Pacific Coast; to publish authentic information concerning them" as well as "enlist the support and cooperation of the people and government in preserving the forests and other natural features of the Sierra Nevada." One hundred and eighty-two inaugural members signed the charter.[35]

Although clearly camaraderie and convivial explorations of nature were part of the Sierra Club's purposes, Muir and his colleagues never sought to form only a social club. Influencing persons in power to protect the environment based on scientific research and data was the organization's raison d'être. To that end, a year after its founding, the group began publishing *The Sierra Club Bulletin*. Renamed *Sierra* in 1977, the magazine reviewed important books about the environment, provided informative accounts of scientific expeditions into the wild, and raised alarms about critical environmental issues. "Any similarity between *Sierra* and the venerable journal of a hundred years ago is proudly admitted," the editors acknowledged in 1993. "The name has changed, but the purpose is the same."[36]

At the outset, club members lobbied government officials to preserve forest resources, notably California's famous redwood and sequoia trees. The group adopted the Sierra sequoia as part of its official seal to illustrate the importance of these rare trees. Early members also joined in weeklong "high trip" outings in the Sierra mountains to appreciate the majesty of their surroundings. Later, John Muir's famous camping trip with President Theodore Roosevelt attracted widespread attention.[37]

Since its origins late in the nineteenth century, the Sierra Club has remained one of the nation's foremost environmental groups. In the twenty-first century, the group claimed to have more than 750,000 members working through state and local chapters throughout the United States. Members were involved in a variety of projects such as promoting clean energy, moving beyond coal-fire power, preventing hydraulic fracturing (fracking) on public lands, and protecting the areas around national parks. As of this writing, the group's headquarters office was located in Oakland, California, but it maintained a legislative office in Washington, D.C., as well as offices in multiple states. A grassroots network coordinated the work of volunteers.[38]

The second group discussed here, the National Audubon Society, derived its name from the celebrated naturalist John James Audubon, discussed in Chapter 6. A prominent Bostonian socialite, Harriet Lawrence

Hemenway, served as the driving force behind the group's creation. She was well known for her support for progressive causes. When the famous black educator Booker T. Washington arrived in Boston and was turned away from a hotel, she opened her home to him. Her most valuable service to environmental causes occurred when she led a boycott against companies that manufactured women's feathered hats. Hemenway was appalled at the slaughter of so many birds simply to meet contemporary fashion needs. By organizing her influential friends as the Massachusetts Audubon Society in 1896, she and fellow activist Mina Hall successfully worked to "discourage buying and wearing for ornamental purposes the feathers of any wild birds."[39]

The organization quickly grew in numbers and influence. Within only a few short years, state-level Audubon Societies sprang up in Pennsylvania, New York, New Hampshire, Illinois, Maine, Wisconsin, New Jersey, Rhode Island, Connecticut, the District of Columbia, Ohio, Indiana, Tennessee, Minnesota, Texas, and California. By 1900, societies existed in 20 states with an estimated membership of 40,000.[40]

Members hailed from all walks of life, everything from high-society women, working journalists, and educators to naturalists and professional lobbyists. State Audubon Societies spent considerable time and money lobbying legislators to enact measures prohibiting anyone from killing nongame birds. They were assisted by the American Ornithologists' Union, which developed model legislation to guide lawmakers in understanding how to draft protective measures.[41]

In addition to changing ladies' fashions, Audubon participants met with several notable legislative successes, beginning with passage of the Lacey Act in 1900. Sponsored by Congressman John B. Lacey of Iowa, the new statute outlawed the interstate shipment of birds killed in violation of state laws. The Audubon Societies also experienced success when Congress passed the Migratory Bird Treaty Act of 1918, an agreement with Great Britain (acting on behalf of Canada) to protect birds traveling across the Canadian-U.S. border.[42]

Building on the successes of state-level societies, a national committee of Audubon Societies originated in 1902. On January 5, 1905, William Dutcher filed papers with the state of New York to form the National Association of Audubon Societies for the Protection of Wild Birds and Animals, a national organization designed to consolidate the gains already achieved in the states. The Audubon Society was on its way to a long and productive career forging partnerships with government leaders. During its long, storied history, the Society has intervened when federal officials could not or would not preserve bird sanctuaries. On those occasions, the Society has purchased the land and established critical habitats without assistance. In 1934, NAS President John H. Baker published the first field guide, a popular resource for ornithologists everywhere. The organization has produced new editions of the *Audubon Field Guides* many times throughout the years.[43]

The Audubon Society of the twenty-first century continues to protect birds, but its purpose is broader. According to the organization's website, "Audubon's mission is to conserve and restore natural ecosystems, focusing on birds, other wildlife, and their habitats for the benefit of humanity and the earth's biological diversity." The NAS achieved the goal by mobilizing a strong network of hundreds of chapters throughout the country to lobby legislators on the importance of protecting wildlife habitats. It also partnered with groups such as BirdLife International to acquire and develop more than 2,500 Audubon-designated Important Bird Areas (IBAs) as well as other wildlife sanctuaries. "We are driven by our belief that local people, working for nature in their own places but connected nationally and internationally through our global Partnership, are the key to sustaining all life on this planet. This unique local-to-global approach delivers high impact and long-term conservation for the benefit of nature and people," the website explained.[44]

The third environmental group examined here is the Natural Resources Defense Council (NRDC), an organization founded by lawyers to pursue legal remedies when government entities cannot or will not take action to rectify environmental problems. The founding dates from 1969, when John H. Adams, a Duke University Law School graduate and former assistant U.S. Attorney for the Southern District of New York, was searching for a new position in the legal world. He had been greatly affected by a series of well-publicized environmental disasters and eventually realized that he wanted to help solve those problems, if he could. "I was ready to move on," he later said of that period in his life, and he needed a new challenge.[45]

That challenge, it turned out, was in the field of environmental law. As he reached out to his network of friends and associates, he met Whitney

North Seymour, a lawyer who was working with a colleague, Stephen Duggan, to create a new organization, the Natural Resources Defense League. Seymour elected to move to a new position before he could fully establish the League. Consequently, Duggan met with Adams to gauge whether Adams would serve as a suitable replacement for the departing founder. The two men hit it off. From their initial discussions, they agreed to collaborate on the new project. Eventually, they changed "League" to "Council," and the NRDC was born.[46]

Adams and Duggan approached the Ford Foundation for funding around the same time that Yale University law students Gus Speth, Dick Ayres, John Bryson, and Edward Strohbehn, along with Harvard Law student and former Rhodes Scholar Tom Stoel, also reached out to the Foundation. When Ford Foundation officials realized that all of these young men were pursuing the same goal, they introduced the parties to each other. Everyone agreed to work within the confines of the new NRDC structure. The resultant organization gained legitimacy and funding following a conference held in Princeton, New Jersey, in February 1970. Adams became the group's first executive director, a position he held for 36 years.[47]

From its inception, the NRDC was influential in legal and policy debates concerning the environment. During the 1970s, the group began filing lawsuits in court as well as participating in federal-level debates on natural resource protection. Government officials took notice. When Jimmy Carter became president in 1977, he asked the NRDC for advice on filling key positions within the administration. Gus Speth served as chairman of the White House Council on Environmental Quality. David Hawkins, an NRDC attorney, became assistant administrator for air at the U.S. Environmental Protection Agency (EPA).[48]

The group's best known legal case, *Chevron U.S.A., Inc. v. Natural Resources Defense Council*, reached the U.S. Supreme Court and resulted in a landmark opinion in administrative law. The issue involved an interpretation of the Clean Air Act of 1977, which required states that failed to meet air quality standards to establish a permit program regulating "new or modified major stationary sources" of air pollution. EPA broadly construed a "source" to include any device installed inside a manufacturing plant that produces air emissions. During the Reagan years, the agency reinterpreted the rule to allow manufacturing plants to meet air quality standards even after new equipment was added, provided that the site's total emissions did not exceed the permit threshold. This "bubble" concept resulted in less stringent air emissions standards, according to the NRDC. The group filed suit against EPA.

The U.S. Court of Appeals for the District of Columbia eventually agreed with the NRDC. EPA appealed to the U.S. Supreme Court. Justice John Paul Stevens, writing for a six-person majority, concluded that Supreme Court would not second-guess EPA's interpretation. Stevens explained that courts should defer to agency interpretations of congressional authority granted by Congress when legislative intent was ambiguous and the agency's interpretation was reasonable. "*Chevron* deference," the major consequence of the case, expanded the power of administrative agencies, ensuring that courts would be reluctant to overrule agencies' statutory interpretations absent a clear abuse of discretionary authority.[49]

In addition to its groundbreaking legal cases, the NRDC has been involved in high-profile media campaigns. Perhaps the most famous, or infamous, issue involved daminozide, a chemical sprayed on fruit to promote growth and enhance its appearance at market. The Uniroyal Chemical Company registered daminozide under the trademarked name "Alar" in 1963. Five years later, the U.S. Food & Drug Administration granted approval for the chemical to be used commercially. In 1989, the NRDC created the Children's Environmental Health Initiative. As part of this initiative, the group retained a public relations firm, Fenton Communications, which targeted Alar, among other chemicals, as an "intolerable risk" to children's health.

The media campaign caught on, with the muckraking CBS television show *60 Minutes* airing an episode about the dangers of Alar. Television personality Phil Donahue noted that Alar was "poisoning our kids." School officials around the country called for a boycott of apples and apple products because they frequently were sprayed with Alar. The U.S. apple industry suffered major economic losses as a result of the negative publicity: orchard owners reportedly lost $250 million and manufacturers of apple products claimed $125 million. Uniroyal stopped manufacturing Alar.

Alar became a case study about the difficulty in identifying genuine environmental risks. The NRDC touted the Alar incident as "a public health win" and defended its decision to target the chemical even decades after daminozide was no longer on the market. Moreover, politically liberal environmental groups questioned whether the apple industry had suffered millions of dollars in damages owing to the Alar scare or because of a glut in the marketplace. For their part, politically conservative commentators questioned whether Alar was the environmental villain that the NRDC claimed. The scientific evidence on the chemical's dangerous properties was anything but clear. NRDC critics cited the episode as proof of the environmental hysteria that ensues when NGOs seize on a crisis *du jour* and publicize supposedly negative effects in a concerted effort to scare a scientifically illiterate public about imaginary dangers. For a skeptical public, it is difficult to determine who is right and who is wrong based on the data, which means that individuals typically lapse into political ideology—with liberals (environmentalists) supporting the NRDC and conservatives (industry representatives) supporting industry.[50]

Early in the twenty-first century, long after John Adams had retired, the Council remained a potent force in the environmental field. "We combine the power of more than two million members and online activists with the expertise of some 500 scientists, lawyers, and policy advocates across the globe to ensure the rights of all people to the air, the water, and the wild," the group's website explained. As for its reputation, numerous sources have attested to the group's effectiveness, even if the persons and organizations offering the testimonials have not been fans of the NRDC's confrontational, "take no prisoners" style. According to *The Wall Street Journal*, the "NRDC is, by many accounts, the most effective lobbying and litigating group on environmental issues." The *New York Times* characterized it as "One of the nation's most powerful environmental groups." "Even by environmentalist standards," *Worth* magazine concluded, "this is a relentless group of lawyers and scientists." For better or worse, the NRDC remains a fixture in American environmentalism.[51]

THE VERDICT ON INTEREST GROUPS

The debate over the necessity of interest group involvement in public policy is older than the republic. The Founders certainly voiced their doubts about their desire for factions to participate in governance. At the same time, they understood that human nature propels men to join with other like-minded individuals in the pursuit of common causes. The trick is to ensure that factional strife does not get out of hand. The structure of American institutions presumably limits the mischief of self-interested groups by pitting rival ambition against rival ambition in a game of forced cooperation. If my opponent hopes to succeed in acting on his preferences, he must work with me to accomplish my own ends. If we can discover points of mutual agreement, perhaps efficacious policies will result from our collaboration.

What the Founders failed to appreciate was how organized interests would work outside of the institutional structure of government to influence the formulation as well as the implementation of public policy. Making a virtue of necessity, Alexis de Tocqueville and his intellectual successors argued that interest groups need not be villains. To the extent that they represent genuine, dynamic pluralism, groups are positive features in a political system where discovering the will of the people is problematic. If persons support voluntary associations that reflect their views, group membership can be an important resource for affecting public policy.

The question of whether groups are genuine mouthpieces for pluralism goes to the heart of the problem. The question is whether elite groups drown out the voices of smaller, less politically connected and poorly funded groups. If so, interest groups are not the saving grace of American politics. They exist as one more fractious source of divisiveness, exactly as the Founders envisioned when they disdained the existence of factions. Perhaps interest groups are no worse than other sources of ideological polarization, but they are no better.

Aside from the value of interest groups as a positive or negative feature of politics, inarguably they are numerous. As interest groups have proliferated in the public policy arena, it is natural that they have branched into the realm of environmental policy. Three of the more influential and famous of these groups—the Sierra Club, the Audubon Society, and the Natural Resources Defense Council—provide a snapshot into the kinds of issues and the tactics used by environmental interest groups. These and many other organizations outside of government seek to influence the political process and, to a great extent, they have succeeded. Yet for all that has been accomplished in environmental protection during the past half century, one question lingers. Where do we go from here?

NOTES

1. James Madison, "Federalist 10," in Alexander Hamilton, James Madison, and John Jay, *The Federalist Papers*, Clinton Rossiter, ed. (New York: New American Library, 1961): 79.
2. Alexander Rosenthal-Pubul, "Reflections on Ancient and Modern Freedom," *Modern Age* 58 (Winter 2016): 35–45; Barry Strauss, "American Democracy through Greek Eyes," *History Today* 44 (April 1994): 32–37.
3. Madison, "Federalist 10," 79. The literature on the perfectibility, or lack thereof, of human nature is voluminous. See, for example, Harold Coward, *The Perfectibility of Human Nature in Eastern and Western Thought* (Albany, N.Y.: State University of New York Press, 2008); Kenneth Schmitz, "Towards the Reciprocity of Man and Nature: Receptivity, Normativity, and Procreativity," *Nova et Vetera* (English Edition) 10 (Winter 2012): 81–94.
4. Madison, "Federalist 10," 81.
5. Madison, "Federalist 10," 82. See also Jeremy David Engels, "The Trouble with 'Public Bodies': On the Anti-Democratic Rhetoric of *The Federalist*," *Rhetoric & Public Affairs* 18 (Fall 2015): 505–38.
6. Madison, "Federalist 10," 84. See also Anthony Johnstone, "The Federalist Safeguards of Politics," *Harvard Journal of Law & Public Policy* 39 (2016): 415–85; Harvey Mansfield, "The Wisdom of 'The Federalist,'" *The New Criterion* 29 (February 2011): 9–13.
7. Alexander Hamilton, "Federalist 9," 72. See also, for example, Martin Diamond, "Democracy and *The Federalist*: A Reconsideration of the Framers' Intent," *American Political Science Review* 53 (March 1959): 52–68; David F. Epstein, *The Political Theory of The Federalist* (Chicago: The University of Chicago Press, 1984): 4, 60–76; Gottfried Dietze, *The Federalist: A Classic on Federalism and Free Government* (Westport, CT.: Greenwood Press, 1960): 316.
8. Madison, "Federalist 51," 322. See also Maynard Smith, "Reason, Passion, and Political Freedom in *The Federalist*," *Journal of Politics* 22 (August 1960): 525–44.
9. Quoted in James L. Nolan, Jr., *What They Saw in America: Alexis de Tocqueville, Max Weber, G.K. Chesterton, and Sayyid Qutb* (Cambridge and New York: Cambridge University Press, 2016): 42.
10. Alexis de Tocqueville, "Individualism and Free Institutions," in *Theories of Social Order: A Reader*, eds. Michael Hechter and Christine Horne (Stanford, CA: Stanford University Press, 2003): 323.
11. Alexis de Tocqueville, *Democracy in America*, translated by Arthur Goldhammer (New York: Library of America, 2004), Book II, Chapter 4, 215–23. See also Sarah R. Adkins, "Democracy's Quite Virtues," in *Ethics and Character: The Pursuit of Democratic Virtues*, eds. William D. Richardson, J. Michael

Martinez, and Kerry R. Stewart (Durham, N.C.: Carolina Academic Press, 1998): 203–23; Arthur Goldhammer, "Tocqueville, Associations, and the Law of 1834," *Historical Reflections* 35 (Winter 2009): 74–75; Henk E.S. Woldring, "State and Civil Society in the Political Philosophy of Alexis de Tocqueville," *Voluntas: International Journal of Voluntary and Nonprofit Organizations* 9 (December 1998): 363–73.

12. David B. Truman, *The Governmental Process: Political Interests and Public Opinion* (New York: Knopf, 1971 [1951]). For more on the interest group theory of democracy, see, for example, Martin Gilens and Benjamin I. Page, "Testing Theories of American Politics: Elites, Interest Groups, and Average Citizens," *Perspectives on Politics* 12 (September 2014): 564–81; Terry M. Moe, "Vested Interests and Political Institutions," *Political Science Quarterly* 130 (June 2015): 277–318.

13. Mancur Olson, *The Logic of Collective Action: Public Goods and the Theory of Groups* (Cambridge, Mass.: Harvard University Press, 1971).

14. E.E. Schattschneider, *The Semisovereign People: A Realist's View of Democracy in America* (Belmont, Calif.: Wadsworth, 1975): 30, 36.

15. Theodore J. Lowi, *The End of Liberalism: The Second Republic of the United States* (New York: W.W. Norton, 2009). See also Brian J. Cook, "Curing the Mischiefs of Faction in the Administrative State," *American Review of Public Administration* 46 (January 2016): 3–27; Brigham Daniels, "Agency as Principal," *Georgia Law Review* 48 (Winter 2014): 335–423; J.R. DeShazo and Jody Freeman, "The Congressional Competition to Control Delegated Power," *Texas Law Review* 81 (May 2003): 1443–1519; Kevin M. Stack, "An Administrative Jurisprudence: The Rule of Law in the Administrative State," *Columbia Law Review* 115 (November 2015): 1985–2018.

16. Robert D. Putnam, *Bowling Alone: The Collapse and Revival of American Community* (New York: Simon & Schuster, 2000).

17. Robert J. Samuelson, "Join the Club," *Washington Post National Weekly Edition* (April 15–21, 1996): 5. See also Steven N. Durlauf, "*Bowling Alone*: A Review Essay," *Journal of Economic Behavior and Organization* 47 (March 2002): 259–73; Nicholas Lemann, "Kicking in Groups," *Atlantic Monthly* 277 (April 1996): 22–26; Leslie Lenowsky, "Still 'Bowling Alone'?" *Commentary* 110 (October 2000): 57–60.

18. Matt Grossmann, "Environmental Advocacy in Washington: A Comparison with Other Interest Groups," *Environmental Policy* 15 (August 2006): 630.

19. The leading source on Theodore Roosevelt's environmentalism is Douglas Brinkley, *The Wilderness Warrior: Theodore Roosevelt and the Crusade for America* (New York: HarperCollins, 2009). See also Benjamin W. Redekop, "Embodying the Story: Theodore Roosevelt's Conservation Leadership," *Leadership* 12 (April 2016): 159–85; Charles Wilkinson, "'The Greatest Good of the Greatest Number in the Long Run': TR, Pinchot, and the Origins of

Sustainability in America," *Colorado Natural Resources, Energy & Environmental Law Review* 26 (2016): 69–79.

20. Quoted in David K. Hecht, "Constructing a Scientist: Expert Authority and Public Images of Rachel Carson," *Historical Studies in the Natural Sciences* 41 (Summer 2011): 286. See also Bill Devall, "The End of American Environmentalism?" *Nature and Culture* 1 (Autumn 2006): 159.

21. Robert Isenberg, "The Book That Changed the World," *E: The Environmental Magazine* 23 (September/October 2012): 21; *Charles* T. Rubin, *The Green Crusade: Rethinking the Roots of Environmentalism* (Lanham, MD.: Rowman & Littlefield, 1998): 30–31; William Souder, *On a Farther Shore: The Life and Legacy of Rachel Carson* (New York: Crown Publishers, 2012); 24–25.

22. Linda J. Lear, "Rachel Carson's *Silent Spring*," *Environmental History Review* 17 (Summer 1993): 24–25; Souder, *On a Farther Shore*, 86–87.

23. Isenberg, "The Book That Changed the World," 22; Souder, *On a Farther Shore*, 89–95, 140–63.

24. Reed Karaim, "Not So Fast with the DDT: Rachel Carson's Warnings Still Apply," *The American Scholar* 74 (Summer 2005): 53–59; Souder, *On a Farther Shore*, 244–64, 273–302.

25. Rubin, *The Green Crusade*, 30–32; Souder, *On a Farther Shore*, 142–60.

26. Rachel Carson, *Silent Spring*, 40th Anniversary Edition (Boston: Houghton Mifflin Harcourt, 2002 [1962]): 2. See also Souder, *On a Farther Shore*, 307–08.

27. Carson, *Silent Spring*, 22.

28. Robert Gottlieb, "Reconstructing Environmentalism: Complex Movements, Diverse Roots," in *American Environmental History*, eds. Louis S. Warren (Oxford, U.K.: B.H. Blackwell, 2004): 253–54; Lear, "Rachel Carson's *Silent Spring*," 32–34.

29. Lear, "Rachel Carson's *Silent Spring*," 36. See also Isenberg, "The Book That Changed the World," 22.

30. Lear, "Rachel Carson's *Silent Spring*," 36, 38–40; Rubin, *The Green Crusade*, 32–33; Souder, *On a Farther Shore*, 3–4.

31. Quoted in Michael B. Smith, "'Silence, Miss Carson!' Science, Gender, and the Reception of *Silent Spring*," *Feminist Studies* 27 (Fall 2001): 738, 739.

32. David K. Hecht, "How to Make a Villain: Rachel Carson and the Politics of Anti-Environmentalism," *Endeavour* 36 (December 2012): 149–55; Isenberg, "The Book That Changed the World," 22–23; Kline, *First Along the River*, 73–74; Lear, "Rachel Carson's *Silent Spring*," Souder, *On a Farther Shore*, 16.

33. Linnie Marsh Wolfe, *Son of the Wilderness: The Life of John Muir*, 2nd. edition (Madison: The University of Wisconsin Press, 2003), 260–61; Donald Worster, *The Passion for Nature: The Life of John Muir* (Oxford and New York: Oxford University Press, 2011); 3, 311–12.

34. Quoted in Paul Brooks, *Speaking for Nature: The Literary Naturalists, from Transcendentalism to the Birth of the American Environmental Movement* (Lincoln, MA.: The Walden Woods Project, 1980): 30. See also Peter Carlson, "TR Goes Camping with John Muir," *American History* 51 (June 2016): 14–15; Wolfe, *Son of the Wilderness*, 262–63, 283–87, 320–22; Worster, *The Passion for Nature*, 334, 368–69.

35. "A Centennial Celebration, 1892–1992," *Sierra* 77 (May/June 1992): 52. See also Brinkley, *The Wilderness Warrior*, 541; Sierra Club Website: "Sierra Club History." Accessed May 12, 2016. http://vault.sierraclub.org/history.

36. "The *Sierra Club Bulletin*," *Sierra* 78, 5 (September/October 1993): 54.

37. Carlson, "TR Goes Camping with John Muir," 14–15; Sierra Club Website: "Sierra Club History."

38. "A Centennial Celebration, 1892–1992," 52–73.

39. Quoted in Kathy S. Mason, "Out of Fashion: Harriet Hemenway and the Audubon Society, 1896–1905," *Historian* 65 (Fall 2002): 1. See also Frank Graham, Jr., *The Audubon Ark: A History of the Audubon Society* (Austin: University of Texas Press, 1992): 3–10; David J. Miller, "Rich History: Celebrating National Audubon Society's Centennial," *New York State Conservationist* 60 (October 2005): 2–5; Nancy Stamp, "Plumed Hats," *History Magazine* 16 (June/July 2015): 6.

40. Brinkley, *The Wilderness Warrior*, 10–11, 184–89; Mason, "Out of Fashion," 10–11.

41. Brinkley, *The Wilderness Warrior*, 497–99.

42. Graham, *The Audubon Ark*, 107; Mason, "Out of Fashion," 10–11; Miller, "Rich History," 2–3; Stamp, "Plumed Hats," 6–7.

43. Graham, *The Audubon Ark*, 46; Mason, "Out of Fashion," 13; Miller, "Rich History," 2.

44. Audubon Society Website: "About Us." Accessed June 30, 2016. http://www.audubon.org/about/. BirdLife International Website: "About BirdLife." Accessed June 30, 2016. http://www.birdlife.org/worldwide/partnership/about-birdlife. See also Graham, *The Audubon Ark*, 134.

45. John H. Adams and Patricia Adams with George Black, *A Force For Nature: The Story of NRDC and Its Fight to Save Our Planet* (San Francisco, CA: Chronicle Books, 2010): 12–13. See also Susan J. Buck, *Understanding Environmental Administration and Law*, 2nd edition (Washington, D.C. and Covelo, Calif.: Island Press, 1996): 17.

46. Adams, Adams, with Black, *A Force For Nature*, 13–20; Paul J. Allen, "Institutions: Natural Resources Defense Council," *Environment* 32 (December 1990): 2.

47. Adams, Adams, with Black, *A Force For Nature*, 12–21; Allen, "Institutions," 2; Philip Shabecoff, *Earth Rising: American Environmentalism in the 21st Century* (Washington, D.C., and Covelo, CA.: Island Press, 2001): 38–39.

48. Bonnie R. Cohen, "Natural Resources Defense Council—Weapons in the Environmentalist Arsenal: Lawsuits, Blacklists and Publicity," in *Organization Trends* (Washington, D.C.: Capital Research Center, August 2003): 2.

49. *Chevron v. Natural Resources Defense Council, Inc.*, 467 U.S. 837 (1984). See also Jack M. Beermann, "End the Failed *Chevron* Experiment Now: How *Chevron* Has Failed and Why It Can and Should be Overruled," *Administrative & Regulatory Law News* 35 (Winter 2010): 3–15; Eric M. Braun, "Coring the Seedless Grape: A Reinterpretation of *Chevron U.S.A. v. NRDC*," *Columbia Law Review* 87 (June 1987): 986–1008; Thomas W. Merrill, "Justice Stevens and the *Chevron* Puzzle," *Northwestern University Law Review* 106 (April 2012): 551–66.

50. Cohen, "Natural Resources Defense Council," 3; Gregg Easterbrook, *A Moment on the Earth: The Coming Age of Environmental Optimism* (New York: Viking, 1995): 117, 249; Wallace Kaufman, *No Turning Back: Dismantling the Fantasies of Environmental Thinking* (New York: Basic Books, 1994): 80–84; Kenneth Smith and Jack Raso, M.S., R.D., *An Unhappy Anniversary: The Alar "Scare" Ten Years Later* (New York: American Council on Science and Health, 1999): 1; Jacqueline Vaughn Switzer, *Green Backlash: The History and Politics of Environmental Opposition in the U.S.* (Boulder, CO: Lynne Rienner Publishers, 1997): 85, 133.

51. Natural Resources Defense Council Website: "About NRDC." Accessed May 18, 2016. https://www.nrdc.org/about.

IV

CONCLUSION

8

SUSTAINABILITY AND AMERICAN PUBLIC ADMINISTRATION

Where Do We Go From Here?

The premise of this book is that the institutions of American government, especially at the federal level, and public administrators who work inside of those institutions have a crucial role to play in developing and implementing environmental sustainability policies. To that end, the book has been organized so that the salient issues can be explored logically. Thus, Part I explores fundamental concepts such as what it means to be environmentally sustainable (Chapter 1), how economic issues affect environmental policy (Chapter 2), and the philosophical schools of thought about what policies ought to be considered sustainable (Chapter 3). From there, the book focuses on processes and institutions affecting public administration and its role in the policy process. Accordingly, Chapter 4 summarizes the rise of the administrative state in the United States. Chapter 5 reviews the development of federal environmental laws and policies with an emphasis on late twentieth-century developments. Part III discusses the evolution of American environmentalism by outlining the history of the environmental movement (Chapter 6) as well as the growth of the environmental lobby (Chapter 7). In this chapter, the goal is to synthesize the information in the book and explain how public administration can promote environmental sustainability, assuming *arguendo* that this is an appropriate goal.

POTENTIAL IMPEDIMENTS TO IMPROVING
SUSTAINABILITY

Anyone conversant with environmental policy in the United States since the 1970s immediately notices the challenges inherent in crafting and implementing public policy. Three potential impediments immediately appear. Although the obstacles are related, the first is political, the second is economic, and the third is technological. With respect to the first impediment, the fragmented nature of a federal system of government where political authority is divided into distinct branches ensures that multiple actors at multiple levels of government play a part in the policy process. Moreover, elected and unelected officials are involved, and they respond to different incentives and pressure points. Policies also vary by type—distributive, redistributive, and self-regulating—and by stages of development, such as policy formulation and policy implementation. Navigating these shoals is complex and difficult, to say the least.

In the meantime, proponents of industrial development argue with environmentalists in a seemingly never-ending battle over the economics of sustainability. Industrialists often are unabashed anthropocentrists who belittle environmentalists as self-absorbed idealists flaunting abstract, unproven theories about all manner of environmental crises to scare the public into donating money and supporting ludicrous causes. Environmentalists frequently denounce industry workers as greedy and self-serving, little more than short-sighted, narrow-minded capitalists who care more about their own short-term interests than the long-term public good. Although both sides make compelling points, they often talk past each other, vilifying opponents and emphasizing their vast differences rather than attempting to find common ground.

On top of these complexities, the quest for abundant, efficient, reliable, inexpensive sources of energy complicates the dispute about what constitutes efficacious environmental policy. A highly industrialized, technologically sophisticated, "power-hungry" society such as the United States possesses enormous energy needs to operate residences containing the latest electronic gadgetry, large and small business offices, and energy-intensive factories reliant on the latest technology to churn out consumer products at a record pace. Fossil fuels historically have met these needs because they have been reliable, plentiful, and relatively inexpensive sources of energy. Unfortunately, locating, extracting, refining, shipping, using, and disposing of by-products from fossil fuels have created a multitude of environmental problems that have been dealt with inadequately, or not at all. Indeed, environmentalists repeatedly have pointed out the hazards of relying on fossils fuels as the nation's primary energy source. Their denunciations of the petroleum and coal industries, in particular, have resonated among Americans who decry the despoliation of the land, water, and air.[1]

Yet even as environmentally conscious citizens promote policies to reduce or eliminate fossil fuels, they cannot seem to wean themselves from their dependence on those sources. The prominent environmental ethicist Mark Sagoff described Americans' seemingly contradictory feelings about environmental policies in a thoughtful 1981 essay, "At the Shrine of Our Lady of Fatima, or Why Political Questions Are Not All Economic." "I love my car; I hate the bus. Yet I vote for candidates who promise to tax gasoline to pay for public transportation," he wrote. "I send my dues to the Sierra Club to protect areas in Alaska I shall never visit … . And of course I applaud the Endangered Species Act, although I have no earthly use for the Colorado Squawfish or the Indiana bat. I support almost any political cause that I think will defeat my consumer interests. This is because I have contempt for—although I act upon—those interests. I have an 'Ecology Now' sticker on a car that leaks oil everywhere it's parked."[2]

Assuming that environmentally-conscious citizens are not merely hypocrites, Sagoff's point is that many Americans appreciate environmental policies even if those policies harm their interests, yet they are loath to surrender the technology and creature comforts that enrich their lives. Sometimes they shrug and ask, "What can be done?" Perhaps renewable resources can provide an answer to the conundrum. Renewables are characterized as any source of energy that is readily replaced and does not harm the natural environment as much as fossil fuels do. Wind energy and solar energy are cited as excellent replacements for far-dirtier fossil fuels. Biomass energy, which uses dung, decaying wood, and plant material to generate heat for producing electricity, and advanced biofuels such as ethanol and biodiesel, which can replace gasoline, are much cleaner sources than traditional fossil fuels. Geothermal energy uses hot water pumped from underground sources to turn turbines in electricity-generating plants. Hydropower uses falling or pressurized water to drive turbines.[3]

All hail renewables as the wave of the future. Alas, given the current state of technology, renewables, while they have their place in the schemata, cannot meet the needs of an energy-hungry nation. Renewables simply do not provide a big enough bang for the buck.[4]

Renewables produce a low power density, such as horsepower or kilowatts, in a specific geographic area. Yes, wind farms generate electricity, but at a tremendous cost. They require large swaths of vacant land to site turbines, but they create relatively little power compared with fossil fuels. Renewable resources contain low energy density (e.g., joules per cubic meter or watt hours per pound). A very small amount of wind or solar energy can be contained and stored. Yet storing energy is crucial for making the energy affordable and available on demand. Using batteries for renewables is not currently feasible because the number and size of the batteries would be enormous. Most technology grows smaller and more affordable as improvements are made and the technology is perfected. Renewables go against the trend. Heavy reliance on renewable energy would require large investments in land and technology, which would increase energy costs into the foreseeable future.

Robert Bryce explained the dilemma in his 2010 book, *Power Hungry*. "We use hydrocarbons—coal, oil, and natural gas—not because we like them, but because they produce lots of heat energy, from small spaces, at prices we can afford, and in the quantities that we demand," he wrote. "And that's the absolutely critical point. The energy business is ruthlessly policed by the Four Imperatives: power density, energy density, cost, and scale." Until renewable resources can meet the needs of a highly industrialized society, their use will remain problematic. Perhaps these issues will be resolved in the decades to come, but early in the twenty-first century, the search of energy sources keeps advanced societies tied to traditional carbon-based fuels.[5]

ENVIRONMENTAL EDUCATION

There is a need for thoughtful, deliberative, science-based, data-driven, environmental education. So much of what passes for education in the environmental field consists of thinly disguised polemics aimed at defending a particular ideology and excoriating opponents. As an example, a well-known book dating from 1989, *50 Simple Things You Can Do to Save the Earth*, is filled with tidbits to help the average person cut back on resource consumption. Much of the practical advice is useful—flushing the toilet fewer times to save water and turning off the lights when no one is in a room—but some of the data, compiled by environmental NGOs, is exaggerated, outdated, or unreliable. For example, the book recommends that consumers replace disposable plastic foodservice products with compostable products. Yet the recommendation does not mention whether the replacement items cost more than the original items, how the replacements will affect the current recycling infrastructure, or whether any commercial composting facilities exist in the area, nor does it mention the life cycle environmental impacts of the manufacturing processes of compostable and noncompostable products. Simple answers are not always wise answers; in fact, they are not always simple, nor are they necessarily answers to meaningful questions. Any advice that is dispensed with no explanation of the bases for the conclusions or an analysis of costs and options is not education. It is ideology.[6]

A quick perusal of libraries and online bookstores reveals that numerous environmental "self-help" manuals are available in the marketplace. They appeal to consumers' desires for easy, quick, painless solutions to complex, multifaceted problems. The titles promise all sorts of wonderful, easy solutions: *Living Green: A Practical Guide to Simple Sustainability*; *Easy Green Living: The Ultimate Guide to Simple, Eco-Friendly Choices for You and Your Home*; *Green Made Easy: The Everyday Guide for Transitioning to a Green Lifestyle*; *Green Living: Green Lifestyle— Green Living Guide for Beginners*; and on and on. Regrettably, many such publications substitute homilies and proverbs for sound scientific discourse. No doubt chatty, anecdotal booklets packaged in slim, affordably priced paperbacks or e-book formats are far more appealing to the general reader than thick, heavy, data-filled tomes. Popular works need not be light on credible science or useful assessments of environmental problems, but often they are. Any environmental scientist worth his or her salary will explain that "green" living, whatever that means, is not easy. It requires work.[7]

Yet even for the conscientious environmentalist, the journey is difficult. The accumulation of scientific data, of course, is never a neutral, uncontested process. Invariably, value-laden choices must be made. Researchers must develop a working hypothesis, build a credible research design, collect data in a methodical, scientifically accepted manner, and prepare and defend a reasonable interpretation. At every step in the process, researchers must make choices that are open to criticism and even derision. If the process is clear, transparent, and scientifically defensible, the researcher contributes to the body of knowledge. If he or she traffics in polemical conclusions or ideological diatribes, the scientific process is polluted.

As discussed in Chapter 1, the politicization of science early in the twenty-first century has ensured that traditional scientific discourse, theoretically designed to improve environmental education, masks a hidden agenda. Presenting a compelling tale has become the primary goal for some pseudoscientists. When Rachel Carson penned *Silent Spring*, she was denounced as an ideologue, but her methods were sound and she freely admitted flaws in the data and places where contrary interpretations might be valid. If she were alive today, she probably would cringe at the bastardization of her work and the manipulation of her memory. She was not the patron saint of a politically liberal agenda, although sometimes she has been portrayed that way. She was a scientist struggling to reach defensible conclusions based on the data she collected. Environmental education is supposed to be about using data to draw conclusions, come what may. So often in twenty-first scientific discourse, unfortunately, the conclusions drive the data.[8]

PRIVATE SECTOR INVOLVEMENT

Proponents of industrialization frequently are cast as villains in a morality play where selfless environmentalists seek to protect nature from the depredations of evil men. Yet even some captains of industry have come to appreciate the benefits of environmental sustainability. Whether they embrace the concept because it provides a market advantage for their products or because they genuinely believe that their manufacturing processes need to be clean and more efficient to preserve natural resources remains an open question. Perhaps most corporate executives act on the basis of both base and noble motives. In any case, increasingly large numbers of top managers and American corporations have embraced the concept of sustainability.

Recall that Chapter 1 detailed the challenges in finding an agreed-upon definition of sustainability. Not surprisingly, corporations tend to define sustainability as the efficient production of their goods and/or services. Reducing air emissions, water usage, and waste material from manufacturing processes becomes the corporate mantra. Such reductions, if undertaken in good faith, certainly improve environmental quality compared with the corporation's past practices. For environmentalists who question the production of particular goods in the first place, however, simply reducing the harmful effects of manufacturing is insufficient. The goods should never be produced. In such situations, the environmental community and the industrial community reach an impasse. Environmentalists long to see the manufacturer go out of business while the manufacturer seeks to ensure economic viability in perpetuity.

To the extent that sustainability practices are incorporated into the private sector world of product manufacturing and sales, such practices are most often implemented within the supply chain. When large companies such as WalMart, Target, and McDonald's inform their suppliers that products must contain recycled content, reduce greenhouse house emissions, and be easily recycled or composted, the changes are likely to be made. Suppliers have an incentive to incorporate these factors into their products to gain a competitive advantage.[9]

Similarly, companies that seek to earn a profit in a marketplace that values sustainable practices will examine the entire life cycle of the product. They will assess the environmental impacts of the raw materials that go into the manufacturing process as well as the effects of the process itself. In addition, they will delve into the costs and benefits of disposing of the product. All of these considerations, along with the economic impacts, will determine whether some products continue to be made or, if they are made, whether they can be made more efficiently with an eye toward environmental protection. Presumably, products that can be made, transported, used, and disposed of with fewer environmental impacts than their competitors—assuming the cost differential is not seen as significant in a particular sector of the marketplace—will gain greater market share.[10]

LEADERSHIP IN THE PUBLIC SECTOR

As early as 1963, Professor Lynton K. Caldwell, a political scientist who later assisted in preparing the National Environmental Policy Act (NEPA), suggested that the environment was a natural and much needed focus for public administration. Arguing that "intellectual foundations for an environmental policy focus are being laid," he posited a central role for unelected government experts to provide leadership in overcoming the impediments discussed in this chapter. "A policy focus on environment in its fullest practicable sense would make more likely the consideration of all the major elements relevant to an environment-affecting decision," he wrote. "Whatever content is being ascribed to the adjective 'good,' it becomes daily more evident that public administration of the environment will not be 'good' if it fails to deal environmental problems in comprehensive terms."[11]

Forty-seven years after Caldwell's thought-provoking article appeared in *Public Administration Review*, Daniel J. Fiorino argued in the same academic journal that "Sustainability must move from being a concept that is debated and analyzed to one that guides decision making and action at all scales of governance and across policy sectors." He concluded the article with a suggestion. "What better way is there to integrate sustainability into decision making and action than by making it a conceptual focus for public administration?"[12]

The first question to address here is whether Caldwell and Fiorino are correct that sustainability should be a focus of the field of public administration. As discussed in Chapter 4 of this book, the literature on public administration cites social equity as a goal notwithstanding possible disputes about what the term "equity" means in the context of day-to-day administration. Assuming that equity encompasses a desire to improve the quality of life for all citizens within the regime by treating like cases alike, environmental sustainability can be considered equitable, even if it is not *necessarily* a part of the field. (The counterargument is that environmental issues belong in departments and fields that address substantive environmental issues, whereas public administration is a loosely organized field—if it is a field at all—that brings together a variety of disciplines without digging too deeply into the content of any one discipline.)

Sustainability, while not essential, certainly *can* be a part of the field of public administration. In fact, because public administration is the nexus of diverse disciplines such as public policy, political science, business management, economics, and statistics, among others, incorporating sustainability into the field is an effective means of ensuring that the issue is discussed among public administrators. Perhaps the topic will inform their work at all levels of government. If public administrators are in some sense guardians of the citizenry, ensuring that current and future generations enjoy a reasonable quality of life, including a healthy environment, is an appropriate goal for all public servants to pursue.[13]

Politically conservative critics who question the role of "big government" blanch at the suggestion that public administrators have a leadership role to play in environmental sustainability. Since the earliest days of the republic, a substantial portion of the citizenry has expressed outrage that governments engage in collective action. The Founders feared powerful, centralized forces would oppress individuals and destroy their liberty. It is a fear that has survived in one form or another for centuries.[14]

Aside from philosophical qualms, politically conservative anthropocentric industrialists argue that government should not tip the scales on environmental issues when those issues are contentious and open to legitimate scientific debate—a debate best waged outside the walls of government institutions. According to this view, for unelected officials to assume that an industrial product or a manufacturing process creates negative environmental consequences is presumptuous unless the agency is tasked with conducting or evaluating peer-reviewed scientific studies. (Even then, some private sector parties question whether government is acting appropriately by intervening into markets under any circumstances.) As an example, career scientists working within the U.S. Environmental Protection Agency and tasked to overhaul the Toxic Substances Control Act (TSCA) possess the expertise and access to data to determine that some chemicals carry more risk than other chemicals. (Even this proposition is contentious for some critics of the administrative state, but presumably a great many citizens accept the premise that experts can weigh in on subjects they are competent to analyze and evaluate.) The problem occurs when government officials accept the conclusions of their colleagues in other agencies with no independent analysis. To allow public administrators working in a completely different field and lacking the educational background and scientific expertise to judge the risk of that same chemical by adopting sustainability best practices that, for example, assert that the chemical is dangerous, can be worrisome. In a political system where the consent of the governed and the right to petition for a redress of grievances are foundational principles, having public administrators use their discretion to make decisions beyond their expertise with little or no direct public accountability is exactly the great fear of opponents of a large administrative state.[15]

The concern about public administrators incorporating sustainability concepts into their decision-making is exactly the same debate about the legitimacy of public administration in the first place. If individuals fear placing too much power in too few hands, they see a public bureaucracy, with its indirect relationship to the electorate, as detrimental to individual rights. Critics argue that if government agents resolve to address questions of environmental sustainability, policy options must begin with elected officials, who will be held accountable by the people.

The rejoinder to the critics of incorporating sustainability practices into public administration is the same rejoinder to critics of bureaucracy in general. Elected officials retain oversight authority. The question of whether Congress or state legislatures effectively exercise this authority or whether they commit "legiscide," to use Theodore Lowi's term, is another matter. Bureaucratic accountability, while not directly tied to the electorate, does exist.[16]

A great deal of the public administration literature delves into the costs and benefits of a highly developed bureaucracy. Even if one agrees that a well-developed bureaucracy is anathema—and this is by no means a settled proposition—a highly industrialized, complex, technologically sophisticated country requires sufficient expertise to operate. Like it or not, a bureaucracy performs this function. Anti government partisans who vehemently object to a large bureaucracy must recognize that no matter how many reforms and cuts are instituted, bureaucracy is here to stay in the American polity. The pragmatic question is not whether a highly developed bureaucracy ought to exist. Rather, the issue is whether public agencies can operate in an optimal manner, and whether their staffs are held accountable for their actions.[17]

One method of determining accountability is to gauge the extent that public administrators represent the general public. If a large plurality of Americans expresses concern about industrial processes damaging the natural environment, presumably that view will be reflected by the individuals working inside of government. This notion of public administrators as responsible stewards possessing responsibility for more than simply their narrow position within a hierarchical institutional structure leads to the concept of representative bureaucracy. Building on the ideas about the representative nature of interests groups discussed in Chapter 7, the concept of representative bureaucracy suggests that social groups reflect the interests of large numbers of people. When individuals who subscribe to their groups' views assume positions within the bureaucracy at all levels of government, they reflect group values as they perform their tasks.[18]

With the death of politics-administration dichotomy, as discussed in Chapter 4, it became clear that policies are not formulated by a legislative body and delegated to administrative agencies for implementation. Instead, policies are formulated and implemented at all stages and levels of government. If unelected administrators are to legitimize their roles formulating as well as implementing policy in a republican form of government, they must make a case that members of agencies are not radically different from the people outside of government. Although public administrators do not stand for periodic elections, they are evaluated, at least in part, by how well they represent the views of groups that share the values of large portions of the general public, according to this view.[19]

"Representative bureaucracy" has been debated at great length since J. Donald Kingsley coined the term in his 1944 book on the subject. A wide range of opinion exists. One criticism is that representative bureaucracy does not exist because the vast majority of public administrators are working in nonpolicymaking roles and therefore possess little influence on substantive policy matters. Even if these administrators can exercise some measure of control over the policy process, their institutional position inside a bureaucracy is designed to reduce or eliminate personal preferences from policymaking. As Max Weber noted, the purpose of a bureaucracy is to ensure that decision-making will not be contaminated by the biases that infect a political spoils system. To suggest that representative bureaucracy is desirable is to undermine the original concept of bureaucracy. (Of course, Max Weber and proponents of the Scientific Management School wrote during the politics-administration heyday when administrators were thought to be efficient implementation cogs in an impersonal machine. Their concerns about legitimizing public administration were different than the theorists who wrote after the advent of a humanistic approach to administration.)[20]

When sustainability becomes a part of the public administration field, the perennial problem of pinning down a definition also becomes an overriding concern. Recall that Chapter 1 reviewed the various definitions as well as their relative strengths and weaknesses. Definitional problems stem from many factors, not the least of which is the vagueness and generality of the sustainability concept. Suggesting that sustainability consists of protecting resources for future generations, or balancing social, political/economic, and ecological factors, or public administrators acting in an equitable manner is so generic as to be almost meaningless. These features must be fleshed out. Otherwise, multiple parties will insist that they are acting in a sustainable fashion even when they are behaving in mutually exclusive ways. If the definition of "sustainability" is so broad and diverse that each party can argue in good faith that he is meeting the goal even as he works at cross-purposes from other parties, the concept has little value. As the dodo bird says in *Alice's Adventures in Wonderland*, "Everybody has won, and all must have prizes!" If everyone sees what he wants to see, all parties claim a prize.[21]

To resolve the differences among competing definitions and ensure commonality in understanding sustainability throughout the field of public administration, associations such as the American Society for Public Administration (ASPA) and the Network of Schools of Public Policy, Affairs, and Administration (NASPAA) can develop guidance documents. Just as the American Bar Association has developed model legal rules adopted by some states, ASPA and NASPAA can guide students and practitioners on how to recognize sustainability when they see it. The definition will always remain vague and perhaps contentious, but developing a working definition is valuable in ensuring consistency.[22]

If environmental sustainability is to become a conceptual focus in the academic world of public administration, the process is relatively clear, although many steps are involved. Requirements can be established and model curricula can be developed within schools of public administration and public policy to increase the likelihood that future public sector leaders will be well versed in the literature and theories of public administration. Books (such as this one!) can be assigned so that students will know something of the history of the environmental movement, the basic foundations of environmental law and public policy, and the pressing issues of the field. ASPA and NASPAA can host conferences, or sections of conferences, on the importance of sustainability education. (In fact, a major theme of the 2013 ASPA annual conference focused on best practices in sustainability.)[23]

A number of substantive changes to a curriculum can be instituted, ranging from inserting examples of sustainable practices into existing courses or inviting guest speakers to discuss salient sustainability issues, providing new courses specifically on the topic, changing the department's mission statement to include sustainability goals, to requiring service learning so that students actively participate in a sustainability project within the community. As referenced above, substantive information on sustainability must be data driven and, to the extent possible, devoid of polemics advancing a specific ideology. These steps are valuable beginnings. The importance of leadership in education cannot be overemphasized.

Yet implementing environmental sustainability into the field of public administration cannot, and should not, be left only to schools of public administration or policy. Aside from taking years, perhaps decades, to implement—at least until the current crop of students graduates and assumes positions of authority inside federal agencies—not all administrators are graduates of schools of public administration or policy. If, in Daniel J. Fiorino's words, sustainability is to affect "decision making and action at all scales of governance and across policy sectors"—and the assumption here is that it should—something more is needed than changes to the educational curriculum, as important as such changes are.[24]

It is axiomatic that administrators working within agencies at the federal, state, and local levels specifically devoted to addressing environmental issues should be aware of sustainability goals and work to achieve them. Even in this area, however, challenges exist. During the process of working with each other, administrators engage in complex relationships. Federal administrators must work with their counterparts in regional offices. State administrators work with colleagues scattered across the state. Both federal and state administrators work with local administrators who exercise the most direct control over implementation because municipal officials labor at the street level. Internecine struggles over the appropriate method of implementing a policy, concerns about the budgetary impacts of one policy versus another policy, misinterpretations about the scope and nature of a policy, and differing political environments at each level of government ensure that formulating and implementing environmental sustainability policies will be difficult.[25]

Systems theory provides one potential method of uniting the disparate elements and participants to encourage environmental sustainability in public administration. At its core, systems theory is a holistic approach that places the role of administrators into a larger conceptual framework. The advantage of this approach is that it requires administrators to consider factors beyond their usual day-to-day operations. Many systems theories call for participants to develop process models where inputs, throughputs, and outputs are illustrated using boxes and arrow diagrams. By showing the steps involved as well as the relationships among stakeholders at each stage, the illustration identifies relevant variables to assist in decision-making. Systems theory can be used to encourage environmental sustainability policymaking writ large or it can model part of the system, such as the recycling process for specific commodities, solid waste management systems, transportation systems, and so forth.[26]

Systems theory also reduces the complexity inherent in environmental decision-making. Facing multiple variables and an open-ended time frame, administrators may be dissuaded from acting owing to the volume of information and the belief that the issue is too large and complex to be tackled. Analysis paralysis is a familiar concept to decision-makers who face large, multifaceted problems with no clear decision rule. The uncertainties appear daunting, and the administrator must determine how to proceed. As discussed in Chapter 1, where consensus exists about the evidence and data, a decision generally will be made according to a clear decision rule. If consensus does not exist, the decision may be delayed or avoided altogether. If a decision is reached, it probably will be based on a variety of criteria, including readily available resources, decision-process constraints, and the available knowledge base, among other things.

Ideally, system theory supplies a clear decision rule that reduces uncertainty in environmental decision-making. Nonetheless, uncertainty cannot be eliminated. Systems theory is abstract and must be modified as situations change and unforeseen events occur. Public administrators must remain sensitive to the political and technical environments and plan accordingly. They must also consider the benefits that accrue from collaborating with corporations and other private parties in promoting environmental sustainability.[27]

PUBLIC-PRIVATE PARTNERSHIPS

If incorporating environmental sustainability into the field of public administration extends beyond establishing a conceptual framework as well as curricula changes inside schools of public administration and public policy, it will require cooperation and collaboration between the public and private sectors. The regulators and the regulated community must find mutually agreeable solutions if environmental problems are to be resolved. It will not be easy. These two sectors are organized differently and pursue distinct goals. Occasionally, the sectors clash. Collaboration, while not impossible, presents a series of challenges that must be met and overcome.

For at least a quarter century, the public administration literature has urged practitioners to champion public-private partnerships (PPPs). The reinventing government movement and the New Public Management were attempts to break out of the barriers of traditional public administration and introduce flexibility into the field. Part of the new emphasis was to use the private sector to perform services more efficiently than public agencies could perform them. Under these conditions, public agencies would oversee private entities and direct their work, but the actual labor would be performed outside of government. Prison administration became the quintessential example of a PPP.

Critics of the PPP arrangement have fretted that public values suffer when private entities act in the public stead. For all of the concerns that antigovernment detractors express about the lack of direct accountability of administrative agencies, the agencies are subject to legislative oversight as well as constitutional correctives. Administrative accountability exists in theory, if not always in practice. When abuses occur, steps can be undertaken to correct problems; officers within the elected branches of government possess the legal authority and institutional controls to prevent future occurrences.

Critics also have voiced concerns about the quality, or lack thereof, of private sector actions. Despite the well-known assertions that the private sector can administer services far more efficiently and effectively than public sector entities can, the record is mixed. A major reason why private sector organizations can reduce costs and act more efficiently than government entities is because they are bound by fewer rules than public sector entities are. Yet one person's rules are another person's accountability procedures. If private sector entities act in strict accordance with public sector accountability rules, the supposed advantages in private sector involvement disappear or are curtailed.[28]

Another concern involves the transparency of actions undertaken at the behest of public agencies. Public administrators must be prepared to defend the record in the event of questions raised by the citizenry or from congressional audits of how time and money are spent. Therefore, a significant portion of many a public administrator's time is devoted to protecting the record so that detailed information exists to show what was done, why it was done, and how it came to be done in precisely that manner. Private sector entities generally provide less information on decision-making than a government agency provides unless the private enterprise is a public company reporting to shareholders. Even in those situations, much of the information is protected through confidential business records laws. While it is true that private sector entities acting on public business cannot shield information that is necessary to determine whether they acted in a lawful manner, often the information is not readily available and requires multiple steps to discover.[29]

In light of these legitimate concerns, a PPP arrangement must specify the type of arrangement involved in the collaboration. Calling for a partnership necessitates sharing responsibility, but the nature and extent of the sharing must be delineated. In the past, privatizing services has meant that ownership, control, and decision-making authority transfers from public agencies to the private sector. Although not as extensive as full privatization, outsourcing is a similar concept whereby public agencies transfer activities such as manufacturing components or working on portions of a large public works project to private sources.

A genuinely collaborative PPP is not as extensive as privatization or outsourcing, each of which transfers significant responsibilities to private parties and raises the concerns already discussed above. Moreover, collaboration between public and private organizations is not based on the premise that private sector involvement is desirable because the public sector cannot act efficiently or effectively enough to meet its goals. PPP collaboration is a genuine partnership where each entity brings something to the relationship. The public sector entity associates with the private entity because the latter is a necessary to solve the problem. In the case of environmental sustainability, so much pollution and waste is the result of private sector activities that an effective solution must involve the private sector.

In traditional public administration scenarios, government entities crafted a policy solution and developed programs that imposed costs on the private sector. This approach, adopted by neoclassical economists who famously championed a Pigouvian tax, favored a top-down or command-and-control process that allowed little direct input from affected parties. Supporters of PPP reject heavy-handed administration. Instead, they argue that allowing private entities to participate in finding solutions and absorbing costs as the project is formulated and implemented is preferable to the old ways of operating. When the source of many environmental problems is involved in the solution, efficiencies exist for all parties. As an example, if an automotive manufacturer works on sustainability plans with administrators from the U.S. Environmental Protection Agency as well as the transportation agencies, the solution is likely to be more palatable and less cumbersome to implement than if the agency imposes the solution on the manufacturer without input.[30]

Administrative law already recognizes the value of involving stakeholders in decision-making through negotiated rulemaking (Reg Neg). The benefit of this process is that members of a regulated community are consulted extensively before a regulatory agency promulgates a rule (or in lieu of the agency promulgating a rule) governing the operation of that community. Because regulators do not necessarily understand the intricacies of a particular business operation, they can learn much valuable information by consulting with stakeholders throughout the rulemaking process. Parties to a negotiation also are more likely to buy into the final result. For their part, members of the regulated community can communicate their concerns and operational challenges to regulators before a final rule is announced. Bargaining and negotiation, whenever possible, is less costly and time consuming than engaging in administrative disputes or litigation.

Reg Neg has generated its share of criticism as commentators worry about the advantages and disadvantages of allowing regulated parties to negotiate their own rules. Perhaps regulators are too cozy with the regulated community. Environmental groups have expressed their disdain for large manufacturing companies that seek to influence regulators by suggesting a relatively lenient regulatory scheme. Even if the regulated community and the regulators are not overly friendly, private sector experts may withhold crucial information or subtly manipulate the negotiation process, resulting in a more favorable ruling than might otherwise have resulted. For exactly these reasons, debates persist about whether Reg Neg works as promised. It is supposed to reduce litigation and expedite the rulemaking process, but the data have been mixed. Whatever its problems, Reg Neg in some instances has allowed stakeholders to benefit from cordial face-face meetings with public administrators instead of always pitting private and public sector representatives against each other in a confrontational setting.[31]

Just as Reg Neg promises a less confrontational, more collaborative approach than the traditional regulatory process, encouraging collaboration between public agencies and private entities in environmental decision-making is an enticing prospect. Underlying the concept of a PPP for environmental sustainability is an insight that neither sector enjoys an advantage over the other. The collaboration is desired because both sectors possess responsibility for formulating and implementing a workable sustainability policy. PPPs have been used more or less successfully for large transportation infrastructure projects. It is not unthinkable that such a partnership would work for environmental policymaking.

Public administration scholars have begun to recognize the important role of sustainability in the public sector. Executive branch agencies at the state and federal levels increasingly are discussing issues such as intergenerational equity, reduction of risk, and conservation of resources in long-range administrative planning. To the extent that these considerations promote bureaucratic goals of efficiency, effectiveness, and citizen participation, they reflect a healthy trend in public administration. The overriding question for the future is whether these issues will exist only as intellectual food for thought or whether environmental sustainability can become an integral part of the public administration field.[32]

NOTES

1. Robert Bryce, *Power Hungry: The Myths of "Green" Energy and the Real Fuels of the Future* (New York: Public Affairs Books, 2010): 13–20; Robert P. Taylor, *et al.*, *Financing Energy Efficiency: Lessons from Brazil, China, India, and Beyond* (Washington, D.C.: The International Bank for Reconstruction and Development/The World Bank, 2008): 3–20; Daniel Yergin, *The Quest: Energy, Security, and the Remaking of the Modern World* (New York: The Penguin Press, 2011): 12–13, 17–18.

2. Mark Sagoff, "At the Shrine of Our Lady of Fatima, or Why Political Questions Are Not All Economic," in *The Environmental Ethics & Policy Book*, 2nd edition, Donald VanDeVeer and Christine Pierce, eds. (Belmont, Calif.: Wadsworth, 1998): 303.

3. Severin Borenstein, "The Private and Public Economics of Renewable Electricity Generation," *Journal of Economic Perspectives* 26 (Winter 2012): 67–92; Bryce, *Power Hungry*, 39–42; "Publisher Llewellyn King on Energy Policy," *Southern Energy Report* 35 (July 1989): 2–3, 4; Yergin, *The Quest*, 523–26.

4. Bryce, *Power Hungry*, 21–23; Thomas L. Friedman, *Hot, Flat, and Crowded: Why We Need a Green Revolution—And How It Can Renew America* (New York: Farrar, Straus and Giroux, 2008): 228–30; Amory B. Lovins and the Rocky Mountain Institute, *Reinventing Fire: Bold Business Solutions for the New Energy Era* (White River Junction, VT: Chelsea Green Publishing Company, 2011): 228–51; Can Tansel Tugcu, Iihan Ozturk, and Alper Aslan, "Renewable and Non-renewable Energy Consumption and Economic Growth Relationship Revisited: Evidence from G7 Countries," *Energy Economics* 34 (November 2012): 1942–50.

5. Quoted at Bryce, *Power Hungry*, 4. See also 3–6, 285–302; Borenstein, "The Private and Public Economics of Renewable Electricity Generation," 67–92; Yergin, *The Quest*, 13–14, 711–17.

6. The Earthworks Group, *50 Simple Things You Can Do to Save the Earth* (Berkeley, CA.: Earthworks Press, 1989): 86–87.

7. Greg Horn, *Living Green: A Practical Guide to Simple Sustainability* (Topanga, CA.: Freedom Press, 2006); Renée Loux, *Easy Green Living:*

The Ultimate Guide to Simple, Eco-Friendly Choices for You and Your Home (Emmaus, PA.: Rodale Books, 2008); Chris Prelitz, *Green Made Easy: The Everyday Guide for Transitioning to a Green Lifestyle* (Carlsbad, CA.: Hay House, 2009); Clara Taylor, *Green Living: Green Lifestyle—Green Living Guide for Beginners* (Seattle, WA.: Amazon Digital Services, 2015).

8. See, for example, William H. Rodgers, Jr., "Giving Voice to Rachel Carson: Putting Science into Environmental Law," *Journal of Land Use & Environmental Law* 28 (Fall 2012): 61–69.

9. Cristina Gimenez and Vicenta Sierra, "Sustainable Supply Chains: Governance Mechanisms to Greening Suppliers," *Journal of Business Ethics* 116 (August 2013): 189–203; Richard M. Kashmanian and Justin R. Moore, "Building Greater Sustainability in Supply Chains," *Environmental Quality Management* 23 (Summer 2014): 13–37; Georgiana Marin, Alexandra Mateiu, and Werner Mailinger, "Collaborative Practices within the Supply Chain Area, as a Solution for Logistic Enterprises to Solve the Challenges in Obtaining Sustainability," *International Journal of Economic Practices and Theories* 5 (May 2015): 222–32.

10. Holger Buxel, Gökçe Esenduran, and Scott Griffin, "Strategic Sustainability: Creating Business Value with Life Cycle Analysis," *Business Horizons* 58 (January–February 2015): 109–22; Selin Gundes, "The Use of Life Cycle Techniques in the Assessment of Sustainability," *Urban Planning and Architectural Design for Sustainable Development (UPADSD), Procedia—Social and Behavioral Sciences* 216 (January 2016): 916–22.

11. Lynton K. Caldwell, "Environment: A New Focus for Public Policy?" *Public Administration Review* 23 (September 1963): 138.

12. Daniel J. Fiorino, "Sustainability as a Conceptual Focus for Public Administration," *Public Administration Review* 70 Supplement (December 2010): s86.

13. See, for example, Deniz Zeynep Leuenberger and John R. Battle, *Sustainable Development for Public Administration* (Armonk, NY.: M.E. Sharpe, Inc., 2009).

14. Nicholas Lemann, "Notorious Big: Why the Spectre of Size Has Always Haunted American Politics," *The New Yorker* 92 (March 28, 2016): 72–75; James Welch IV and Nita Clark, "The Problematic Nature of Civic Participation in Sustainability Initiatives: The Case of the Arlington Hike and Bike Master Plan," *Public Integrity* 17 (Winter 2014–15): 37–54.

15. Alexandru Roman, "The Roles Assumed by Public Administrators: The Link Between Administrative Discretion and Representation," *Public Administration Quarterly* 39 (Winter 2015): 595–644.

16. Susan E. Dudley, "Improving Regulatory Accountability: Lessons from the Past and Prospects for the Future," *Case Western Reserve Law Review* 65 (Summer 2015): 1027–57; David J. Houston and Lauren Howard Harding, "Public Trust in Government Administrators: Explaining Citizen Perceptions

of Trustworthiness and Competence," *Public Integrity* 16 (Winter 2013–14): 53–75; Peter Triantafillou, "The Politics of Neutrality and the Changing Role of Expertise in Public Administration," *Administrative Theory & Praxis* 37 (July 2015): 174–87.

17. See, for example, Aaron J. Ley, "The Costs and Benefits of American Policy-Making Values," *Law & Society Review* 48 (March 2014): 91–126; Kenneth J. Meier, "Proverbs and the Evolution of Public Administration," *Public Administration Review* 75 (January–February 2015): 15–24.

18. Leuenberger and Battle, *Sustainable Development for Public Administration*, 127–28.

19. Neale Smith, "The Public Administrator as Collaborative Citizen: Three Conceptions," *Public Administration Quarterly* 34 (Summer 2010): 238–61.

20. J. Donald Kingsley, *Representative Bureaucracy: An Interpretation of the British Civil Service* (Yellow Springs, OH.: The Antioch Press, 1944). See also Nicole M. Rishel Elias, "Shifting Diversity Perspectives and New Avenues for Representative Bureaucracy," *Public Administration Quarterly* 37 (Fall 2013): 331–73; Brandy A. Kennedy, "Sorting Through: The Role of Representation in Bureaucracy," *Journal of Public Administration Research & Theory* 23 (October 2013): 791–816.

21. Lewis Carroll, *Alice's Adventures in Wonderland* (Mineola, NY: Courier Dover Publications, 1993 [1865]): 16.

22. Tom Lininger, "Green Ethics for Lawyers," *Boston College Law Review* 57 (January 2016): 61–115; Anthony DeForest Molina and Cassandra L. McKeown, "The Heart of the Profession: Understanding Public Service Values," *Journal of Public Affairs Education* 18 (Spring 2012): 375–96.

23. American Society for Public Administration Website. Accessed July 1, 2016. http://www.aspanet.org/public/ASPA/Home/ASPA/Home.aspx?hkey=5d5de8d7-63f5-4ecd-a151-3af1541471f6.

24. Geoffrey W. Chase and Peggy F. Barlett, *Sustainability in Higher Education: Stories and Strategies for Transformation* (Cambridge, MA.: MIT Press, 2013); Leuenberger and Battle, *Sustainable Development for Public Administration*, 103–14.

25. Christopher McGrory Klyza and David J. Sousa, *American Environmental Policy, 1990–2006: Beyond Gridlock* (Cambridge, MA.: MIT Press, 2008); George B. Wyeth and Beth Termini, "Regulating for Sustainability," *Environmental Law* 45 (Summer 2015): 663–712.

26. Leuenberger and Battle, *Sustainable Development for Public Administration*, 9–11.

27. Keith H. Hirokawa, "Saving Sustainability," *Environmental Law Reporter: News & Analysis* 46 (February 2016): 10151–57.

28. Elisabetta Iossa and David Martimort, "The Simple Microeconomics of Public-Private Partnerships," *Journal of Public Economic Theory* 17 (February 2015): 4–48; Anne-Marie Reynaers, "Public Values in Public-Private

Partnerships," *Public Administration Review* 74 (January–February 2014): 41–50; Mohamed Ismail Sabry, "Good Governance, Institutions and Performance of Public Private Partnerships," *International Journal of Public Sector Management* 28 (2015): 566–82.

29. Anne-Marie Reynaers and Stephan Grimmelikhuijsen, "Transparency in Public-Private Partnerships: Not So Bad After All?" *Public Administration* 93 (September 2015): 609–26.

30. Lea Stadtler, "Scrutinizing Public-Private Partnerships for Development: Towards a Broad Evaluation Conception," *Journal of Business Ethics* 135 (April 2016): 71–86; United States General Accountability Office, *Public-Private Partnerships: Pilot Program Needed to Demonstrate the Actual Benefits of Using Partnerships* (Washington, D.C.: U.S. Government Printing Office. GAO Publication No. GAO-01-096, July 2001).

31. Paul Calcott, "Negotiating versus Consultation in the Development of a Regulation," *Environmental & Resource Economics* 39 (February 2008): 75–82; Peter H. Schuck and Steven Kochevar, "Reg Neg Redux: The Career of a Procedural Reform," *Theoretical Inquiries in Law* 15 (July 2014): 417–46.

32. See, for example, Leuenberger and Battle, *Sustainable Development for Public Administration*, 3–16, 127–28; Laurie Kaye Nijaki, "Justifying and Juxtaposing Environmental Justice and Sustainability: Towards an Inter-Generational and Intra-Generational Analysis of Environmental Equity in Public Administration," *Public Administration Quarterly* 39 (Spring 2015): 85–116; Welch and Clark, "The Problematic Nature of Civic Participation in Sustainability Initiatives," 37–54.

REFERENCES

40 CFR § 1503.13.

Abbott, Alden F. "U.S. Government Antitrust Intervention in Standard-Setting Activities and the Competitive Process." *Vanderbilt Journal of Entertainment & Technology Law* 18 (Winter 2016): 225–46.

Abbot Laboratories v. Gardner, 387 U.S. 136 (1967).

Ackerman, Bruce A., and Richard B. Stewart. "Reforming Environmental Law: The Democratic Case for Market Incentives." *Columbia Journal of Environmental Law* 13 (1987): 171–99.

Adams, Henry. *The United States in 1800*. Ithaca, NY.: Cornell University Press, 1974.

Adams, John H., and Patricia Adams with George Black. *A Force For Nature: The Story of NRDC and Its Fight to Save Our Planet*. San Francisco, CA.: Chronicle Books, 2010.

Adkins, Sarah R. "Democracy's Quite Virtues." In *Ethics and Character: The Pursuit of Democratic Virtues*. Edited by William D. Richardson, J. Michael Martinez, and Kerry R. Stewart, 203–23. Durham, N.C.: Carolina Academic Press, 1998.

Adler, Jonathan H., and Andrew P. Morriss. "Common Law Environmental Protection." *Virginia Law Review* 101 (September 2015): 575–82.

Aflaki, Sam. "The Effect of Environmental Uncertainty on the Tragedy of the Commons." *Games and Economic Behavior* 82 (November 2013): 240–53.

Agar, Nicholas. "Biocentrism and the Concept of Life." *Ethics* 108 (October 1997): 147–68.

Aikins, Stephen K. "Political Economy of Government Intervention in the Free Market System." *Administrative Theory & Praxis* 31 (September 2009): 403–8.

Aldred, Jonathan. "Climate Change Uncertainty, Irreversibility and the Precautionary Principle." *Cambridge Journal of Economics* 36 (September 2012): 1051–72.

Alexander, Jack. "Reformer in the Promised Land." *Saturday Evening Post* 212 (July 22, 1939): 5–7, 66–71.

Allen, Paul J. "Institutions: Natural Resources Defense Council." *Environment* 32 (December 1990): 2–4.

Altman, Ida. "The Revolt of Enriquillo and the Historiography of Early Spanish America." *The Americas* 63 (April 2007): 587–614.

Altman, Morris. "When Green Isn't Mean: Economic Theory and the Heuristics of the Impact of Environmental Regulations on Competitiveness and Opportunity Cost." *Ecological Economics* 36 (January 2001): 31–44.

Al-Wagdani, Abdullah M. "Beyond Weberian Bureaucracy: Max Weber on Bureaucracy and His Critics." *Journal of the Social Sciences* 38 (2010): 11–28.

Ambrose, Stephen E. *Undaunted Courage: Meriwether Lewis, Thomas Jefferson, and the Opening of the American West.* New York: Touchstone Books, a Division of Simon & Schuster, 1996.

American Society for Public Administration Website. Accessed July 1, 2016. http://www.aspanet.org/public/ASPA/Home/ASPA/Home.aspx?hkey=5d5de8d7-63f5-4ecd-a151-3af1541471f6.

Amstutz, David Lee. "Nebraska's Live Stock Sanitary Commission and the Rise of Progressivism." *Great Plains Quarterly* 28 (Fall 2008): 259–75.

"Analytical Framework for Evaluating the Costs and Benefits of Extended Producer Responsibility Programmes: Executive Summary." *OECD Papers* 5 (2005): 4–57.

Anand, Sudhir, and Kara Hanson. "DALYs: Efficiency Versus Equity." *World Development* 26 (February 1998): 307–10.

Andersen, Robert, and Josh Curtis. "Social Class, Economic Inequality, and the Convergence of Policy Preferences: Evidence from 24 Modern Democracies." *Canadian Review of Sociology* 52 (August 2015): 266–88.

Anderson, Jed. "The Disappearing Distinction." *The Environmental Forum* 29 (December 2012): 30–33.

Anderson, Paul. "Which Direction for International Environmental Law?" *Journal of Human Rights & The Environment* 6 (March 2015): 98–126.

Andreoni, James. "Warm-Glow Versus Cold-Pickle: The Effects of Positive and Negative Framing on Cooperation in Experiments." *Quarterly Journal of Economics* 110 (February 1995): 1–21.

Andrews, Richard N.L. "The EPA at 40: An Historical Perspective." *Duke Environmental Law & Policy Forum* 21 (Spring 2011): 223–58.

Ang, Frederic, and Steven Van Passel. "Beyond the Environmentalist's Paradox and the Debate on Weak versus Strong Sustainability." *BioScience* 62 (March 2012): 251–59.

Appel, Peter A. "Wilderness, the Courts, and the Effect of Politics on Judicial Decision-making." *Harvard Environmental Law Review* 35 (2011): 275–312.

Appleby, Paul H. *Big Democracy*. New York: Knopf, 1945.

Appleby, Paul H. *Policy and Administration*. University, AL.: University of Alabama Press, 1949.

Applegate, Alexis. "Common Law Preclusion and Environmental Citizen Suits: Are Citizen Groups Losing Their Standing?" *Boston College Environmental Affairs Law Review* 39 Supplement (2012): 1–14.

Applegate, John S. "The Perils of Unreasonable Risk: Information, Regulatory Policy, and Toxic Substances Control." *Columbia Law Review* 91 (March 1991): 261–333.

Arenas, Daniel, and Pablo Rodrigo. "On Firms and the Next Generations: Difficulties and Possibilities for Business Ethics Inquiry." *Journal of Business Ethics* 133 (January 2016): 165–78.

Argersinger, Peter H. *Populism and Politics: William Alfred Peffer and the People's Party*. Lexington: University Press of Kentucky, 2015.

Arnold, Peri E. "The Brownlow Committee, Regulation, and the Presidency: Seventy Years Later." *Public Administration Review* 67 (November/December 2007): 1030–40.

Aronovsky, Ronald G. "Federalism and CERCLA: Rethinking the Role of Federal Law in Private Cleanup Cost Disputes." *Ecology Law Quarterly* 33 (2006): 1–104.

Arrow, Kenneth J. "Thorstein Veblen as an Economic Theorist." *American Economist* 19 (Spring 1975): 5–9.

Asano, Takao. "Precautionary Principle and the Optimal Timing of Environmental Policy under Ambiguity." *Environmental and Resource Economics* 47 (October 2010): 173–96.

Asheim, Geir B., and Tapan Mitra. "Sustainability and Discounted Utilitarianism in Models of Economic Growth." *Mathematical Social Sciences* (Special Issue on Sustainability) 59 (March 2010): 148–69.

Asimow, Michael. "Five Models of Administrative Adjudication." *American Journal of Comparative Law* 63 (Winter 2015): 3–31.

Association of Data Processing Service Organizations v. Camp, 397 U.S. 150 (1970).

Atkinson, Scott E., and T.H. Tietenberg. "Approaches for Reaching Ambient Standards in Non-Attainment Areas: Financial Burden and Efficiency Considerations." *Land Economics* 60 (May 1984): 148–59.

Audi, Robert. "Can Utilitarianism be Distributive? Maximization and Distribution as Criteria in Managerial Decisions." *Business Ethics Quarterly* 17 (October 2007): 593–611.

Audubon Society Website: "About Us." Accessed June 30, 2016. http://www.audubon.org/about/.

Bachmann, John. "Will the Circle Be Broken? A History of the U.S. National Ambient Air Quality Standards." *Journal of the Air & Waste Management Association* 57 (June 2007): 652–97.

Baiardi, Donatella, and Mario Menegatti. "Pigouvian Tax, Abatement Policies and Uncertainty in the Environment." *Journal of Economics* 103 (July 2011): 221–51.

Balogh, Brian. "Scientific Forestry and the Roots of the Modern American State: Gifford Pinchot's Path to Progressive Reform." *Environmental History* 7 (April 2002): 198–225.

Barde, Robert. "Arthur E. Morgan, First Chairman of TVA." *Tennessee Historical Quarterly* 30 (Fall 1971): 299–314.

Barnard, Steve, and Michael Elliott. "The 10-Tenets of Adaptive Management and Sustainability: An Holistic Framework for Understanding and Managing the Socioecological System." *Environmental Science & Policy* 51 (August 2015): 181–91.

Barnes, Barry. *T.S. Kuhn and Social Sciences*. New York: Columbia University Press, 1982.

Barnett, A.H. "The Pigouvian Tax Rule under Monopoly." *The American Economic Review* 70 (December 1980): 1037–41.

Barnett, Harold C. "The Allocation of Superfund." *Land Economics* 61 (August 1985): 255–62.

Barnett, Michael L.; Nicole Darnall; and Bryan W. Husted. "Sustainability Strategy in Constrained Economic Times." *Long Range Planning* 48 (April 2015): 63–68.

Bass, Melissa. "The Success and Contradictions of New Deal Democratic Populism: The Case of the Civilian Conservation Corps." *The Good Society* 21 (2012): 250–60.

Bateman, Bradley W. "Bringing in the State? The Life and Times of Laissez-Faire in the Nineteenth-Century United States." *History of Political Economy* 37 (Supplement 2005): 175–99.

Beck, Glenn. *Agenda 21: Into the Shadows*. New York: Threshold Books, 2015. Accessed May 25, 2016. http://www.glennbeck.com/agenda21/.

Becker, Robert A. "Intergenerational Equity: The Capital-Environment Tradeoff." *Journal of Environmental Economics and Management* 9 (June 1982): 165–85.

Beckerman, Wilfred. "'Sustainable Development': Is It a Useful Concept?" In *The Environmental Ethics & Policy Book*. 2nd edition. Edited by Donald VanDeVeer and Christine Pierce, 462–74. Belmont, CA.: Wadsworth, 1998.

Beermann, Jack M. "End the Failed *Chevron* Experiment Now: How *Chevron* Has Failed and Why It Can and Should be Overruled." *Administrative & Regulatory Law News* 35 (Winter 2010): 3–15.

Bergeson, Lynn L. "The Federal Trade Commission Brings Actions Regarding Misleading and Unsubstantiated Environmental Marketing Claims." *Environmental Quality Management* 23 (Spring 2014): 75–79.

Berry, Christopher J. "Adam Smith's 'Science of Human Nature.'" *History of Political Economy* 44 (Fall 2012): 471–92.

Berry, Christopher J. *The Idea of Commercial Society in the Scottish Enlightenment.* Edinburgh: Edinburgh University Press, 2013.

Berry, Michael A., and Dennis A. Rondinelli, "Proactive Corporate Environmental Management: A New Industrial Revolution." *Academy of Management Executive* 12 (May 1998): 38–50.

Besharat, Ali; Daniel M. Ladik; and François A. Carrillat. "Are Maximizers Blind to the Future? When Today's Best Does Not Make for a Better Tomorrow." *Marketing Letters* 25 (March 2014): 77–91.

Bianchi, Francesco, and Leonardo Melosi. "Modeling the Evolution of Expectations and Uncertainty in General Equilibrium." *International Economic Review* 57 (May 2016): 717–56.

Biasetti, Pierfrancesco. "From Beauty to Love: A Kantian Way to Environmental Moral Theory?" *Environmental Philosophy* 12 (Fall 2015): 139–60.

Biles, Blake A., and Lawrence E. Culleen. "TSCA, Redux." *The Environmental Forum* 27 (January/February 2010): 30–34.

Bird, Alexander. "Kuhn, Naturalism, and the Positivist Legacy." *Studies in History & Philosophy of Science Part A* 35 (June 2004): 337–56.

BirdLife International Website: "About BirdLife." Accessed June 30, 2016. http://www.birdlife.org/worldwide/partnership/about-birdlife.

Bish, Robert L. "Vincent Ostrom's Contributions to Political Economy." *Publius: The Journal of Federalism* 44 (April 2014): 227–48.

Black, Harvey. "Imperfect Protection: NEPA at 35 Years." *Environmental Health Perspectives* 112 (April 2004): A292–95.

Block, Robert H. "Frederick Jackson Turner and American Geography." *Annals of the Association of American Geographers* 70 (March 1980): 31–42.

Blumm, Michael C., and Andrea Lang. "Shared Sovereignty: The Role of Expert Agencies in Environmental Law." *Ecology Law Quarterly* 42 (2015): 609–50.

Boime, Albert. "John James Audubon: A Birdwatcher's Fanciful Flights." *Art History* 22 (December 1999): 728–55.

Bokulich, Alisa. "Heisenberg Meets Kuhn: Closed Theories and Paradigms." *Philosophy of Science* 73 (January 2006): 90–107.

Bolis, Ivan. "Review: When Sustainable Development Risks Losing Its Meaning; Delimiting the Concept with a Comprehensive Literature Review." *Journal of Cleaner Production* 83 (November 2014): 7–20.

Bookchin, Murray. "Will Ecology Become 'The Dismal Science'?" In *The Environmental Ethics & Policy Book.* 2nd edition. Edited by Donald VanDeVeer and Christine Pierce, 230–35. Belmont, Calif.: Wadsworth, 1998.

Booth, Bibi. "Robert Marshall (1901–1939)." In *Environmental Activists*. Edited by John Mongillo and Bibi Booth, 173–78. Westport, CT.: Greenwood Press, 2001.

Borenstein, Severin. "The Private and Public Economics of Renewable Electricity Generation." *Journal of Economic Perspectives* 26 (Winter 2012): 67–92.

Bosse, Douglas A., and Robert A. Phillips. "Agency Theory and Bounded Self-Interest." *Academy of Management Review* 41 (April 2016): 276–97.

Bostwick, Peg. "Integrating State and Federal Needs Under the Clean Water Act." *National Wetlands Newsletter* 33 (July/August 2011): 5–6.

Botkin, Daniel. *No Man's Garden: Thoreau and a New Vision of Civilization and Nature*. Washington, D.C. and Covelo, CA.: Island Press/Shearwater Books, 2001.

Bourdeaux, Carolyn. "Politics versus Professionalism: The Effect of Institutional Structure on Democratic Decision-making in a Contested Policy Area." *Journal of Public Administration Research and Theory* 18 (July 2008): 349–73.

Boyle, Kevin. *The Arc of Justice: A Saga of Race, Civil Rights, and Murder in the Jazz Age*. New York: Henry Holt, 2004.

Brands, H.W. *Traitor to His Class: The Privileged Life and Radical Presidency of Franklin Delano Roosevelt*. New York: Doubleday, 2008.

Braun, Eric M. "Coring the Seedless Grape: A Reinterpretation of *Chevron U.S.A. v. NRDC*." *Columbia Law Review* 87 (June 1987): 986–1008.

Breuilly, John. "Max Weber, Charisma and Nationalist Leadership." *Nations and Nationalism* 17 (July 2011): 477–99.

Brewster, Rachel. "Stepping Stone or Stumbling Block: Incrementalism and National Climate Change Legislation." *Yale Law & Policy Review* 28 (April 1, 2010): 245–312.

Brinkley, Douglas. *Cronkite*. New York: Harper, 2012.

Brinkley, Douglas. *Rightful Heritage: Franklin D. Roosevelt and the Land of America*. New York: Harper, 2016.

Brinkley, Douglas. *The Wilderness Warrior: Theodore Roosevelt and the Crusade for America*. New York: HarperCollins, 2009.

Brooks, Paul. *Speaking for Nature: The Literary Naturalists, from Transcendentalism to the Birth of the American Environmental Movement*. Lincoln, MA.: The Walden Woods Project, 1980.

Brown, Darryl K. "The Perverse Effects of Efficiency in Criminal Process." *Virginia Law Review* 100 (March 2014): 183–223.

Brown, James D. "Prospects for the Open Treatment of Uncertainty in Environmental Research." *Progress in Physical Geography* 34 (February 2010): 75–100.

Brown, Phil. "Wilderness Advocate." *New York Conservationist*, 62 (August 2007): 2–6.

Brown, Ph.D, Phil, and Richard Clapp, DSc. "Looking Back on Love Canal." *Public Health Reports* 117 (March/April 2002): 95–98.

Brunacini, Alan. "POSDCORB." *Fire Engineering* 168 (March 2015): 54–56.

Bruno, Jonathan R. "Note: Immunity for 'Discretionary' Functions: A Proposal to Amend the Federal Tort Claims Act." *Harvard Journal on Legislation* 49 (July 2012): 411–50.

Bryce, Robert. *Power Hungry: The Myths of "Green" Energy and the Real Fuels of the Future.* New York: Public Affairs Books, 2010.

Buck, Susan J. *Understanding Environmental Administration and Law.* 2nd edition Washington, D.C. and Covelo, Calif.: Island Press, 1996.

Butler, Henry N. "A Defense of Common Law Environmentalism: The Discovery of Better Environmental Policy." *Case Western Reserve Law Review* 58 (Spring 2008): 705–52.

Buxel, Holger; Gökçe Esenduran; and Scott Griffin. "Strategic Sustainability: Creating Business Value with Life Cycle Analysis." *Business Horizons* 58 (January–February 2015): 109–22.

Byrch, Christine; Kate Kearins; Markus J. Milne; and Richard K. Morgan. "Sustainable Development: What Does It Really Mean?" *University of Auckland Business Review* 11 (Autumn 2009): 1–7.

Cagle, M. Christine, J. Michael Martinez, and William D. Richardson. "Privatizing Professional Licensing Boards: Self-Governance or Self-Interest?" *Administration & Society* 30 (January 1999): 734–70.

Cahnman, Werner J. "Ideal Type Theory: Max Weber's Concept and Some of Its Derivations." *The Sociological Quarterly* 6 (Summer 1965): 268–80.

Calcott, Paul. "Negotiating versus Consultation in the Development of a Regulation." *Environmental & Resource Economics* 39 (February 2008): 75–82.

Caldwell, Lynton K. "Environment: A New Focus for Public Policy?" *Public Administration Review* 23 (September 1963): 132–39.

Caldwell, Lynton K. *Science and the National Environmental Policy Act: Redirecting Policy through Procedural Reform.* Tuscaloosa: University of Alabama Press, 1982.

Callicott, J. Baird. "Genesis and John Muir." *ReVision* 12 (Winter 1990): 31–47.

Callicott, J. Baird. *In Defense of the Land Ethic: Essays in Environmental Philosophy.* Albany, NY.: State University of New York Press, 1989.

Callicott, J. Baird. "Non-Anthropocentric Value Theory and Environmental Ethics." *American Philosophical Quarterly* 21 (October 1984): 299–309.

Campbell, John Angus. "Charles Darwin and the Crisis of Ecology: A Rhetorical Perspective." *Quarterly Journal of Speech* 60 (December 1974): 442–49.

Capper, Charles. "'A Little Beyond': The Problem of the Transcendentalist Movement in American History." *The Journal of American History* 85 (September 1998): 502–39.

Carlson, Peter. "TR Goes Camping with John Muir." *American History* 51 (June 2016): 14–15.

Carmody, Christine. "Considering Future Generations: Sustainability in Theory and Practice." *Economic Round-Up* 3 (November 2012): 65–92

Carpenter, Ronald H. "Frederick Jackson Turner and the Rhetorical Impact of the Frontier Thesis." *Quarterly Journal of Speech* 63 (April 1977): 117–129.

Carroll, Lewis. *Alice's Adventures in Wonderland*. Mineola, NY.: Courier Dover Publications, 1993 [1865].

Carson, Rachel. *Silent Spring*. 40th Anniversary Edition. Boston: Houghton Mifflin Harcourt, 2002 [1962].

Catlin, George. *Letters and Notes on the Manners, Customs, and Condition of the North American Indians*. Vol. I. London: Tosswell and Myers, 1841.

Cawley, R. McGreggor. "Inserting Frontier into Dichotomies: Politics, Administration, and Agonistic Pluralism." *Administrative Theory & Praxis* 37 (December 2015): 227–41.

"A Centennial Celebration, 1892–1992." *Sierra* 77 (May/June 1992): 52–73.

Chakravarty, Satya R. "Equity and Efficiency as Components of a Social Welfare Function." *International Journal of Economic Theory* 5 (June 2009): 181–99.

Chase, Geoffrey W., and Peggy F. Barlett. *Sustainability in Higher Education: Stories and Strategies for Transformation*. Cambridge, MA.: MIT Press, 2013.

Chevron v. Natural Resources Defense Council, 467 U.S. 837 (1984).

Christofferson, Bill. *The Man From Clear Lake: Earth Day Founder Senator Gaylord Nelson*. Madison: The University of Wisconsin Press, 2004.

Citizens to Preserve Overton Park, Inc. v. Volpe, 401 U.S. 402 (1971).

The Clean Air Act (CAA) of 1970. 42 U.S.C. § 7401 *et seq.* (1970).

The Clean Water Act (CWA) (Federal Water Pollution Control Amendments of 1972). 33 U.S.C. § 1251 *et seq.* (1972).

Coase, Ronald H. "The Institutional Structure of Production." *The American Economic Review* 82 (September 1992): 713–19.

Cohen, Bonnie R. "Natural Resources Defense Council—Weapons in the Environmentalist Arsenal: Lawsuits, Blacklists and Publicity." In *Organization Trends*, 1–5. Washington, D.C.: Capital Research Center, August 2003.

Cohen, Sheila Terman. *Gaylord Nelson: Champion for Our Earth*. Madison: Wisconsin Historical Society Press, 2010.

Cohen, Steven. "What is Stopping the Renewable Energy Transformation and What Can the U.S. Government Do about It?" *Social Research* 82 (Fall 2015): 689–710.

Colburn, Jamison E. "Administering the National Environmental Policy Act." *Environmental Law Reporter: News & Analysis* 45 (April 2015): 10287–323.

"Communicating Results to Community Residents: Lessons from Recent ATSDR Health Investigations." *Journal of Exposure Analysis and Environmental Epidemiology* 14 (November 2004): 484–91.

The Comprehensive Environmental Response, Compensation and Liability Act (CERCLA) of 1980. 42 U.S.C. § 9601 et seq. (1980).

Comstock, Gary. "Intuitive Level System Rules: Commentary on 'Utilitarianism and the Evolution of Ecological Ethics.'" Science and Engineering Ethics 14 (December 2008): 575–79.

Conrad, Klaus. "Applied General Equilibrium Modeling for Environmental Policy Analysis." Annals of Operations Research 54 (1994): 129–42.

Cook, Brian J. "Curing the Mischiefs of Faction in the Administrative State." American Review of Public Administration 46 (January 2016): 3–27.

Copeland, Claudia. Clean Water Act: A Summary of the Law. Washington, D.C.: Congressional Research Service, April 23, 2010.

Corcoran, Peter B., and Eric Sievers. "Reconceptualizing Environmental Education: Five Possibilities." Journal of Environmental Education 25 (Summer 1994): 4–8.

Corsa, Andrew J. "Henry David Thoreau: Greatness of Soul and Environmental Virtue." Environmental Philosophy 12 (Fall 2015): 161–84.

Costanza, Robert; Cutler Cleveland, and Charles Perrings. The Development of Ecological Economics. Cheltenham, UK.: Edward Elgar Publishing, 1997.

Coward, Harold. The Perfectibility of Human Nature in Eastern and Western Thought. Albany, NY.: State University of New York Press, 2008.

Cox, James C., and Vjollca Sadiraj. "Direct Tests of Individual Preferences for Efficiency and Equity." Economic Inquiry 50 (October 2012): 920–31.

Coyle, Kevin A. "Standing of Third Parties to Challenge Administrative Agency Actions." California Law Review 76 (October 1988): 1061–107.

Crampton, Roger C., and Richard K. Berg. "On Leading a Horse to Water: NEPA and the Federal Bureaucracy." Michigan Law Review 71 (January 1973): 511–36.

Crane, Daniel A. "Is More Antitrust the Answer to Wealth Inequality?" Regulation 38 (Winter 2015–2016): 18–21.

"Creation of the Executive Departments." Congressional Digest 40 (November 1961): 258–60.

Cushing, Lincoln. "Posters about Ecology and the Environment Before and During the 1970s." Electronic Green Journal 1 (December 2010): 1–5.

Dahl, Robert A. A Preface to Democratic Theory. Chicago: The University of Chicago Press, 1956.

Dahl, Robert A. "The Science of Public Administration: Three Problems." Public Administration Review 7 (Winter 1947): 1–11.

Daniels, Brigham. "Agency as Principal." Georgia Law Review 48 (Winter 2014): 335–423.

Danziger, Sheldon. "Do Rising Tides Lift All Boats? The Impact of Secular and Cyclical Changes on Poverty." The American Economic Review 76 (May 1986): 405–10.

Daston, Lorraine. "Simon and the Sirens: A Commentary." *ISIS: Journal of the History of Science in Society* 106 (September 2015): 669–76.

"David E. Lilienthal is Dead at 81; Led U.S. Effort in Atomic Power." *New York Times*, January 16, 1981: A1.

Davidson, Jonathan, and Joseph M. Norbeck. *An Interpretive History of the Clean Air Act: Scientific and Policy Perspectives*. Waltham, Mass.: Elsevier, 2012.

Deckers, Jan. "Christianity and Ecological Ethics: The Significance of Process Thought and a Panexperientialist Critique of Strong Anthropocentrism." *Ecotheology: Journal of Religion, Nature & the Environment* 9 (December 2004): 359–87.

Delborne, Jason; Jen Schneider; Ravtosh Bal; Susan Cozzens; and Richard Worthington. "Policy Pathways, Policy Networks, and Citizen Deliberation: Disseminating the Results of World Wide Views on Global Warming in the USA." *Science and Public Policy* 40 (2013): 378–92.

Delmas, Magali A., and Maria J. Montes-Sancho. "An Institutional Perspective on the Diffusion of International Management System Standards: The Case of the Environmental Management Standard ISO 14001." *Business Ethics Quarterly* 21 (January 2011): 103–32.

Derksen, Maarten. "Turning Men into Machines? Scientific Management, Industrial Psychology, and the 'Human Factor.'" *Journal of the History of Behavioral Sciences* 50 (Spring 2014): 148–65.

Derman, Joshua. "Max Weber and Charisma: A Transatlantic Affair." *New German Critique* 113 (Summer 2011): 51–88.

DeShazo, J. R., and Jody Freeman. "The Congressional Competition to Control Delegated Power." *Texas Law Review* 81 (May 2003): 1443–1519.

DesJardins, Joseph. "Is It Time to Jump Off the Sustainability Bandwagon?" *Business Ethics Quarterly* 26 (January 2016): 117–35.

Devall, Bill. "The End of American Environmentalism?" *Nature and Culture* 1 (Autumn 2006): 157–80.

Devall, Bill, and George Sessions. "Deep Ecology." In *The Environmental Ethics & Policy Book*. 2nd edition, Edited by Donald VanDeVeer and Christine Pierce, 221–26. Belmont, CA.: Wadsworth, 1998.

DeWitt, Calvin. *The Environment and the Christian: What Does the New Testament Say About the Environment?* Grand Rapids, MI.: Baker Academic, 1991.

Diamond, Martin. "Democracy and *The Federalist*: A Reconsideration of the Framers' Intent." *The American Political Science Review* 53 (March 1959): 52–68.

Diehm, Christian. "Darwin and Deep Ecology." *Ethics & The Environment* 19 (Spring 2014): 73–93.

Dietze, Gottfried. *The Federalist: A Classic on Federalism and Free Government*. Westport, CT.: Greenwood Press, 1960.

Diggins, John Patrick. *The Lost Soul of American Politics: Virtue, Self-Interest, and the Foundations of Liberalism.* Chicago and London: University of Chicago Press, 1986.

Diggins, John Patrick. *Thorstein Veblen: Theorist of the Leisure Class.* Princeton, N.J.: Princeton University Press, 1999.

Dimock, Marshall E. *Free Enterprise and the Administrative State.* Westport, CT.: Greenwood Press, 1972.

Dimock, Marshall E. "The Study of Administration." *The American Political Science Review* 31 (February 1937): 28–40.

Djulbegovic, Benjamin. "Articulating and Responding to Uncertainties in Clinical Research." *Journal of Medicine and Philosophy* 32 (March/April 2007): 79–98.

Dobel, J. Patrick. "Stewards of the Earth's Resources: A Christian Response to Ecology." *Christian Century* 94 (October 12, 1977): 906–9.

Dobusch, Leonhard, and Jakob Kapeller. "Why is Economics not an Evolutionary Science? New Answers to Veblen's Old Question." *Journal of Economic Issues* 43 (December 2009): 867–989.

Doerrenberg, Philipp, and Andreas Peichl. "The Impact of Redistributive Policies on Inequality in OECD Countries." *Applied Economics* 46 (June 2014): 2066–86.

Donnelly, Bebhinn, and Patrick Bishop. "Natural Law and Ecocentrism." *Journal of Environmental Law* 19 (2007): 89–101.

Donovan, Frank. *Mr. Madison's Constitution: The Story Behind the Constitutional Convention.* New York: Dodd Mead & Company, 1965.

Dow, Alexander; Sheila Dow; and Alan Hutton. "The Scottish Political Economy Tradition and Modern Economics." *Scottish Journal of Political Economy* 44 (September 1997): 368–83.

Dow, Dustin M. "The Unambiguous Supremacy Clause." *Boston College Law Review* 53 (May 2012): 1009–44.

Dreier, Peter. "The Fifty Most Influential Progressives of the Twentieth Century." *Nation* 291 (October 4, 2010): 11–21.

Drengson, Alan; Bill Devall; and Mark A. Schroll. "The Deep Ecology Movement: Origins, Development, and Future Prospects (Toward a Transpersonal Ecosophy)." *International Journal of Transpersonal Studies* 30 (June 2011): 101–17.

Driouchi, Tarik; Michel Leseure; and David Bennett. "A Robustness Framework for Monitoring Real Options under Uncertainty." *Omega* 37 (June 2009): 698–710.

D'Souza, Jeevan, and Michael Gurin. "The Universal Significance of Maslow's Concept of Self-Actualization." *The Humanistic Psychologist* 44 (June 2016): 210–14.

Dudley, Susan E. "Improving Regulatory Accountability: Lessons from the Past and Prospects for the Future." *Case Western Reserve Law Review* 65 (Summer 2015): 1027–57.

Duke Power Company v. Carolina Environmental Study Group, Inc., 438 U.S. 59 (1978).

Dunlap, Riley E., and Angela G. Mertig. "The Evolution of the U.S. Environmental Movement from 1970 to 1990: An Overview." *Society & Natural Resources: An International Journal* 4 (1991): 209–18.

Dunning, Mike. "Manifest Destiny and the Trans-Mississippi South: Natural Laws and the Extension of Slavery into Mexico." *Journal of Popular Culture* 35 (Fall 2001): 111–27.

Durlauf, Steven N. *"Bowling Alone*: A Review Essay." *Journal of Economic Behavior and Organization* 47 (March 2002): 259–73.

Dwyer, John. "Ethics and Economics: Bridging Adam Smith's *Theory of Moral Sentiments* and *Wealth of Nations.*" *Journal of British Studies* 44 (October 2005): 662–87.

The Earthworks Group. *50 Simple Things You Can Do to Save the Earth.* Berkeley, CA.: Earthworks Press, 1989.

Easterbrook, Gregg. *A Moment on the Earth: The Coming Age of Environmental Optimism.* New York: Viking, 1995.

Eccleston, Charles H. "Does NEPA Suffer from the Pike Syndrome?" *Environmental Practice* 4 (March 2002): 8–9.

Eccleston, Charles H., and Frederic March. *Global Environmental Policy: Concepts, Principles, and Practices.* Boca Raton, FL.: CRC Press, 2011.

Egerton, Frank N., and Laura Dassow Walls. "Rethinking Thoreau and the History of American Ecology." *Concord Saunterer* 5 (Fall 1997): 5–20.

Eidelson, Benjamin. "The Majoritarian Filibuster." *Yale Law Journal* 122 (January 2013): 980–1023.

Eisenach, Eldon J. "Progressivism as a National Narrative in Biblical-Hegelian Times." *Social Philosophy & Policy* 24 (January 2007): 59–83.

Ekbladh, David. "'Mr. TVA': Grass-Roots Development, David Lilienthal, and the Rise and Fall of the Tennessee Valley Authority as a Symbol for U.S. Overseas Development, 1933–1973." *Diplomatic History* 26 (Summer 2002): 335–74.

Ellefson, Paul V. "The Safety of Our Forests and the Prosperity of Out People." *Journal of Forestry* 98 (May 2000): 14–22.

Elias, Nicole M. Rishel. "Shifting Diversity Perspectives and New Avenues for Representative Bureaucracy." *Public Administration Quarterly* 37 (Fall 2013): 331–73.

Elias, Roni A. "The Legislative History of the Administrative Procedure Act." *Fordham Environmental Law Review* 27 (Winter 2016): 207–24.

Elshtain, Jean Bethke. "A Return to Hull House: Reflections on Jane Addams." *Feminist Issues* 15 (1997): 105–13.

Emigh, Rebecca Jean; Dylan Riley; and Patricia Ahmed. "The Racialization of Legal Categories in the First U.S. Census." *Social Science History* 39 (2015): 485–519.

The Endangered Species Act (ESA) of 1973. 16 U.S.C. § 1531, *et seq.* (1973).

Engels, Jeremy David. "The Trouble with 'Public Bodies': On the Anti-Democratic Rhetoric of *The Federalist*." *Rhetoric & Public Affairs* 18 (Fall 2015): 505–38.

Enting, Ian G. "Assessing the Information Content in Environmental Modelling: A Carbon Cycle Perspective." *Entropy* 10 (December 2008): 556–75.

Epstein, David F. *The Political Theory of The Federalist*. Chicago: The University of Chicago Press, 1984.

Evans, David. "Clean Water Act § 404 Assumption: What Is It, How Does It Work, and What are the Benefits?" *National Wetlands Newsletter* 31 (May–June 2009): 18–21.

Evensky, Jerry. "Adam Smith's *Theory of Moral Sentiments*: On Morals and Why They Matter to a Liberal Society of Free People and Free Markets." *Journal of Economic Perspectives* 19 (Summer 2005): 109–30.

"Evolution of Present Federal Law." *Congressional Digest* 49 (August/September 1970): 194–97.

Farber, Daniel A. "Coping with Uncertainty: Cost-Benefit Analysis, the Precautionary Principle, and Climate Change." *Washington Law Review* 90 (December 2015): 1659–726.

Farber, Daniel A., and Anne Joseph O'Connell. "The Lost World of Administrative Law." *Texas Law Review* 92 (April 2014): 1137–89.

Farrell, Joseph. "Information and the Coase Theorem." *The Journal of Economic Perspectives* 1 (Autumn 1987): 113–29.

Fears, Darryl. "EPA Gains Power to Block Harmful Chemicals in Products." *The Washington Post*, June 23, 2016: A3.

Fechner, Robert. "The Civilian Conservation Corps Program." *The Annals of the American Academy of Political and Social Science* 194 (November 1937): 129–40.

The Federal Insecticide, Fungicide and Rodenticide Act (FIFRA). As amended by the Federal Environmental Pesticide Control Act of 1972. 7 U.S.C. § 136 *et seq.* (1972).

Feinstein, Nick. "Learning from Past Mistakes: Future Regulation to Prevent Greenwashing." *Boston College Environmental Affairs Law Review* 40 (2013): 229–57.

Feldman, Ira R. "ISO Standards, Environmental Management Systems, and Ecosystem Services." *Environmental Quality Management* 21 (Spring 2012): 69–79.

Ferrey, Steven. *Environmental Law: Examples and Explanations*. New York: Aspen Law & Business, 1997.

Ferrey, Steven. "Inverting the Law: Superfund Hazardous Substance Liability and Supreme Court Reversal of All Federal Circuits." *William & Mary Environmental Law & Policy Review* 33 (May 2009): 633–722.

Finer, Herman. "Administrative Responsibility in Democratic Government." In *Combating Corruption/ Encouraging Ethics: A Sourcebook for Public Service Ethics.* Edited by William L. Richter, Francis Burke, and Jameson W. Doig, 44. Washington, D.C.: The American Society for Public Administration, 1990.

Fiori, Stefano. "Forms of Bounded Rationality: The Reception and Redefinition of Herbert A. Sion's Perspective." *Review of Political Economy* 23 (October 2011): 587–612.

Fiorino, Daniel J. "Rethinking Environmental Regulation: Perspectives on Law and Governance." *Harvard Environmental Law Review* 23 (1999): 441–68.

Fiorino, Daniel J. "Sustainability as a Conceptual Focus for Public Administration." *Public Administration Review* 70 Supplement (December 2010): s78–s88.

Fiorino, Daniel J. "Streams of Environmental Innovation: Four Decades of EPA Policy Reform," *Environmental Law* 44 (Summer 2014): 723–60.

Fisher, Elizabeth; Pasky Pascual; and Wendy Wagner. "Rethinking Judicial Review of Expert Agencies." *Texas Law Review* 93 (June 2015): 1681–721.

Fitzpatrick, Jody; Malcolm Goggin; Tanya Heikkila; Donald Klingner; Jason Machado; and Christine Martell. "A New Look at Comparative Public Administration: Trends in Research and an Agenda for the Future." *Public Administration Review* 71 (November/December 2011): 821–30.

Fleming, Louise Conn. "Civic Participation: A Curriculum for Democracy." *American Secondary Education* 40 (Fall 2011): 39–50.

Fleming, Thomas J. "The Murder Trial of Dr. Ossian Sweet." *Ebony* 25 (October 1970): 106–8, 110–12, 114.

Flint, Richard. *No Settlement, No Conquest: A History of the Coronado Entrada.* Albuquerque: University of New Mexico Press, 2008.

Fontana, Giuseppe, and Malcolm Sawyer. "Towards Post-Keynesian Ecological Macroeconomics." *Ecological Economics* 121 (January 2016): 186–95.

Foote, Christopher L.; Kristopher Gerardi; Lorenz Goette; and Paul S. Willen. "Just the Facts: An initial Analysis of Subprime's Role in the Housing Crisis." *Journal of Housing Economics* 17 (December 2008): 291–305.

Fowler, Luke. "Assessing the Framework of Policy Outcomes: The Case of the U.S. Clean Air Act and Clean Water Act." *Journal of Environmental Assessment Policy and Management* 16 (December 2014): 1–19.

Frahm, Sally. "The Cross and the Compass: Manifest Destiny, Religious Aspects of the Mexican-American War." *Journal of Popular Culture* 35 (Fall 2001): 83–99.

Fredericks, Sarah E. "Ethics in Agenda 21." *Ethics, Policy & Environment* 17 (October 2014): 324–38.

Frederickson, H. George. *New Public Administration/* Tuscaloosa, AL.: University of Alabama Press, 1980.

Free, Andrew, and Nicholas H. Barton. "Do Evolution and Ecology Need the Gaia Hypothesis?" *Trends in Ecology and Evolution* 22 (November 2007): 611–19.

Freeland, Cynthia. "Imagery in the *Phaedrus*: Seeing, Growing, Nourishing." *Symbolae Osloenses* 84 (2010): 62–72.

Frese, Stephen J. "Aldo Leopold: An American Prophet." *History Teacher* 37 (November 2003): 99–118.

Frick, Karen Trapenberg; David Weinzimmer; and Paul Waddell. "The Politics of Sustainable Development Opposition: State Legislative Efforts to Stop the United Nations' Agenda 21 in the United States." *Urban Studies* 52 (February 2015): 209–32.

Friedman, Thomas L. *Hot, Flat, and Crowded: Why We Need a Green Revolution—And How It Can Renew America*. New York: Farrar, Straus and Giroux, 2008.

Friedrich, Carl J. "Public Policy and the Nature of Administrative Responsibility." In *Combating Corruption/ Encouraging Ethics: A Sourcebook for Public Service Ethics*. Edited by William L. Richter, Francis Burke, and Jameson W. Doig, 43. Washington, D.C.: The American Society for Public Administration, 1990.

Frueh, Joseph. "Comment: Pesticides, Preemption, and the Return of Tort Protection." *Yale Journal on Regulation* 23 (2006): 299–309.

Gaba, Jeffrey M. "Generally Illegal: NPDES General Permits Under the Clean Water Act." *Harvard Environmental Law Review* 31 (March 2007): 409–73.

Gaffney, Brian P. "A Divided Duty: The EPA's Dilemma under the Endangered Species Act and Clean Water Act Concerning the National Pollutant Discharge Elimination System." *The Review of Litigation* 26 (April 2007): 487–524.

Gahvari, Firouz. "Second-Best Pigouvian Taxation: A Clarification." *Environmental and Resource Economics* 59 (December 2014): 525–35.

Gaido, Daniel. "The Populist Interpretation of American History: A Materialist Revision." *Science & Society* 65 (Fall 2001): 350–75.

Garry, Patrick M. *Liberalism and American Identity*. Kent, Ohio: Kent State University Press, 1992.

Gazell, James A. "Authority-Flow Theory and the Impact of Chester Barnard." *California Management Review* 13 (Fall 1970): 68–74.

Gellhorn, Walter. "The Administrative Procedure Act: The Beginnings." *Virginia Law Review* 72 (March 1986): 219–33.

Getzner, Michael. "Uncertainties and the Precautionary Principle in Cost-Benefit Environmental Policies." *Journal of Policy Modeling* 30 (2008): 1–17.

Gherasim, Gabriel. "Introductory Sketch to the Analytics and Pragmatism of American Progressivism." *Studia Universitatis Babes-Bolyai. Studia Europaea* 56 (September 2011): 119–42.

Giannantonio, Cristina M., and Amy E. Hurley-Hanson. "Frederick Winslow Taylor: Reflections on the Relevance of *The Principles of Scientific Management* 100 Years Later." *Journal of Business & Management* 17 (April 2011): 7–10.

Gibbs, Lois Marie. "Housewife's Data." *American Journal of Public Health* 101 (September 2011): 1556–59.

Gilens, Martin, and Benjamin I. Page. "Testing Theories of American Politics: Elites, Interest Groups, and Average Citizens." *Perspectives on Politics* 12 (September 2014): 564–81.

Gimenez, Cristina, and Vicenta Sierra. "Sustainable Supply Chains: Governance Mechanisms to Greening Suppliers." *Journal of Business Ethics* 116 (August 2013): 189–203.

Gitler, Stefanie. "Settling the Tradeoffs Between Voluntary Cleanup of Contaminated Sites and Cooperation with the Government Under CERCLA." *Ecology Law Quarterly* 35 (2008): 337–61.

Glover, James A. *A Wilderness Original: The Life of Bob Marshall.* Seattle, WA.: The Mountaineers Book, 1986.

Goldhammer, Arthur. "Tocqueville, Associations, and the Law of 1834." *Historical Reflections* 35 (Winter 2009): 74–84.

Goldsteen, Raymond L.; Karen Goldsteen; and John K. Schorr. "Trust and Its Relationship to Psychological Distress: The Case of Three Mile Island." *Political Psychology* 13 (December 1992): 693–707.

Golembiewski, Robert T. *Men, Management, and Morality: Toward a New Organizational Ethic.* New York: McGraw-Hill, 1965.

Golinski, Jan. "Science in the Enlightenment, Revisited." *History of Science* 49 (June 2011): 217–31.

González, Thalia, and Giovanni Saarman. "Regulating Pollutants, Negative Externalities, and Good Neighbor Agreements: Who Bears the Burden of Protecting Communities?" *Ecology Law Quarterly* 41 (2014): 37–79.

Goodland, Robert. "The Concept of Environmental Sustainability." *Annual Review of Ecology and Systematics* 26 (1995): 1–24.

Goodnow, Frank J. *Politics and Administration: A Study in Government.* New York and London: The MacMillan Company, 1900.

Gottlieb, Robert. "Reconstructing Environmentalism: Complex Movements, Diverse Roots." In *American Environmental History.* Edited by Louis S. Warren, 245–56. Oxford, U.K.: B.H. Blackwell, 2004.

Graham, Jr., Frank. *The Audubon Ark: A History of the Audubon Society.* Austin: University of Texas Press, 1992.

Greve, Michael S., and Ashley C. Parrish. "Administrative Law without Congress." *George Mason Law Review* 22 (Spring 2015): 501–47.

Grisinger, Joanna. "Law in Action: The Attorney General's Committee on Administrative Procedure." *The Journal of Policy History* 20 (July 2008): 379–418.

Grizzle, Raymond E., Paul E. Rothrock, and Christopher B. Barrett. "Evangelicals and Environmentalism: Past, Present, and Future." *Trinity Journal* 19 (Spring 1998): 3–27.

Grossmann, Matt. "Environmental Advocacy in Washington: A Comparison with Other Interest Groups." *Environmental Policy* 15 (August 2006): 628–38.

Gruner, Hans Peter. "Redistributive Policy, Inequality, and Growth." *Journal of Economics* 62 (February 1995): 1–23.

Guéant, Olivier; Roger Guesnerie; and Jean-Michel Lasry. "Ecological Intuition versus Economic 'Reason.'" *Journal of Public Economic Theory* 14 (March 2012): 245–72.

Gulick, Luther, and Lyndall Urwick, Editors. *Papers on the Science of Administration.* New York: Institute of Public Administration, 1937.

Gundes, Selin. "The Use of Life Cycle Techniques in the Assessment of Sustainability." *Urban Planning and Architectural Design for Sustainable Development (UPADSD), Procedia—Social and Behavioral Sciences* 216 (January 2016): 916–22.

Guo, Robert M. "Reasonable Bases for Apportioning Harm under CERCLA." *Ecology Law Quarterly* 37 (2010): 317–52.

Guyer, Paul. "Kant's Answer to Hume?" *Philosophical Topics* 31 (Spring and Fall 2003): 127–64.

Habib, Benjamin. "Sustainability is Not Enough: A Call for Regeneration." *Ethos* 23 (June 2015): 7–10.

Habich, Robert D. "Emerson, Thoreau, Fuller, and Transcendentalism." In *American Literary Scholarship 2013: An Annual.* Edited by Gary Scharnhorst, 3–21. Durham, NC.: Duke University Press, 2015.

Hacker, Jacob S., and Paul Pierson. "Making America Great Again: The Case for the Mixed Economy." *Foreign Affairs* 95 (May/June 2016): 69–90.

Hall, Joshua C. "Positive Externalities and Government Involvement in Education." *Journal of Private Enterprise* 21 (Spring 2006): 165–75.

Hamilton, Alexander; James Madison; and John Jay. *The Federalist Papers.* Edited by Clinton Rossiter. New York: New American Library, 1961 [1788].

Hands, D. Wade. "Economics, Psychology and the History of Consumer Choice Theory." *Cambridge Journal of Economics* 34 (July 2010): 633–48.

Harcourt, Edward. "Integrity, Practical Deliberation and Utilitarianism." *The Philosophical Quarterly* 48 (April 1998): 189–98.

Harmon, M. Judd. "Some Contributions of Harold L. Ickes." *The Western Political Quarterly* 7 (June 1954): 238–52.

Hart, David K. "Social Equity, Justice, and the Equitable Administrator." *Public Administration Review* 34 (January 1974): 3–11.

Hashmi, M. Anaam; Amal Damanhouri; and Divya Rana. "Evaluation of Sustainability Practices in the United States and Large Corporations." *Journal of Business Ethics* 127 (March 2015): 673–81.

Haufler, Virginia. *A Public Role for the Private Sector: Industry Self-Regulation in a Global Economy*. Washington, D.C.: Carnegie Endowment for International Peace, 2001.

Haugh, Helen M., and Alka Talwar, "How Do Corporations Embed Sustainability Across the Organization?" *Academy of Management Learning and Education* 9 (September 2010): 384–96.

Hausdoerffer, John. *Catlin's Lament: Indians, Manifest Destiny, and the Ethics of Nature*. Lawrence: University Press of Kansas, 2009.

Hauskeller, Michael. "No Philosophy for Swine: John Stuart Mill on the Quality of Pleasures." *Utilitas* 23 (December 2011): 428–46.

Hawkins, Christopher V., and XiaoHu Wang. "Policy Integration for Sustainable Development and the Benefits of Local Adoption." *Cityscape: A Journal of Policy Development and Research* 15 (2013): 63–82.

Hawkins, Christopher V., and XiaoHu Wang. "Sustainable Development Governance: Citizen Participation and Support Networks in Local Sustainability Initiatives." *Public Works Management & Policy* 17 (January 2012): 7–29.

Hayes, Denis. "Earth Day! A Call to Unite in Defense of Our Planet." *Mother Earth News* 309 (April/May 2005): 24–31.

Heal, Geoffrey. "Defining and Measuring Sustainability." *Review of Environmental Economics and Policy* 6 (Winter 2012): 147–63.

Hearn, Michael F. "One Person's Waste is Another Person's Liability: Closing the Liability Loophole in RCRA's Citizen Enforcement Action." *McGeorge Law Review* 42 (April 2011): 467–97.

Hecht, David K. "Constructing a Scientist: Expert Authority and Public Images of Rachel Carson." *Historical Studies in the Natural Sciences* 41 (Summer 2011): 277–302.

Hecht, David K. "How to Make a Villain: Rachel Carson and the Politics of Anti-Environmentalism." *Endeavour* 36 (December 2012): 149–55.

Heise, Ursula K. "Environmental Literature and the Ambiguities of Science." *Anglia* 133 (March 2015): 22–36.

Heitman, Danny. "Earthy Wisdom: Aldo Leopold's Land Ethic." *Humanities* 34 (November/December 2013): 28–35.

Heitman, Danny. "Not Exactly a Hermit: Henry David Thoreau." *Humanities* 33 (September/October 2012): 14–17, 50.

Hemmingsen, Michael. "Anthropocentrism, Conservatism, and Green Political Thought." In *The Peace of Nature and the Nature of Peace: Essays on Ecology, Nature, Nonviolence, and Peace*. Edited by Andrew Fiala, 81–90. Boston: Brill, 2015.

Herman, Arthur. "How America Got Rich: It Was Tax Relief, Not Keynesianism, That Propelled American Prosperity after World War II." *Commentary* 134 (September 2012): 20–25.

Hernandez, Morela; Laura J. Noval; and Kimberly A. Wade-Benzoni. "How Leaders Can Create Intergenerational Sustainability Systems to Promote

Organizational Sustainability." *Organizational Dynamics* (Special Issue: Sustainability and Corporate Social Responsibility) 44 (April–June 2015): 104–111.

Hertsgaard, Mark. "Save Earth Day." *The Nation* 294 (May 7, 2012): 3–4.

Hilbert, Richard A. "Bureaucracy as Belief, Rationalization as Repair: Max Weber in a Post-Functionalist Age." *Sociological Theory* 5 (Spring 1987): 70–86.

Hill, Peter J. "Environmental Theology: A Judeo-Christian Defense." *Journal of Markets and Morality* 3 (Fall 2000): 158–72.

Hirokawa, Keith H. "Saving Sustainability." *Environmental Law Reporter: News & Analysis* 46 (February 2016): 10151–57.

Hitler, Adolf . "Selections from *Mein Kampf*." In *The Quest for Justice: Readings in Political Ethics* 3rd. edition. Edited by Leslie G. Rubin and Charles T. Rubin, 237–54. Needham Heights, MA.: Ginn Press, 1992.

Hodder, Alan D. "The Gospel According to this Moment: Thoreau, Wildness, and American Nature Religion." *Religion and the Arts* 15 (September 2011): 460–85.

Hoffman, Andrew J. "Institutional Evolution and Change: Environmentalism and the U.S. Chemical Industry." *The Academy of Management Journal* 42 (August 1999): 351–71.

Hoffman, Andrew J. "An Uneasy Rebirth at Love Canal." *Environment* 37 (March 1995): 4–9, 25–31.

Holden, Erling; Kristin Linnerud; and David Banister. "Sustainable Development: *Our Common Future* Revisited." *Global Environmental Change* 26 (May 2014): 130–39.

Hollis, Sacha. "Old Solutions to New Problems: Providing for Intergenerational Equity in National Institutions." *New Zealand Journal of Environmental Law* 14 (2010): 25–61.

Holmes, Oliver Wendell. "A Farewell to Agassiz." In *The Complete Poetical Works of Oliver Wendell Holmes*, 203–4. Boston and New York: Houghton Mifflin and Company, the Riverside Press, Cambridge, 1895.

Holmes, Oliver Wendell. "At the Saturday Club." In *The Poetical Works of Oliver Wendell Holmes in Three Volumes. Vol. III*, 119–25. Boston and New York: Houghton Mifflin and Company, the Riverside Press, Cambridge, 1891.

Holmes, Steven J. *The Young John Muir: An Environmental Biography*. Madison: The University of Wisconsin Press, 1999.

Hoogenboom, Ari. "The Pendleton Act and the Civil Service." *The American Historical Review* 64 (January 1959): 301–18.

Horn, Greg. *Living Green: A Practical Guide to Simple Sustainability*. Topanga, CA.: Freedom Press, 2006.

Hou, Shen. "*Garden and Forest*: A Forgotten Magazine and the Urban Roots of American Environmentalism." *Environmental History* 17 (October 2012): 813–42.

Hough, Palmer, and Morgan Robertson. "Mitigation Under Section 404 of the Clean Water Act: Where It Comes From, What It Means." *Wetlands Ecology & Management* 17 (January 2009): 15–33.

Houghton, Jeffrey D. "Does Max Weber's Notion of Authority Still Hold in the Twenty-first Century?" *Journal of Management History* 16 (September 2010): 449–53.

Houston, David J., and Lauren Howard Harding. "Public Trust in Government Administrators: Explaining Citizen Perceptions of Trustworthiness and Competence." *Public Integrity* 16 (Winter 2013–14): 53–75.

Howe, Daniel Walker. *What Hath God Wrought: The Transformation of America*. Oxford and New York: Oxford University Press, 2007.

Hsueh, Lily. "Regulatory Effectiveness and the Long-Run Policy Horizon: The Case of U.S. Toxic Chemical Use." *Environmental Science and Policy* 52 (October 2015): 6–22.

Hubbard, Raymond C., and C. Kenneth Meyer. "The Rise of Statistical Significance Testing in Public Administration Research and Why This is a Mistake." *Journal of Business and Behavioral Sciences* 25 (Spring 2013): 4–20.

Hultman Nathan, and Jonathan Koomey. "Three Mile Island: The Driver of U.S. Nuclear Power's Decline?" *Bulletin of the Atomic Scientists* 69 (May 1, 2013): 63–70.

Hundley, Meredith, and Gary Wamsley. "John Rohr's Legacy: Constitutional Literacy and the Public Service." *Administrative Theory & Praxis* 34 (December 2012); 642–47.

Hunt, E.K., and Mark Lautzenheiser. *History of Economic Thought: A Critical Perspective*. 3rd edition Armonk, N.Y.: M.E. Sharpe, Inc., 2011.

Hussain, A.M. Tanvir, and John Tschirhart. "Economic/Ecological Tradeoffs among Ecosystem Services and Biodiversity Conservation." *Ecological Economics* 93 (September 2013): 116–27.

Hutton, T.R.C. "Beating a Dead Horse: The Continuing Presence of Frederick Jackson Turner in Environmental and Western History." *International Social Science Review* 77 (January 2002): 47–57.

Ickes, Harold L. "A Department of Conservation." *Vital Speeches of the Day* 3 (September 1, 1937): 693–95.

Illinois Central Railroad v. Illinois, 146 U.S. 387 (1892).

Imran, Sophia; Khorshed Alam; and Narelle Beaumont. "Reinterpreting the Definition of Sustainable Development for a More Ecocentric Reorientation." *Sustainable Development* 22 (March/April 2014): 134–44.

Iossa, Elisabetta, and David Martimort. "The Simple Microeconomics of Public-Private Partnerships." *Journal of Public Economic Theory* 17 (February 2015): 4–48.

Irmscher, Christoph. "The Ambiguous Agassiz." *Humanities* 34 (November/December 2013): 16–19, 51.

Irmscher, Christoph. *Louis Agassiz: Creator of American Science*. Boston: Houghton Mifflin Harcourt, 2013.

Isenberg, Robert. "The Book That Changed the World." *E: The Environmental Magazine* 23 (September/October 2012): 20–26.

Jackson, Donald Dale. "Just Plain Bob was the Best Friend Wilderness Ever Had." *Smithsonian* 25 (August 1994): 92–100.

Jackson, James R., and William C. Kimler. "Taxonomy and the Personal Equation: The Historical Fates of Charles Girard and Louis Agassiz." *Journal of the History of Biology* 32 (Winter 1999): 509–55.

Jackson, Michael. "Responsibility versus Accountability in the Friedrich-Finer Debate." *Journal of Management History* 15 (January 2009): 66–77.

Jacobs, J. Roger. "The Precautionary Principle as a Provisional Instrument in Environmental Policy: The Montreal Protocol Case Study." *Environmental Science & Policy* 37 (March 2014): 161–71.

Jaffray, Jean-Yves, and Peter Wakker. "Decision-making with Belief Functions: Compatibility and Incompatibility with the Sure-Thing Principle." *Journal of Risk & Uncertainty* 7 (December 1993): 255–71.

Jankunis, Frank J. "Milgram and the Prevalence of Anthropocentrism." *Theoretical and Applied Ethics* 2 (Winter 2013): 93–104.

Jefferson, Thomas. *The Portable Thomas Jefferson*. Edited by Merrill D. Peterson. New York: Penguin Classics, 1977.

Jekic, Milos. "Lowering the Jurisdictional Bar: A Call for an Equitable-Factors Analysis Under CERCLA's Timing-of-Review Provision." *Kansas Law Review* 59 (2011): 157–90.

Jenkins, Robin R.; Elizabeth Kopits; and David Simpson. "The Evolution of Solid and Hazardous Waste in the United States." *Review of Environmental Economics and Policy* 3 (Winter 2009): 104–20.

John, Stephen. "In Defense of Bad Science and Irrational Policies: An Alternative Account of the Precautionary Principle." *Ethical Theory & Moral Practice* 13 (February 2010): 3–18.

Johnson, Douglas R., and David G. Hoopes. "Managerial Cognition, Sunk Costs, and the Evolution of Industry Structure." *Strategic Management Journal* 24 (October 2003): 1057–68.

Johnson, Herbert A. *Gibbons v. Ogden: John Marshall, Steamboats, and the Commerce Clause*. Lawrence: University Press of Kansas, 2010.

Johnstone, Anthony. "The Federalist Safeguards of Politics." *Harvard Journal of Law & Public Policy* 39 (2016): 415–85.

Jones, Bryan D. "Bounded Rationality and Public Policy: Herbert A. Simon and the Decisional Foundation of Collective Choice." *Policy Sciences* 35 (September 1, 2002): 269–84.

Jones, Eileen Gay. "Risky Assessments: Uncertainties in Science and the Human Dimensions of Environmental Decision-making." *William and Mary Environmental Law and Policy Review* 22 (Fall 1997): 1–70.

Jreisat, Jamil E. "Commentary—Comparative Public Administration: A Global Perspective." *Public Administration Review* 71 (November/December 2011): 834–38.

"Judicial Review of Agency Change." *Harvard Law Review* 127 (May 2014): 2070–91.

Jung, Chan Su, and Soo-Young Lee. "The Hawthorne Studies Revisited: Evidence from the U.S. Federal Workforce." *Administration & Society* 47 (July 2015): 507–31.

Kaminitz, Shiri Cohen. "Economics and Ethics under the Same Umbrella: Edgeworth's 'Exact Utilitarianism,' 1877–1881." *Utilitas* 25 (December 2013): 487–503.

Kaminitz, Shiri Cohen. "J.S. Mill and the Value of Utility." *History of Political Economy* 46 (Summer 2014): 231–46.

Karaim, Reed. "Not So Fast with the DDT: Rachel Carson's Warnings Still Apply." *The American Scholar* 74 (Summer 2005): 53–59.

Karkkainen, Bradley C. "Toward a Smarter NEPA: Monitoring and Managing Government's Environmental Performance." *Columbia Law Review* 102 (May 2002): 903–72.

Kashmanian Richard M., and Justin R. Moore. "Building Greater Sustainability in Supply Chains." *Environmental Quality Management* 23 (Summer 2014): 13–37.

Kaufman, Wallace. *No Turning Back: Dismantling the Fantasies of Environmental Thinking.* New York: Basic Books, 1994.

Kay, Jeanne. "Human Dominion over Nature in the Hebrew Bible." *Annals of the Association of American Geographers* 79 (June 1989): 214–33.

Keita, L.D. *Science, Rationality, and Neoclassical Economics.* Cranbury, N.J.: Associated University Presses, Inc., 1992.

Kellstedt, Paul M.; Suzanna Linn; and A. Lee Hannah. "The Polls-Review: The Usefulness of Consumer Sentiment: Assessing Construct and Measurement." *Public Opinion Quarterly* 79 (Spring 2015): 181–203.

Kennedy, Brandy A. "Sorting Through: The Role of Representation in Bureaucracy." *Journal of Public Administration Research & Theory* 23 (October 2013): 791–816.

Kent, Curtis. "The Virtue of Thoreau: Biography, Geography, and History in Walden Woods." *Environmental History* 15 (January 2010): 31–53.

Khalil, Elias L. "Beyond Self-Interest and Altruism: A Reconstruction of Adam Smith's Theory of Human Conduct." *Economics and Philosophy* 6 (October 1990): 255–73.

Khondker, Habibul Haque. "From 'The Silent Spring' to Globalization of the Environmental Movement." *Journal of International and Global Studies* 6 (April 2015): 25–37.

Kim, Zooh, and Vijay P. Singh. "Assessment of Environmental Flow Requirements by Entropy-Based Multi-Criteria Decision." *Water Resources Management* 28 (January 2014): 459–74.

King, Andrew A., and Michael J. Lenox. "Industry Self-Regulation Without Sanctions: The Chemical Industry's Responsible Care Program." *The Academy of Management Journal* 43 (August 2000): 698–716.

King, James T. "The Moral Theories of Kant and Hume: Comparisons and Polemics." *Hume Studies* 18 (November 1992): 441–66.

Kingsley, J. Donald. *Representative Bureaucracy: An Interpretation of the British Civil Service.* Yellow Springs, OH.: The Antioch Press, 1944.

Kirchner, James W. "The Gaia Hypothesis: Can It Be Tested?" *Reviews of Geophysics* 27 (May 1989): 223–35.

Kirchner, James W. "The Gaia Hypothesis: Fact, Theory, and Wishful Thinking." *Climatic Change* 52 (2002): 391–408.

Kitcher, Patricia. "Kant's Argument for the Categorical Imperative," *Noûs* 38 (December 2004): 555–84.

Klass, Alexandra B. "The Public Trust Doctrine in the Shadow of State Environmental Rights Laws: A Case Study." *Environmental Law* 45 (April 2015): 431–62.

Klauer, Bernd; Reiner Manstetten, Thomas Petersen; and Johannes Schiller. "The Art of Long-Term Thinking: A Bridge between Sustainability Science and Politics." *Ecological Economics* 93 (September 2013): 79–84.

Kline, Benjamin, Ph.D. *First Along the River: A Brief History of the U.S. Environmental Movement.* 3rd. edition Lanham, MD.: Rowman & Littlefield, 2007.

Klopf, Sonja; Nada Wolff Culver; and Pete Morton. "A Road Map to a Better NEPA: Why Environmental Risk Assessments Should Be Used to Analyze the Environmental Consequences of Complex Federal Actions." *Sustainable Development Law & Policy* 8 (Fall 2007): 38–43, 84–85.

Klyza, Christopher McGrory, and David J. Sousa. *American Environmental Policy, 1990–2006: Beyond Gridlock.* Cambridge, MA: MIT Press, 2008.

Knowles, Dudley. "Conservative Utilitarianism." *Utilitas* 12 (July 2000): 155–75.

Knudsen, Steven; Larry Jakus; and Maida Metz. "The Civil Service Reform Act of 1978." *Public Personnel Management* 8 (May/June 1979): 170–81.

Koelsch, William A. "Thomas Jefferson, Geographers, and the Uses of Geography." *Geographical Review* 98 (April 2008): 260–79.

Koppl, Roger, and Meghan Sacks. "The Criminal Justice System Creates Incentives for False Convictions." *Criminal Justice Ethics* 32 (August 2013): 126–62.

Kotzé, Louis J. "Rethinking Global Environmental Law and Governance in the Anthropocene." *Journal of Energy & Natural Resources Law* 32 (May 2014): 121–56.

Koumakhov, Rouslan. "Conventions in Herbert Simon's Theory of Bounded Rationality." *Journal of Economic Psychology* 30 (June 2009): 293–306.

Kowlasky, Nathan. "Whatever Happened to Deep Ecology?" *The Trumpeter: Journal of Ecosophy* 30 (2014): 95–100.

Kuehn, Manfred. "Kant's Conception of 'Hume's Problem.'" *Journal of the History of Philosophy* 21 (January 1983): 175–93.

Kuhn, Thomas S. *The Structure of Scientific Revolutions.* 2nd edition. Chicago: The University of Chicago Press, 1970.

Kveton, Viktor; Jiri Louda; and Martin Pelucha. "Contribution of Local Agenda 21 to Practical Implementation of Sustainable Development: The Case of the Czech Republic." *European Planning Studies* 22 (March 2014): 515–36.

Kwoka, Margaret B. "FOIA, Inc." *Duke Law Journal* 65 (2016): 1361–1437.

Lara, Michel; Vincent Martinet; and Luc Doyen. "Satisficing versus Optimality: Criteria for Sustainability." *Bulletin of Mathematical Biology* 77 (February 2015): 281–97.

Larsen, Christina. "Is the Glass Half Empty or Half Full? Challenging Incomplete Agency Action under Section 706(1) of the Administrative Procedure Act." *Public Land & Resources Law Review* 25 (April 2004): 113–30.

Larson, Edward J. "The Reception of Darwinism in the Nineteenth Century: A Three Part Story." *Science & Christian Belief* 21 (April 2009): 3–24.

Lawson, Tony. "What is This 'School' Called Neoclassical Economics?" *Cambridge Journal of Economics* 37 (September 2013): 947–83.

Lear, Linda J. "Rachel Carson's *Silent Spring.*" *Environmental History Review* 17 (Summer 1993): 23–48.

Lee, Jongkon. "Environmental Legislative Standstill and Bureaucratic Politics in the USA." *Policy Studies* 35 (January 2014): 40–58.

Leighninger, Jr., Robert D. *Building Louisiana: The Legacy of the Public Works Administration.* Jackson: University Press of Mississippi, 2007.

Lemann, Nicholas. "Kicking in Groups." *Atlantic Monthly* 277 (April 1996): 22–26.

Lemann, Nicholas. "Notorious Big: Why the Spectre of Size Has Always Haunted American Politics." *The New Yorker* 92 (March 28, 2016): 72–75.

Lenowsky, Leslie. "Still 'Bowling Alone'?" *Commentary* 110 (October 2000): 57–60.

Leopold, Aldo. *A Sand County Almanac; with Essays on Conservation from Round River.* New York: Ballatine Books, 1990 [1949].

Lerner, Michael A. "Going Dry." *Humanities* 32 (September/October 2011): 10–13, 48.

Leuenberger, Deniz Zeynep, and John R. Battle. *Sustainable Development for Public Administration.* Armonk, NY.: M.E. Sharpe, Inc., 2009.

Levy, Jason M. "Conflicting Enforcement Mechanisms under RCRA: The Abstention Battleground Between State Agencies and Citizen Suits." *Ecology Law Quarterly* 39 (2012): 373–404.

Ley, Aaron J. "The Costs and Benefits of American Policy-Making Values." *Law & Society Review* 48 (March 2014): 91–126.

Lienhoop, Nele; Bartosz Bartkowski; and Bernd Hansjürgens. "Informing Biodiversity Policy: The Role of Economic Valuation, Deliberative Institutions and Deliberative Monetary Valuation." *Environmental Science and Policy* 54 (December 2015): 522–32.

Lilienthal, David E. "The Citizen as Public Servant." *Vital Speeches of the Day* 14 (July 15, 1948): 578–81.

Lilienthal, David E. *TVA: Democracy on the March.* New York: Penguin Books, 1944.

Lininger, Tom. "Green Ethics for Lawyers." *Boston College Law Review* 57 (January 2016): 61–115.

Link, Arthur S. "Woodrow Wilson and the Study of Administration." *Proceedings of the American Philosophical Society* 112 (December 9, 1968): 431–33.

Lion, Hermann; Jerome D. Donovan; and Rowan E. Bedggood. "Environmental Impact Assessments from a Business Perspective: Extending Knowledge and Guiding Business Practice." *Journal of Business Ethics* 117 (November 2013): 789–805.

Lipford, Jody W., and Bruce Yandle. "Determining Economic Freedom: Democracy, Political Competition, and the Wealth Preservation Struggle." *The Journal of Private Enterprise* 30 (Fall 2015): 1–18.

Lipshitz, Raanan, and Leon Mann. "Leadership and Decision Making: William R. Ruckelshaus and the Environmental Protection Agency." *Journal of Leadership and Organizational Studies* 11 (June 23, 2005): 41–53.

Lipshitz, Raanan, and Orna Strauss. "Coping With Uncertainty: A Naturalistic Decision-making Analysis." *Organizational Behavior and Human Decision Processes* 69 (February 1997): 149–63.

Liu, Xinyu; Gengyuan Liu; Zhifeng Yang; Bin Chen; and Sergio Ulgiati. "Comparing National Environmental and Economic Performances through Emerging Sustainability Indicators: Moving Environmental Ethics beyond Anthropocentrism toward Ecocentrism." *Renewable and Sustainable Energy Reviews* 58 (May 2016): 1532–42.

Lock, Reiner H., and J.B. Ruhl. "Interview: William Ruckelshaus." *Natural Resources & Environment* 5 (Summer 1990): 36–39, 62–66.

Longaker, Mark Garrett. "Adam Smith on Rhetoric and Phronesis, Law and Economics." *Philosophy and Rhetoric* 47 (2014): 25–47.

Longhofer, Wesley; Evan Schofer; Natasha Miric; and David John Frank. "NGOs, INGOs, and Environmental Policy Reform, 1970–2010." *Social Forces* 94 (June 2016): 1743–68.

Lough, Alex Wagner. "Henry George, Frederick Jackson Turner, and the 'Closing' of the American Frontier." *California History* 89 (March 2012): 4–23.

Loux, Renée. *Easy Green Living: The Ultimate Guide to Simple, Eco-Friendly Choices for You and Your Home.* Emmaus, PA.: Rodale Books, 2008.

Lovelock, James. *Gaia: A New Look at Life on Earth.* New York and Oxford: Oxford University Press, 2000.

Lovins, Amory B., and the Rocky Mountain Institute. *Reinventing Fire: Bold Business Solutions for the New Energy Era.* White River Junction, VT.: Chelsea Green Publishing Company, 2011.

Lowi, Theodore J. *The End of Liberalism: The Second Republic of the United States.* New York: W.W. Norton, 2009.

Lu, Jiahuan. "Intellectual Paradigms in Public Administration: Why So Many and How to Bridge Them?" *Administrative Theory & Praxis* 35 (June 2013): 308–13.

Lujan v. Defenders of Wildlife, 504 U.S. 555 (1992).

Lujan v. National Wildlife Federation, 497 U.S. 871 (1990).

Luna, Marcos. *The Environment since 1945.* New York: Facts on File, an Imprint of Infobase Learning, 2012.

Luria, Amy. "CERCLA Contribution: An Inquiry into What Constitutes An Administrative Settlement." *North Dakota Law Review* 84 (2008): 333–64.

Luttig, Matthew. "The Structure of Inequality and Americans' Attitudes toward Redistribution." *Public Opinion Quarterly* 77 (Fall 2013): 811–21.

Lynn, Jr., Laurence E. "Restoring the Rule of Law to Public Administration: What Frank Goodnow Got Right and Leonard White Didn't." *Public Administration Review* 69 (September/October 2009): 803–12.

MacKenzie, Ian A., and Markus Ohndorf. "Coasean Bargaining in the Presence of Pigouvian Taxation." *Journal of Environmental Economics Management* 75 (January 2016): 1–11.

Mackintosh, Barry. "Harold L. Ickes and the National Park Service." *Journal of Forest History* 29 (April 1985): 78–84.

Maher, Neil M. *Nature's New Deal: The Civilian Conservation Corps and the Roots of the American Environmental Movement.* Oxford and New York: Oxford University Press, 2008.

Maher, Neil M. "A New Deal Body Politic: Landscape, Labor, and the Civilian Conservation Corps." *Environmental History* 7 (July 2002): 435–61.

Maidani, Ebrahim A. "Comparative Study of Herzberg's Two-factor Theory of Job Satisfaction among Public and Private Sectors." *Public Personnel Management* 20 (Winter 1991): 441–48.

Manning, John F. "The Necessary and Proper Clause and Its Legal Antecedents." *Boston University Law Review* 92 (July 1, 2012): 1349–80.

Mansfield, Harvey. "The Wisdom of 'The Federalist.'" *The New Criterion* 29 (February 2011): 9–13.

Marin, Georgiana; Alexandra Mateiu; and Werner Mailinger. "Collaborative Practices within the Supply Chain Area, as a Solution for Logistic Enterprises to Solve the Challenges in Obtaining Sustainability." *International Journal of Economic Practices and Theories* 5 (May 2015): 222–32.

Marini, Frank. "The Minnowbrook Perspective and the Future of Public Administration." In *Toward a New Public Administration: The Minnowbrook Perspective.* Edited by Frank Marini, 346–67. New York: Chandler, 1971.

Marsh, George Perkins. *Man and Nature; or Physical Geography as Modified by Human Action.* New York: Charles Scribner, 1864.

Marshall, Gary S., and Orion F. White, Jr. "The Blacksburg Manifesto and the Postmodern Debate: Public Administration in a Time Without a Name." *American Review of Public Administration* 20 (June 1990): 61–76.

Marshall, Robert. *The People's Forests.* Iowa City: University of Iowa Press, 2002 [1933].

Marshall, Robert. *The Social Management of American Forests.* New York: League for Industrial Democracy, 1930.

Martella, Roger, and Kim Smacziak. "Introduction to Rio + 20: A Reflection on Progress Since the First Earth Summit and the Opportunities That Lie Ahead." *Sustainable Development Law & Policy* 12 (Spring 2012): 4–7.

Martin v. Reynolds Metal Company, 221 Or. 86, 342 P.2d 790 (1959); *cert. denied* 362 U.S. 918 (1960).

Martin, Edward J. "Economic Rights, Sustainable Development, and Environmental Management." *Public Administration & Management* 16 (April 2011): 121–44.

Martin, Roscoe Coleman, editor. *Public Administration and Democracy: Essays in Honor of Paul H. Appleby.* Syracuse, NY.: Syracuse University Press, 1965.

Martinelli, Dario. "Anthropocentrism as a Social Phenomenon: Semiotic and Ethical Implications." *Social Semiotics* 18 (March 2008): 79–99.

Martinez, J. Michael. *American Environmentalism: Philosophy, History, and Public Policy.* Boca Raton, FL.: CRC Press, 2014.

Martins, Nuno Ornelas. "Classical Surplus Theory and Heterodox Economics." *American Journal of Economics and Sociology* 72 (November 2013): 1205–31.

Mashaw, Jerry L. "Federal Administration and Administrative Law in the Gilded Age." *Yale Law Journal* 119 (May 2010): 1362–1472.

Masnavi, M.R. "Environmental Sustainability and Ecological Complexity: Developing an Integrated Approach to Analyse the Environment and Landscape Potentials to Promote Sustainable Development." *International Journal of Environmental Research* 7 (Autumn 2013): 995–1006.

Mason, Kathy S. "Out of Fashion: Harriet Hemenway and the Audubon Society, 1896–1905." *Historian* 65 (Fall 2002): 1–14.

Massarutto, Antonio. "The Long and Winding Road to Resource Efficiency—An Interdisciplinary Perspective on Extended Producer Responsibility." *Resources, Conservation & Recycling* 85 (April 2014): 11–21.

Masur, Jonathan S., and Eric A. Posner. "Toward a Pigouvian State." *University of Pennsylvania Law Review* 164 (December 2015): 93–147.

McCrory, Martin A. "Who's on First: CERCLA Cost Recovery, Contribution, and Protection." *American Business Law Journal* 37 (Fall 1999): 3–33.

McCullough, David. *Brave Companions: Portraits in History.* New York: Simon & Schuster, 1992.

McDaniel, Dennis K. "The First Congressman Martin Dies of Texas." *Southwestern Historical Quarterly* 102 (October 1998): 130–61.

McGrath, Robert J. "The Rise and Fall of Radical Civil Service Reform in the U.S. States." *Public Administration Review* 73 (July/August 2013): 638–49.

McGregor, Douglas. *The Human Side of Enterprise.* New York: McGraw-Hill, 1960.

McNollgast. "The Political Origins of the Administrative Procedure Act." *Journal of Law, Economics, & Organization* 15 (April 1999): 180–217.

Meadowcroft, James. "What about Politics? Sustainable Development, Transition Management, and Long Term Energy Transitions." *Policy Sciences* 42 (November 2009): 323–40.

Medema, Steven G. "The Curious Treatment of the Coase Theorem in the Environmental Economics Literature, 1960–1979." *Review of Environmental Economics and Policy* 8 (January 2014): 39–57.

Meehan, Sean Ross. "Ecology and Imagination: Emerson, Thoreau, and the Nature of Metonymy." *Criticism* 55 (Spring 2013): 299–329.

Meier, Kenneth J. "Governance, Structure, and Democracy: Luther Gulick and the Future of Public Administration." *Public Administration Review* 70 Supplement (December 2010): s284–s291.

Meier, Kenneth J. "Proverbs and the Evolution of Public Administration." *Public Administration Review* 75 (January–February 2015): 15–24.

Meinard, Yves; Malgorzata Dereniowska; and Jean-Sebastien Gharbi. "Discussion: The Ethical Stakes in Monetary Valuation Methods for Conservation Purposes." *Biological Conservation* 199 (July 2016): 67–74.

Menand, Louis. *The Metaphysical Club: A Story of Ideas in America.* New York: Farrar, Straus and Giroux, 2001.

Merchant, Carolyn. *American Environmental History: An Introduction.* New York: Columbia University Press, 2007.

Mercuro, Nicholas. "Interdisciplinary Paradigms for Environmental Policy: Interrelationships Among Ecology, Law, and Economics." In *Property Rights, Economics, and the Environment: The Economics of Legal Relationships.* Edited by Michael D. Kaplowitz, 247–79. New York and London: Routledge, an Imprint of the Taylor & Francis Group, 2000.

Merrill, Thomas W. "Justice Stevens and the *Chevron* Puzzle." *Northwestern University Law Review* 106 (April 2012): 551–66.

Metzger, Gillian. "The Constitutional Duty to Supervise." *Yale Law Journal* 124 (April 2015): 1836–1933.

Michaelson v. United States, 266 U.S. 42 (1924).

Mignaqui, Vera. "Sustainable Development as a Goal: Social, Environmental and Economic Dimensions." *International Journal of Social Quality* 4 (Summer 2014): 57–77.

Mihaylov, Nikolay L., and Douglas D. Perkins. "Local Environmental Grassroots Activism: Contributions from Environmental Psychology, Sociology and Politics." *Behavioral Sciences* 5 (2015): 121–53.

Mikkelson, Gregory M., and Colin A. Chapman. "Individualistic Environmental Ethics: A Reductio ad Exstinctum?" *Environmental Ethics* 36 (Fall 2014): 333–38.

Millard, Candice. *Destiny of the Republic: A Tale of Madness, Medicine and the Murder of a President.* New York: Doubleday, 2011.

Miller, Char. "Thinking Like a Conservationist." *Journal of Forestry* 100 (December 2002): 42–45.

Miller, Char, and V. Alaric Sample. "Gifford Pinchot: A Life in Progress." *Journal of Forestry* 97 (January 1999): 27–32.

Miller, David J. "Rich History: Celebrating National Audubon Society's Centennial." *New York State Conservationist* 60 (October 2005): 2–5.

Miller, Susan M. "Administering Representation: The Role of Elected Administrators in Translating Citizens' Preferences into Public Policy." *Journal of Public Administration Research and Theory* 23 (October 2013): 865–97.

Millner, Antony; Simon Dietz; and Geoffrey Heal. "Scientific Ambiguity and Climate Policy." *Environmental and Resource Economics* 55 (May 2013): 21–46.

Minan, John H., and Tracy M. Frech. "Pesticides as 'Pollutants' Under the Clean Water Act." *San Diego Law Review* 47 (Winter 2010): 109–44.

Minteer, Ben A., and Stephen J. Pyne. "Restoring the Narrative of American Environmentalism." *Restoration Ecology* 21 (January 2013): 6–11.

Moe, Terry M. "Vested Interests and Political Institutions." *Political Science Quarterly* 130 (June 2015): 277–318.

Molina, Anthony DeForest, and Cassandra L. McKeown. "The Heart of the Profession: Understanding Public Service Values." *Journal of Public Affairs Education* 18 (Spring 2012): 375–96.

"Momentum for Plastic Bag Bans Spreading; Recycling Programs Earn Mixed Reviews." *Solid Waste Report* 45 (April 25, 2014): 5–6.

Moritz, Joshua M. "Animals and the Image of God in the Bible and Beyond." *Dialog: A Journal of Theology* 48 (Summer 2009): 134–46.

Morrison, Michael A. *Slavery and the American West: The Eclipse of Manifest Destiny and the Coming of the Civil War.* Chapel Hill: University of North Carolina Press, 1997.

Morss, Rebecca E.; Olga V. Wilhelmi; Mary W. Downton; and Eve Gruntfest. "Flood Risk, Uncertainty, and Scientific Information for Decision Making: Lessons from an Interdisciplinary Project." *American Meteorological Society* 86 (November 2005): 1593–1601.

Moya, Olga L., and Andrew L. Fono. *Federal Environmental Law: The User's Guide.* St. Paul, MN: West, 1997.

Muir, John. *The Mountains of California.* New York: Penguin Books, 1985 [1894].

Mulgan, Tim. "Utilitarianism for a Broken World." *Utilitas* 27 (March 2015): 92–114.

Munda, Giuseppe. *Multicriteria Evaluation in a Fuzzy Environment: Theory and Applications in Ecological Economics*. Berlin: Springer Science + Business Media, 2012.

Murphy, Brian L. "Allocation by Contribution to Cost and Risk at Superfund Sites." *Journal of Environmental Forensics* 1 (September 2000): 117–20.

Myers, Jr., Donald B., and Paul A. Locke. "Modernizing U.S. Chemical Laws: How the Application of Twenty-first Century Toxicology Can Help Drive Legal Reform." *New York Environmental Law Journal* 40 (2012): 35–78.

Myers, Nancy. "The Rise of the Precautionary Principle." *Multinational Monitor* 25 (September 2004): 9–15.

Nadeau, Robert L. "Methodological and Ideological Options: The Unfinished Journey of Ecological Economics." *Ecological Economics* 109 (January 2015): 101–108.

Naess, Arne. "The Shallow and the Deep, Long-range Ecology Movements." In *Deep Ecology for the 21st Century*. Edited by George Sessions, 151–55. Boston: Shambala, 1995.

Nathan, Richard P. "There Will Always be a New Federalism." *Journal of Public Administration Research and Theory* 16 (October 2006): 499–510.

National Audubon Society v. Superior Court, 33 Cal.3d 419, 452 (1983).

The National Environmental Policy Act (NEPA) of 1969. 42 U.S.C. § 4321 *et seq.* (1969).

Natural Resources Defense Council Website: "About NRDC." Accessed May 18, 2016. https://www.nrdc.org/about.

Nelson, Douglas T.; Joshua Saltzman; William K. Rawson; Claudia O'Brien; and Bart J. Kempf. "Real Environmental Protection: Not a Paper Exercise." *Environmental Law Reporter: News & Analysis* 42 (February 2012): 10166–71.

Nelson, Gaylord. "Earth Day Speech, Denver, Colorado." In *The Environmental Movement, 1968–1972*. Edited by David Stradling, 85–86. Seattle: University of Washington Press, 2012.

Neuse, Steven M. *David E. Lilienthal: The Journey of an American Liberal*. Knoxville: University of Tennessee Press, 1996.

Newbold, Stephanie P. *All But Forgotten: Thomas Jefferson and the Development of Public Administration*. Albany: State University of New York Press, 2010.

Newbold, Stephanie P. "Toward a Constitutional School for American Public Administration." *Public Administration* 70 (July/August 2010): 538–46.

Newcomer, Kathryn E., and James Edwin Kee. "*Federalist* No. 23: Can the Leviathan be Managed?" *Public Administration Review* 71 (November 2011): s37–s46.

Ngosso, Thierry. "The Right to Development of Developing Countries: An Argument Against Environmental Protection?" *Public Reason* 5 (December 2013): 41–60.

Nievergelt, Yves. "The Concept of Elasticity in Economics." *SIAM Review* 25 (April 1983): 261–65.

Nijaki, Laurie Kaye. "Justifying and Juxtaposing Environmental Justice and Sustainability: Towards an Inter-Generational and Intra-Generational Analysis of Environmental Equity in Public Administration." *Public Administration Quarterly* 39 (Spring 2015): 85–116.

Nobles, W. Scott. "Harold L. Ickes: New Deal Hatchet Man." *Western Speech* 22 (Summer 1958): 158–63.

Nolan, Jr., James L. *What They Saw in America: Alexis de Tocqueville, Max Weber, G.K. Chesterton, and Sayyid Qutb.* Cambridge and New York: Cambridge University Press, 2016.

Nordhaus, William D. *Managing the Global Commons: The Economics of Climate Change.* Cambridge, Mass.: MIT Press, 1994.

Norton, Bryan G. "Beyond Positivist Ecology: Toward an Integrated Ecological Ethics." *Science and Engineering Ethics* 14 (December 2008): 581–92.

Norton, Bryan G. "Population and Consumption: Environmental Problems as Problems of Scale." *Ethics and the Environment* 5 (Spring 2000): 23–45.

Norton, Richard K. "Agenda 21 and Its Discontents: Is Sustainable Development a Global Imperative or Globalized Conspiracy?" *Urban Lawyer* 46 (Spring 2014): 325–60.

"Notes: Rationalizing Hard Look Review After the Fact." *Harvard Law Review* 122 (May 2009): 1909–30.

O'Dair, Sharon. "'To Fright the Animals and To Kill Them Up': Shakespeare and Ecology." *Shakespeare Studies* 39 (October 2011): 74–83.

Oelschlaeger, Max. "Ecological Restoration, Aldo Leopold, and Beauty: An Evolutionary Tale." *Environmental Philosophy* 4 (Fall/Spring 2007): 149–61.

Oksanen, Markku. "The Moral Value of Biodiversity." *Ambio* 26 (December 1997): 541–45.

Okun, Arthur M. *Equality and Efficiency: The Big Tradeoff.* Washington, D.C.: The Brookings Institution, 1975.

Olson, Mancur. *The Logic of Collective Action: Public Goods and the Theory of Groups.* Cambridge, Mass.: Harvard University Press, 1971.

Olsson, J. Mikael. "Higher Pleasures, Civic Virtue, and Democracy: A Reconstruction of Millian Themes." *Kritike* 8 (December 2014): 193–260.

O'Riordan, Tim. "Environmental Science, Sustainability and Politics." *Transactions of the Institute of British Geographers* 29 (June 1, 2004): 234–47.

Ostrom, Vincent. *The Political Theory of a Compound Republic: Designing the American Experiment.* 2nd. edition Lincoln: University of Nebraska Press, 1987.

O'Toole, Jr., Laurence J. and Kenneth I. Hanf. "American Public Administration and Impacts of International Governance." *Public Administration Review* 62, Special Issue (September 2002): 158–69.

Overeem, Patrick. "Beyond Heterodoxy: Dwight Waldo and the Politics-Administration Dichotomy." *Public Administration Review* 68 (January/February 2008): 36–45.

Overeem, Patrick. "The Value of the Dichotomy: Politics, Administration, and the Political Neutrality of Administrators." *Administrative Theory & Praxis* 27 (July 2005): 311–29.

Paganelli, Maria Pia. "The Adam Smith Problem in Reverse: Self-Interest in *The Wealth of Nations* and *The Theory of Moral Sentiments*." *History of Political Economy* 40 (Summer 2008): 365–82.

Paganelli, Maria Pia. "The Moralizing Role of Distance in Adam Smith: *The Theory of Moral Sentiments* as Possible Praise of Commerce." *History of Political Economy* 42 (Fall 2010): 425–41.

Parr, Adrian. *Hijacking Sustainability*. Cambridge, MA: MIT Press, 2009.

Pearce, Trevor. "'A Great Complication of Circumstances'—Darwin and the Economy of Nature." *Journal of the History of Biology* (August 2010): 493–528.

Pearson, Susan J. *The Rights of the Defenseless: Protecting Animals and Children in Gilded Age America*. Chicago and London: The University of Chicago Press, 2011.

Percival, Robert V. "Checks without Balance: Executive Office Oversight of the Environmental Protection Agency." *Law and Contemporary Problems* 54 (Fall 1991): 127–204.

Petrişor, Alexandru-Ionuţ, and Liliana Petrişor. "25 Years of Sustainability: A Critical Assessment." *Present Environment & Sustainable Development* 8 (2014): 175–90.

Phillips, Alicia Saunte; Yung-Tse Hung; and Paul A. Bosela. "Love Canal Tragedy." *Journal of Performance of Constructed Facilities* 21 (July/August 2007): 313–19.

Piatek, Zdzislawa. "Ecophilosophy as a Philosophical Underpinning of Sustainable Development." *Sustainable Development* 16 (March/April 2008): 91–99.

Pinchot, Gifford. "The Economic Significance of Forestry." *The North American Review* 213 (February 1921): 157–67.

Plato. *Phaedrus*. Millis, MA.: Agora Publications, 2009.

Pollitt, Christopher. "Not Odious but Onerous: Comparative Public Administration." *Public Administration* 89 (March 2011): 114–27.

Port of Boston Marine Terminal v. Rederiaktiebolaget Transatlantic, 400 U.S. 62 (1970).

Portier, Ph.D, Christopher J. "ATSDR in the 21st Century." *Journal of Environmental Health* 74 (March 2012): 30–31.

Potter, Van Rensselaer. "Real Bioethics: Biocentric or Anthropocentric?" *Ethics and the Environment* 1 (Fall 1996): 177–83.

Powell, John Wesley. *The Exploration of the Colorado River and Its Canyons*. New York: Penguin Books, 2003 [1875].

Prelitz, Chris. *Green Made Easy: The Everyday Guide for Transitioning to a Green Lifestyle*. Carlsbad, CA.: Hay House, 2009.

President's Committee on Administrative Management. *Report of the Committee*. Washington, D.C.: U.S. Government Printing Office, 1937.

Price, Courtney M., and Jennifer M. Smart. "Understanding the Toxic Substances Control Act: The Significance of Reporting and Recordkeeping Requirements." *William & Mary Environmental Law & Policy Review* 16 (1991): 1–29.

Priel, Dan. "Toward Classical Legal Positivism." *Virginia Law Review* 101 (June 2015): 987–1022.

"Progress of the Civil Service System in the United States." *Congressional Digest* 16 (November 1937): 261–65.

"Publisher Llewellyn King on Energy Policy." *Southern Energy Report* 35 (July 1989): 2–3, 4.

Purcell, Aaron D. "Undermining the TVA: George Berry, David Lilienthal, and Arthur Morgan." *Tennessee Historical Quarterly* 57 (Fall 1998): 168–89.

Putnam, Robert D. *Bowling Alone: The Collapse and Revival of American Community*. New York: Simon & Schuster, 2000.

Raadschelders, Jos C.N. "The Future Study of Public Administration: Embedding Research Object and Methodology in Epistemology and Ontology." *Public Administration Review* 71 (November/December 2011): 916–24.

Rațiu, Simina. "The Anti-Utopian Pessimism of the Late Nineteenth and Early Twentieth Century." *Caietele Echinox* 25 (December 2013): 65–75.

"RCRA Questions and Answers Provide Regulatory Insight." *Hazardous Waste Consultant* 30 (2012): 4.1–4.23.

Redclift, Michael. "Sustainable Development (1987–2005): An Oxymoron Comes of Age." *Sustainable Development* 13 (October 2005): 212–27.

Redish, Martin H., and Matthew Heins. "Premodern Constitutionalism." *William & Mary Law Review* 57 (April 2016): 1825–1912.

Redekop, Benjamin W. "Embodying the Story: Theodore Roosevelt's Conservation Leadership." *Leadership* 12 (April 2016): 159–85.

Redman, Charles L. "Should Sustainability and Resilience be Combined or Remain Distinct Pursuits?" *Ecology & Society* 19 (2014): 398–408.

Reitze, Jr., Arnold W. "Emergency Response and Planning Requirements Applicable to Unpermitted Air Pollution Releases." *Brigham Young University Law Review* 2005 (2005): 1075–193.

Rejeski, David. "Any Big Ideas Left?" *The Environmental Forum* 28 (September/October 2011): 36–41.

Reséndez, Andrés. *A Land So Strange: The Epic Journey of Cabeza de Vaca: The Extraordinary Tale of a Shipwrecked Spaniard Who Walked Across America in the Sixteenth Century*. New York: Basic Books, 2007.

The Resource Conservation and Recovery Act (RCRA) of 1976. 42 U.S.C. § 6901 *et seq.* (1976).

Reynaers, Anne-Marie. "Public Values in Public-Private Partnerships." *Public Administration Review* 74 (January-February 2014): 41–50

Reynaers, Anne-Marie, and Stephan Grimmelikhuijsen. "Transparency in Public-Private Partnerships: Not So Bad After All?" *Public Administration* 93 (September 2015): 609–26.

Richardson, William D. *Democracy, Bureaucracy, & Character: Founding Thought*. Lawrence: University Press of Kansas, 1997.

Richardson, William D., and Lloyd G. Nigro. "Administrative Ethics and Founding Thought: Constitutional Correctives, Honor, and Education." *Public Administration Review* 47 (September/October 1987): 376–76.

Richey, Robert Glenn, Jr. "The Effects of Environmental Focus and Program Timing on Green Marketing Performance and the Moderating Role of Resource Commitment." *Industrial Marketing Management* 43 (October 2014): 1246–57.

Ridge, Michael. "Consequentialist Kantianism." *Philosophical Perspectives* 23 (December 2009): 421–38.

Rietti, Sophie. "Utilitarianism and Psychological Realism." *Utilitas* 21 (September 2009): 347–67.

Riley, D.D. *Controlling the Federal Bureaucracy*. Philadelphia: Temple University Press, 1987.

Rizzo, Christopher. "RCRA's 'Imminent and Substantial Endangerment' Citizen Suit Turns 25." *National Resources & Environment* 23 (Fall 2008): 50–51.

Robert, Thomas. "Darwinian Ethology and Naess' Principles of Deep Ecology." *The Trumpeter: Journal of Ecosophy* 31 (2015): 39–57.

Robinson, Nicholas A. "Fundamental Principles of Law for the Anthropocene?" *Environmental Policy and Law* 44 (2014): 13–27.

Rodgers, Jr., William H. "Giving Voice to Rachel Carson: Putting Science into Environmental Law." *Journal of Land Use & Environmental Law* 28 (Fall 2012): 61–69.

Rodrigues, João. "Where to Draw the Line between the State and Markets? Institutionalist Elements in Hayek's Neoliberal Political Economy." *Journal of Economic Issue* 46 (December 2012): 1007–33.

Rohr, John A. *Ethics for Bureaucrats: An Essay on Law and Values*. 2nd. edition. New York and Bessel: Marcel Dekker, 1989.

Rohr, John A. "Ethics and Comparative Administration: A Constitutional Commentary." *Public Integrity* 10 (Winter 2007–8): 65–74.

Roman, Alexandru. "The Roles Assumed by Public Administrators: The Link Between Administrative Discretion and Representation." *Public Administration Quarterly* 39 (Winter 2015): 595–644.

Romar, Edward J. "Noble Markets: The Noble/Slave Ethic in Hayek's Free Market Capitalism." *Journal of Business Ethics* 85 (March 2009): 57–66.

Rome, Adam. *The Genius of Earth Day: How a 1970 Teach-In Unexpectedly Made the First Green Generation*. New York: Hill and Wang, 2013.

Rootes, Christopher, and Liam Leonard. "Environmental Movements and Campaigns against Waste Infrastructure in the United States." *Environmental Politics* 18 (November 2009): 835–50.

Rose, Carol M. "Liberty, Property, Environmentalism." *Social Philosophy & Policy* 26 (July 2009): 1–25.

Rosenbaum, Walter A. *Environmental Politics and Policy*. 4th edition. Washington, D.C.: Congressional Quarterly Press, 1998.

Rosenberg, Michael M. "The Conceptual Articulation of the Reality of Life: Max Weber's Theoretical Constitution of Sociological Ideal Types." *Journal of Classical Sociology* 16 (February 2016): 84–101.

Rosenbloom, David H. "The Politics-Administration Dichotomy in U.S. Historical Context." *Public Administration Review* 68 (January/February 2008): 57–60.

Rosenkranz, Stephanie, and Patrick W. Schmitz. "Can Coasean Bargaining Justify Pigouvian Taxation?" *Economica* 74 (November 2007): 573–85.

Rosenthal-Pubul, Alexander. "Reflections on Ancient and Modern Freedom." *Modern Age* 58 (Winter 2016): 35–45.

Rosser, Christian. "Examining Frank J. Goodnow's Hegelian Heritage: A Contribution to Understanding Progressive Administrative Theory." *Administration & Society* 45 (November 2013): 1063–94.

Rottman, Joshua. "Breaking Down Biocentrism: Two Distinct Forms of Moral Concern for Nature." *Frontiers in Psychology* 5 (July 2014): 1–5.

Rowley, Gwyn. "On 'Human Dominion over Nature in the Hebrew Bible' by Kay." *Annals of the Association of American Geographers* 80 (September 1990): 447–51.

Rubin, Charles T. *The Green Crusade: Rethinking the Roots of Environmentalism*. Lanham, MD.: Rowman & Littlefield, 1998.

Ruhl, J. B. "The Endangered Species Act's Fall from Grace in the Supreme Court." *Harvard Environmental Law Review* 36 (2012): 487–532.

RUS, Dana. "The Role of Transcendentalism in Shaping American Cultural Ideology." *Studia Universitatis Petru Maior—Philologia* 14 (January 2013): 247–54.

Rutgers, Mark R. "Beyond Woodrow Wilson: The Identity of the Study of Public Administration in Historical Perspective." *Administration & Society* 29 (July 1997): 276–300.

Rylands v. Fletcher, 3 H.C. 774, 159 Eng. Rep. 737 (1865).

Sabry, Mohamed Ismail. "Good Governance, Institutions and Performance of Public Private Partnerships." *International Journal of Public Sector Management* 28 (2015): 566–82.

Sager, Fritz, and Christian Rosser. "Weber, Wilson, and Hegel: Theories of Modern Bureaucracy." *Public Administration Review* 69 (November/December 2009): 1136–47.

Sagoff, Mark. "At the Shrine of Our Lady of Fatima, or Why Political Questions Are Not All Economic." In *The Environmental Ethics & Policy Book*.

2nd edition. Edited by Donald VanDeVeer and Christine Pierce, 301–10. Belmont, Calif.: Wadsworth, 1998.

Sahni, Isher-Paul. "Max Weber's Sociology of Law." *Journal of Classical Sociology* 9 (May 2009): 209–33.

Sajeva, Maurizo; Parminder Singh Sahota; and Mark Lemon. "Giving Sustainability a Chance: A Participatory Framework for Choosing between Alternative Futures." *Journal of Organisational Transformation & Social Change* 12 (April 2015): 57–89.

Salanie, Bernard. *The Economics of Taxation*. Cambridge, MA.: MIT Press, 2003.

Samuelson, Robert J. "Join the Club." *Washington Post National Weekly Edition* (April 15–21, 1996): 5.

Schaeffer, Francis A., and Udo W. Middelmann. *Pollution and the Death of Man*. Wheaton, IL.: Crossway, 1970.

Schattschneider, E.E. *The Semisovereign People: A Realist's View of Democracy in America*. Belmont, Calif.: Wadsworth, 1975.

Schlag, Pierre. "Coase Minus the Coase Theorem—Some Problems with Chicago Transaction Analysis." *Iowa Law Review* 99 (November 2013): 175–223.

Schmitz, Kenneth. "Towards the Reciprocity of Man and Nature: Receptivity, Normativity, and Procreativity." *Nova et Vetera* (English Edition) 10 (Winter 2012): 81–94.

Schnapf, Larry. "How the CERCLA Notification Requirements Facilitate the Creation of Brownfields and What EPA Can Do to Address the Problem." *Sustainable Development Law & Policy* 11 (2010): 19–26, 63–65.

Schneider, Anne, and Helen Ingram. "Social Construction of Target Populations: Implications for Politics and Policy." *The American Political Science Review* 87 (June 1993): 334–47.

Schneider, Richard J. *Thoreau's Sense of Place: Essays in American Environmental Writing*. Iowa City: University of Iowa Press, 2000.

Schofield, Philip. "Jeremy Bentham on Utility and Truth." *History of European Ideas* (December 2015): 1125–42.

Schreurs, Miranda A. "20th Anniversary of the Rio Summit: Taking a Look Back and at the Road Ahead." *GAIA: Ecological Perspectives for Science & Society* 21 (March 2012): 13–16.

Schuck, Peter H., and Steven Kochevar. "Reg Neg Redux: The Career of a Procedural Reform." *Theoretical Inquiries in Law* 15 (July 2014): 417–46.

Schulze, Christin; Don van Ravenzwaaij; and Ben R. Newell. "Of Marchers and Maximizers: How Competition Shapes Choice under Risk and Uncertainty." *Cognitive Psychology* 78 (May 2015): 78–98.

Schwarz, Ingo. "Alexander von Humboldt's Visit to Washington and Philadelphia, His Friendship with Jefferson, and His Fascination with the United States." *Northeastern Naturalist* 8 (2001): 43–56.

Schwartz, Scott. "The Hapless Ecosystem: A Federalist Argument in Favor of an Ecosystem Approach to the Endangered Species Act." *Virginia Law Review* 95 (September 2009): 1325–60.

Scott, Emilee Mooney. "Bona Fide Protection: Fulfilling CERCLA's Legislative Purpose by Applying Differing Definitions of 'Disposal.'" *Connecticut Law Review* 42 (February 2010): 957–90.

Seed, John; Joanna Macy; Pat Fleming; and Arne Naess. *Thinking Like a Mountain: Towards a Council of All Beings.* Gabriola Island, B.C., Canada: New Society Publishers, 1988.

Segal, Howard. "Down in the Valley: David Lilienthal's *TVA: Democracy on the March.*" *American Scholar* 64 (Summer 1995): 423–28.

Segerson, Kathleen. "The Role of Economics in Interdisciplinary Environmental Policy Debates: Opportunities and Challenges." *American Journal of Agricultural Economics* 9 (March 2015): 374–89.

Sensen, Oliver. "Kant's Conception of Inner Value." *European Journal of Philosophy* 19 (June 2011): 262–80.

Sessions, George. "The Deep Ecology Movement: A Review." *Environmental Review: ER* 1 (Summer 1987): 105–25.

Shabecoff, Philip. *Earth Rising: American Environmentalism in the 21st Century.* Washington, D.C., and Covelo, CA.: Island Press, 2001.

Shabecoff, Philip. *A Fierce Green Fire: The American Environmental Movement.* Washington, D.C., and Covelo, CA.: Island Press, 2003.

Shakespeare, William. *The Tragedy of Hamlet: King of Denmark.* New York: Airmont Books, 1965 [1603].

Shaw, Chris. "The Dangerous Limits of Dangerous Limits: Climate Change and the Precautionary Principle." *Sociological Review* 57 (October 2009): 103–23.

Sherman, William R. "The Deliberation Paradox and Administrative Law." *Brigham Young University Law Review* 2015 (January 2016): 413–69.

Shinkuma, Takayoshi. "Reconsideration of an Advance Disposal Fee Policy for End-of-Life Durable Goods." *Journal of Environmental Economics and Management* 53 (2007): 110–21.

Shores, James W. "A Win-Lose Situation: Historical Context, Ethos, and Rhetorical Choices in John Muir's 1908 'Hetch Hetchy Valley' Article." *The Journal of American Culture* 29 (June 2006): 191–201.

Shoven, John B., and John Whalley. "Applied General-Equilibrium Models of Taxation and International Trade: An Introduction and Survey." *Journal of Economic Literature* 22 (September 1984): 1007–51.

Shugerman, Jed Handelsman. "The Creation of the Department of Justice: Professionalization without Civil Rights or Civil Service." *Stanford Law Review* 66 (January 2014): 121–71.

Sierra Club v. Morton, 405 U.S. 727 (1972).

Sierra Club Website: "Sierra Club History." Accessed May 12, 2016. http://vault.sierraclub.org/history.

Simon, Herbert A. *Administrative Behavior.* 4th edition. New York: The Free Press, 1997.

Simon, Herbert A. "The Proverbs of Administration." *Public Administration Review* 6 (Winter 1946): 53–67.

Skelley, B. Douglas. "The Persistence of the Politics-Administration Dichotomy: An Additional Explanation." *Public Administration Quarterly* 32 (Winter 2008): 549–70.

Skinner, Daniel J.C.; Sophie A. Rocks; and Simon J.T. Pollard. "A Review of Uncertainty in Environmental Risk: Characterizing Potential Natures, Locations and Levels." *Journal of Risk Research* 17 (February 2014): 195–219.

Smith, Adam. *An Inquiry into the Nature and Causes of the Wealth of Nations.* London: J.M. Dent & Sons, Ltd., 1921.

Smith, Craig. "Adam Smith's 'Collateral' Inquiry: Fashion and Morality in *The Theory of Moral Sentiments* and *The Wealth of Nations.*" *History of Political Economy* 45 (Fall 2013): 505–22.

Smith, II, George P., and David M. Steenburg. "Environmental Hedonism or, Securing the Environment Through the Common Law." *William & Mary Law & Policy Review* 40 (Fall 2015): 65–114.

Smith, Joseph Wayne, and Gary Sauer-Thompson. "Civilization's Wake: Ecology, Economics and the Roots of Environmental Destruction and Neglect." *Population and Environment: A Journal of Interdisciplinary Studies* 19 (July 1998): 541–75.

Smith, Kenneth, and Jack Raso, M.S., R.D. *An Unhappy Anniversary: The Alar "Scare" Ten Years Later.* New York: American Council on Science and Health, 1999.

Smith, Maynard . "Reason, Passion, and Political Freedom in *The Federalist.*" *Journal of Politics* 22 (August 1960): 525–44.

Smith, Michael B. "'Silence, Miss Carson!' Science, Gender, and the Reception of *Silent Spring.*" *Feminist Studies* 27 (Fall 2001): 733–52.

Smith, Neale. "The Public Administrator as Collaborative Citizen: Three Conceptions." *Public Administration Quarterly* 34 (Summer 2010): 238–61.

Smulders, Sjak. "Environmental Policy and Sustainable Economic Growth." *De Economist* 143 (May 1995): 163–95.

Smythe, Kathleen R. "Rethinking Humanity in the Anthropocene: The Long View of Humans and Nature." *Sustainability* 7 (June 2014): 146–53.

Solow, Robert M. "Sustainability: An Economist's Perspective." In *The Environmental Ethics & Policy Book.* 2nd edition. Edited by Donald VanDeVeer and Christine Pierce, 450–55. Belmont, CA.: Wadsworth, 1998.

Somogyi, Zoltan. "A Framework for Quantifying Environmental Sustainability." *Ecological Indicators* 61, Part 2 (February 2016): 338–45.

Soranno, Patricia A.; Kendra S. Cheruvelil; Kevin C. Elliott; and Georgina M. Montgomery. "It's Good to Share: Why Environmental Scientists' Ethics Are Out of Date." *BioScience* 65 (January 2015): 69–73.

Sorensen, Paul. "Weak Sustainability and a Post-Industrial Society." *International Journal of Environmental Studies* 70 (December 2013): 872–76.

Souder, William. *On a Farther Shore: The Life and Legacy of Rachel Carson.* New York: Crown Books, 2012.

Spash, Clive L., and Anthony Ryan. "Economic Schools of Thought on the Environment: Investigating Unity and Division." *Cambridge Journal of Economics* 36 (September 2012): 1091–1121.

Spicer, Michael W. "Public Administration in a Disenchanted World: Reflections on Max Weber's Value Pluralism and His Views on Politics and Bureaucracy." *Administration & Society* 47 (January 2015): 24–43.

Stack, Kevin M. "An Administrative Jurisprudence: The Rule of Law in the Administrative State." *Columbia Law Review* 115 (November 2015): 1985–2018.

Stadtler, Lea. "Scrutinizing Public-Private Partnerships for Development: Towards a Broad Evaluation Conception." *Journal of Business Ethics* 135 (April 2016): 71–86.

Stål, Herman I. "Inertia and Change Related to Sustainability—An Institutional Approach." *Journal of Cleaner Production* 99 (July 2015): 354–65.

Stamp, Nancy. "Plumed Hats." *History Magazine* 16 (June/July 2015): 6–7.

Stanley, Harold W., and Richard G. Niemi. *Vital Statistics on American Politics 20011–2012.* Washington, D.C.: CQ Press, 2012.

St. Antoine, Theodore J. "The NLRB, the Courts, the Administrative Procedure Act, and *Chevron*: Now and Then." *Emory Law Journal* 64 Supplement (2015): 1529–52.

Steinberg, Michael K. "Audubon Landscapes in the South." *The Mississippi Quarterly* 63 (Winter 2010): 313–29.

Stensvaag, John-Mark. "Preventing Significant Deterioration Under the Clean Air Act: Area Classification, Initial Allocation, and Redesignation." *Environmental Law Reporter: News & Analysis* 41 (January 2011): 10008–23.

Sterba, James. "A Biocentrist Strikes Back." *Environmental Ethics* 20 (Winter 1998): 361–76.

Stevens, Yee-Wan; Mildred M. Williams-Johnson; and William Cibulas, Jr. "Findings and Accomplishments of ATSDR's Superfund-Mandated Substance-Specific Applied Research Program." *International Journal of Hygiene and Environmental Health* 205 (2002): 29–39.

Stevenson, Dru, and Sonny Eckhart. "Standing as Channeling in the Administrative Age." *Boston College Law Review* 53 (September 2012): 1357–1416.

Stewart, Debra W. "Professional vs. Democracy: Friedrich vs. Finer Revisited." *Public Administration Quarterly* 9 (Spring 1985): 13–25.

Stillman II, Richard J. *American Bureaucracy: The Core of Modern Government.* 3rd. edition. Belmont, CA.: Wadsworth/Thomson, 2004.

Stillman II, Richard J. "The Peculiar 'Stateless' Origins of American Public Administration and the Consequences for Government Today." *Public Administration Review* 90 (March/April 1990): 156–67.

Stillman II, Richard J. "Review Article: Dwight Waldo's *The Administrative State*: A Neglected American Administrative State Theory for Our Times." *Public Administration* 86 (June 2008): 581–90.

Stillman II, Richard J. "Woodrow Wilson and the Study of Administration: A New Look at an Old Essay." *The American Political Science Review* 67 (June 1973): 582–88.

Stivers, Camilla. "The Significance of *The Administrative State*." *Public Administration Review* 68 (January/February 2008): 53–56.

Stone, Deborah. *Policy Paradox: The Art of Political Decision Making*. Revised Edition. New York: W.W. Norton, 2002.

Storing, Herbert J. "Leonard D. White and the Study of Public Administration." *Public Administration Review* 25 (March 1965): 38–51.

Stout, Margaret. "Revisiting the (Lost) Art of Ideal-Typing in Public Administration." *Administrative Theory & Praxis* 32 (December 2010): 491–519.

Strand, Margaret "Peggy," and Lowell M. Rothschild. "What Wetlands Are Regulated? Jurisdiction of the § 404 Program." *Environmental Law Reporter: News & Analysis* 40 (April 2010): 10372–93.

Stranlund, John K., and Yakov Ben-Haim. "Price-based versus Quantity-based Environmental Regulation under Knightian Uncertainty: An Info-gap Robust Satisficing Perspective." *Journal of Environmental Management* 87 (2008): 443–49.

Strauss, Barry. "American Democracy through Greek Eyes." *History Today* 44 (April 1994): 32–37.

Sulamoyo, Dalitso. "Building Beyond Already Established OD Success Rates: An Interview with Dr. Robert T. Golembiewski." *Organization Development Journal* 28 (Winter 2010): 11–19.

Sussman, Glen, and Byron W. Daynes. "Spanning the Century: Theodore Roosevelt, Franklin Roosevelt, Richard Nixon, Bill Clinton, and the Environment." *White House Studies* 4 (April 2004): 337–54.

Sutter, Paul S. "The World with Us: The State of American Environmental History." *The Journal of American History* 100 (June 2013): 94–119.

Svara, James H. "Beyond Dichotomy: Dwight Waldo and the Intertwined Politics-Administration Relationship." *Public Administration Review* 68 (January/February 2008): 46–52.

Swain, Donald C. "Harold Ickes, Horace Albright, and the Hundred Days: A Study in Conservation Administration." *Pacific Historical Review* 34 (November 1965): 455–65.

Swanson, Jacinda. "The Economy and Its Relation to Politics: Robert Dahl, Neoclassical Economics, and Democracy." *Polity* 39 (April 2007): 208–33.

Swidler, Ann. "The Concept of Rationality in the Work of Max Weber." *Sociological Inquiry* 43 (January 1973): 35–42.

Switzer, Jacqueline Vaughn. *Green Backlash: The History and Politics of Environmental Opposition in the U.S.* Boulder, CO: Lynne Rienner Publishers, 1997.

Tabatabai, Maryam. "Comparing U.S. and EU Hazardous Waste Liability Frameworks: How the EU Liability Directive Competes with CERCLA." *Houston Journal of International Law* 34 (Summer 2012): 653–85.

Tahmasebi, Reza, and Seyyed Mohammad Mahdi Musavi. "Politics-Administration Dichotomy: A Century Debate." *Administration & Public Management Review* 17 (December 2011): 130–43.

Tausanovitch, Chris, and Christopher Warshaw. "Measuring Constituent Policy Preferences in Congress, State Legislatures, and Cities." *The Journal of Politics* 75 (April 2013): 330–42.

Taylor, Bob Pepperman. "Environmental Ethics and Public Policy." *Polity* 23 (Summer 1991): 567–83.

Taylor, Clara. *Green Living: Green Lifestyle—Green Living Guide for Beginners.* Seattle, WA: Amazon Digital Services, 2015.

Taylor, Frederick Winslow. *The Principles of Scientific Management.* Mineola, NY.: Courier Dover Publications, 2009 [1911].

Taylor, Paul. *Respect for Nature: A Theory of Environmental Ethics.* 25th Anniversary Edition. Princeton, N.J.: Princeton University Press, 2011.

Taylor, Robert P., Chandrasekar Govindarajalu, Anke S. Meyer, and William A. Ward. *Financing Energy Efficiency: Lessons from Brazil, China, India, and Beyond.* Washington, D.C.: The International Bank for Reconstruction and Development/The World Bank, 2008.

Tedsen, Elizabeth, and Gesa Homann. "Implementing the Precautionary Principle for Climate Engineering." *Carbon & Climate Law Review* 2 (April 2013): 90–100.

Thoreau, Henry David. *Walden, or Life in the Woods.* New York: Thomas Y. Crowell & Company, 1910 [1854].

Thoreau, Henry David. "Walking." In *The Writings of Henry David Thoreau.* Vol. V: *Excursions and Poems.* Edited by Bradford Torrey, 217–18. Boston and New York: Houghton Mifflin and Company, the Riverside Press, Cambridge, 1906 [1865]): 205–48.

Thrower, Alex W., and J. Michael Martinez. "Hazardous Materials Transportation in an Age of Devolution." *The American Review of Public Administration* 29 (June 1999): 167–89.

Thrower, Alex W., and J. Michael Martinez. "Reconciling Anthropocentrism and Biocentrism Through Adaptive Management: The Case of the Waste Isolation Pilot Plant and Public Risk Perception." *The Journal of Environment & Development* 9 (March 2000): 68–97.

Tiller, Emerson H. "Controlling Policy by Controlling Process: Judicial Influence on Regulatory Decision Making." *Journal of Law, Economics, and Organization* 14 (April 1998): 114–35.

Tilman, Rick. "Thorstein Veblen and the Disinterest of Neoclassical Economists in Wasteful Consumption." *International Journal of Politics, Culture and Society* 13 (1999): 207–23.

Tisdell, Clem. "Local Communities, Conservation and Sustainability: Institutional Change, Altered Governance and Kant's Social Philosophy." *International Journal of Social Economics* 24 (December 1997): 1361–75.

Tocqueville, Alexis de. *Democracy in America*. Book II. Translated by Arthur Goldhammer. New York: Library of America, 2004.

Tocqueville, Alexis de. "Individualism and Free Institutions." In *Theories of Social Order: A Reader*. Edited by Michael Hechter and Christine Horne, 317–28. Stanford, CA.: Stanford University Press, 2003.

Toren, Nina. "Bureaucracy and Professionalism: A Reconsideration of Weber's Thesis." *Academy of Management Review* 1 (July 1976): 36–46.

The Toxic Substances Control Act (TSCA) of 1976. 15 U.S.C. § 2601 *et seq.* (1976).

"Toxic Substances Control Act Overview: Current Laws and Policies." *Congressional Digest* 89, 8 (October 2010): 226–28; 256.

Triantafillou, Peter. "The Politics of Neutrality and the Changing Role of Expertise in Public Administration." *Administrative Theory & Praxis* 37 (July 2015): 174–87.

Truman, David B. *The Governmental Process: Political Interests and Public Opinion*. New York: Knopf, 1971 [1951].

"TSCA Reform: The Standard of Safety." *Environmental Law Reporter: News & Analysis* 41 (December 2011): 11081–90.

Tsesis, Alexander. "Into the Light of Day: Relevance of the Thirteenth Amendment to Contemporary Law." *Columbia Law Review* 112 (November 2012): 1447–58.

Tugcu, Can Tansel, Iihan Ozturk, and Alper Aslan. "Renewable and Nonrenewable Energy Consumption and Economic Growth Relationship Revisited: Evidence from G7 Countries." *Energy Economics* 34 (November 2012): 1942–50.

Türk, Alexander H. "Oversight of Administrative Rulemaking: Judicial Review." *European Law Journal* 19 (January 2013): 126–42.

Turner, Frederick Jackson. "The Significance of the Frontier in American History." In *Annual Report of the American Historical Association for 1893*, 199–227. Washington, D.C.: U.S. Government Printing Office, 1894.

Tversky, Amos, and Daniel Kahneman. "Judgment under Uncertainty: Heuristics and Biases." *Science* 185 (September 27, 1974): 1124–31.

Twain, Mark, and Charles Dudley Warner. *The Gilded Age: A Tale of Today*. New York: The New American Library, 1985 [1873].

Udall, Stewart L. *The Quiet Crisis*. New York: Holt, Rinehart, and Winston, 1963.

Uhr, John. "John Rohr's Concept of Regime Values: Locating Theory in Public Administration." *Administration & Society* 46 (March 2014): 141–52.

"United Nations Activities: Advances in Sustainability and Democracy." *Environmental Policy and Law* 46 (March 2016): 2–9.

United Nations. *Agenda 21: Earth Summit: The United Nations Programme of Action from Rio*. Heiskell, TN: CrabCube, Inc., 2013.

United Nations. *Universal Declaration of Human Rights*. Carlisle, MA: Applewood Books, 2001.

United States v. Students Challenging Regulatory Agency Procedures (SCRAP), 412 U.S. 669 (1973).

United States Environmental Protection Agency. *RCRA, Superfund & EPCRA Call Center*. Washington, D.C.: U.S. Government Printing Office. Solid Waste and Emergency Response Publication No. EPA530-R-04-010. September 2003.

United States General Accountability Office. *Agency for Toxic Substances and Disease Registry: Policies and Procedures for Public Health Product Preparation Should be Strengthened*. Washington, D.C.: U.S. Government Printing Office. GAO Publication No. GAO-10-449. April 2010.

United States General Accountability Office. *Public-Private Partnerships: Pilot Program Needed to Demonstrate the Actual Benefits of Using Partnerships*. Washington, D.C.: U.S. Government Printing Office. GAO Publication No. GAO-01-096. July 2001.

United States House of Representatives, Committee on Resources, One Hundred Ninth Congress, First Session. Oversight Hearing, Thursday, November 17, 2005. *NEPA: Lessons Learned and Next Steps*. Washington, D.C.: U.S. Government Printing Office, 2006.

United States Senate, Committee on Environment and Public Works, Subcommittee on Clean Air and Nuclear Safety. *Three Mile Island: Looking Back on 30 Years of Lessons Learned: Hearing Before the Subcommittee on Clean Air and Nuclear Safety of the Committee on Environment and Public Works, United States Senate, One Hundred Eleventh Congress, First Session, March 24, 2009*. Washington, D.C.: U.S. Government Printing Office, 2015.

"The Unrealized Potential of SARA." *Environment* 29 (May 1987): 6–11, 40–44.

Urofsky, Melvin I. "Thomas Jefferson and John Marshall: What Kind of Constitution Shall We Have?" *Journal of Supreme Court History* 31 (July 2006): 109–25.

Urpelainen, Johannes. "A Model of Dynamic Climate Governance: Dream Big, Win Small." *International Environmental Agreements* 13 (May 2013): 107–25.

van Egteren, Henry, and R. Todd Smith. "Environmental Regulations under Simple Negligence or Strict Liability." *Environmental & Resource Economics* 21 (April 2002): 369–96.

Van Horn, Gavin. "The (Religious) Naturalist's Eye: An Introduction to 'Aldo Leopold: Ethical and Spiritual Dimensions.'" *Journal for the Study of Religion, Nature, and Culture* 5 (2011): 397–409.

van Soest, Daan; Jan Stoop; and Jana Vyrastekova. "Toward a Delineation of the Circumstances in Which Cooperation Can Be Sustained in Environmental and Resource Problems." *Journal of Environmental Economics and Management* 77 (May 2016): 1–13.

Vardas, Giannis, and Anastasios Xepapadeas. "Model Uncertainty, Ambiguity and the Precautionary Principle: Implications for Biodiversity Management." *Environmental and Resource Economics* 45 (March 2010): 379–404.

Varner, Gary. "A Harean Perspective on Humane Sustainability." *Ethics & The Environment* 15 (Fall 2010): 31–50.

Varner, Gary. "Utilitarianism and the Evolution of Ecological Ethics." *Science and Engineering Ethics* 14 (December 2008): 551–73.

Vermeule, Adrian. "Deference and Due Process." *Harvard Law Review* 129 (May 2016): 1890–1931.

Vermont Yankee Nuclear Power Corporation v. Natural Resources Defense Council, Inc., 435 U.S. 519 (1978).

Viscusi, W. Kip, and Ted Gayer. "Behavioral Public Choice: The Behavioral Paradox of Government Policy." *Harvard Journal of Law & Public Policy* 38 (Summer 2015): 973–1007.

Vitiello, Domenic. "Monopolizing the Metropolis: Gilded Age Growth Machines and Power in American Urbanization." *Planning Perspectives* 28 (January 2013): 71–90.

Vollan, Björn; Sebastian Prediger; and Markus Frölich. "Analysis: Co-managing Common-pool Resources: Do Formal Rules Have to be Adapted to Traditional Ecological Norms?" *Ecological Economics* 95 (November 2013): 51–62.

Wagner, Travis. "Hazardous Waste: Evolution of a National Environmental Problem." *Journal of Policy History* 16 (October 2004): 307–31.

Wakefield, Susan. "Ethics and the Public Service: A Case for Individual Responsibility." *Public Administration Review* 36 (November/December 1976): 661–66.

Waldo, Dwight. *The Administrative State: A Study of the Political Theory of American Public Administration.* New York: Ronald Press, 1948.

Waldron, Maya. "A Proposal to Balance Polluter and Community Intervention in CERCLA Litigation." *Ecology Law Quarterly* 38 (2011): 401–26.

Walker, Samuel J. *Three Mile Island: A Nuclear Crisis in Historical Perspective.* Berkeley: University of California Press, 2004.

Walsh, William J., and Michelle M. Skjoldal. "Sustainability is Driving Toxic Chemicals from Products." *Natural Resources & Environment* 25 (Winter 2011): 16–20.

Walters, Daniel E. "Note: The Justiciability of Fair Balance under the Federal Advisory Committee Act: Toward a Deliberative Process Approach." *Michigan Law Review* 110 (February 2012): 677–708.

Wamsley, Gary L.; Robert N. Bacher; Charles T. Goodsell; Philip S. Kronenberg; John A. Rohr; Camilla M. Stivers; Orion F. White; and James F. Wolf. *Refounding Public Administration*. Newbury Park, CA.: Sage Publications, 1990.

Warke, Tom. "Multi-Dimensional Utility and the Index Number Problem: Jeremy Bentham, J.S. Mill, and Qualitative Hedonism." *Utilitas* 12 (July 2000): 176–203.

Warshaw, Christopher, and Gregory E. Wannier. "Business as Usual? Analyzing the Development of Environmental Standing Doctrine since 1976." *Harvard Law & Policy Review* 5 (July 2011): 289–322.

Watson, Matthew. "Desperately Seeking Social Approval: Adam Smith, Thorstein Veblen and the Moral Limits of Capitalist Culture." *The British Journal of Sociology* 63 (September 2012): 491–512.

Webber, David J. "Earth Day and Its Precursors: Continuity and Change in the Evolution of Midtwentieth-Century U.S. Environmental Policy." *Review of Policy Research* 25 (July 2008): 313–32.

Weidema, Bo. "Has ISO 14040/44 Failed Its Role as a Standard for Life Cycle Assessment?" *Journal of Industrial Ecology* 18 (June 2014): 324–26.

Weinstein, Jack Russell. *Adam Smith's Pluralism: Rationality, Education, and the Moral Sentiments*. New Haven and London: Yale University Press, 2013.

Weisbach, David A. "Should Environmental Taxes Be Precautionary?" *National Tax Journal* 65 (June 2012): 453–74.

Welch IV, James, and Nita Clark. "The Problematic Nature of Civic Participation in Sustainability Initiatives: The Case of the Arlington Hike and Bike Master Plan." *Public Integrity* 17 (Winter 2014–15): 37–54.

West, John G. "The Church Darwin." *First Things: A Monthly Journal of Religion & Public Life* 254 (June/July 2015): 21–23.

Westra, Laura. *Living in Integrity: A Global Ethic to Restore a Fragmented Earth*. Lanham, MD.: Rowman & Littlefield, 1998.

Wettenhall, Roger. "Minnowbrook: Just American or More?" *Administrative Theory & Praxis* 31 (June 2009): 255–60.

White, Leonard D. *Introduction to the Study of Public Administration*. New York and London: The MacMillan Company, 1946 [1926].

White, Jr., Lynn. "The Historical Roots of Our Ecological Crisis." *Science* 155 (March 10, 1967): 1203–1207.

White, Richard. "Discovering Nature in North America." *The Journal of American History* 79 (December 1992): 874–91.

Whitford, Andrew B. "Threats, Institutions and Regulation in Common Pool Resources." *Policy Sciences* 35 (June 2002): 122–39.

Wilde, Norman. "Kant's Relation to Utilitarianism." *The Philosophical Review* 3 (May 1, 1894): 289–304.

Wilkinson, Charles. "'The Greatest Good of the Greatest Number in the Long Run': TR, Pinchot, and the Origins of Sustainability in America." *Colorado Natural Resources, Energy & Environmental Law Review* 26 (2016): 69–79.

Wilkinson, David M. "Is Gaia Really Conventional Ecology?" *Oikos* 84 (March 1999): 533–36.

Willard, Barbara E. "Rhetorical Landscapes as Epistemic: Revisiting Aldo Leopold's *A Sand County Almanac*." *Environmental Communication* 1 (November 2007): 218–35.

Willer, David E. "Max Weber's Missing Authority Type." *Sociological Inquiry* 37 (Spring 1967): 231–39.

Williams, Stephen F. "'Hybrid Rulemaking' under the Administrative Procedure Act: A Legal and Empirical Analysis." *The University of Chicago Law Review* 42 (Spring 1975): 401–56.

Wilson, Woodrow. "The Study of Administration." *Political Science Quarterly* 2 (June 1887): 197–222.

Wirzba, Norman. "Ecology and the Eyes of Faith: All Creatures." *Christian Century* 132 (July 22, 2015): 26–27, 29.

Woldring, Henk E.S. "State and Civil Society in the Political Philosophy of Alexis de Tocqueville." *Voluntas: International Journal of Voluntary and Nonprofit Organizations* 9 (December 1998): 363–73.

Wolfe, Linnie Marsh. *Son of the Wilderness: The Life of John Muir*. 2nd. edition Madison: The University of Wisconsin Press, 2003.

Wolff, Brian G. "Environmental Studies and Utilitarian Ethics." *Bioscene: Journal of College Biology Teaching* 34 (December 2008): 6–11.

Wong, James K. "A Dilemma for Green Democracy." *Political Studies* 64 (2016 Supplement): 136–55.

World Commission on Environment and Development. *Our Common Future*. Oxford and New York: Oxford University Press, 1987.

Worster, Donald. "John Muir and the Modern Passion for Nature." *Environmental History* 10 (January 2005): 8–19.

Worster, Donald. *The Passion for Nature: The Life of John Muir*. Oxford and New York: Oxford University Press, 2011.

Wray, L. Randall, and Marc-Andre Pigeon. "Can a Rising Tide Raise All Boats? Evidence from the Clinton-Era Expansion." *Journal of Economic Issues* 34 (December 2000): 811–45.

Wren, Daniel A. "The Centennial of Frederick W. Taylor's *The Principles of Scientific Management*: A Retrospective Commentary." *Journal of Business & Management* 17 (April 2011): 11–22.

Wyeth, George B., and Beth Termini. "Regulating for Sustainability." *Environmental Law* 45 (Summer 2015): 663–712.

Xepapadeas, Anastasios, and Catarina Roseta-Palma. "Instabilities and Robust Control in Natural Resource Management." *Portuguese Economic Journal* 12 (December 2013): 161–80.

Yackee, Susan Webb. "Participant Voice in the Bureaucratic Policymaking Process." *Journal of Public Administration Research and Theory* 25 (April 2015): 427–49.

Yandle, Bruce. "The Common Law and the Environment in the Courts: Discussion of Code Law and Common Law." *Case Western Reserve Law Review* 58 (Spring 2008): 647–61.

Yergin, Daniel. *The Quest: Energy, Security, and the Remaking of the Modern World*. New York: The Penguin Press, 2011.

Yudanin, Michael. "Can Positive Duties be Derived from Kant's Categorical Imperative?" *Ethical Theory and Moral Practice: An International Forum* 18 (June 2015): 595–614.

Zafirovski, Milan. "A Rational Choice Approach to Human Studies: A Reexamination." *Human Studies* 26 (January 2003): 41–66.

Zelinsky, Wilbur. *The Cultural Geography of the United States*. Englewood Cliffs, N.J.: Prentice Hall, 1973.

INDEX

American Ornithologists' Union, 222

American Society for Public
Administration (ASPA), 246,
247

analysis paralysis, 15, 248

anthropocentric. *See*
anthropocentrism

anthropocentrism, 6, 7, 8, 68–71, 72,
75, 78, 165, 167, 215, 236, 243

Appleby, Paul, 104

arbitrary and capricious standard,
129, 131–32, 134

Aristotle, 74, 205

Arizona State University, xvii

Army Corps of Engineers, 145

Articles of Confederation, 90

*Association of Data Processing
Service Organizations v. Camp*,
127

Athens (Greece), 207

The Atlantic Monthly (magazine), 216

Atomic Energy Commission (AEC),
130–31

"At the Saturday Club" (poem), 170

"At the Shrine of Our Lady of
Fatima, or Why Political
Questions Are Not All
Economic" (essay), 237

Attorney General's Committee on
Administrative Procedure, 111

Audubon, John James, 160–61, 221

Audubon, Lucy, 161

Audubon Field Guides (book), 223

Audubon Society. *See* National
Audubon Society

Ayres, Dick, 224

Bacon, Francis, 205

Baker, John H., 223

Bancroft, George, 160

Barnard, Chester, 107

Beck, Glenn, 11

Bentham, Jeremy, 64

Best Available Control Technology
(BACT), 135.
See also Clean Air Act (CAA)

Bethesda (Maryland), 192

Big Democracy (book), 104

Bill of Rights, 48

bioaccumulation, 217

biocentric. *See* biocentrism

biocentrism, 7, 29, 68, 71–75, 78, 164

biodegradability, 13

biodiesel, 237

biofuels, 237

biomass energy, 237

Black Plague, 206

BirdLife International, 223

Birds in America (book), 161

Blacksburg Manifesto, 105–6

Bob Marshall Wilderness Area, 185

Bonaparte, Napoleon, 93

Bookchin, Murray, 74

The Book-of-the-Month Club, 218

Boston (Massachusetts), 168

bottom up management, 157, 186

bounded rationality, 103

bounty hunter provisions, 121–22

*Bowling Alone: America's Declining
Social Capital* (book), 213–14

Brazil, 9, 19, 169

Brown, Michael, 141

Brownlow Committee, 102–3, 111

Brundtland, Gro Harlem, 5

Brundtland Report. *See Our
Common Future*

Bryce, Robert, 238

Bryson, John, 224

bureaucracy, 100, 244

Bureau of Fisheries. *See* Fish and
Wildlife Service of the United
States

Bureau of Indian Affairs, 183

Burroughs, John, 220

Cabell, John C., 92

Founders (American), 35–36, 89–95,
    104, 106, 173, 204, 205, 206,
    210, 226–27, 243
fracking. *See* hydraulic fracturing
France, 160
Frank R. Lautenberg Chemical
    Safety for the 21st Century Act,
    139
Frederickson, H. George, 105
Freedom of Information Act (FOIA),
    132–33
free rider problem, 211
Friedrich, Carl J., 105
The Functions of the Executive
    (book), 107
Fungible goods, 34, 52, 70

Gaia Meditations (book), 74
Gaia principle, 74
Garfield, James A., 110
general equilibrium, 36
General Public Utilities Nuclear
    energy division. *See* GPU, Inc.
Georgia State University, xvii
Geothermal energy, 237–38
Gilded Age, 163
The Gilded Age: A Tale of Today
    (book), 172
global warming, 20, 30, 50–51
GPU, Inc., 191
Golden Age of Tribunals, 111
Golden Rule, 68
Golembiewski, Robert, 107
Goodnow, Frank, 98
Government in the Sunshine Act, 133
The Governmental Process (book),
    209–10, 211
Grand Canyon (Arizona), 70, 164
Grand Tetons National Park, 177
Gray, Asa, 171
Great Britain, 222
Great Depression, 178, 179
Great Society, 111

Greeks, 205, 206
greenhouse gases (GHG), 18, 19, 241
*Green Living: Green Lifestyle—
    Green Living Guide for
    Beginners* (book), 239
*Green Made Easy: The Everyday
    Guide for Transitioning to a
    Green Lifestyle* (book), 239
greenwashing, 13
Grinnell, George Bird, 161
Guggenheimer, Untermeyer, and
    Marshall (law firm), 183
Guiteau, Charles, 110
Gulick, Luther, 102

Haiti, 160
Hall, Mina, 222
Hamilton, Alexander, 92, 93, 94–95,
    206, 207
Hamlet (play), 65
Harding, Warren G., 176
hard look review, 129–30, 132
Harrisburg (Pennsylvania), 191
Hart, David K., 105
Harvard University, 76, 168, 169, 213
Harvard University Law School, 187,
    189, 224
Hawkins, David, 224
Hawthorne, Nathaniel, 169
Hawthorne Studies, 106
Hayek, F. A. von, 39
Hayes, Denis, 187, 189
hazardous materials, 137–46
hazardous waste, 189
Hazard Ranking System (HRS), 143.
    See also Comprehensive
    Environmental Response,
    Compensation, and Liability Act
    of 1980 (CERCLA)
Hemenway, Harriet Lawrence,
    221–22
Herzberg, Frederick, 106
Hetch Hetchy Valley, 166

ABOUT THE AUTHOR

J. Michael Martinez works in Monroe, Georgia, as an environmental affairs representative for a manufacturing company. He also teaches political science as a part-time faculty member at Kennesaw State University in Kennesaw, Georgia. He is the author of 10 previous books, including *American Environmentalism: Philosophy, History, and Public Policy*. Visit him on the Internet at www.jmichaelmartinez.com.